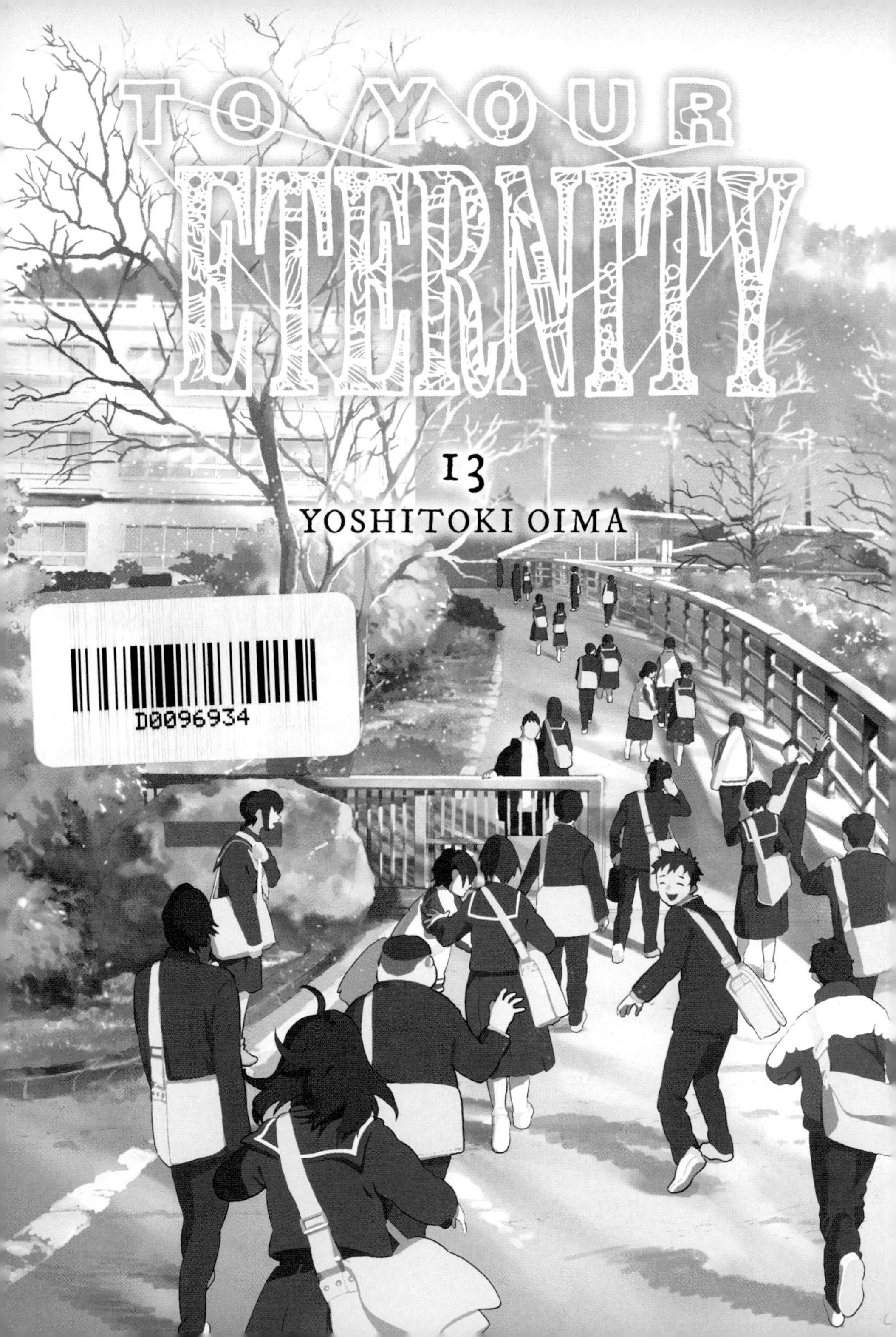
TO YOUR
ETERNITY
13
YOSHITOKI OIMA

CONTENTS

WARNING

This volume contains mentions of suicide.
If you are experiencing suicidal thoughts or feelings,
you are not alone, and there is help.
Call the National Suicide Prevention Lifeline at
1-800-273-TALK (8255) or go to
SuicidePreventionLifeline.org.

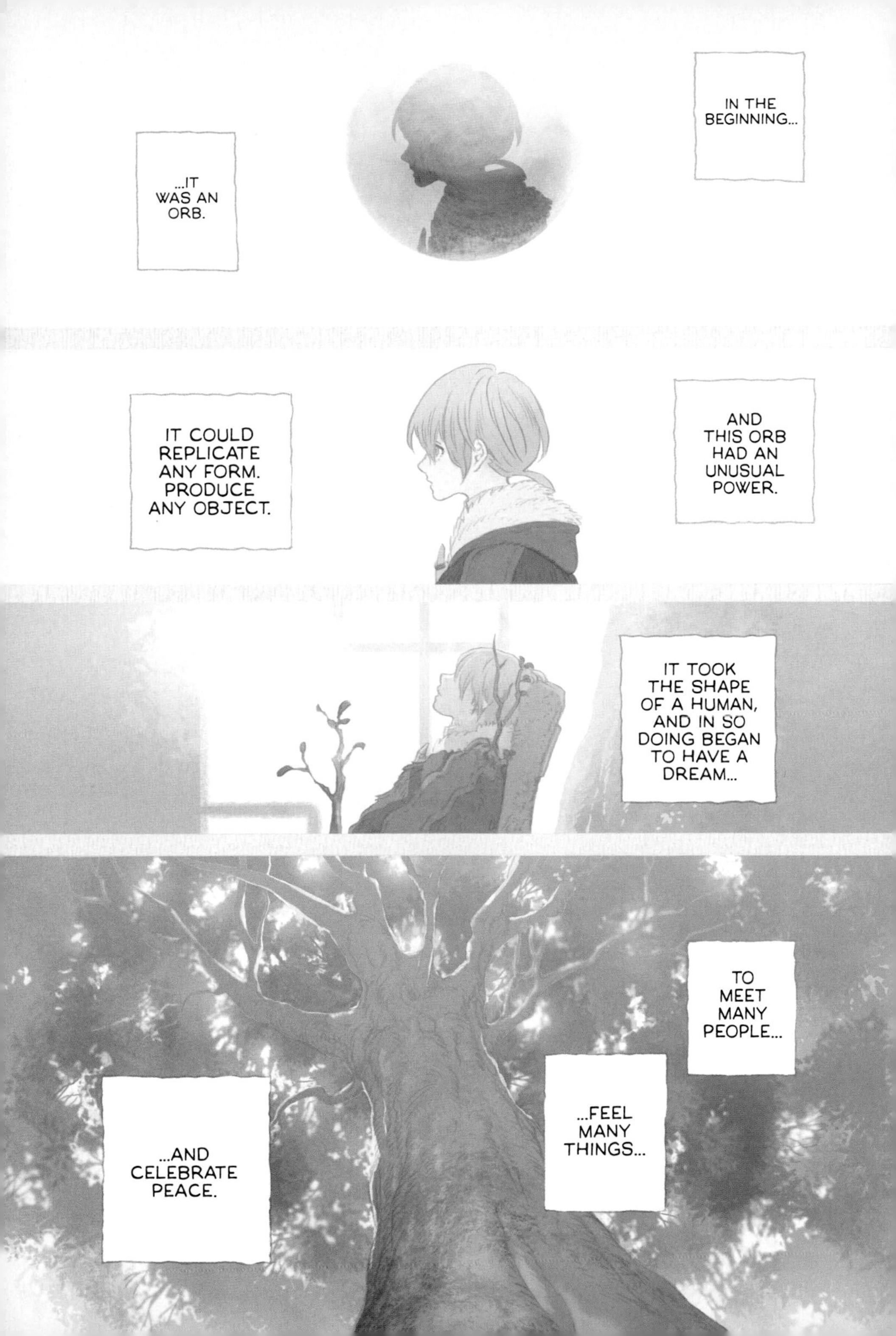
IN THE BEGINNING...
...IT WAS AN ORB.
AND THIS ORB HAD AN UNUSUAL POWER.
IT COULD REPLICATE ANY FORM. PRODUCE ANY OBJECT.
IT TOOK THE SHAPE OF A HUMAN, AND IN SO DOING BEGAN TO HAVE A DREAM...
TO MEET MANY PEOPLE...
...FEEL MANY THINGS...
...AND CELEBRATE PEACE.

TO YOUR ETERNITY

#117 Peaceful World

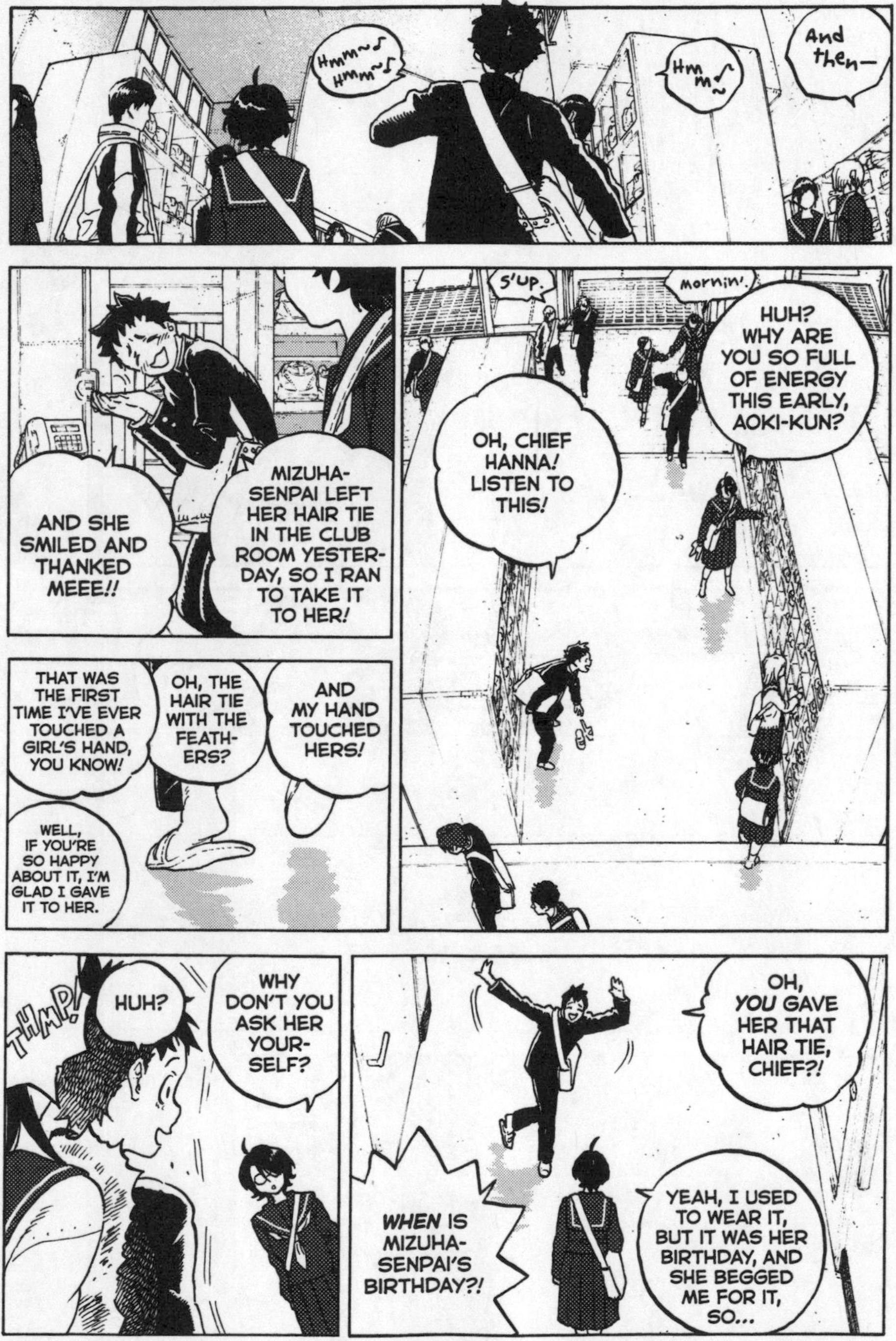

And then—
Hm m~♪
Hmm~♪ Hmm~♪
mornin'.
s'up.
HUH? WHY ARE YOU SO FULL OF ENERGY THIS EARLY, AOKI-KUN?
OH, CHIEF HANNA! LISTEN TO THIS!
MIZUHA-SENPAI LEFT HER HAIR TIE IN THE CLUB ROOM YESTERDAY, SO I RAN TO TAKE IT TO HER!
AND SHE SMILED AND THANKED MEEE!!
AND MY HAND TOUCHED HERS!
OH, THE HAIR TIE WITH THE FEATHERS?
THAT WAS THE FIRST TIME I'VE EVER TOUCHED A GIRL'S HAND, YOU KNOW!
WELL, IF YOU'RE SO HAPPY ABOUT IT, I'M GLAD I GAVE IT TO HER.
OH, *YOU* GAVE HER THAT HAIR TIE, CHIEF?!
YEAH, I USED TO WEAR IT, BUT IT WAS HER BIRTHDAY, AND SHE BEGGED ME FOR IT, SO...
WHEN IS MIZUHA-SENPAI'S BIRTHDAY?!
WHY DON'T YOU ASK HER YOURSELF?
HUH?
THMP!

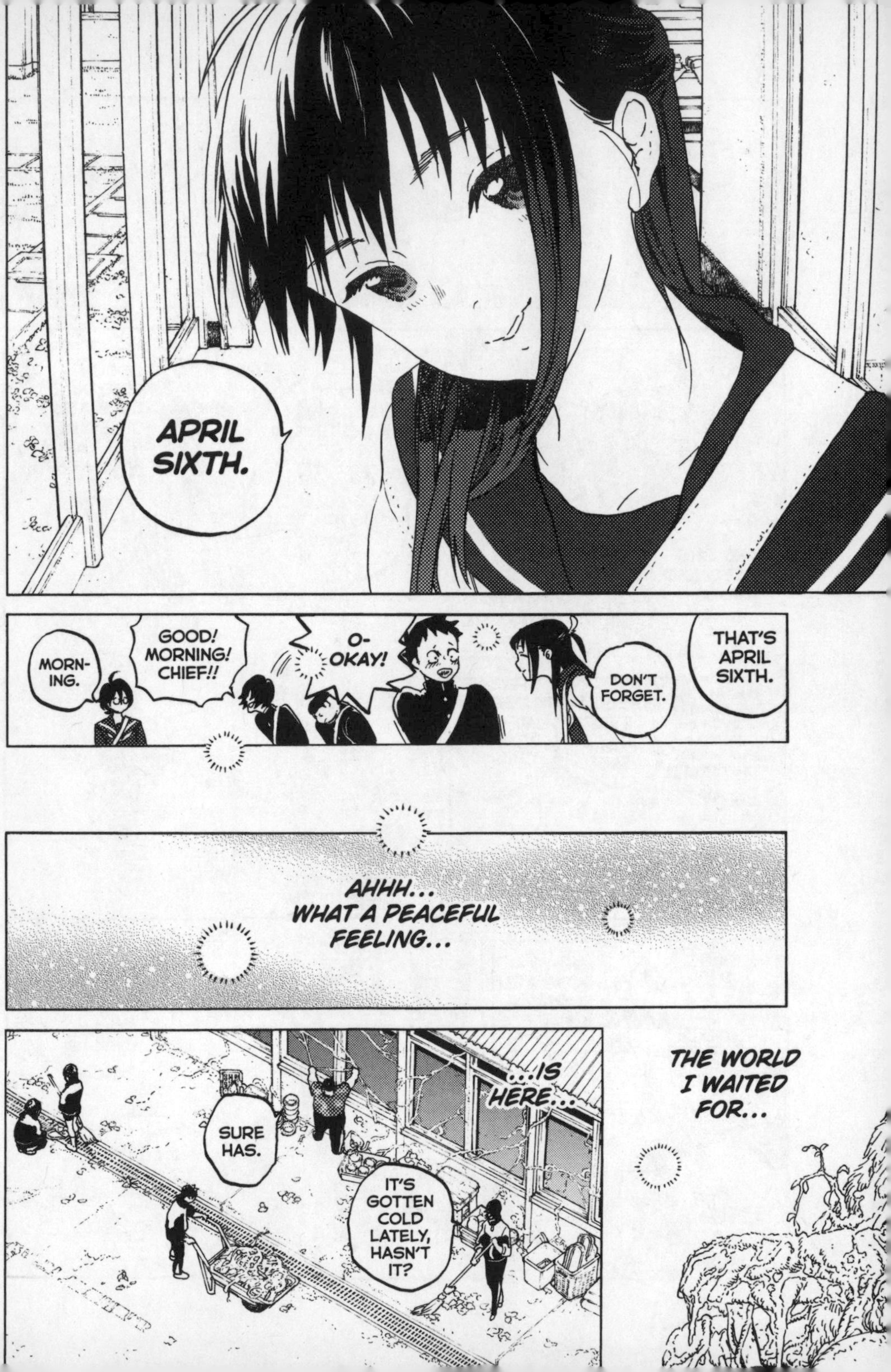
APRIL SIXTH.
THAT'S APRIL SIXTH.
DON'T FORGET.
O-OKAY!
GOOD! MORNING! CHIEF!!
MORN-ING.
AHHH... WHAT A PEACEFUL FEELING...
THE WORLD I WAITED FOR...
...IS HERE...
IT'S GOTTEN COLD LATELY, HASN'T IT?
SURE HAS.

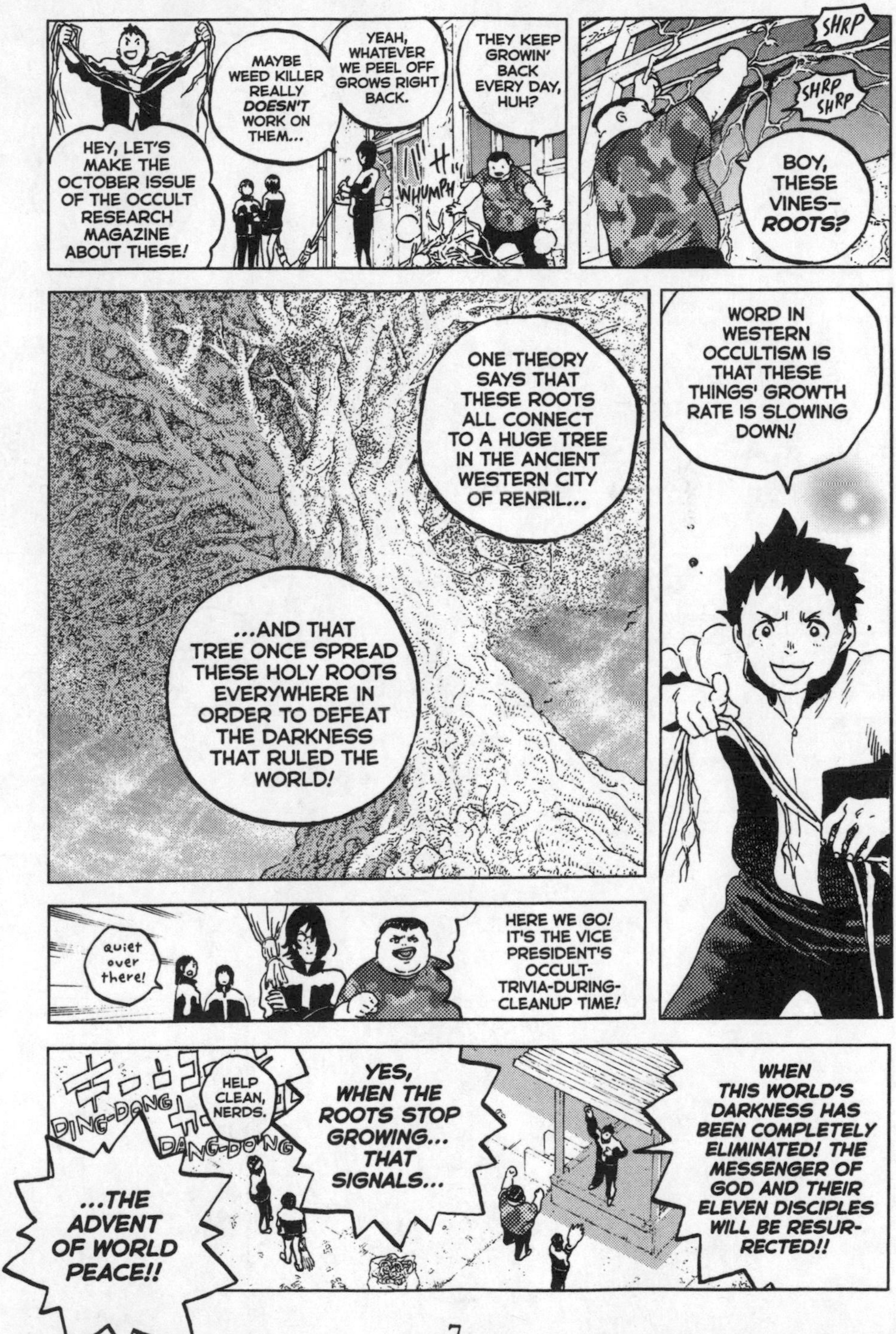
SHRP
SHRP SHRP
BOY, THESE VINES—*ROOTS?*
THEY KEEP GROWIN' BACK EVERY DAY, HUH?
YEAH, WHATEVER WE PEEL OFF GROWS RIGHT BACK.
MAYBE WEED KILLER REALLY *DOESN'T* WORK ON THEM...
WHUMPH
HEY, LET'S MAKE THE OCTOBER ISSUE OF THE OCCULT RESEARCH MAGAZINE ABOUT THESE!
WORD IN WESTERN OCCULTISM IS THAT THESE THINGS' GROWTH RATE IS SLOWING DOWN!
ONE THEORY SAYS THAT THESE ROOTS ALL CONNECT TO A HUGE TREE IN THE ANCIENT WESTERN CITY OF RENRIL...
...AND THAT TREE ONCE SPREAD THESE HOLY ROOTS EVERYWHERE IN ORDER TO DEFEAT THE DARKNESS THAT RULED THE WORLD!
HERE WE GO! IT'S THE VICE PRESIDENT'S OCCULT-TRIVIA-DURING-CLEANUP TIME!
quiet over there!
WHEN THIS WORLD'S DARKNESS HAS BEEN COMPLETELY ELIMINATED! THE MESSENGER OF GOD AND THEIR ELEVEN DISCIPLES WILL BE RESURRECTED!!
YES, WHEN THE ROOTS STOP GROWING... THAT SIGNALS...
HELP CLEAN, NERDS.
DING-DONG
DANG-DONG
...THE ADVENT OF WORLD PEACE!!

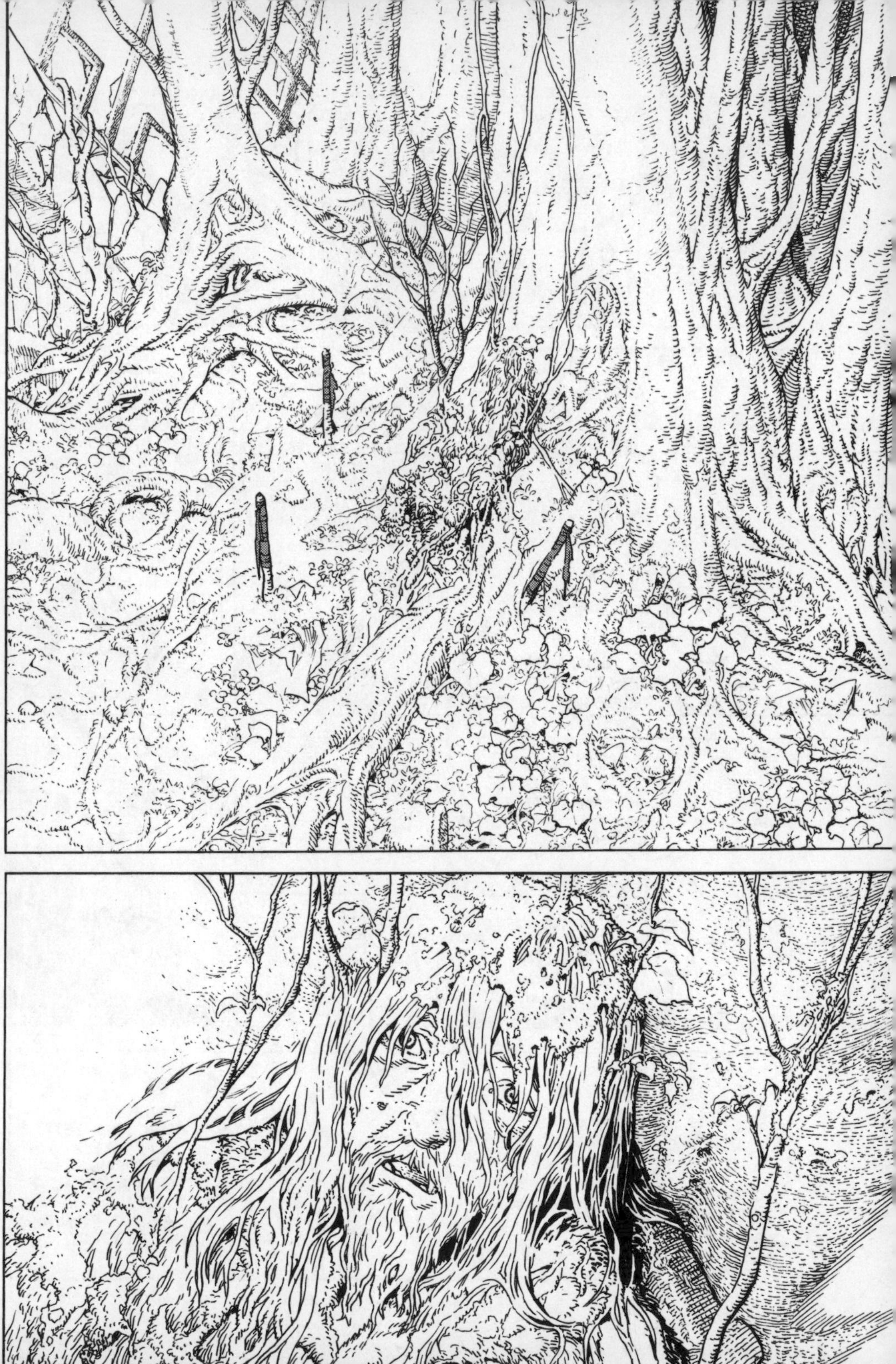

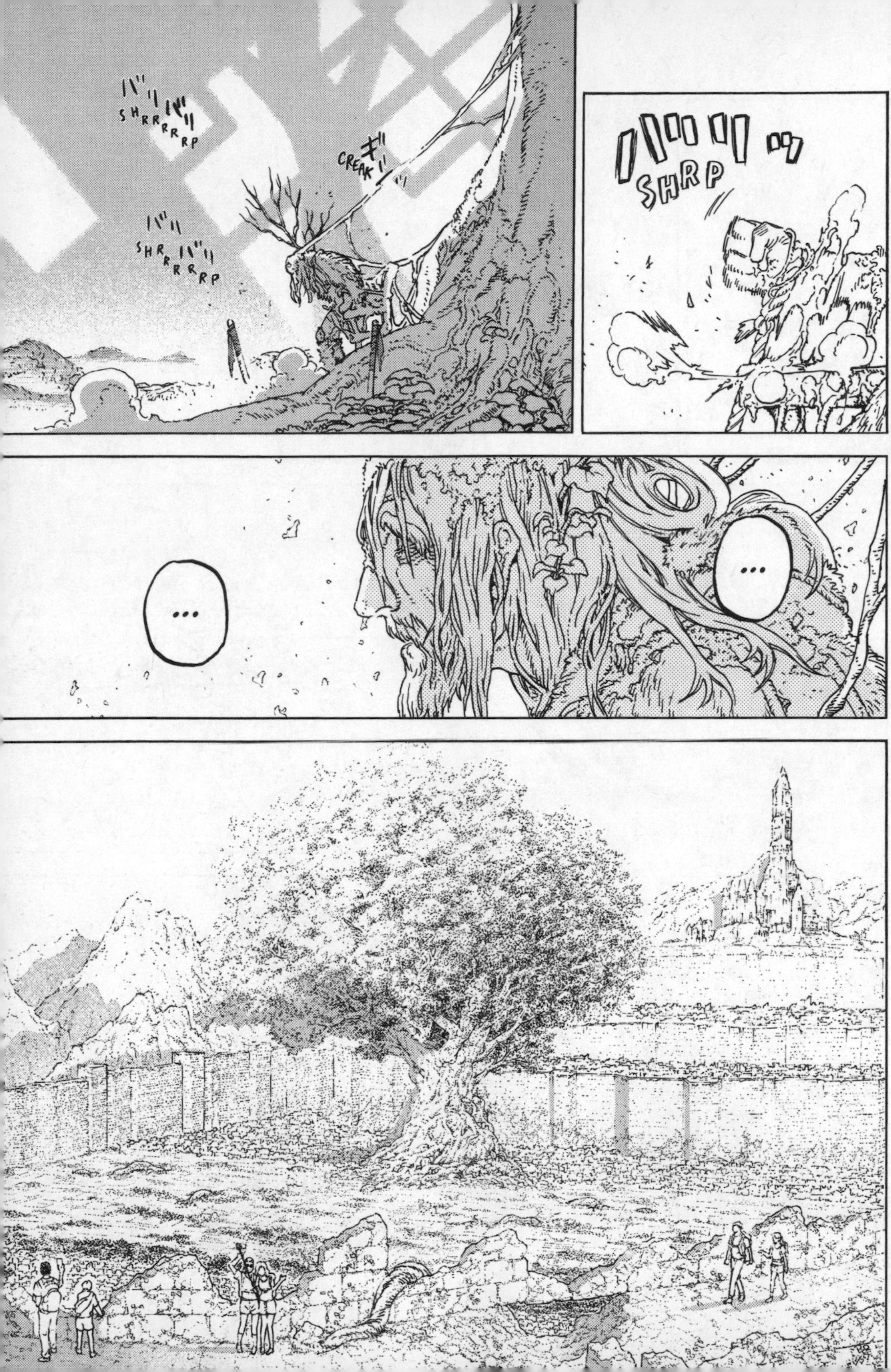

SHRP
SHRRRRRP
CREAK
SHRRRRRP
...
...

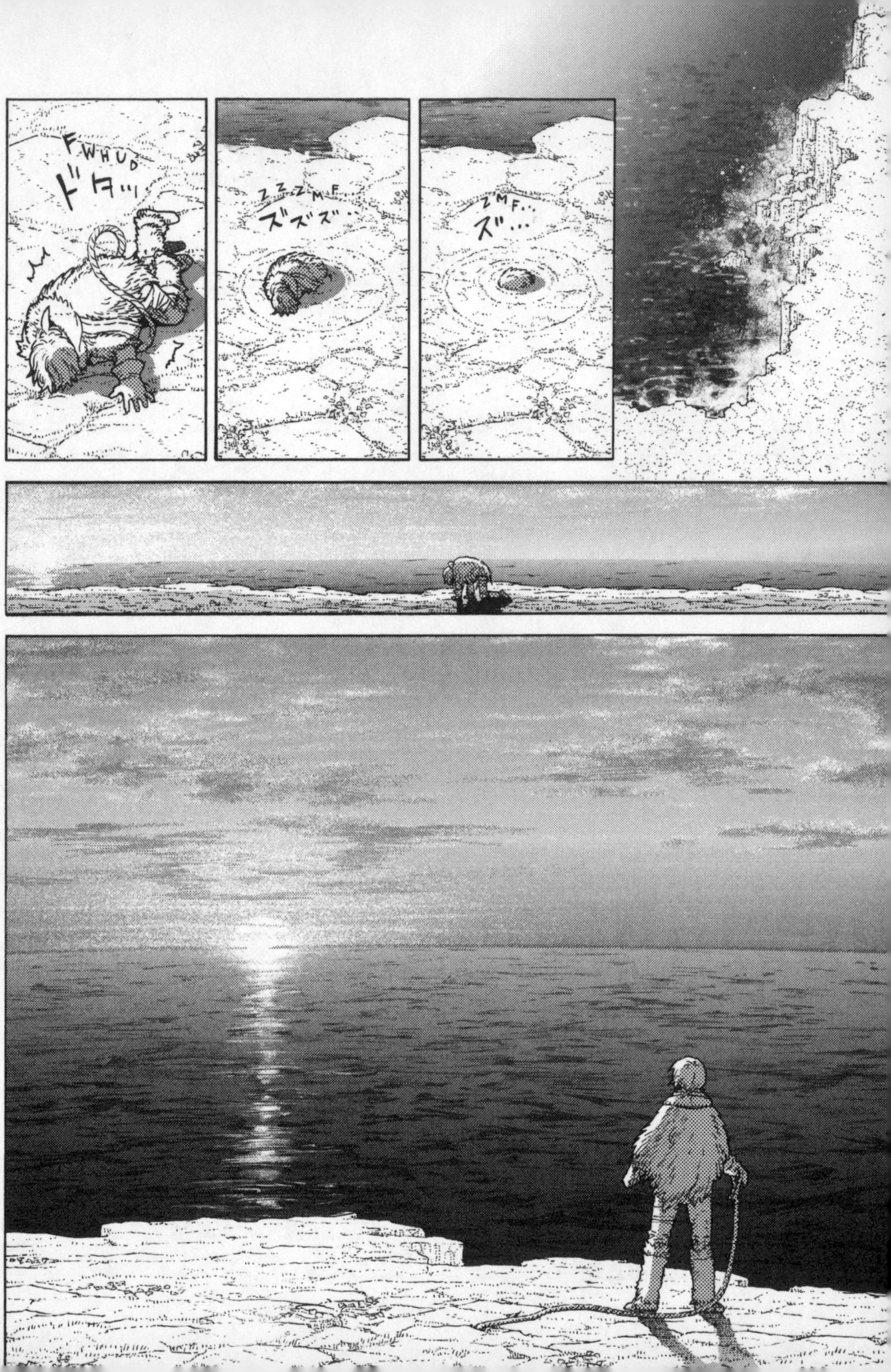
ZMF…
ズ…
ZZZMF
ズズズ…
FWHUD
ドタッ

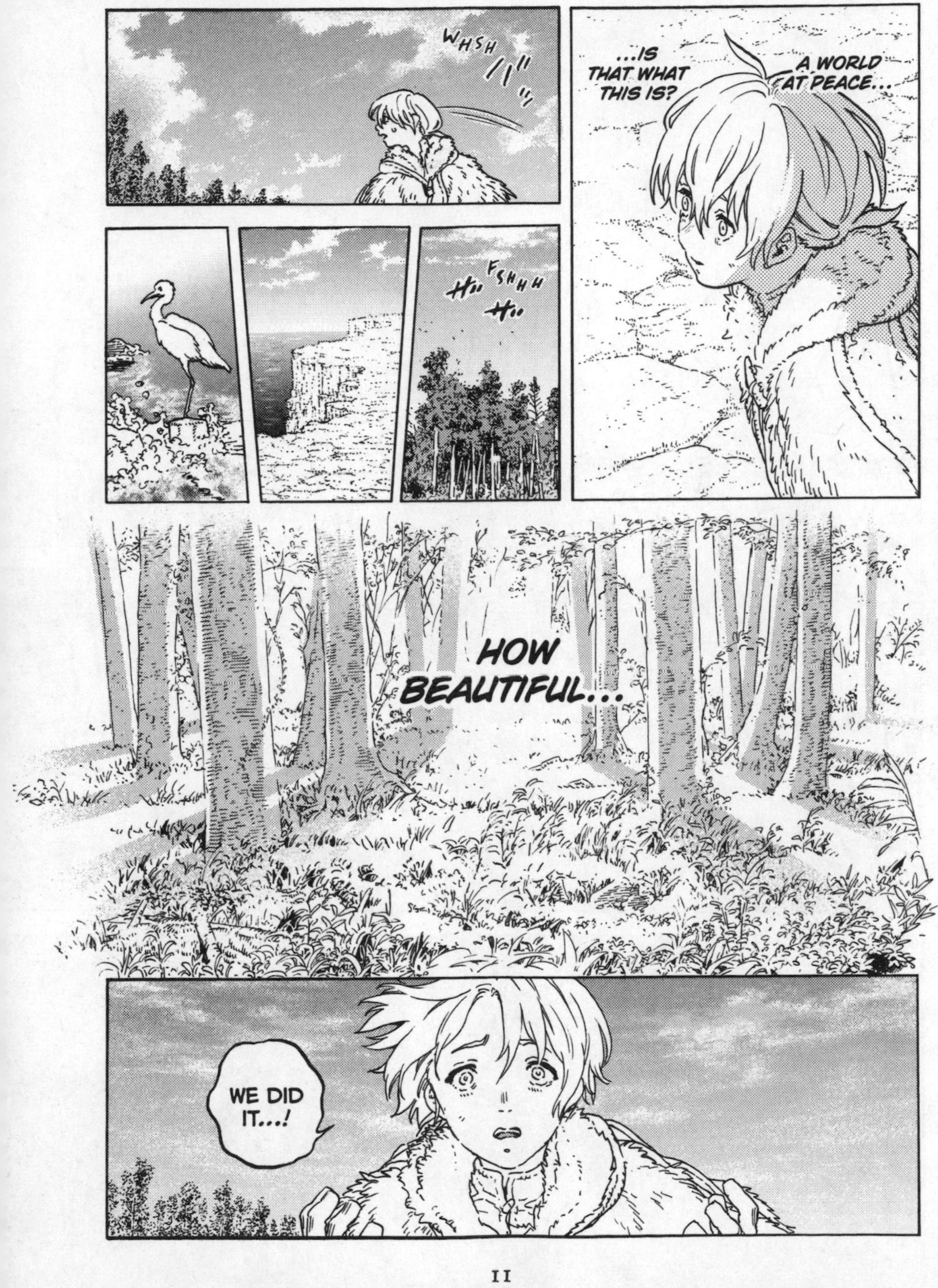
A WORLD AT PEACE...
...IS THAT WHAT THIS IS?
WHSH
FSHHH
HOW BEAUTIFUL...
WE DID IT...!

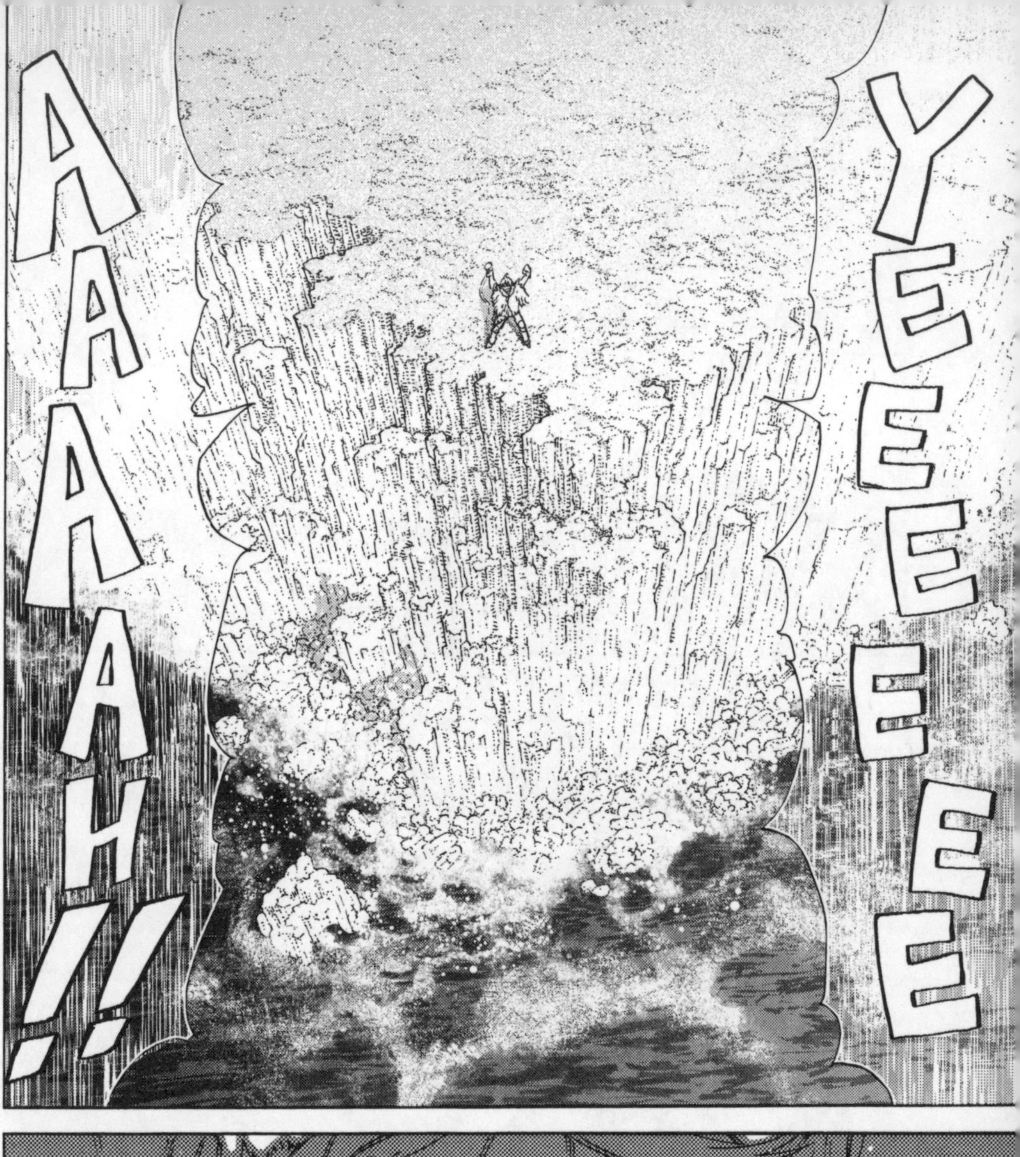
YEEEEEEE
AAAAH!!
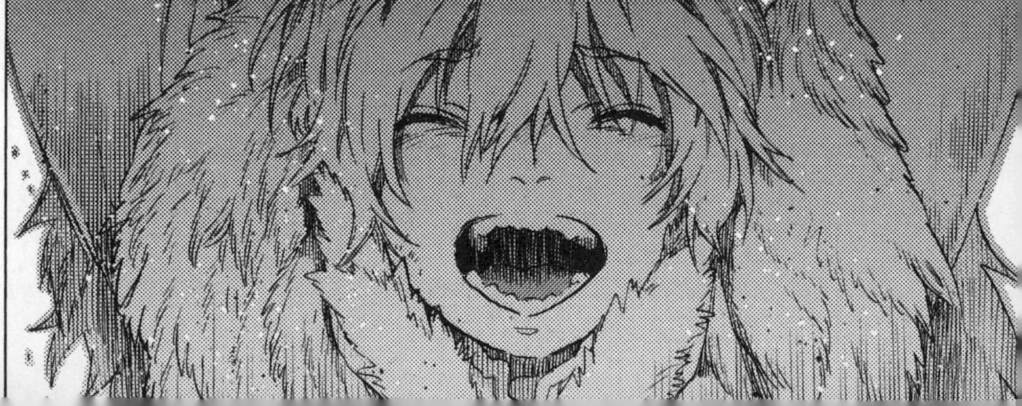

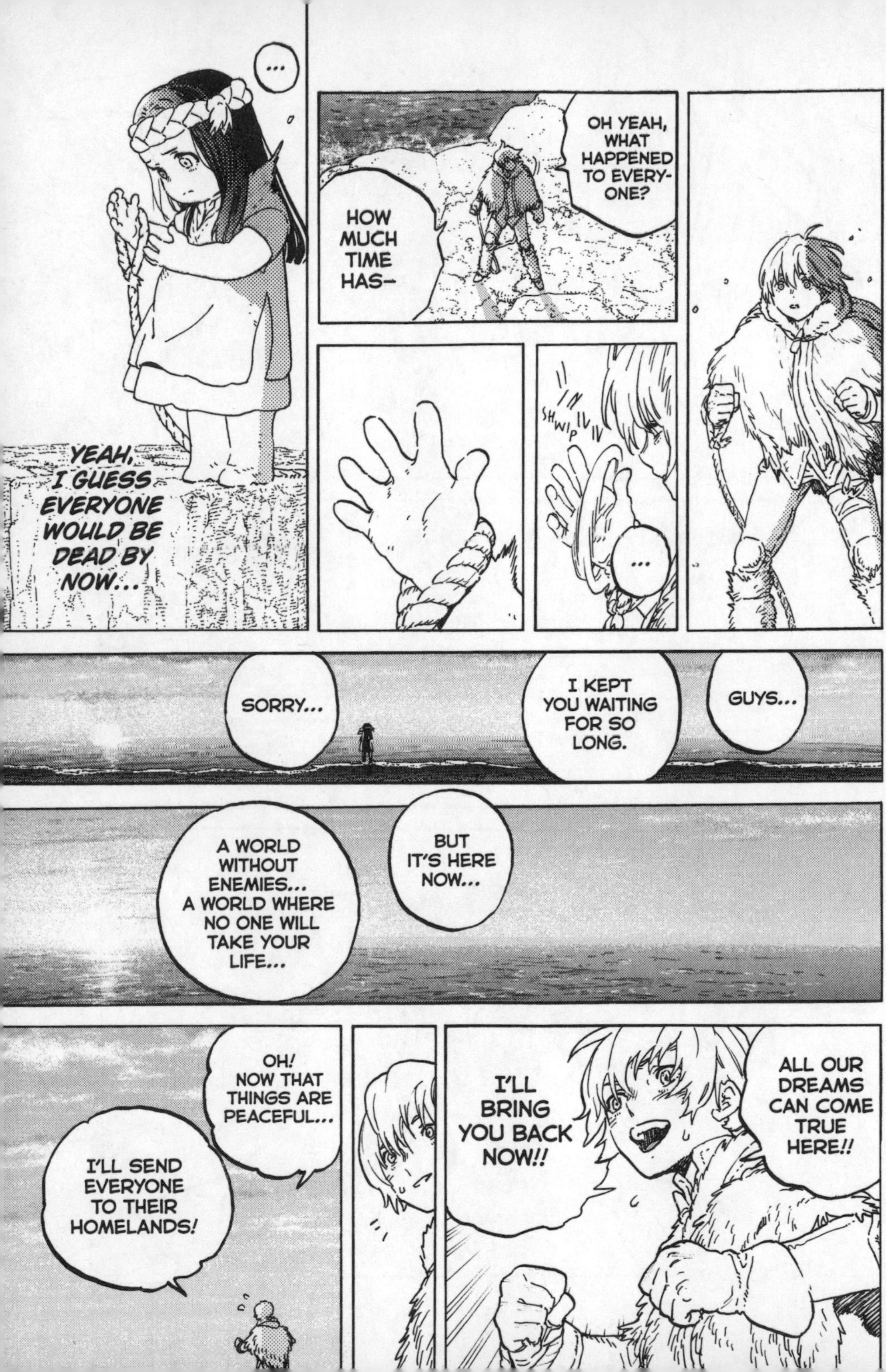
OH YEAH, WHAT HAPPENED TO EVERY-ONE?
HOW MUCH TIME HAS—
SHWIP
...
...
YEAH, I GUESS EVERYONE WOULD BE DEAD BY NOW...
GUYS...
I KEPT YOU WAITING FOR SO LONG.
SORRY...
BUT IT'S HERE NOW...
A WORLD WITHOUT ENEMIES... A WORLD WHERE NO ONE WILL TAKE YOUR LIFE...
ALL OUR DREAMS CAN COME TRUE HERE!!
I'LL BRING YOU BACK NOW!!
OH! NOW THAT THINGS ARE PEACEFUL...
I'LL SEND EVERYONE TO THEIR HOMELANDS!

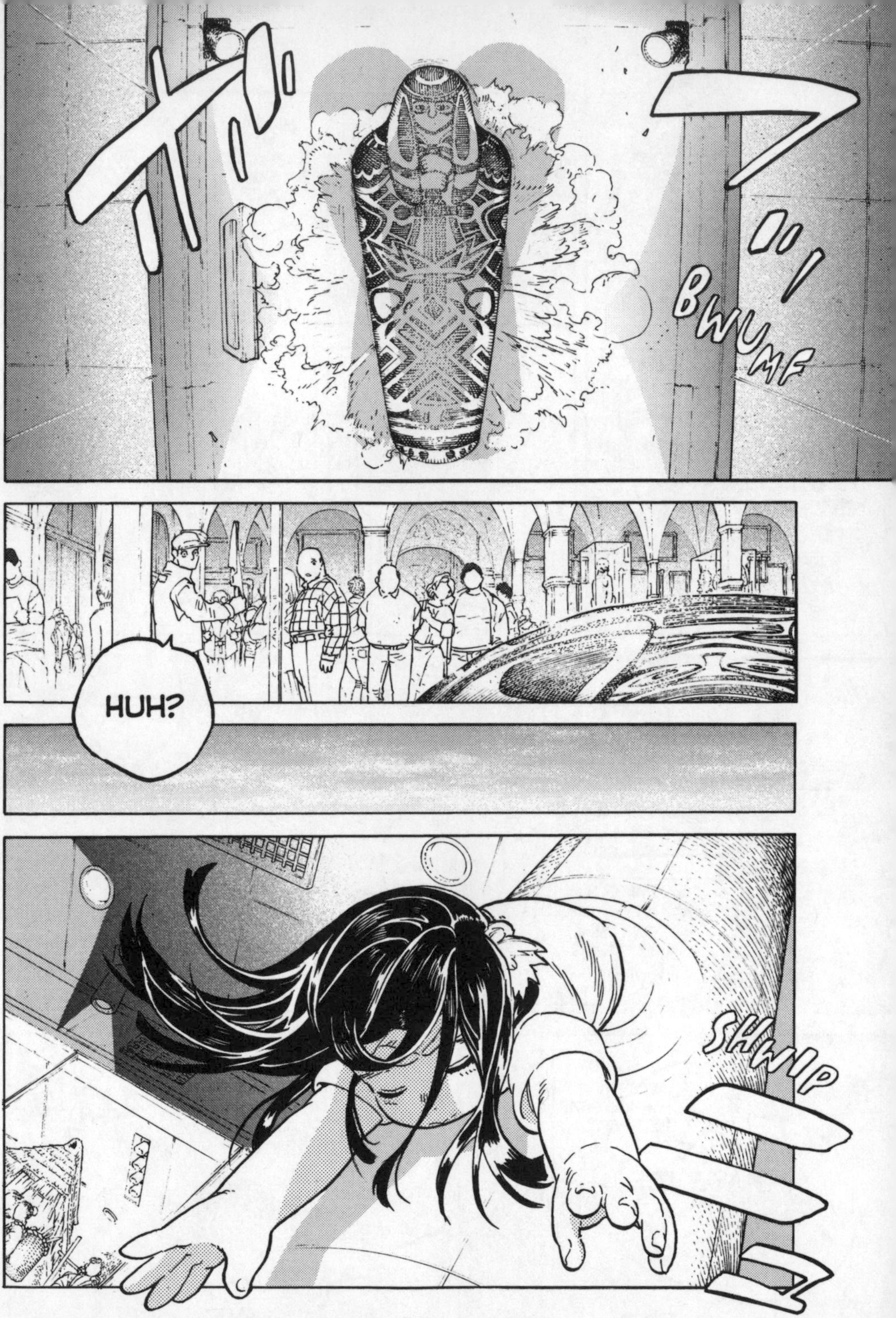
BWUMF
HUH?
SHWIP

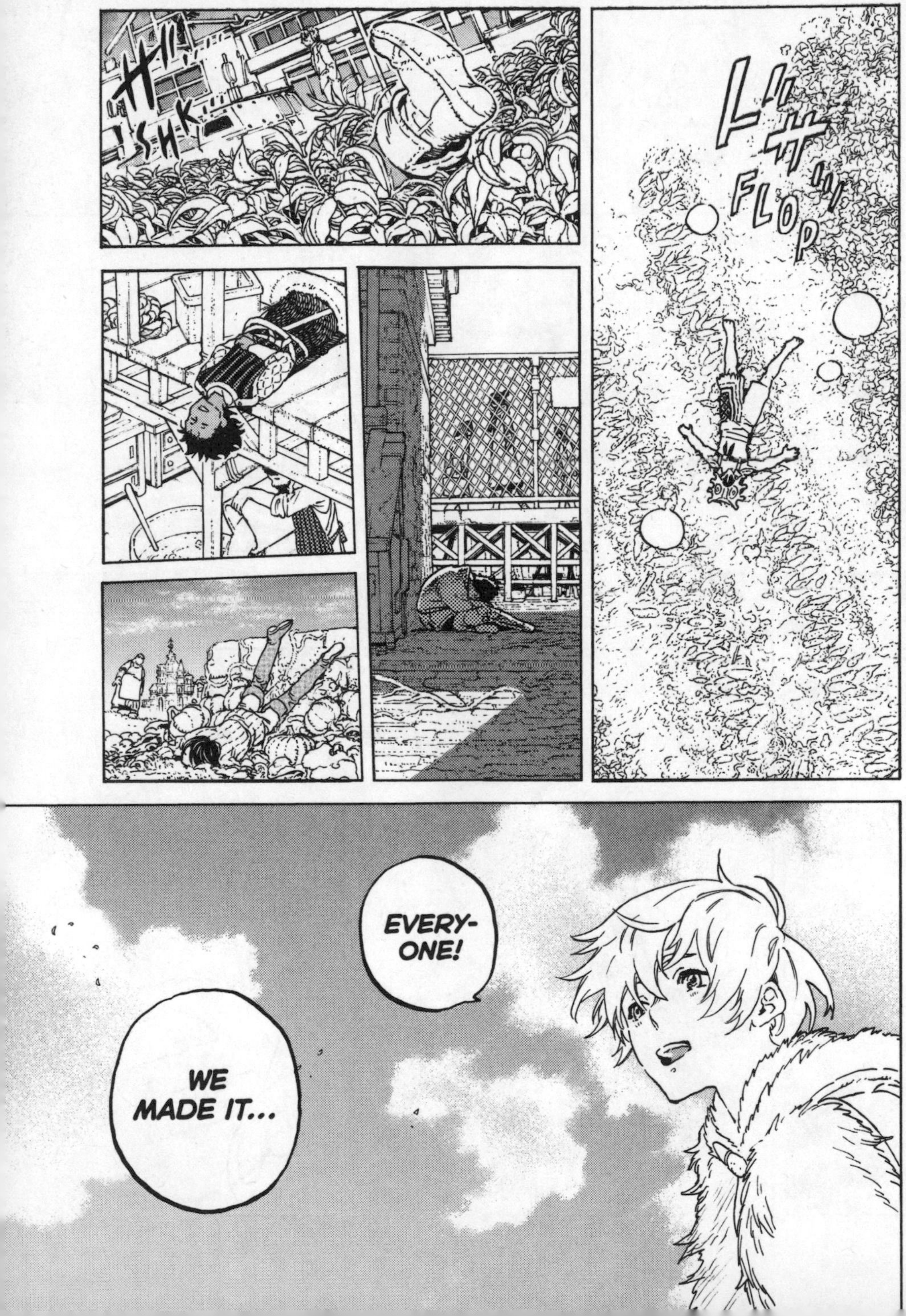
FLOP
SHK
EVERY-ONE!
WE MADE IT...

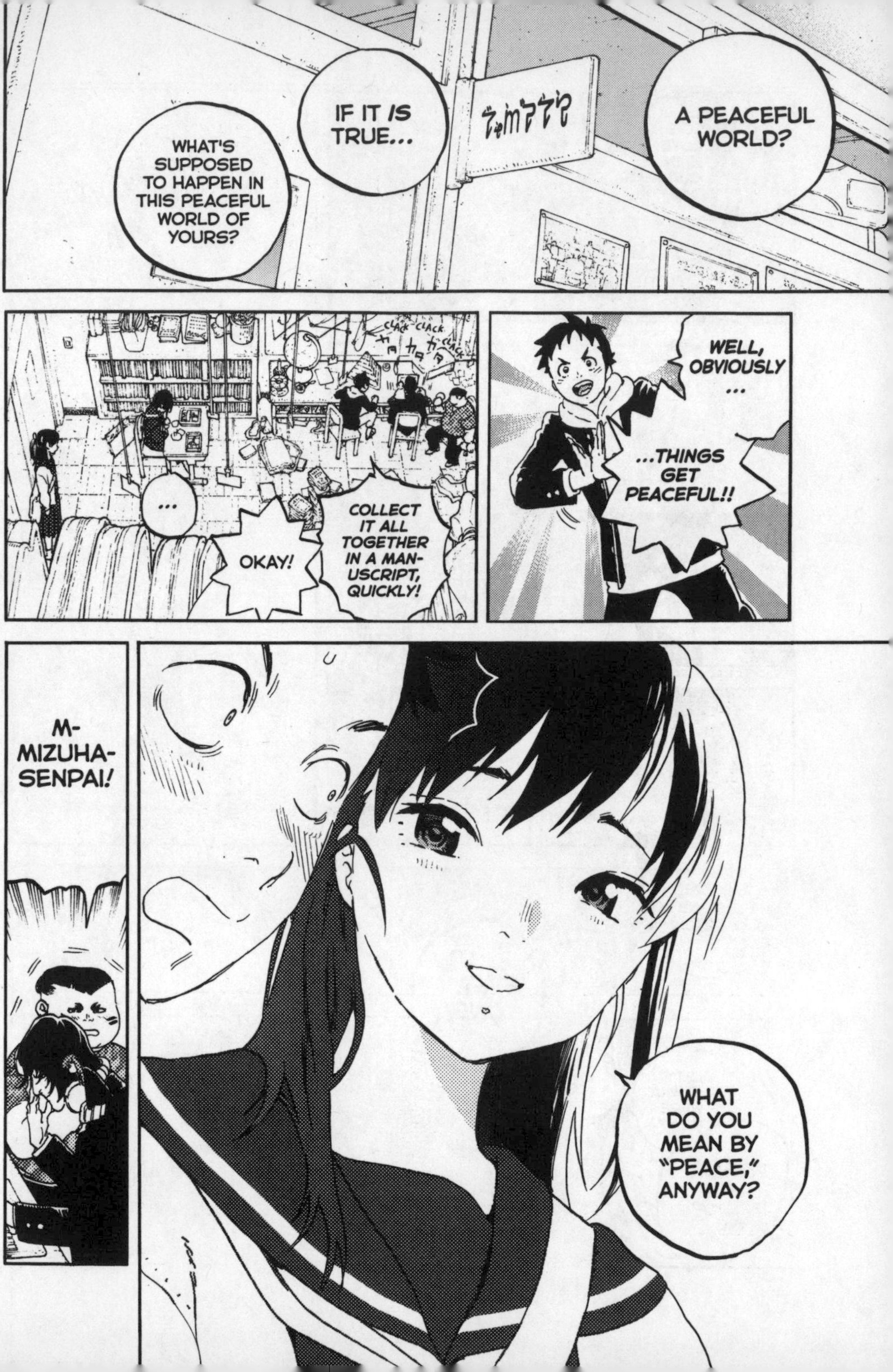
A PEACEFUL WORLD?
IF IT IS TRUE...
WHAT'S SUPPOSED TO HAPPEN IN THIS PEACEFUL WORLD OF YOURS?
WELL, OBVIOUSLY ...
...THINGS GET PEACEFUL!!
CLACK CLACK CLACK
COLLECT IT ALL TOGETHER IN A MAN-USCRIPT, QUICKLY!
OKAY!
...
WHAT DO YOU MEAN BY "PEACE," ANYWAY?
M-MIZUHA-SENPAI!

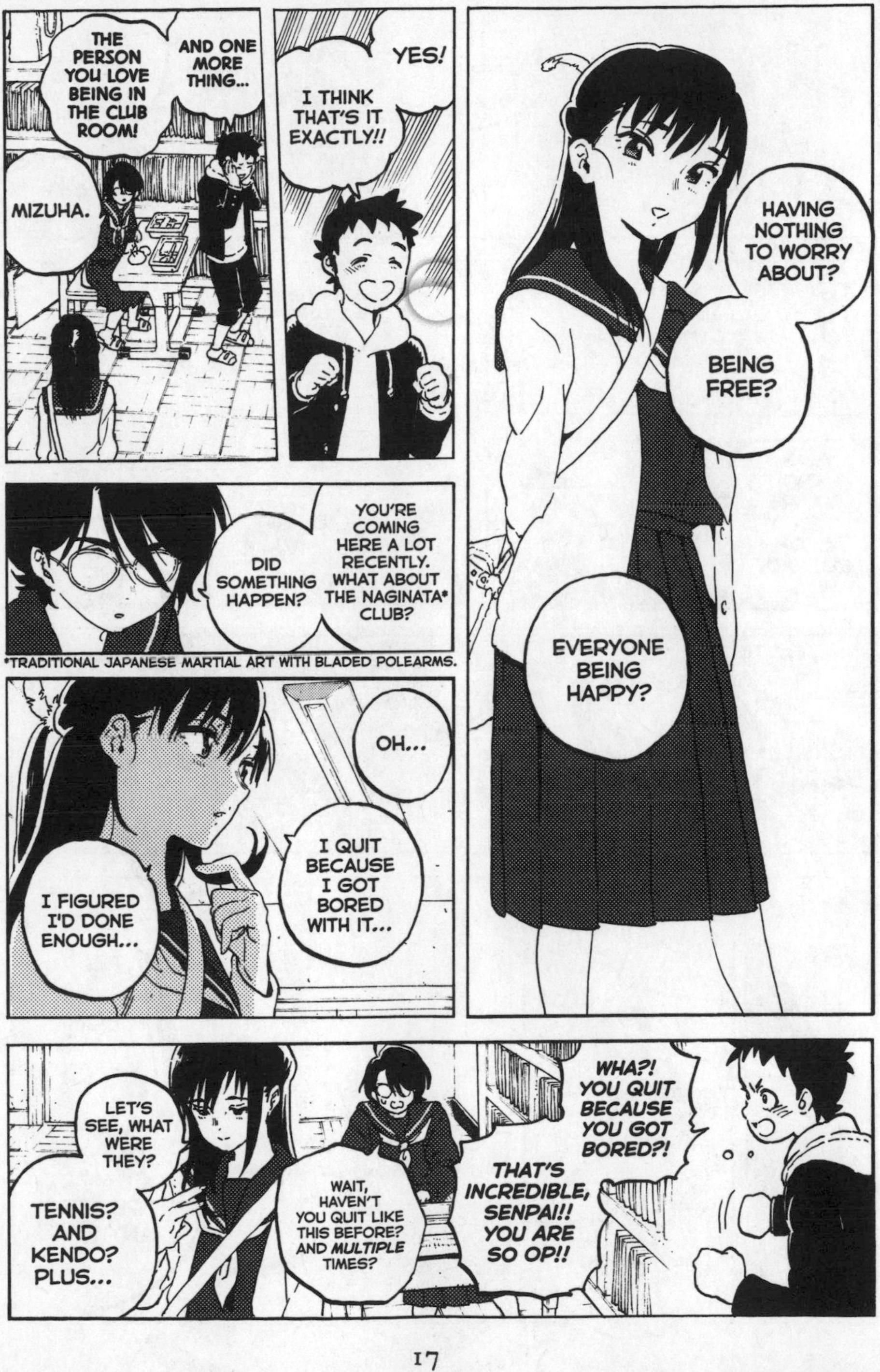
HAVING NOTHING TO WORRY ABOUT?
BEING FREE?
EVERYONE BEING HAPPY?
YES!
I THINK THAT'S IT EXACTLY!!
AND ONE MORE THING...
THE PERSON YOU LOVE BEING IN THE CLUB ROOM!
MIZUHA.
YOU'RE COMING HERE A LOT RECENTLY. WHAT ABOUT THE NAGINATA* CLUB?
DID SOMETHING HAPPEN?
*TRADITIONAL JAPANESE MARTIAL ART WITH BLADED POLEARMS.
OH...
I QUIT BECAUSE I GOT BORED WITH IT...
I FIGURED I'D DONE ENOUGH...
WHA?! YOU QUIT BECAUSE YOU GOT BORED?!
THAT'S INCREDIBLE, SENPAI!! YOU ARE SO OP!!
WAIT, HAVEN'T YOU QUIT LIKE THIS BEFORE? AND *MULTIPLE* TIMES?
LET'S SEE, WHAT WERE THEY?
TENNIS? AND KENDO? PLUS...

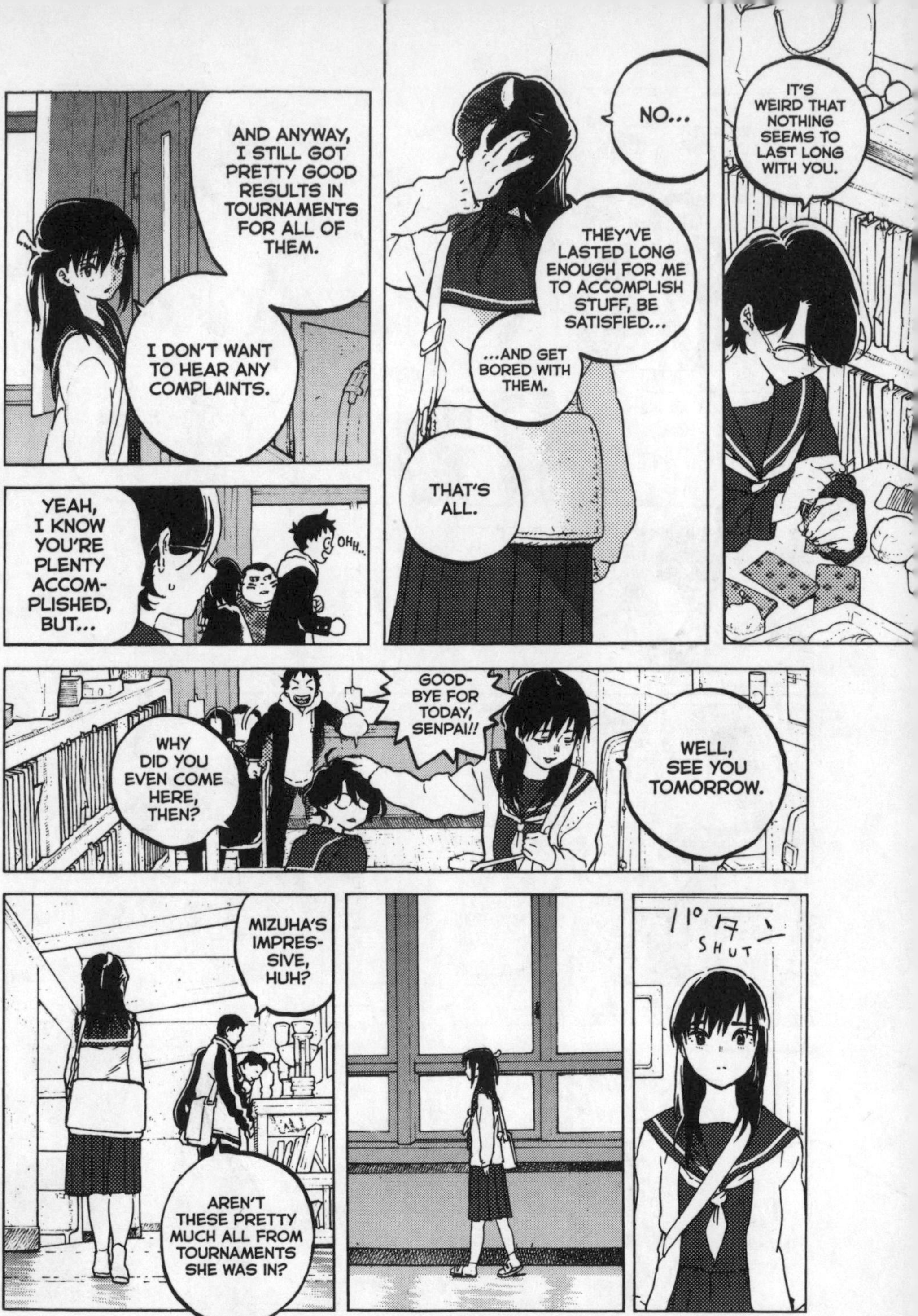
IT'S WEIRD THAT NOTHING SEEMS TO LAST LONG WITH YOU.
NO...
THEY'VE LASTED LONG ENOUGH FOR ME TO ACCOMPLISH STUFF, BE SATISFIED...
...AND GET BORED WITH THEM.
THAT'S ALL.
AND ANYWAY, I STILL GOT PRETTY GOOD RESULTS IN TOURNAMENTS FOR ALL OF THEM.
I DON'T WANT TO HEAR ANY COMPLAINTS.
YEAH, I KNOW YOU'RE PLENTY ACCOM-PLISHED, BUT...
OHH..
WELL, SEE YOU TOMORROW.
GOOD-BYE FOR TODAY, SENPAI!!
WHY DID YOU EVEN COME HERE, THEN?
パタン
SHUT
MIZUHA'S IMPRES-SIVE, HUH?
AREN'T THESE PRETTY MUCH ALL FROM TOURNAMENTS SHE WAS IN?

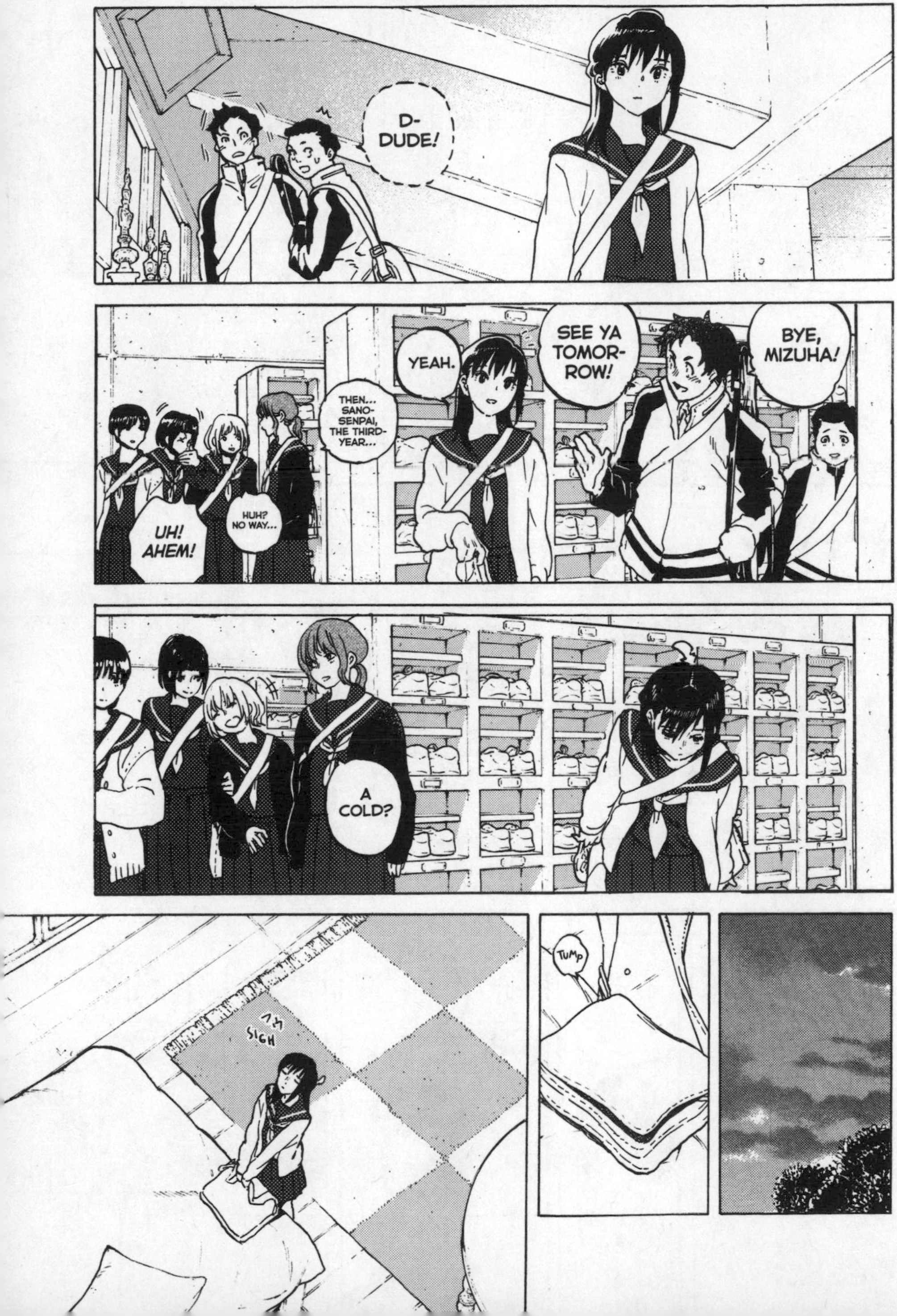
D-DUDE!
BYE, MIZUHA!
SEE YA TOMORROW!
YEAH.
THEN... SANO-SENPAI, THE THIRD-YEAR...
HUH? NO WAY...
UH! AHEM!
A COLD?
TUMP
SIGH

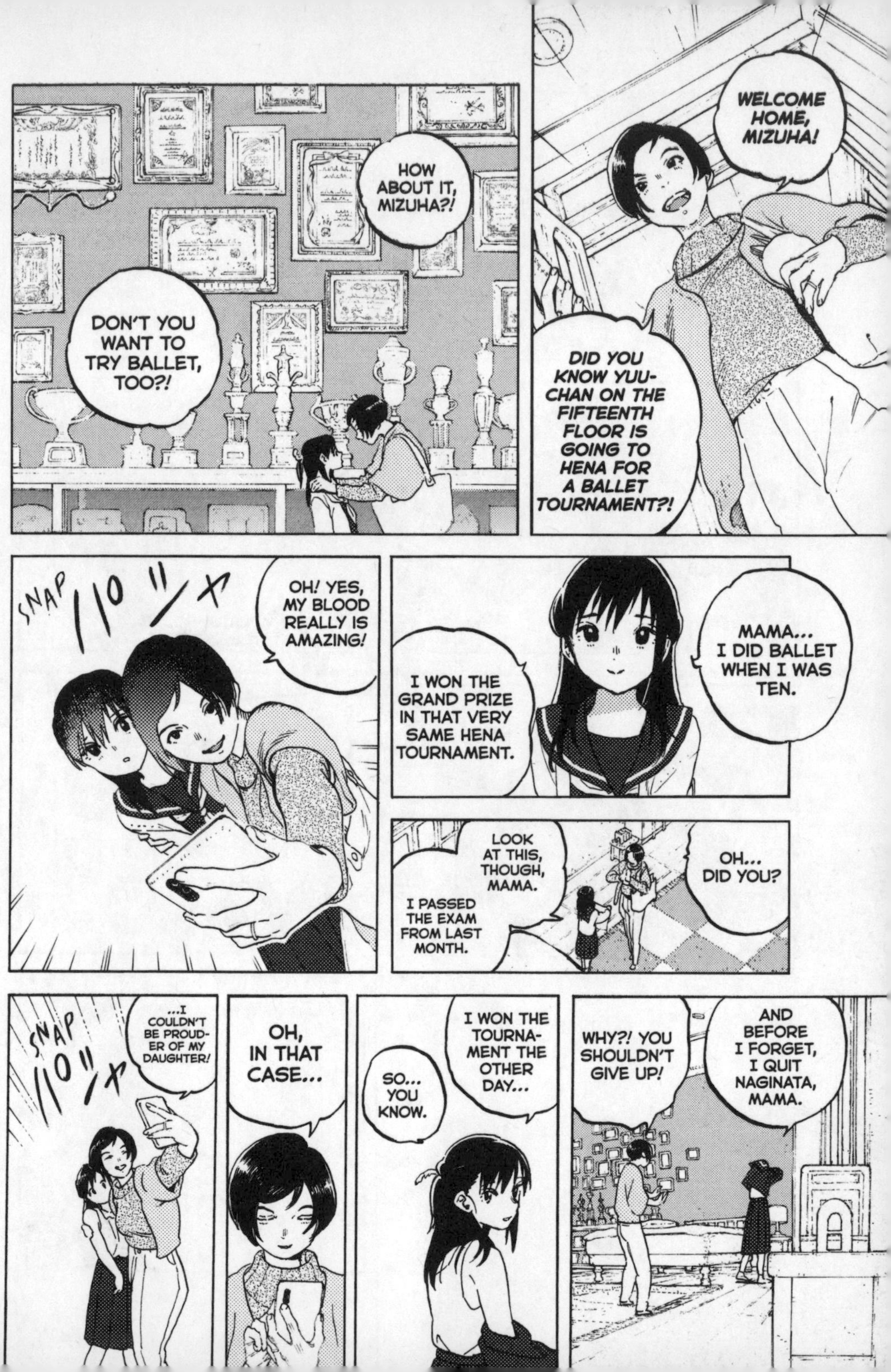
WELCOME HOME, MIZUHA!
DID YOU KNOW YUU-CHAN ON THE FIFTEENTH FLOOR IS GOING TO HENA FOR A BALLET TOURNAMENT?!
HOW ABOUT IT, MIZUHA?!
DON'T YOU WANT TO TRY BALLET, TOO?!
MAMA... I DID BALLET WHEN I WAS TEN.
I WON THE GRAND PRIZE IN THAT VERY SAME HENA TOURNAMENT.
OH... DID YOU?
LOOK AT THIS, THOUGH, MAMA.
I PASSED THE EXAM FROM LAST MONTH.
OH! YES, MY BLOOD REALLY IS AMAZING!
SNAP
AND BEFORE I FORGET, I QUIT NAGINATA, MAMA.
WHY?! YOU SHOULDN'T GIVE UP!
I WON THE TOURNAMENT THE OTHER DAY...
SO... YOU KNOW.
OH, IN THAT CASE...
...I COULDN'T BE PROUDER OF MY DAUGHTER!
SNAP

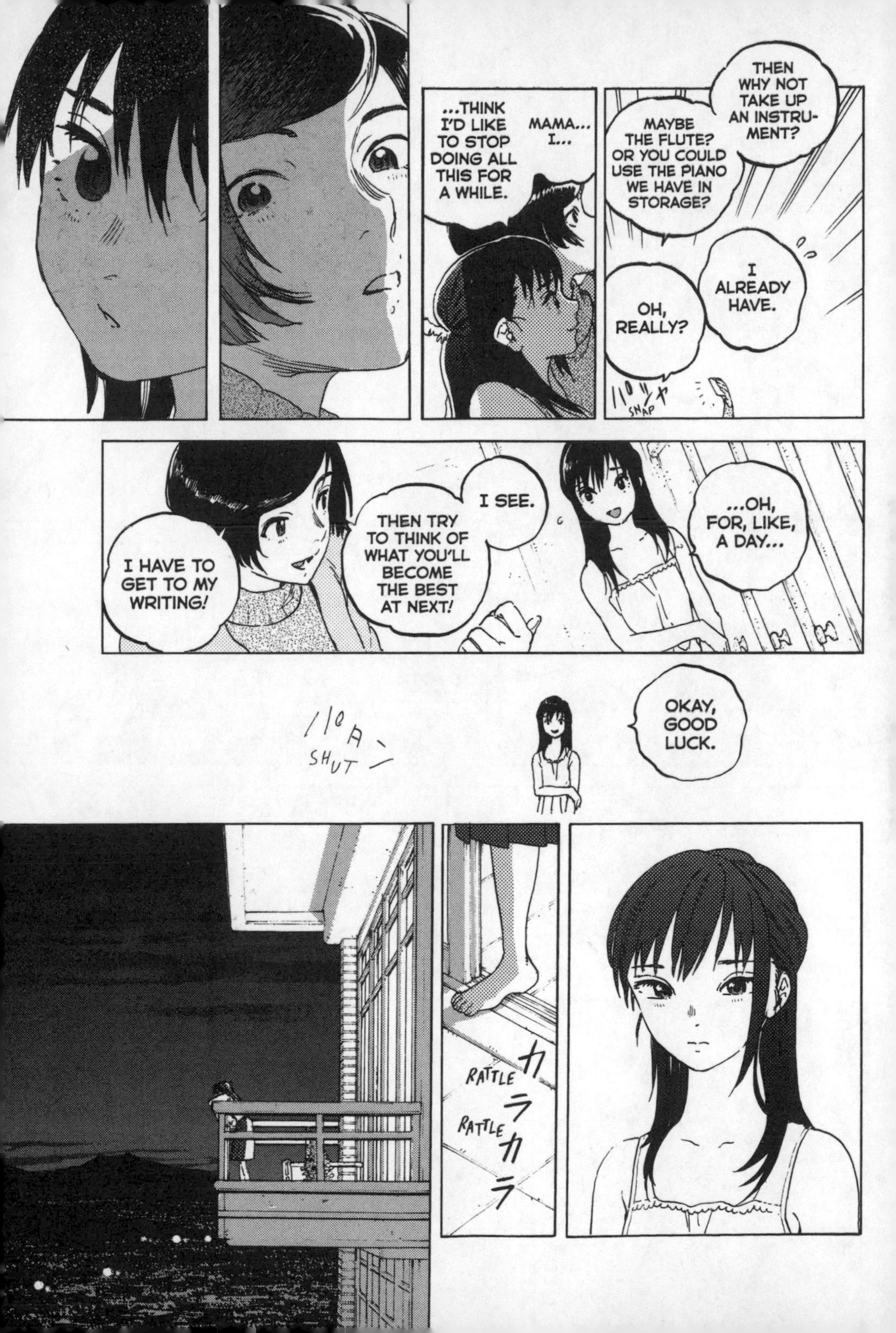
THEN WHY NOT TAKE UP AN INSTRUMENT?
MAYBE THE FLUTE? OR YOU COULD USE THE PIANO WE HAVE IN STORAGE?
I ALREADY HAVE.
OH, REALLY?
SNAP
MAMA... I...
...THINK I'D LIKE TO STOP DOING ALL THIS FOR A WHILE.
...OH, FOR, LIKE, A DAY...
I SEE.
THEN TRY TO THINK OF WHAT YOU'LL BECOME THE BEST AT NEXT!
I HAVE TO GET TO MY WRITING!
OKAY, GOOD LUCK.
SHUT
RATTLE
RATTLE

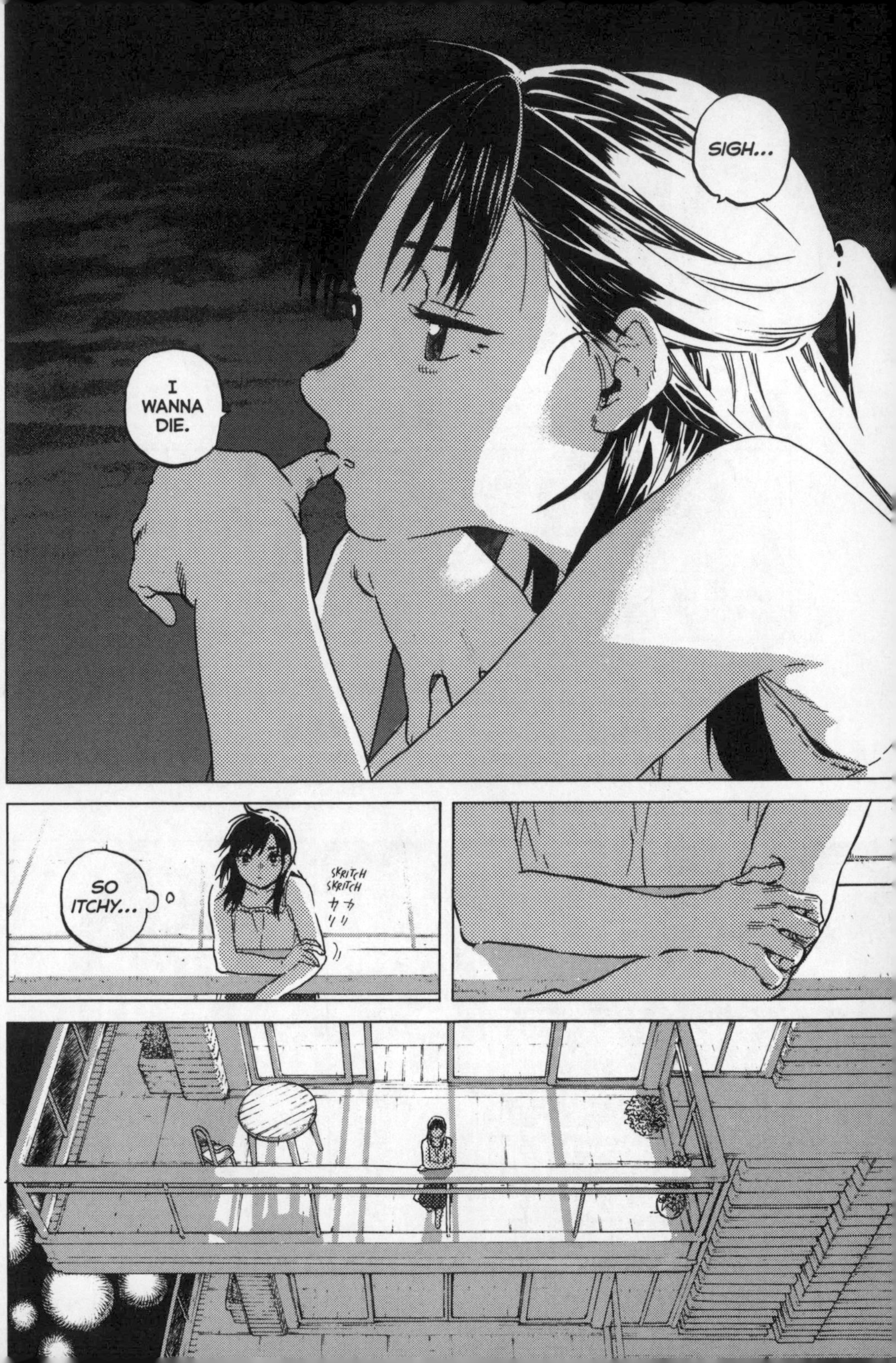
SIGH...
I WANNA DIE.
SO ITCHY...
SKRITCH SKRITCH

TO YOUR
ETERNITY

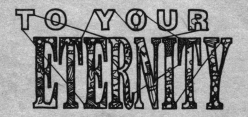

The End of St. Cylira

When he defeated Fushi,
Cylira, the High Cleric of the Church of Bennett,
transcended Ilsarita and became the savior of the entire world.
But the power of Bennett did not protect him.

One day, a lone man appeared before him.
The man led him to a blast furnace, pushed him from behind,
and reduced him to no more than slag.
Then the man used explosives to blow up
both the blast furnace and himself.
Those who saw the red-tinged sky claimed
that a demon had awakened from hell.
Henceforth, Entas was known as a cursed city.

It was later revealed that the man was Kahaku:
The leader of the Guardians and a close associate of Fushi.
These events will be recorded in the New Testament of
the Book of Bennett as the most wicked of all events in history.

UGA CASTLE PRIEST CORCODA'S NOTES

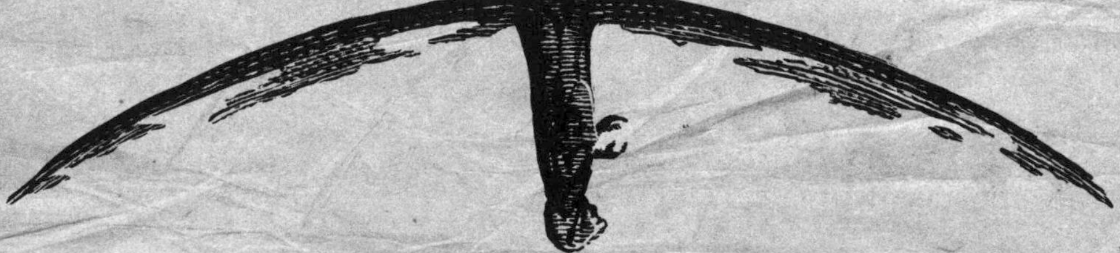

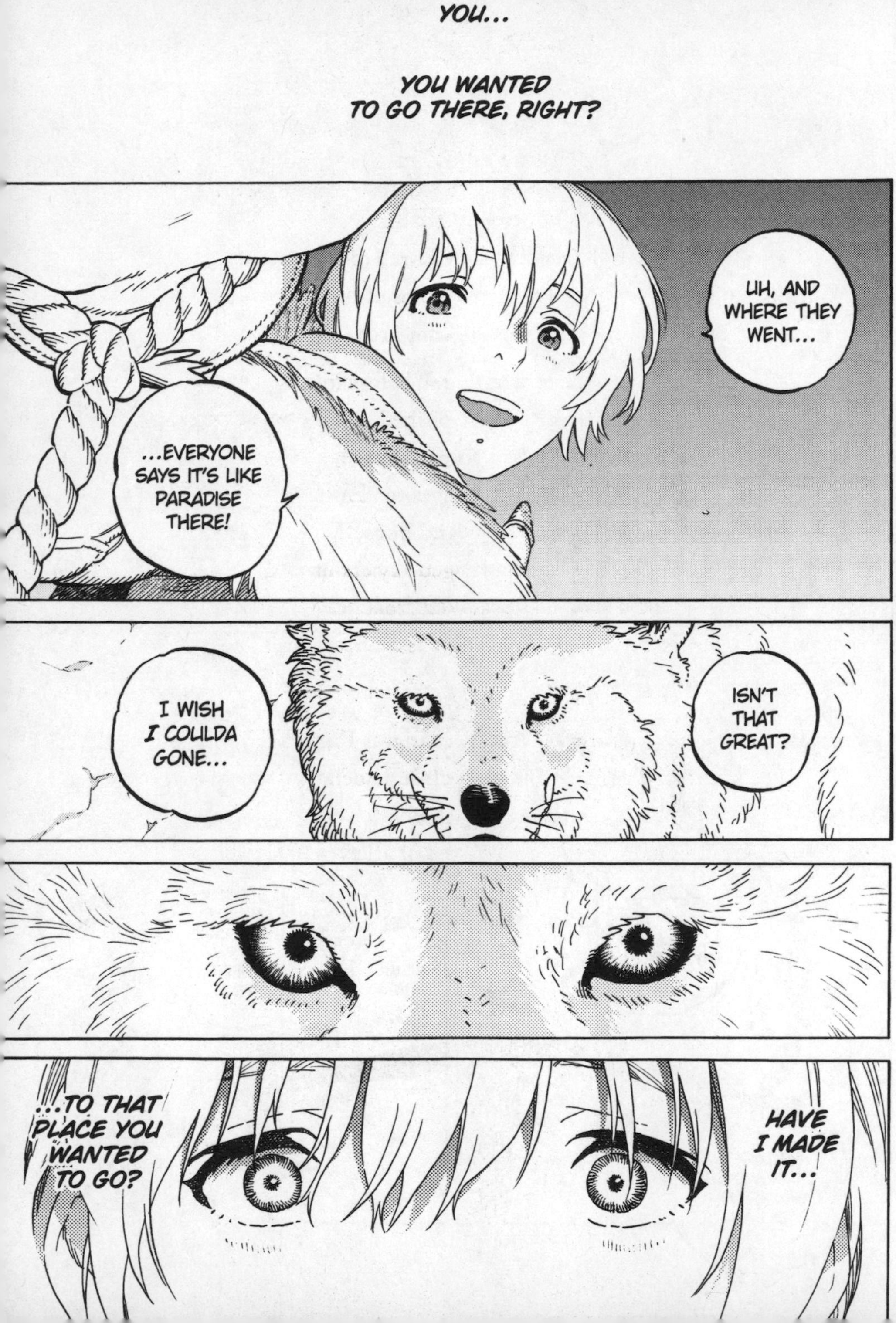
YOU...
YOU WANTED TO GO THERE, RIGHT?
UH, AND WHERE THEY WENT...
...EVERYONE SAYS IT'S LIKE PARADISE THERE!
ISN'T THAT GREAT?
I WISH I COULDA GONE...
HAVE I MADE IT...
...TO THAT PLACE YOU WANTED TO GO?

#118 Reins

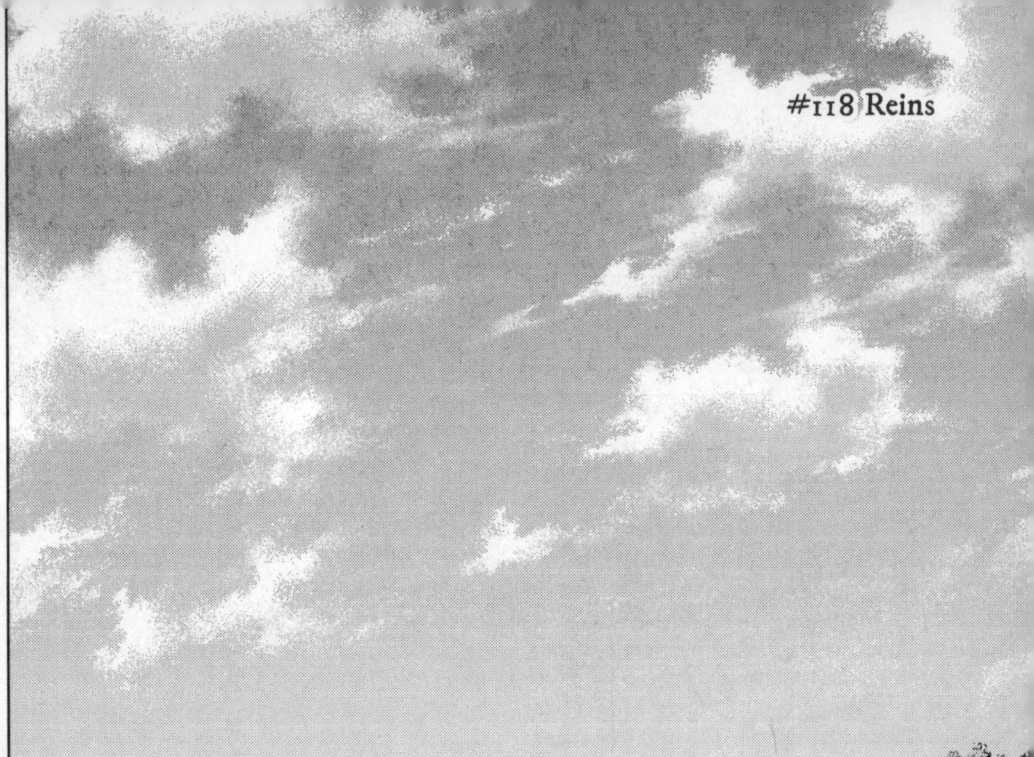

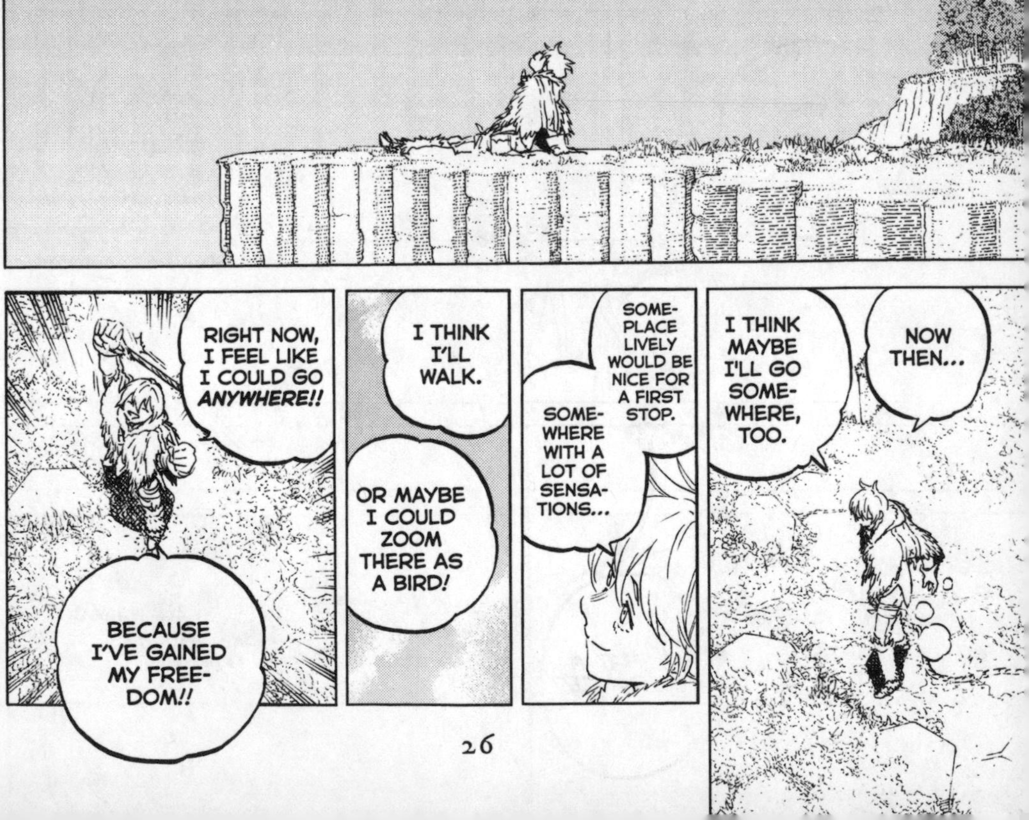
NOW THEN...
I THINK MAYBE I'LL GO SOME-WHERE, TOO.
SOME-PLACE LIVELY WOULD BE NICE FOR A FIRST STOP.
SOME-WHERE WITH A LOT OF SENSA-TIONS...
I THINK I'LL WALK.
OR MAYBE I COULD ZOOM THERE AS A BIRD!
RIGHT NOW, I FEEL LIKE I COULD GO *ANYWHERE!!*
BECAUSE I'VE GAINED MY FREE-DOM!!

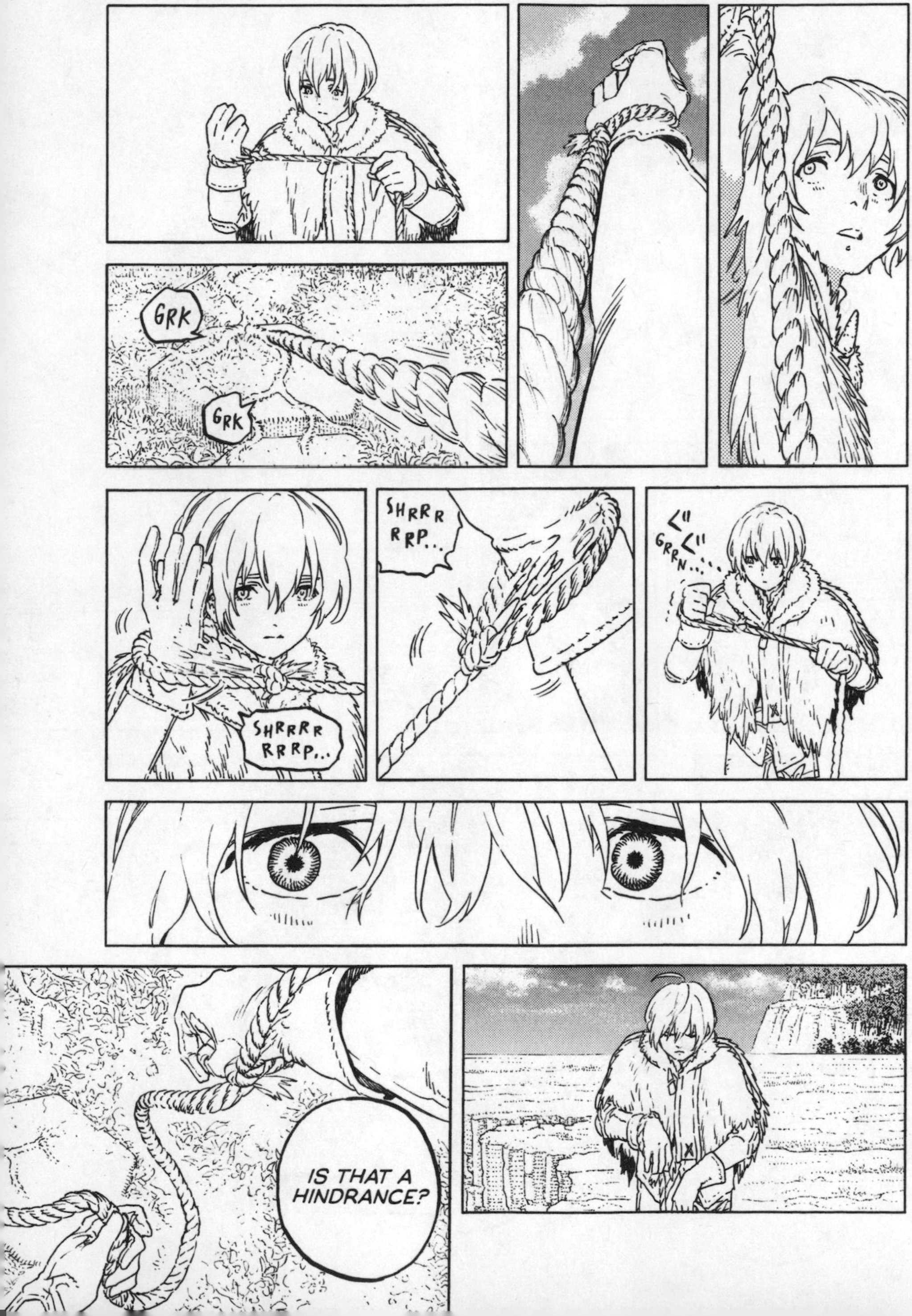
GRK
GRK
ぐぐ
GRRN...
SHRRRRRP...
SHRRRRRRP...
IS THAT A HINDRANCE?

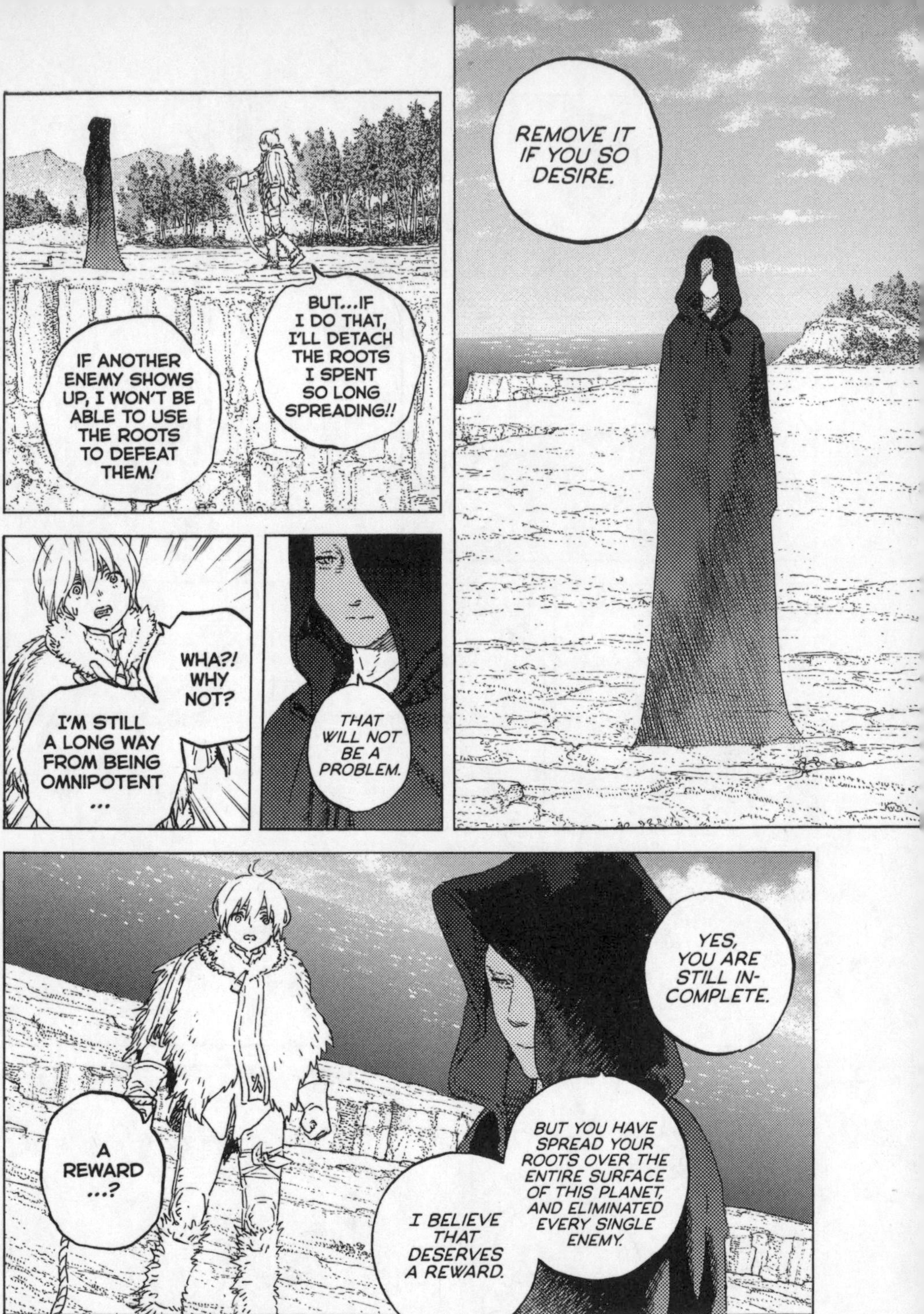
REMOVE IT IF YOU SO DESIRE.
BUT...IF I DO THAT, I'LL DETACH THE ROOTS I SPENT SO LONG SPREADING!!
IF ANOTHER ENEMY SHOWS UP, I WON'T BE ABLE TO USE THE ROOTS TO DEFEAT THEM!
THAT WILL NOT BE A PROBLEM.
WHA?! WHY NOT?
I'M STILL A LONG WAY FROM BEING OMNIPOTENT ...
YES, YOU ARE STILL IN-COMPLETE.
BUT YOU HAVE SPREAD YOUR ROOTS OVER THE ENTIRE SURFACE OF THIS PLANET, AND ELIMINATED EVERY SINGLE ENEMY.
I BELIEVE THAT DESERVES A REWARD.
A REWARD ...?

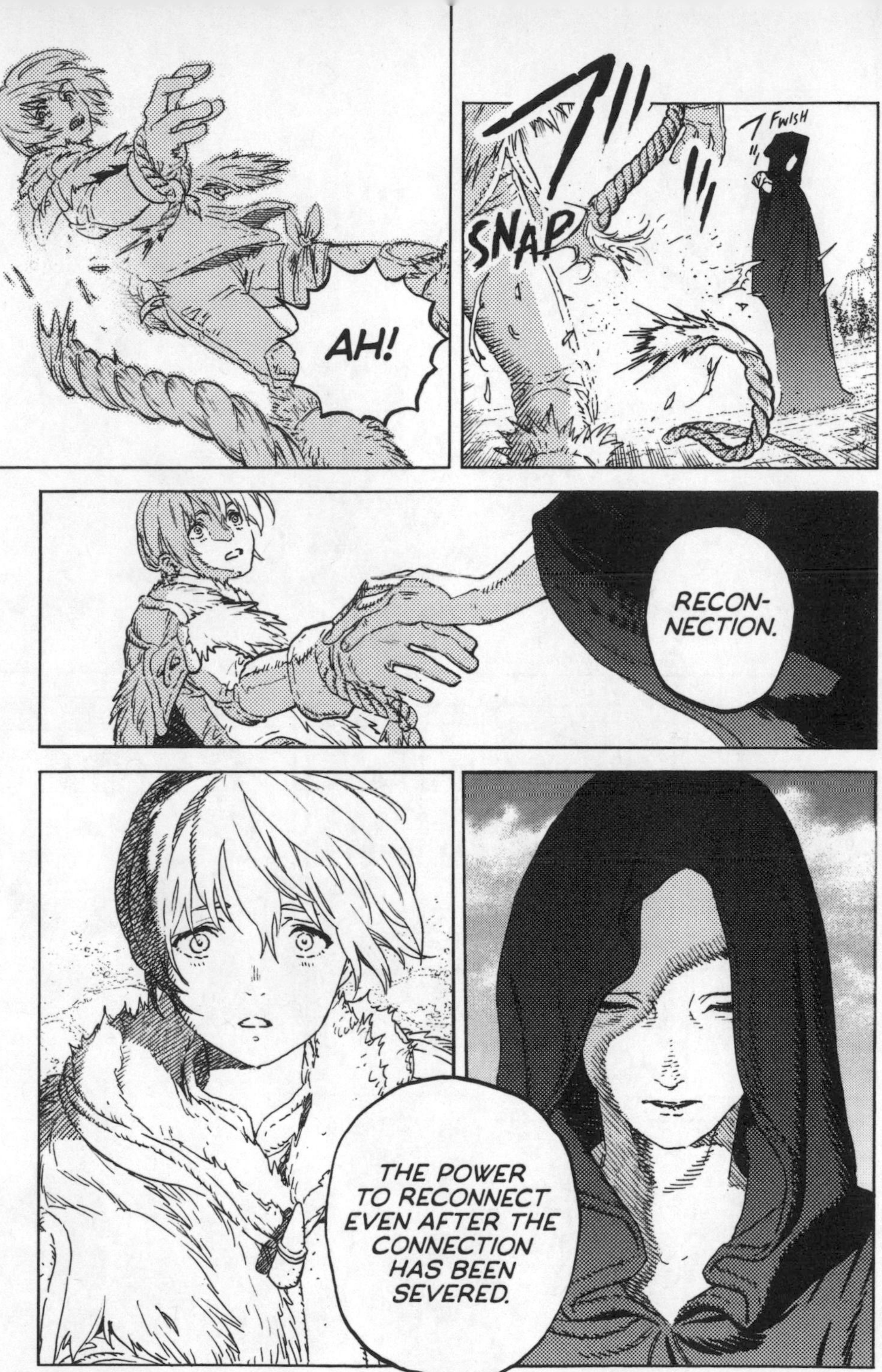
SNAP
FWISH
AH!
RECON-
NECTION.
THE POWER
TO RECONNECT
EVEN AFTER THE
CONNECTION
HAS BEEN
SEVERED.

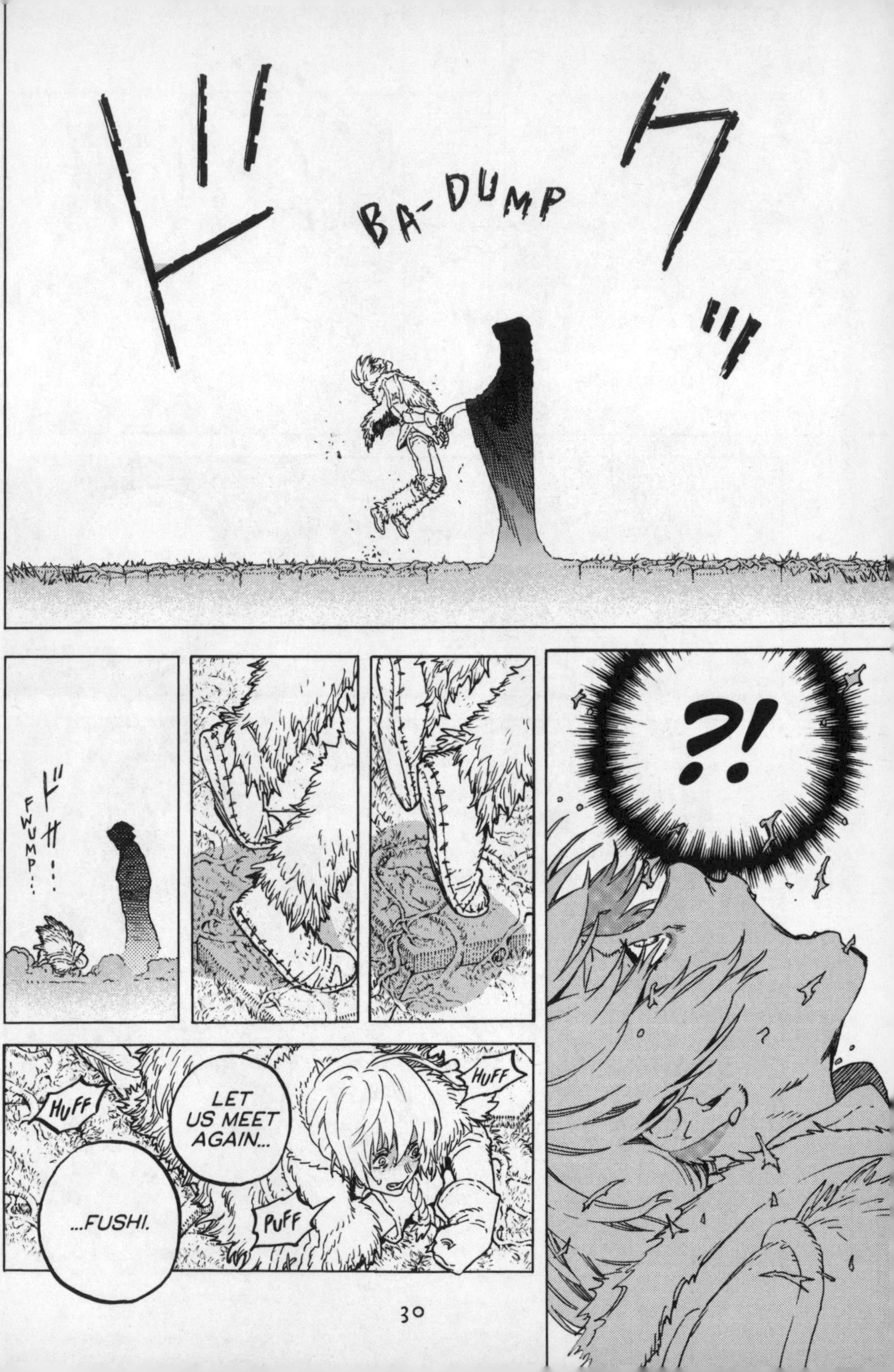
BA-DUMP
?!
FWUMP...
HUFF
LET US MEET AGAIN...
...FUSHI.
PUFF
HUFF

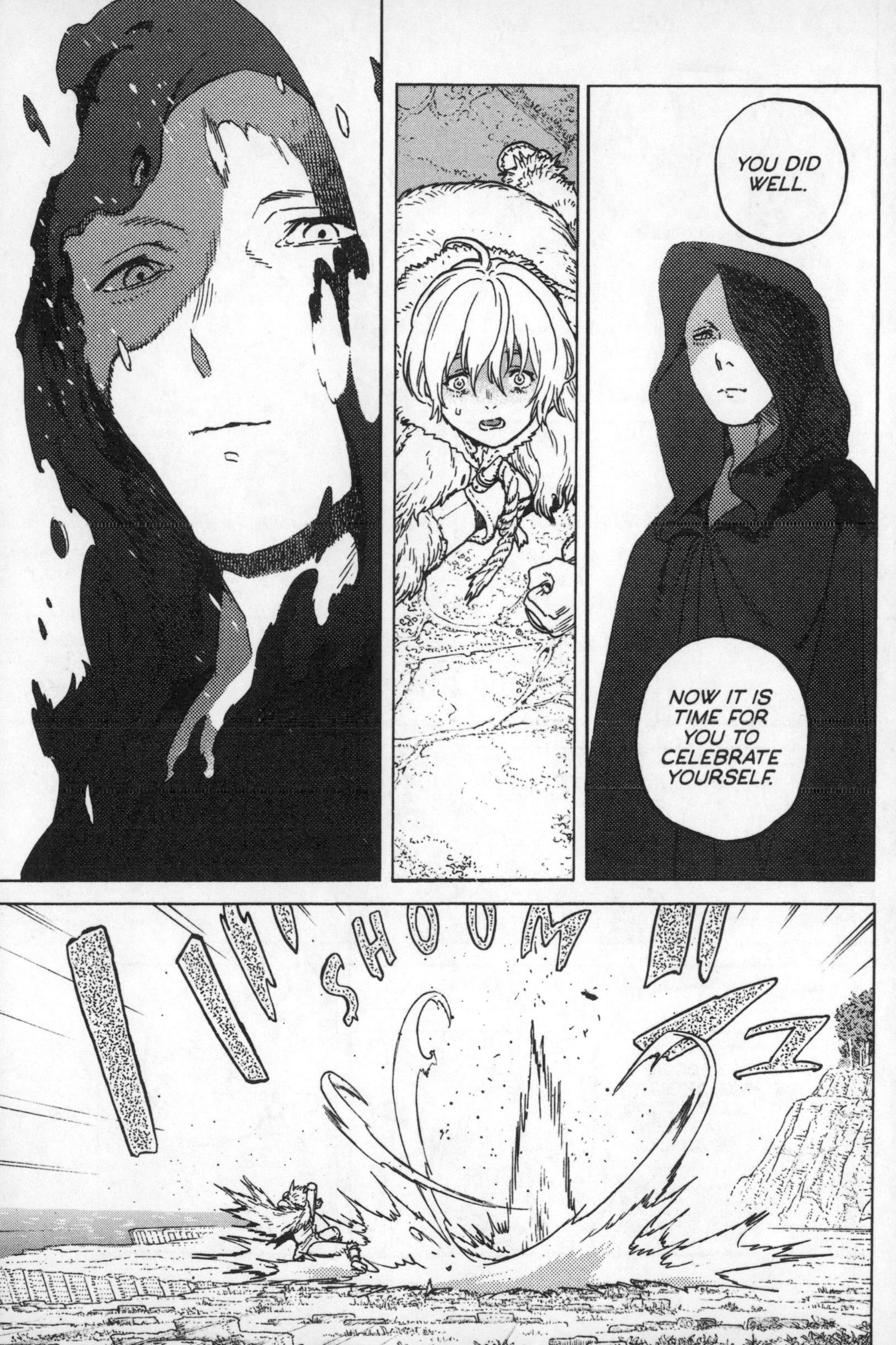
YOU DID WELL.
NOW IT IS TIME FOR YOU TO CELEBRATE YOURSELF.
SHOOM!!

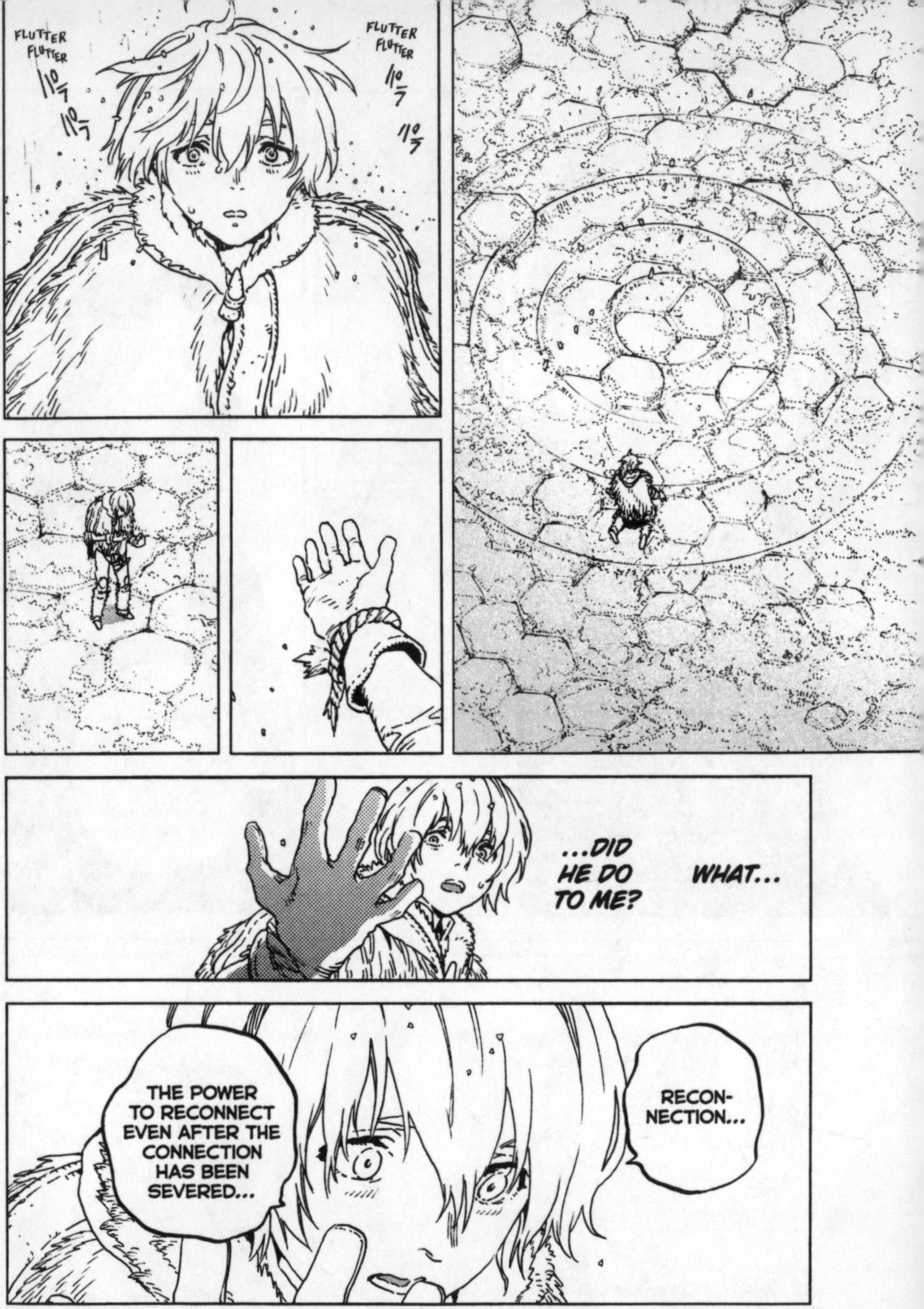
FLUTTER FLUTTER
パタ パタ
FLUTTER FLUTTER
パタ パタ
WHAT...
...DID HE DO TO ME?
RECON-NECTION...
THE POWER TO RECONNECT EVEN AFTER THE CONNECTION HAS BEEN SEVERED...

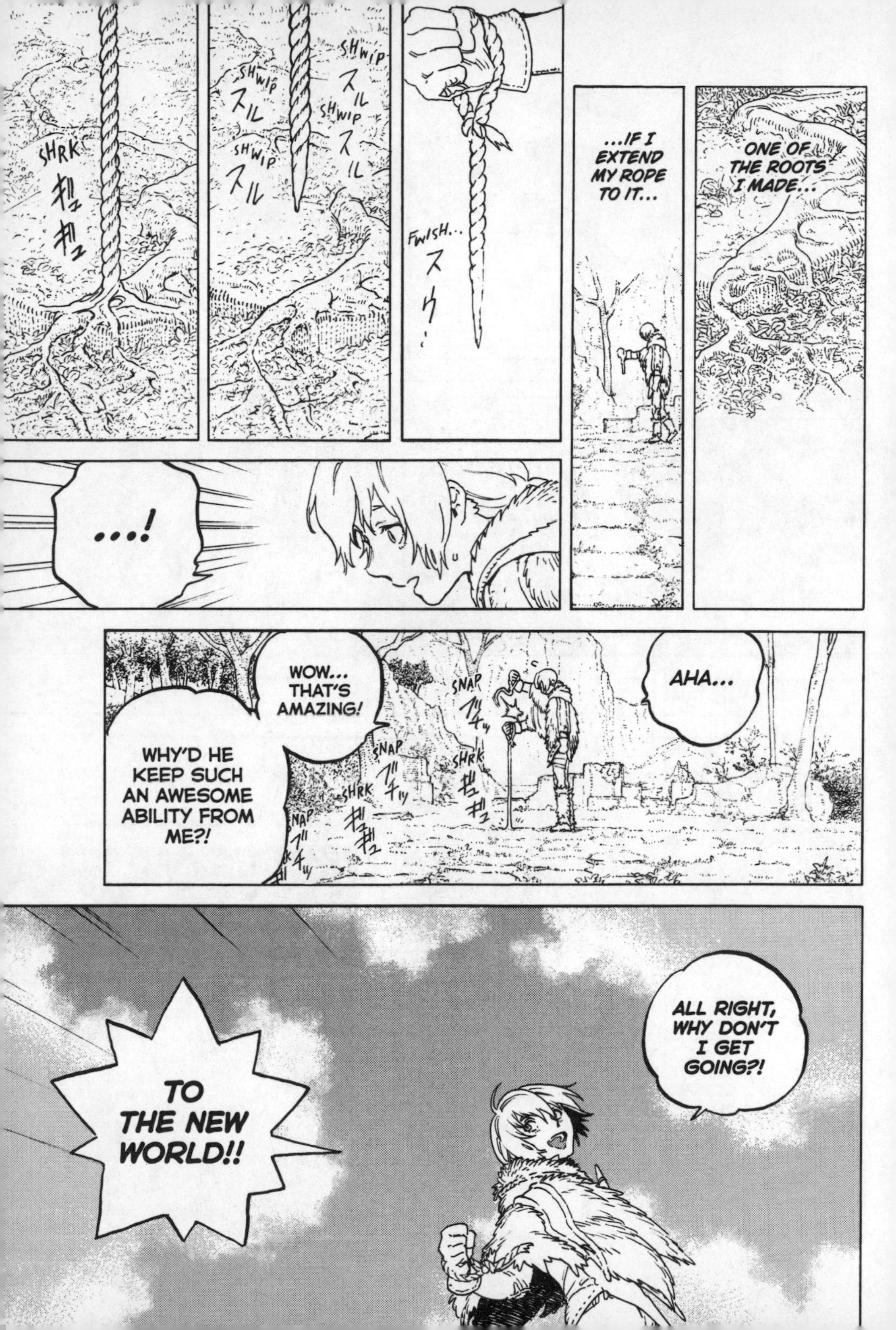

ONE OF THE ROOTS I MADE...
...IF I EXTEND MY ROPE TO IT...
FWISH...
SHWIP
SHWIP
SHWIP
SHRK
...!
AHA...
SNAP
SHRK
WOW... THAT'S AMAZING!
WHY'D HE KEEP SUCH AN AWESOME ABILITY FROM ME?!
SNAP
SHRK
SNAP
ALL RIGHT, WHY DON'T I GET GOING?!
TO THE NEW WORLD!!

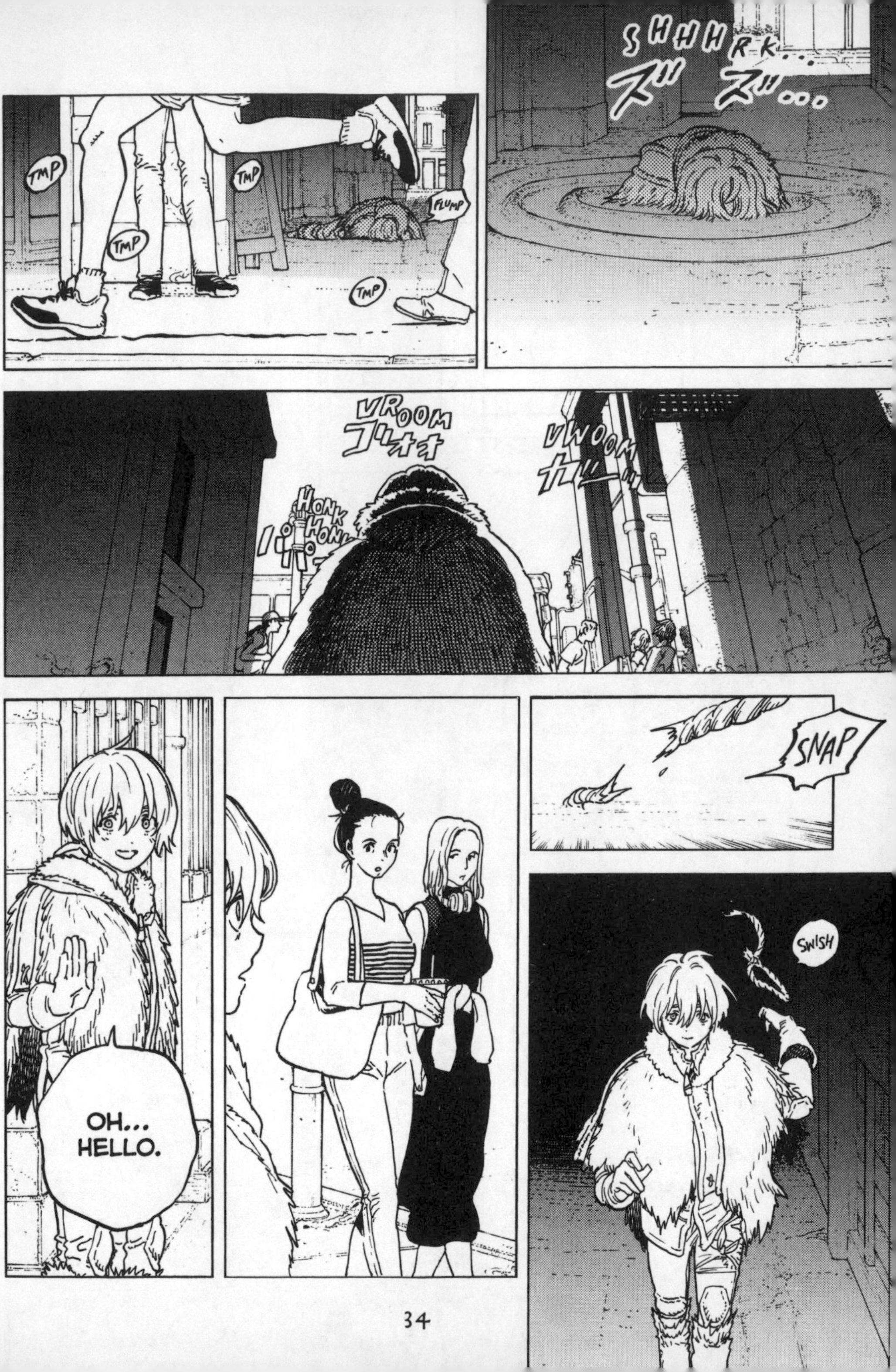
SHHHRK...
TMP
TMP
FLUMP
TMP
TMP
VWOOM
VROOM
HONK HONK
SNAP
SWISH
OH... HELLO.

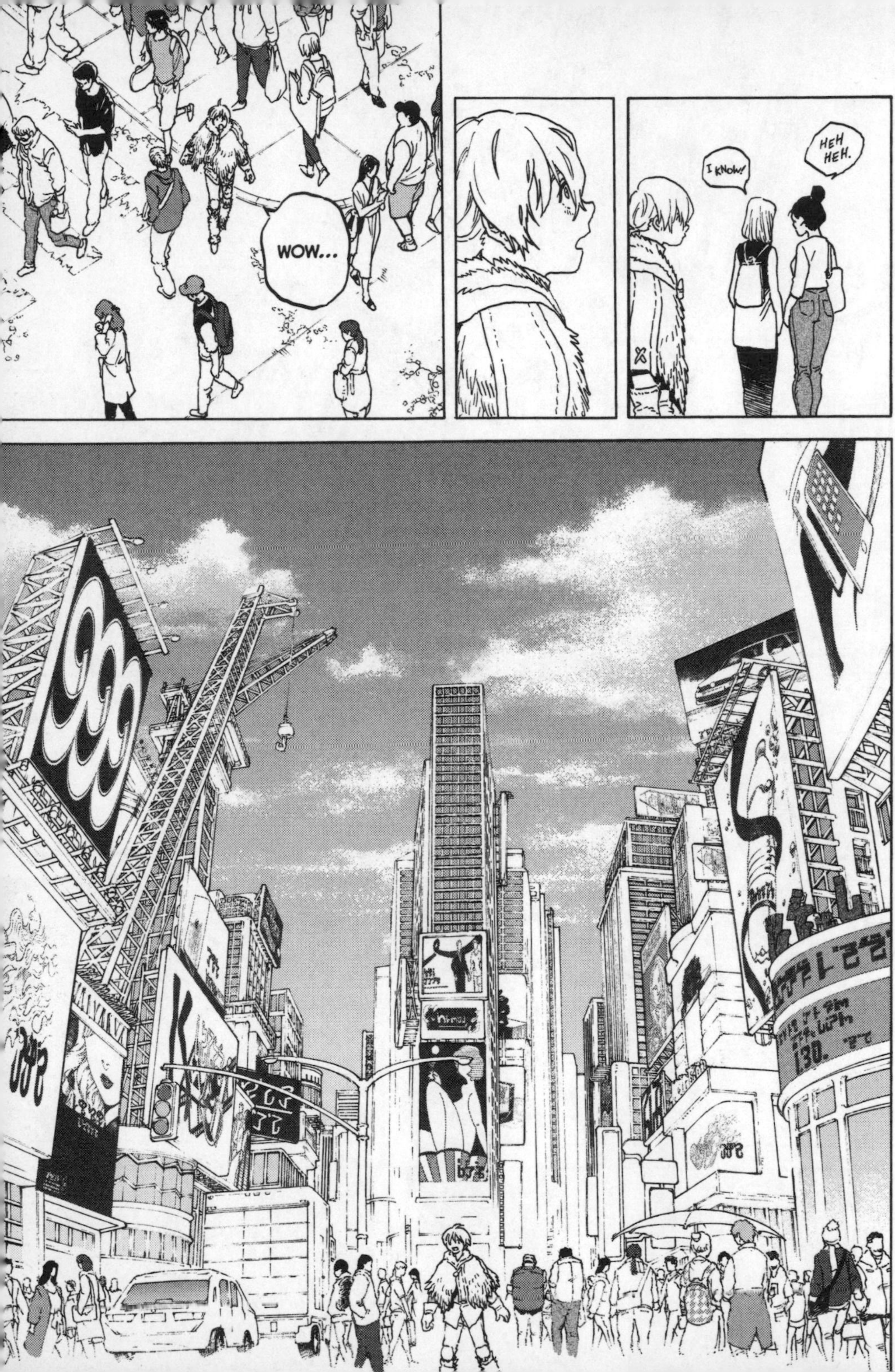
HEH HEH.
I KNOW!!
WOW...

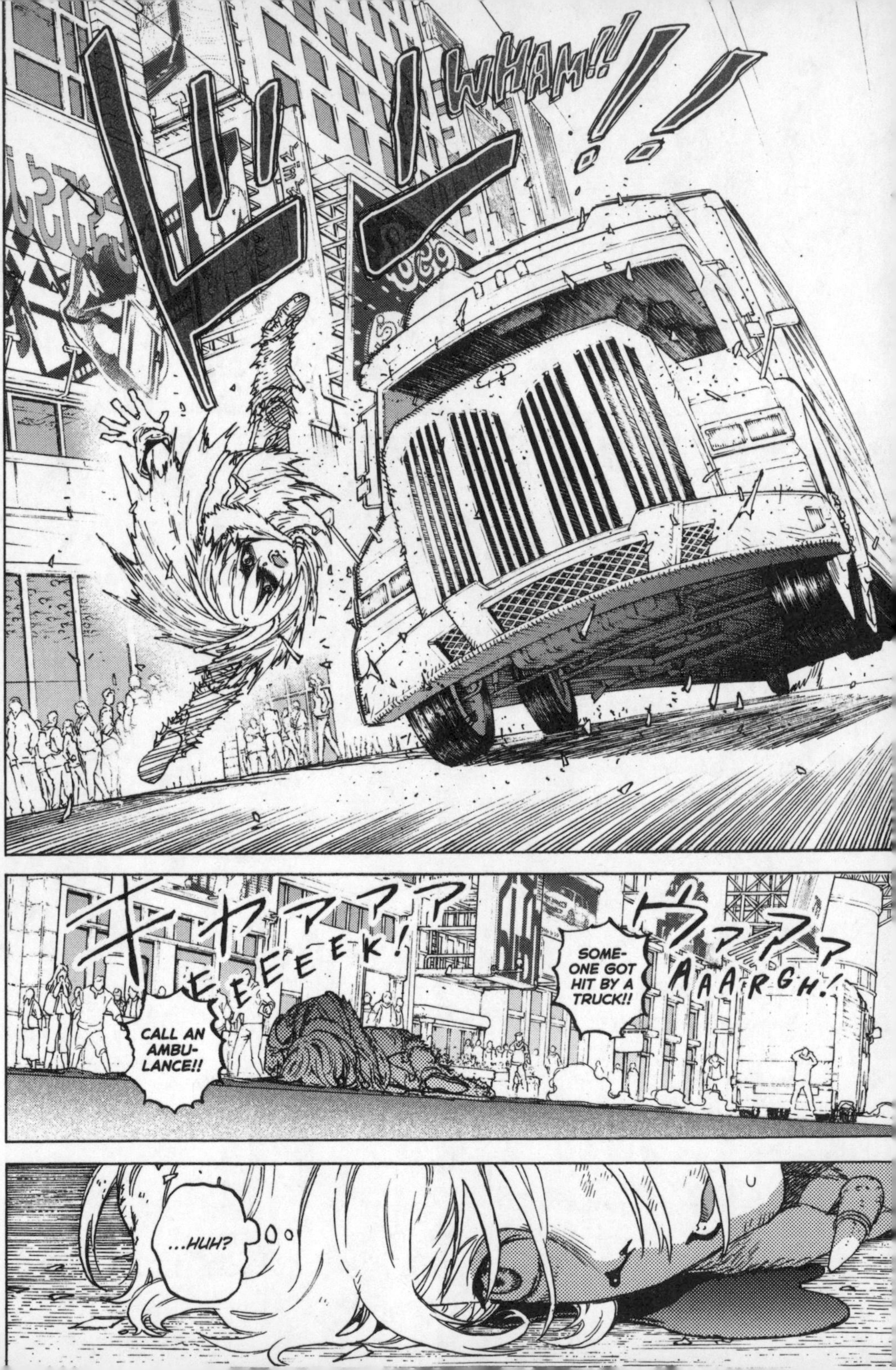
WHAM!!
SOME-ONE GOT HIT BY A TRUCK!!
AAARGH!
EEEEEEK!
CALL AN AMBU-LANCE!!
...HUH?

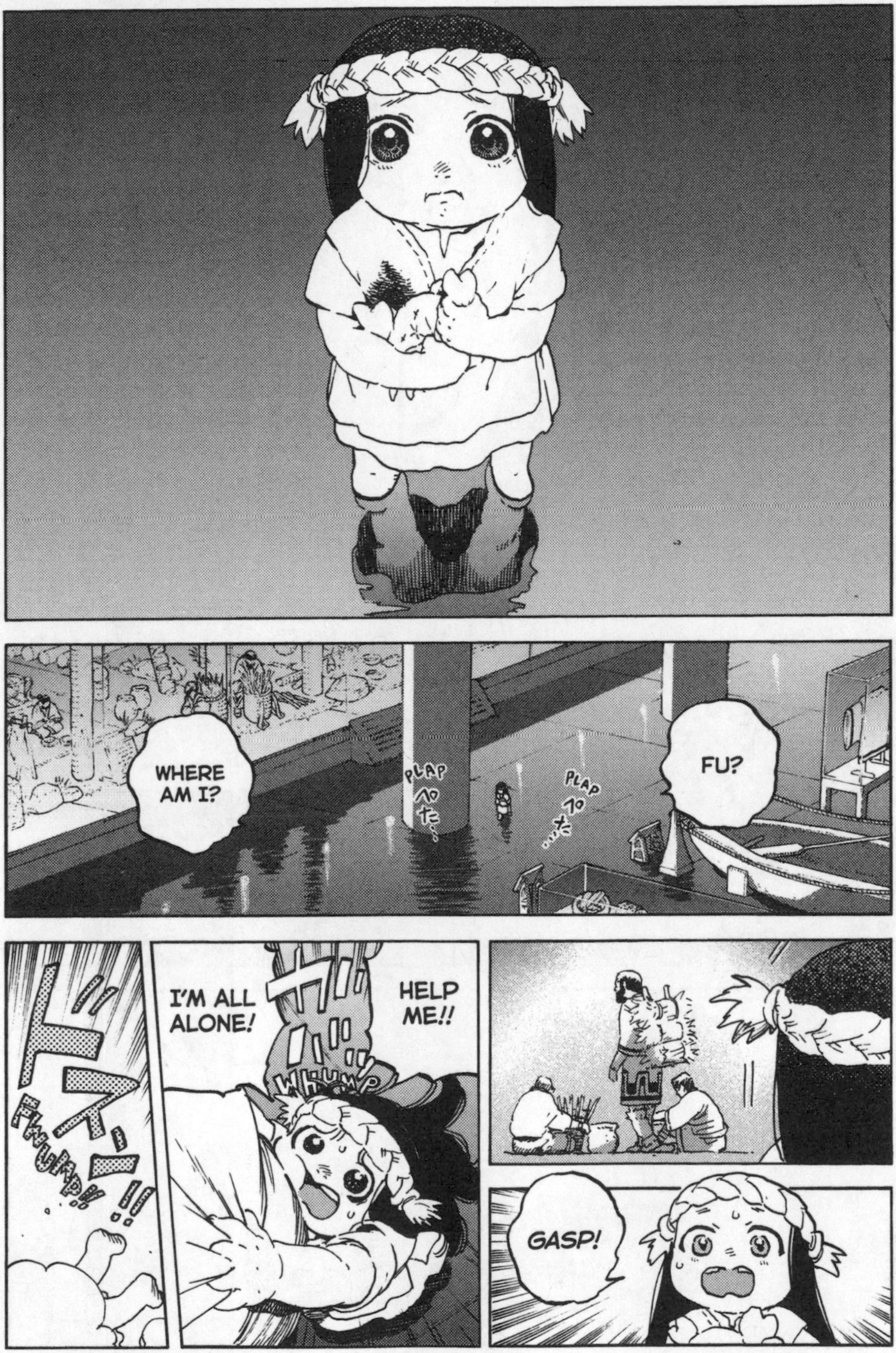
FU?
PLAP
PLAP
WHERE AM I?
GASP!
HELP ME!!
I'M ALL ALONE!
WHUMP
FWUMP!!

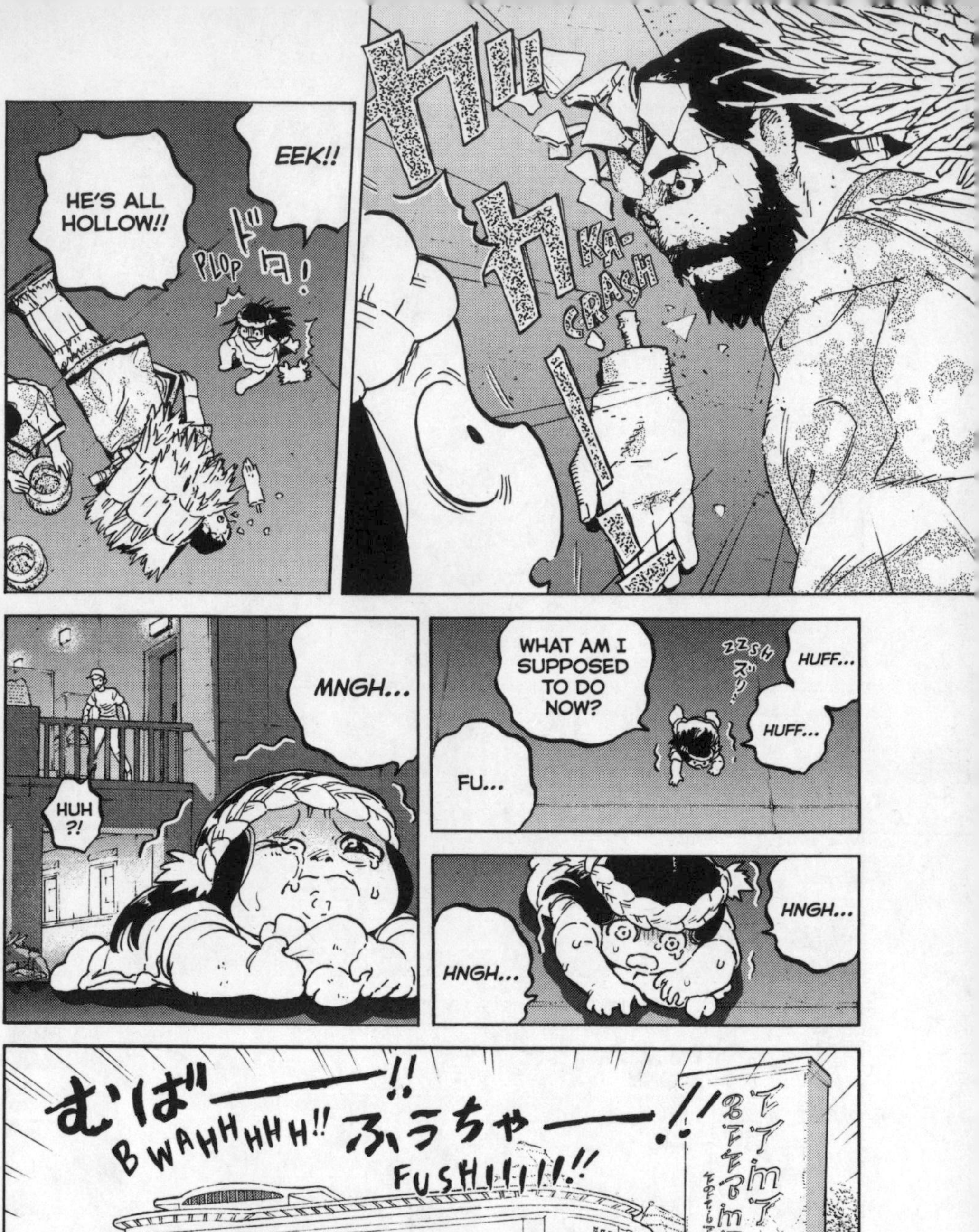
KA-CRASH
EEK!!
HE'S ALL HOLLOW!!
PLOP
WHAT AM I SUPPOSED TO DO NOW?
ZZSH
ズリ…
HUFF...
HUFF...
FU...
HNGH...
HNGH...
MNGH...
HUH?!
むばーー!!
BWAHHHHH!!
ふうちゃーー!!
FUSHIIIIII!!
YANOME HISTORICAL AND CULTURAL MUSEUM
HUH?! WHAT'S THE MATTER, KID?!

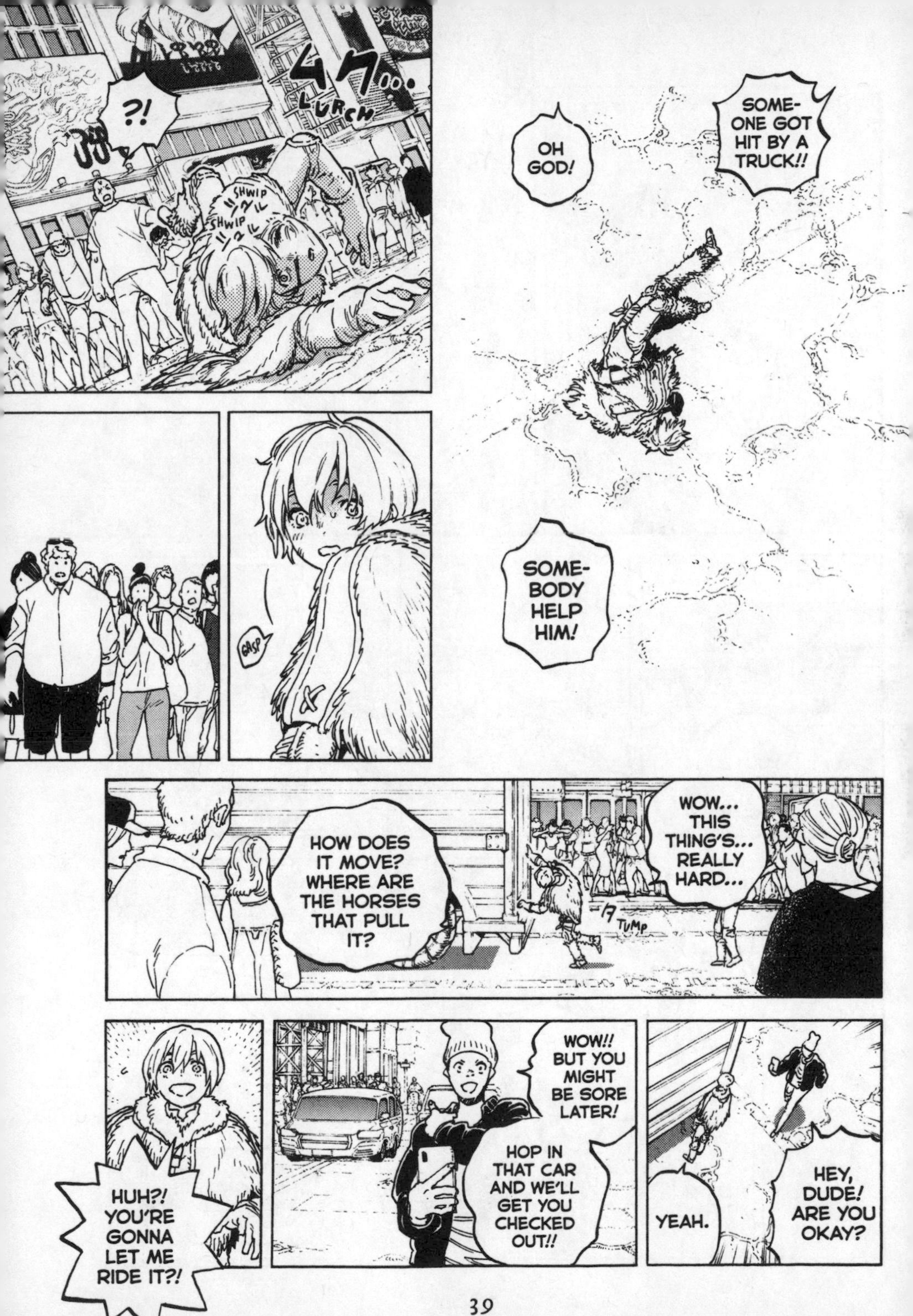
SOME-ONE GOT HIT BY A TRUCK!!
OH GOD!
SOME-BODY HELP HIM!
?!
LURCH
SHWIP
SHWIP
GASP
WOW... THIS THING'S... REALLY HARD...
TUMP
HOW DOES IT MOVE? WHERE ARE THE HORSES THAT PULL IT?
HEY, DUDE! ARE YOU OKAY?
YEAH.
WOW!! BUT YOU MIGHT BE SORE LATER!
HOP IN THAT CAR AND WE'LL GET YOU CHECKED OUT!!
HUH?! YOU'RE GONNA LET ME RIDE IT?!

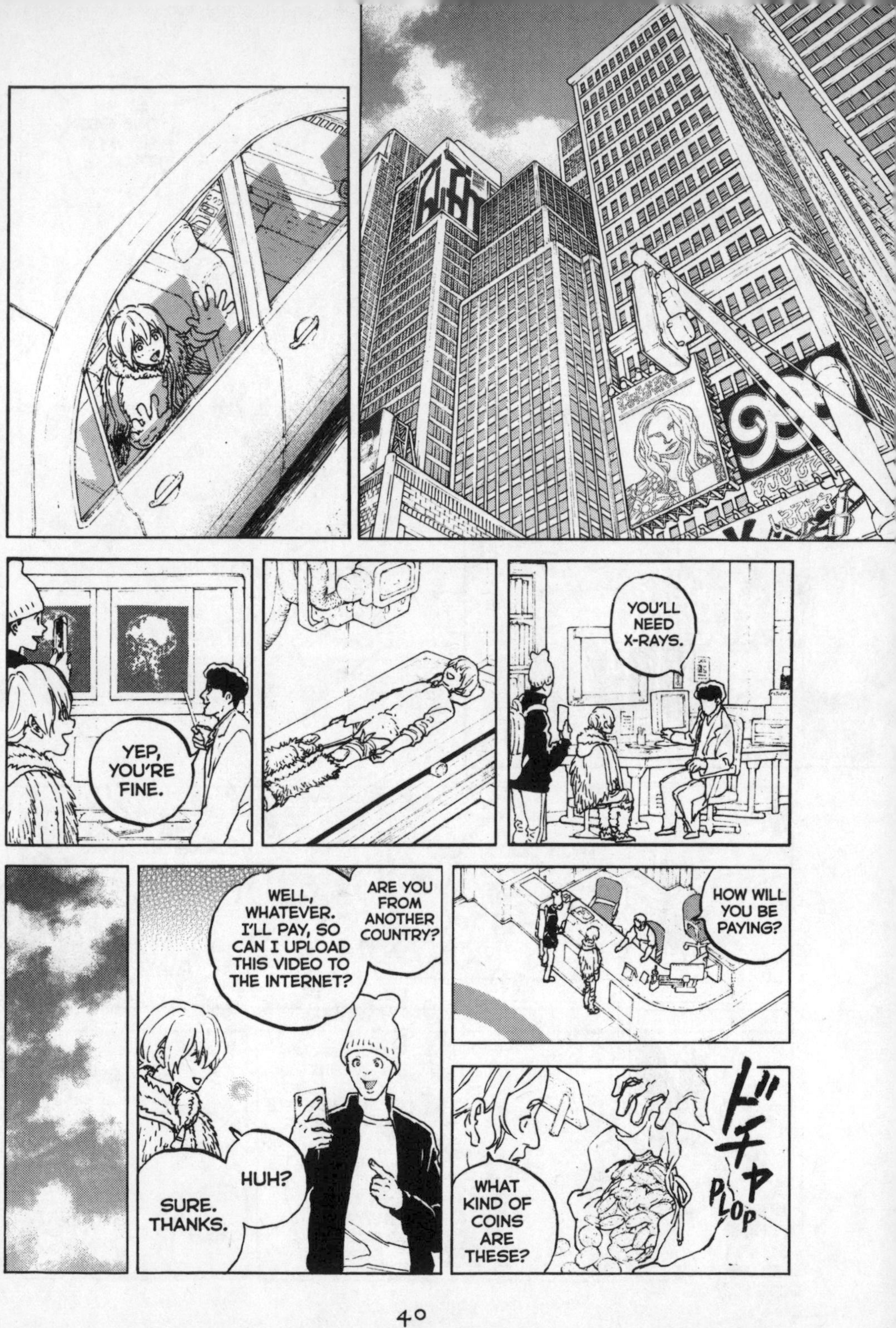
YOU'LL NEED X-RAYS.
YEP, YOU'RE FINE.
HOW WILL YOU BE PAYING?
ドチャ
PLOP
WHAT KIND OF COINS ARE THESE?
ARE YOU FROM ANOTHER COUNTRY?
WELL, WHATEVER. I'LL PAY, SO CAN I UPLOAD THIS VIDEO TO THE INTERNET?
HUH?
SURE. THANKS.

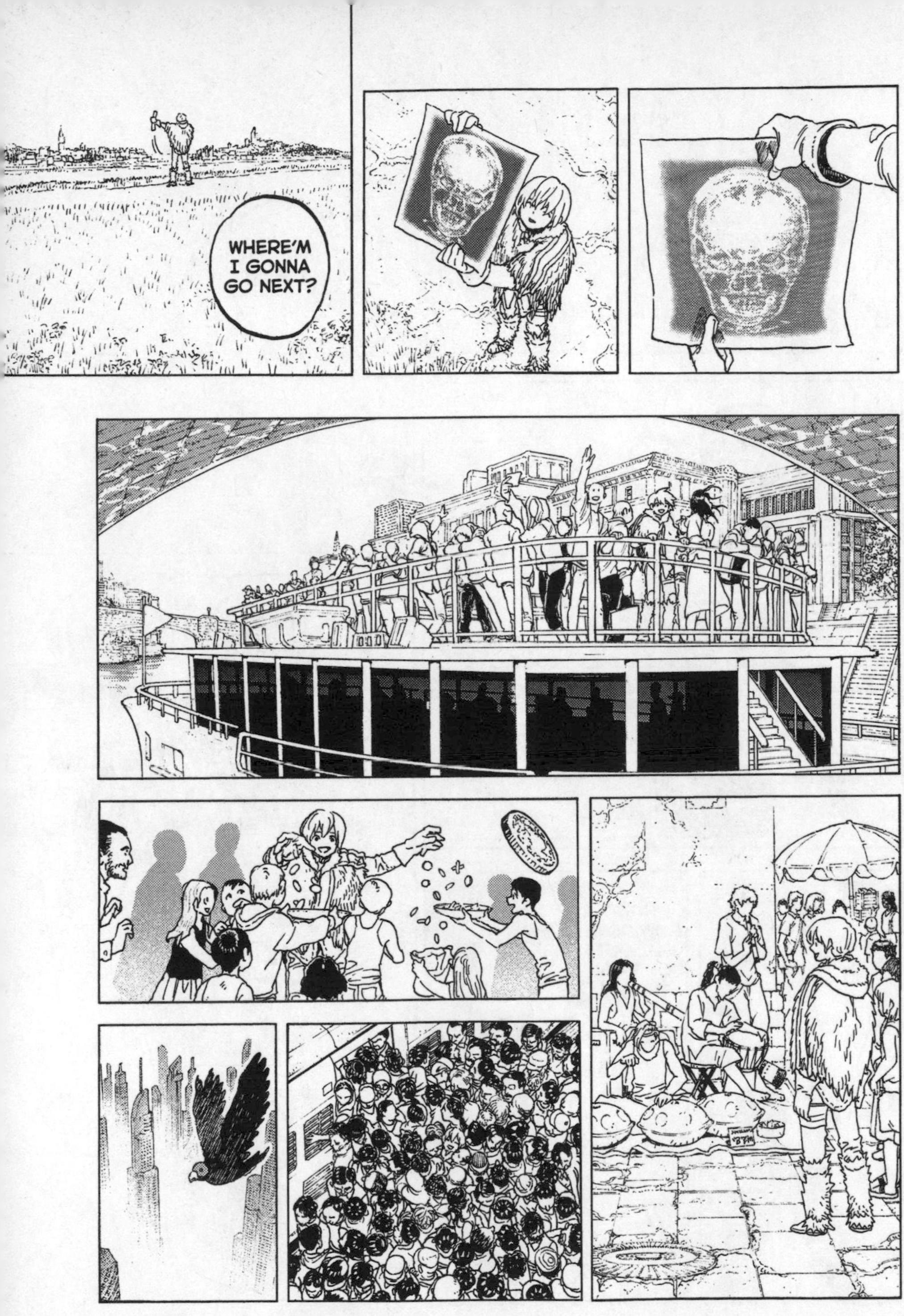
WHERE'M I GONNA GO NEXT?

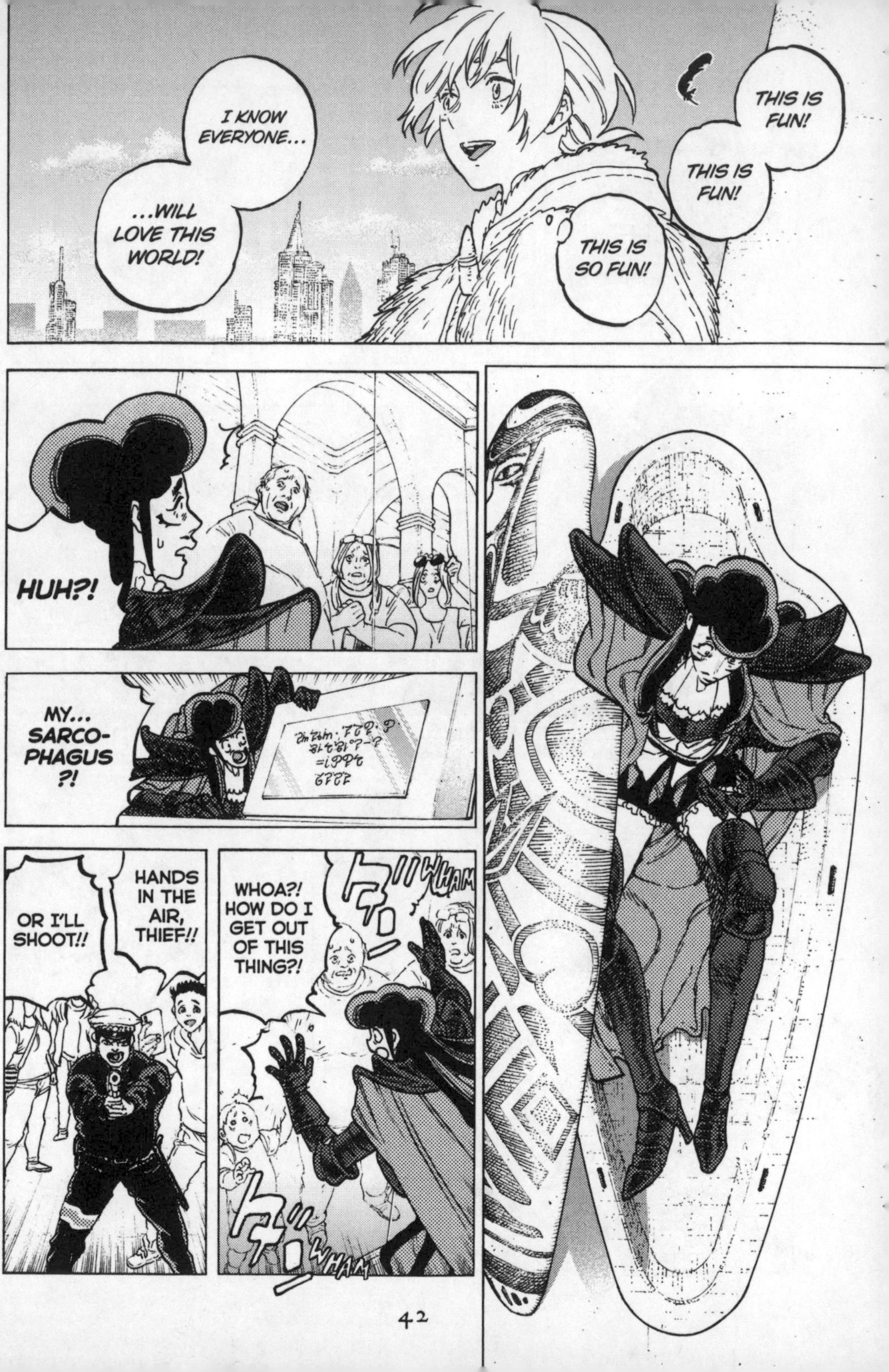
THIS IS FUN!
THIS IS FUN!
THIS IS SO FUN!
I KNOW EVERYONE...
...WILL LOVE THIS WORLD!
HUH?!
MY... SARCOPHAGUS?!
WHOA?! HOW DO I GET OUT OF THIS THING?!
WHAM
WHAM
HANDS IN THE AIR, THIEF!!
OR I'LL SHOOT!!

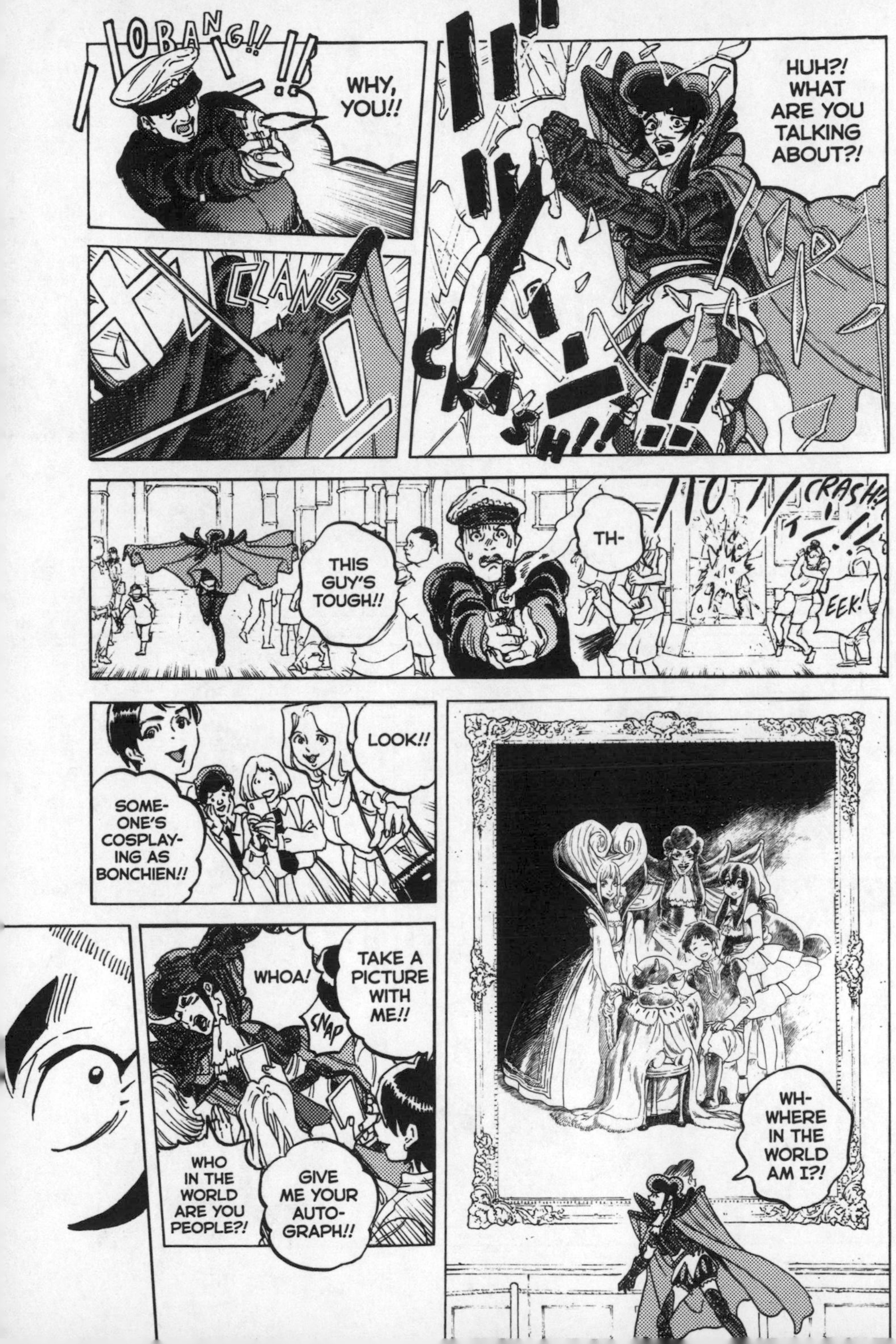
HUH?! WHAT ARE YOU TALKING ABOUT?!
CRASH!!
BANG!!
WHY, YOU!!
CLANG
CRASH!!
EEK!
TH-
THIS GUY'S TOUGH!!
WH- WHERE IN THE WORLD AM I?!
LOOK!!
SOME-ONE'S COSPLAY-ING AS BONCHIEN!!
TAKE A PICTURE WITH ME!!
WHOA!
SNAP
GIVE ME YOUR AUTO-GRAPH!!
WHO IN THE WORLD ARE YOU PEOPLE?!

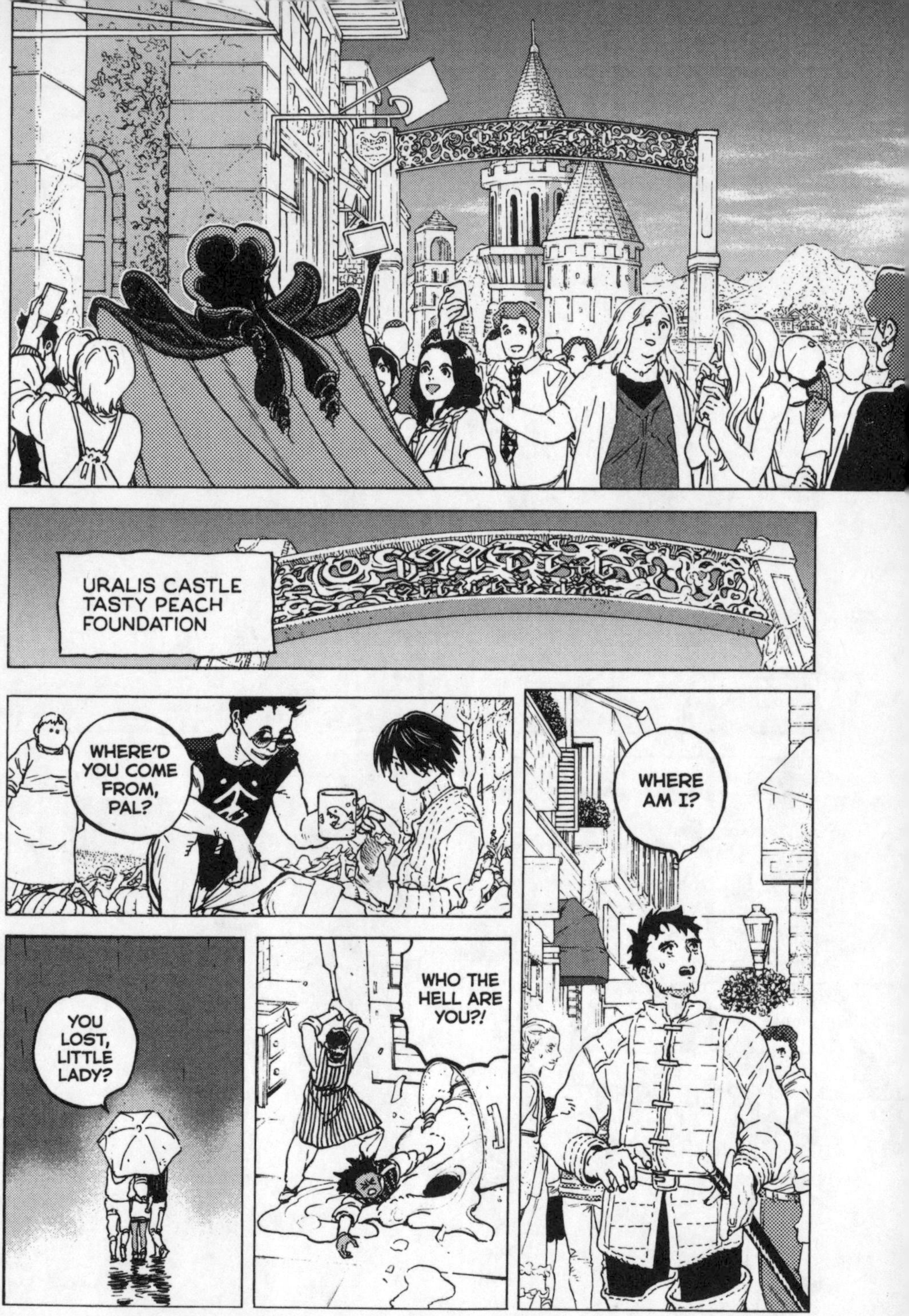
URALIS CASTLE TASTY PEACH FOUNDATION
WHERE AM I?
WHERE'D YOU COME FROM, PAL?
WHO THE HELL ARE YOU?!
YOU LOST, LITTLE LADY?

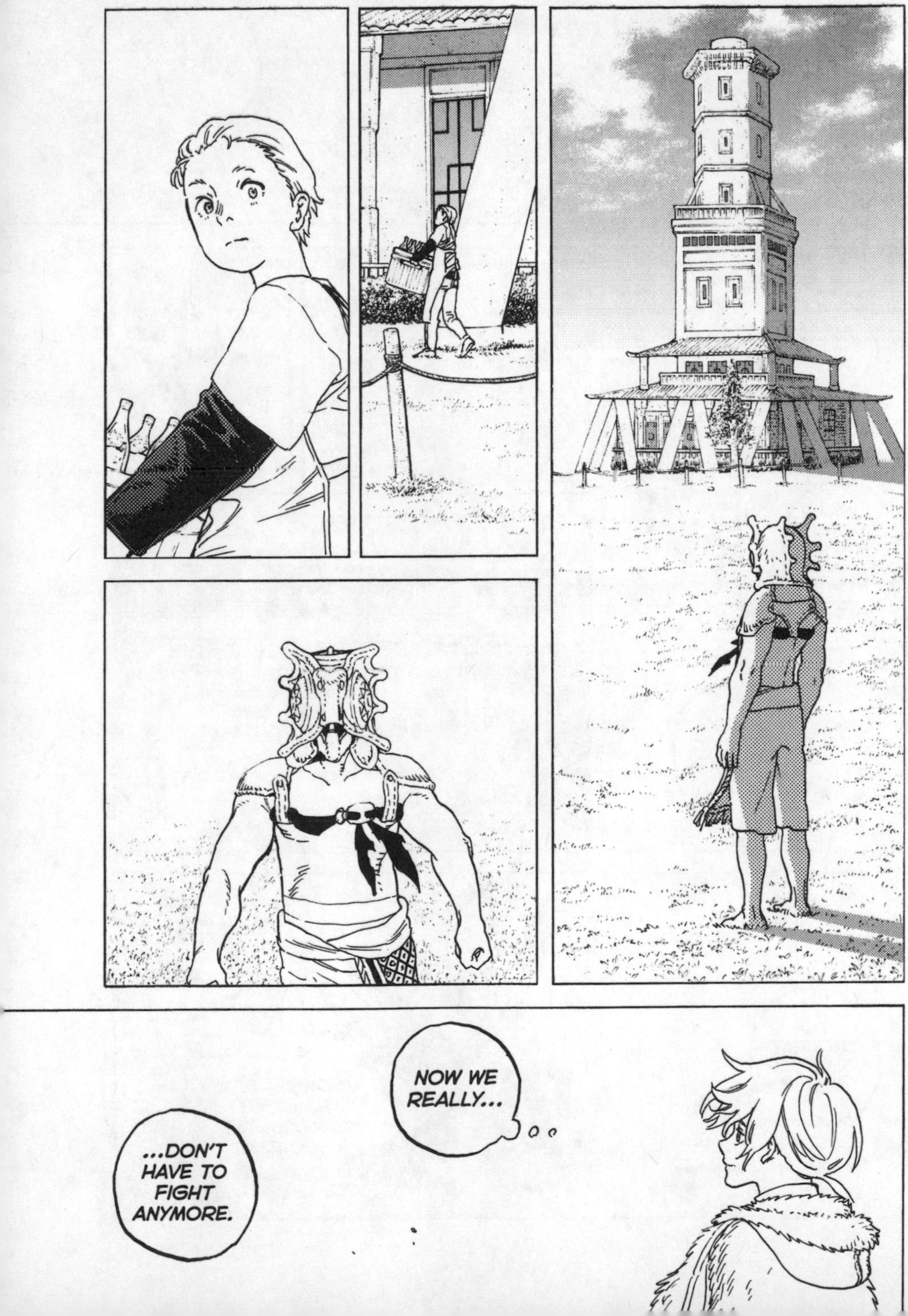
NOW WE REALLY...
...DON'T HAVE TO FIGHT ANYMORE.

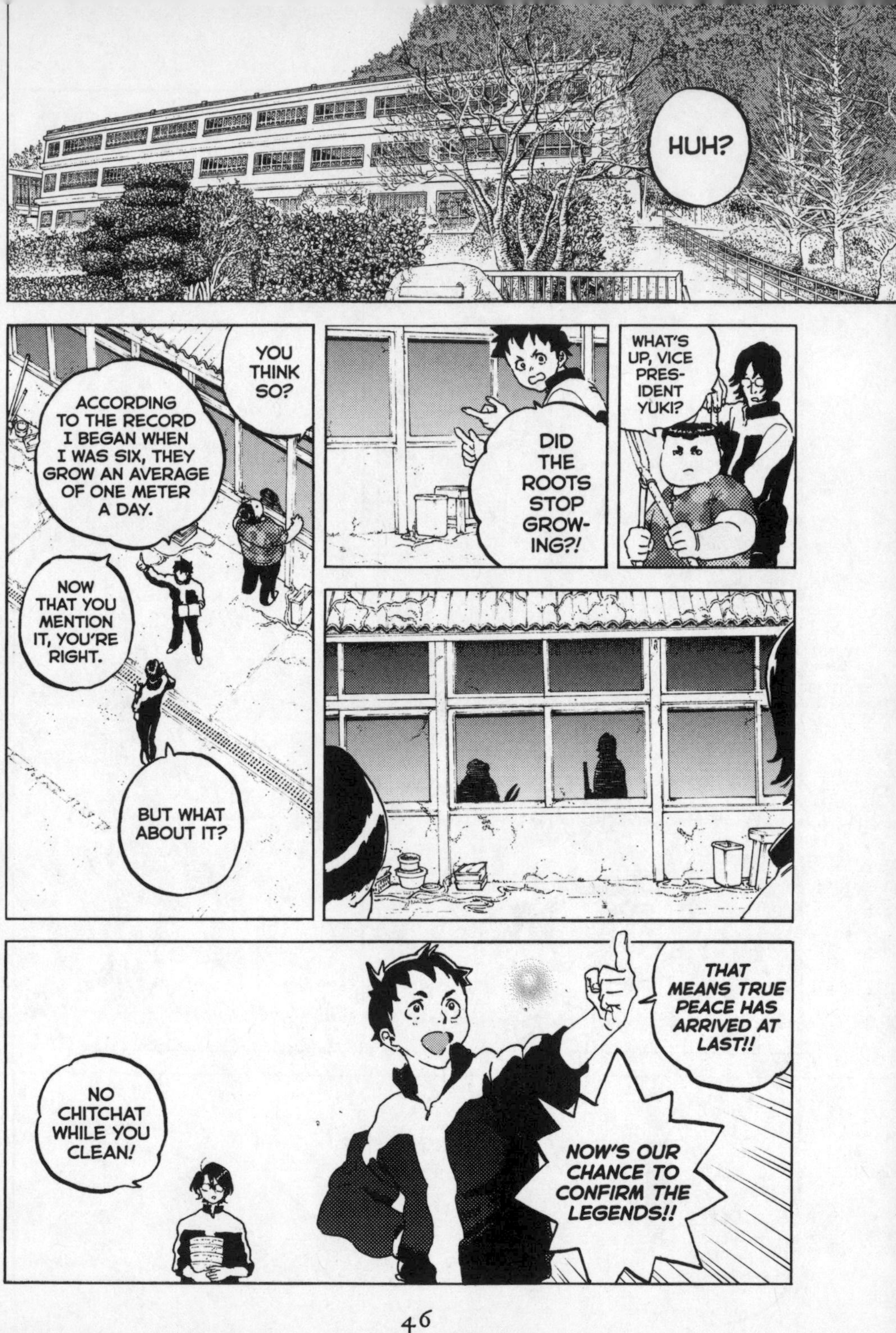

HUH?
WHAT'S UP, VICE PRESIDENT YUKI?
DID THE ROOTS STOP GROWING?!
YOU THINK SO?
ACCORDING TO THE RECORD I BEGAN WHEN I WAS SIX, THEY GROW AN AVERAGE OF ONE METER A DAY.
NOW THAT YOU MENTION IT, YOU'RE RIGHT.
BUT WHAT ABOUT IT?
THAT MEANS TRUE PEACE HAS ARRIVED AT LAST!!
NOW'S OUR CHANCE TO CONFIRM THE LEGENDS!!
NO CHITCHAT WHILE YOU CLEAN!

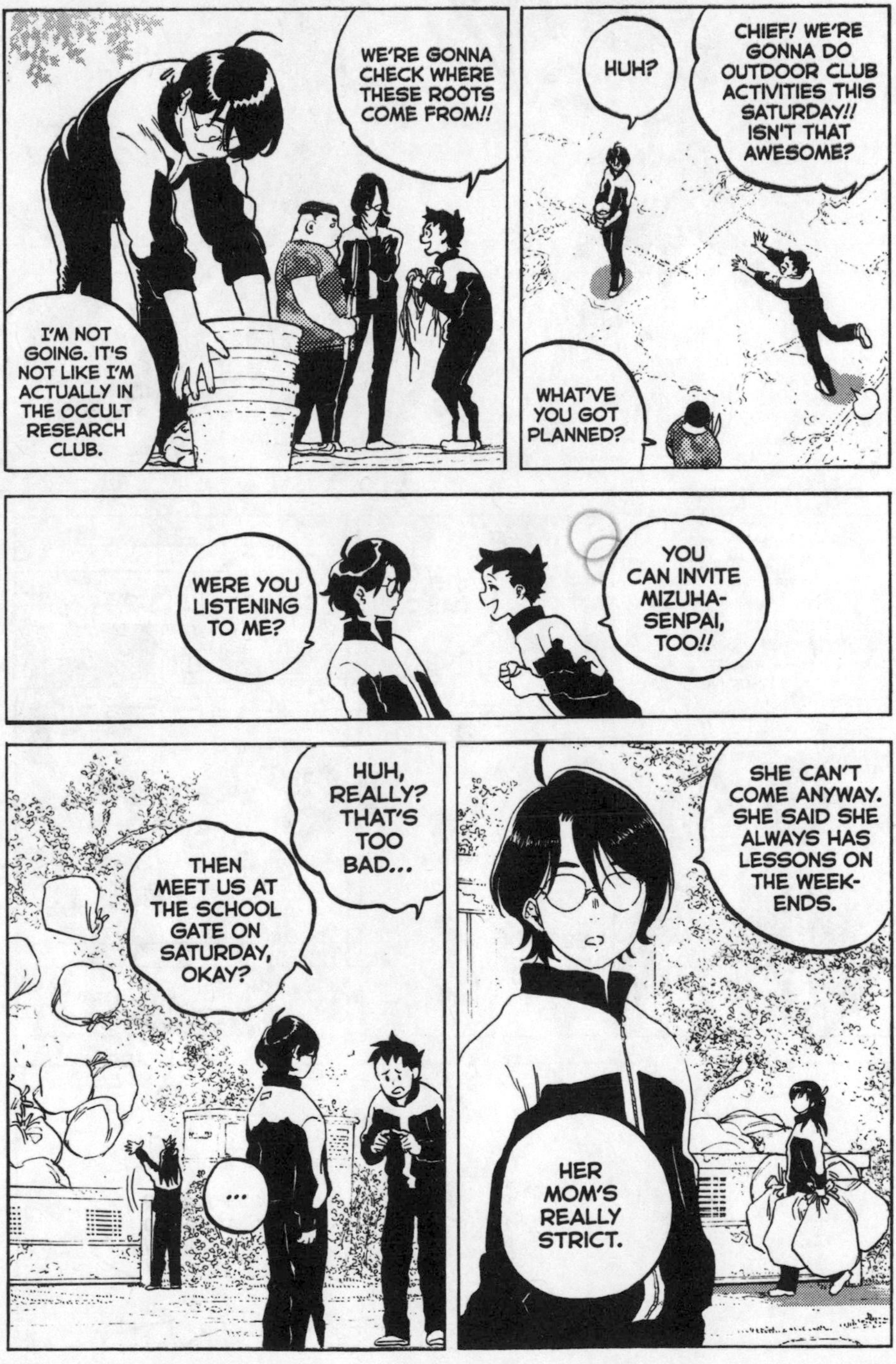
CHIEF! WE'RE GONNA DO OUTDOOR CLUB ACTIVITIES THIS SATURDAY!! ISN'T THAT AWESOME?
HUH?
WHAT'VE YOU GOT PLANNED?
WE'RE GONNA CHECK WHERE THESE ROOTS COME FROM!!
I'M NOT GOING. IT'S NOT LIKE I'M ACTUALLY IN THE OCCULT RESEARCH CLUB.
YOU CAN INVITE MIZUHA-SENPAI, TOO!!
WERE YOU LISTENING TO ME?
SHE CAN'T COME ANYWAY. SHE SAID SHE ALWAYS HAS LESSONS ON THE WEEK-ENDS.
HER MOM'S REALLY STRICT.
HUH, REALLY? THAT'S TOO BAD...
THEN MEET US AT THE SCHOOL GATE ON SATURDAY, OKAY?
...

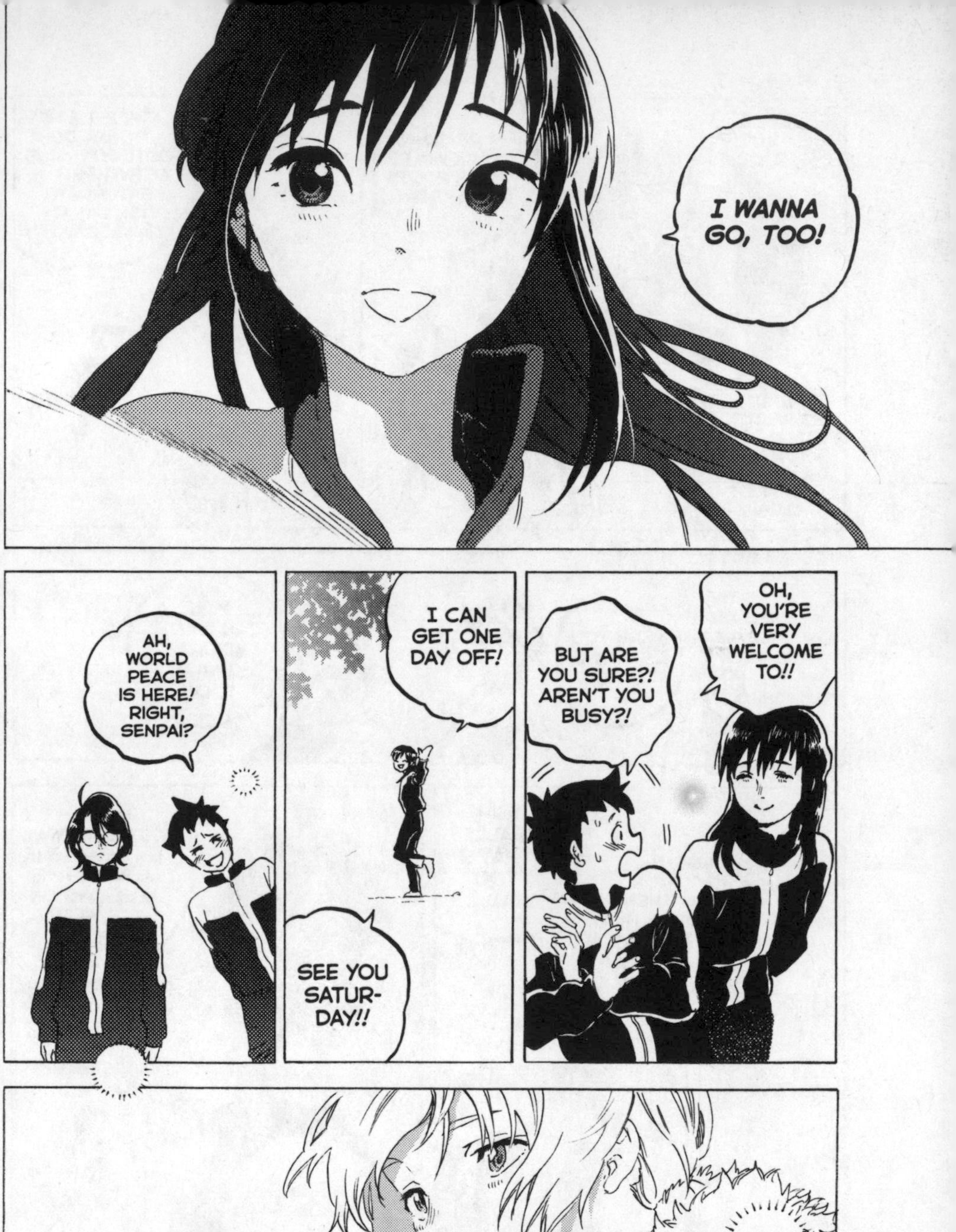
I WANNA GO, TOO!
OH, YOU'RE VERY WELCOME TO!!
BUT ARE YOU SURE?! AREN'T YOU BUSY?!
I CAN GET ONE DAY OFF!
SEE YOU SATUR-DAY!!
AH, WORLD PEACE IS HERE! RIGHT, SENPAI?

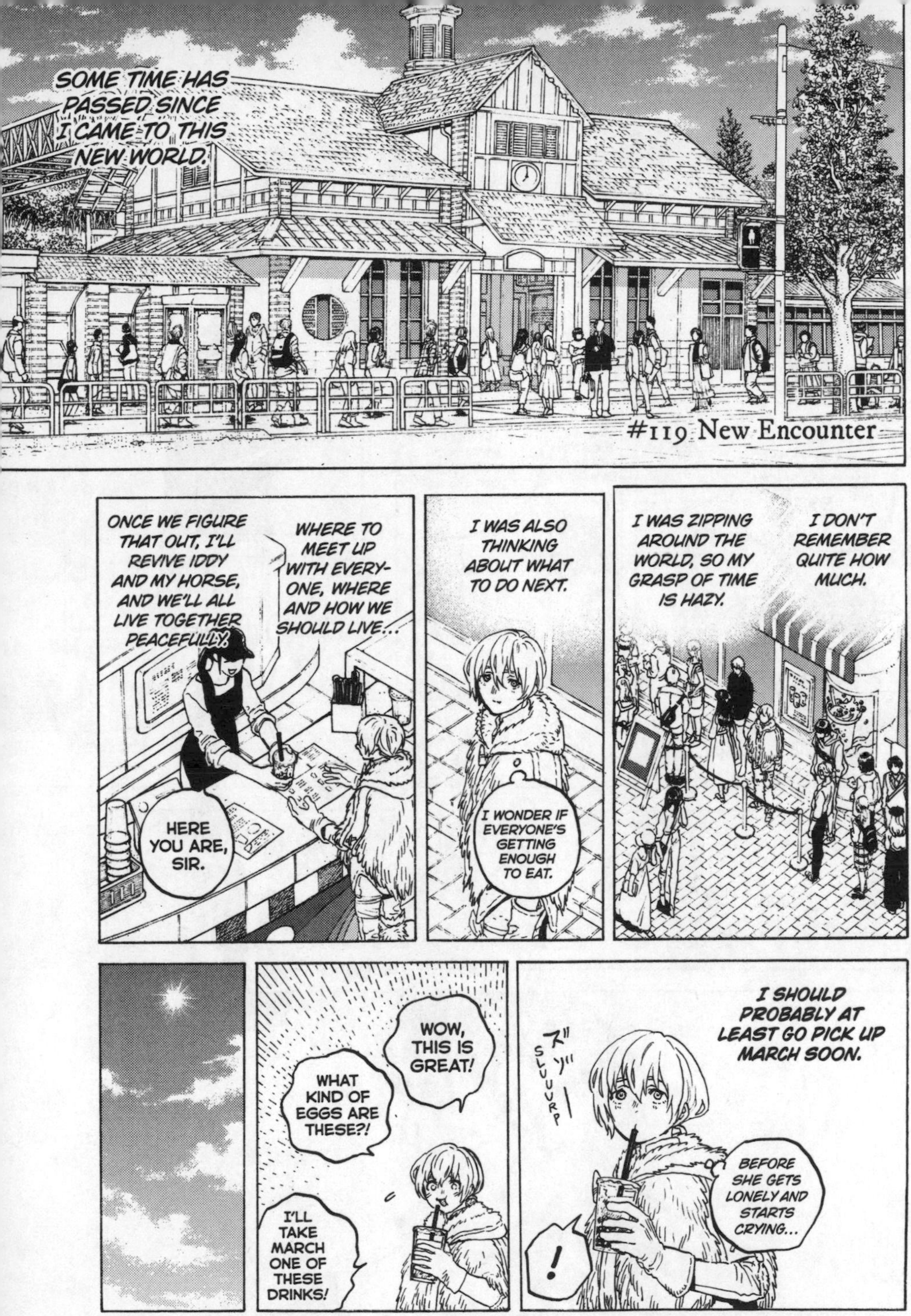
SOME TIME HAS PASSED SINCE I CAME TO THIS NEW WORLD.
#119 New Encounter
I DON'T REMEMBER QUITE HOW MUCH.
I WAS ZIPPING AROUND THE WORLD, SO MY GRASP OF TIME IS HAZY.
I WAS ALSO THINKING ABOUT WHAT TO DO NEXT.
I WONDER IF EVERYONE'S GETTING ENOUGH TO EAT.
WHERE TO MEET UP WITH EVERYONE, WHERE AND HOW WE SHOULD LIVE...
ONCE WE FIGURE THAT OUT, I'LL REVIVE IDDY AND MY HORSE, AND WE'LL ALL LIVE TOGETHER PEACEFULLY.
HERE YOU ARE, SIR.
I SHOULD PROBABLY AT LEAST GO PICK UP MARCH SOON.
SLUUURP
BEFORE SHE GETS LONELY AND STARTS CRYING...
!
WOW, THIS IS GREAT!
WHAT KIND OF EGGS ARE THESE?!
I'LL TAKE MARCH ONE OF THESE DRINKS!

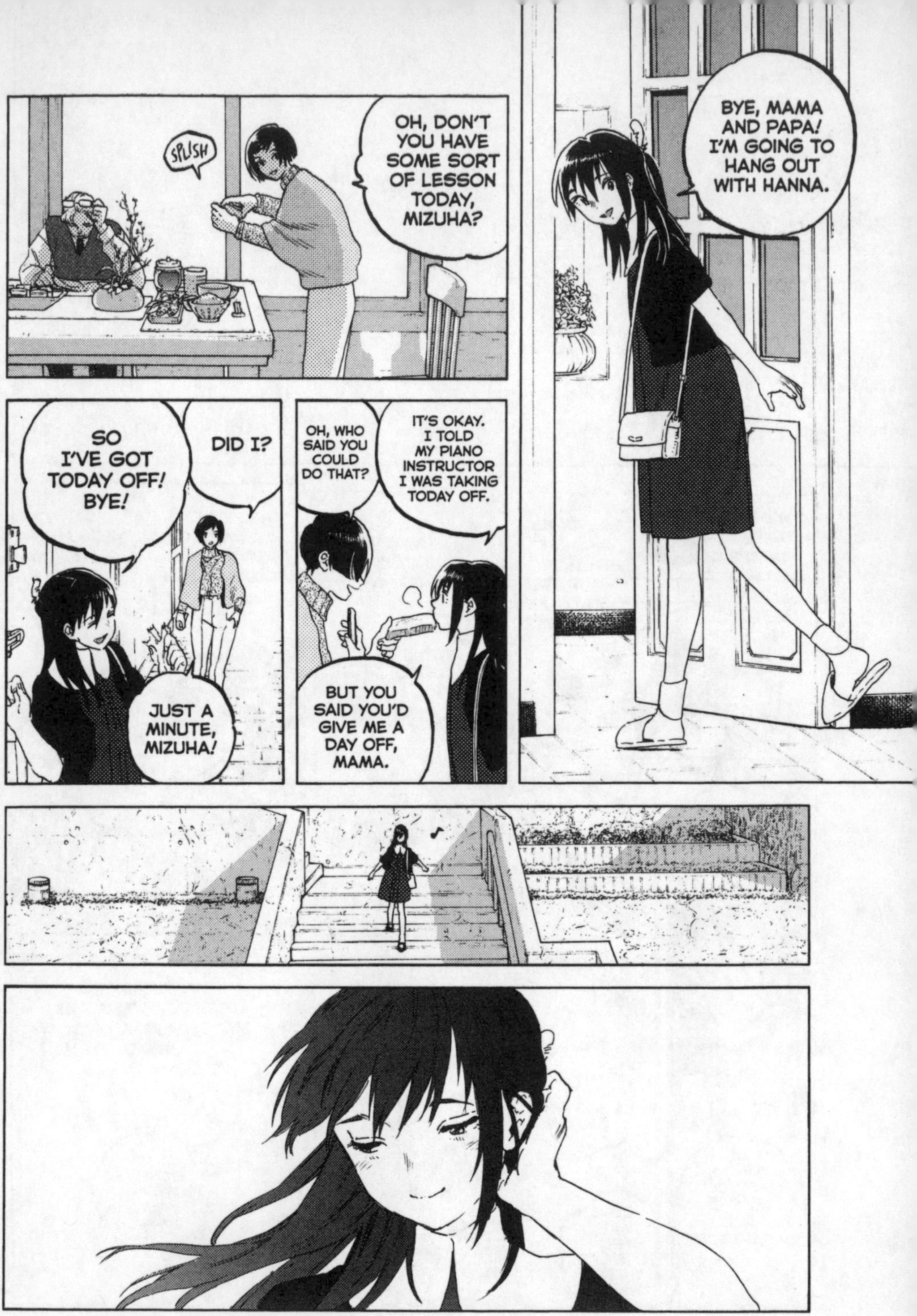
BYE, MAMA AND PAPA! I'M GOING TO HANG OUT WITH HANNA.
OH, DON'T YOU HAVE SOME SORT OF LESSON TODAY, MIZUHA?
SPLISH
IT'S OKAY. I TOLD MY PIANO INSTRUCTOR I WAS TAKING TODAY OFF.
OH, WHO SAID YOU COULD DO THAT?
BUT YOU SAID YOU'D GIVE ME A DAY OFF, MAMA.
DID I?
SO I'VE GOT TODAY OFF! BYE!
JUST A MINUTE, MIZUHA!

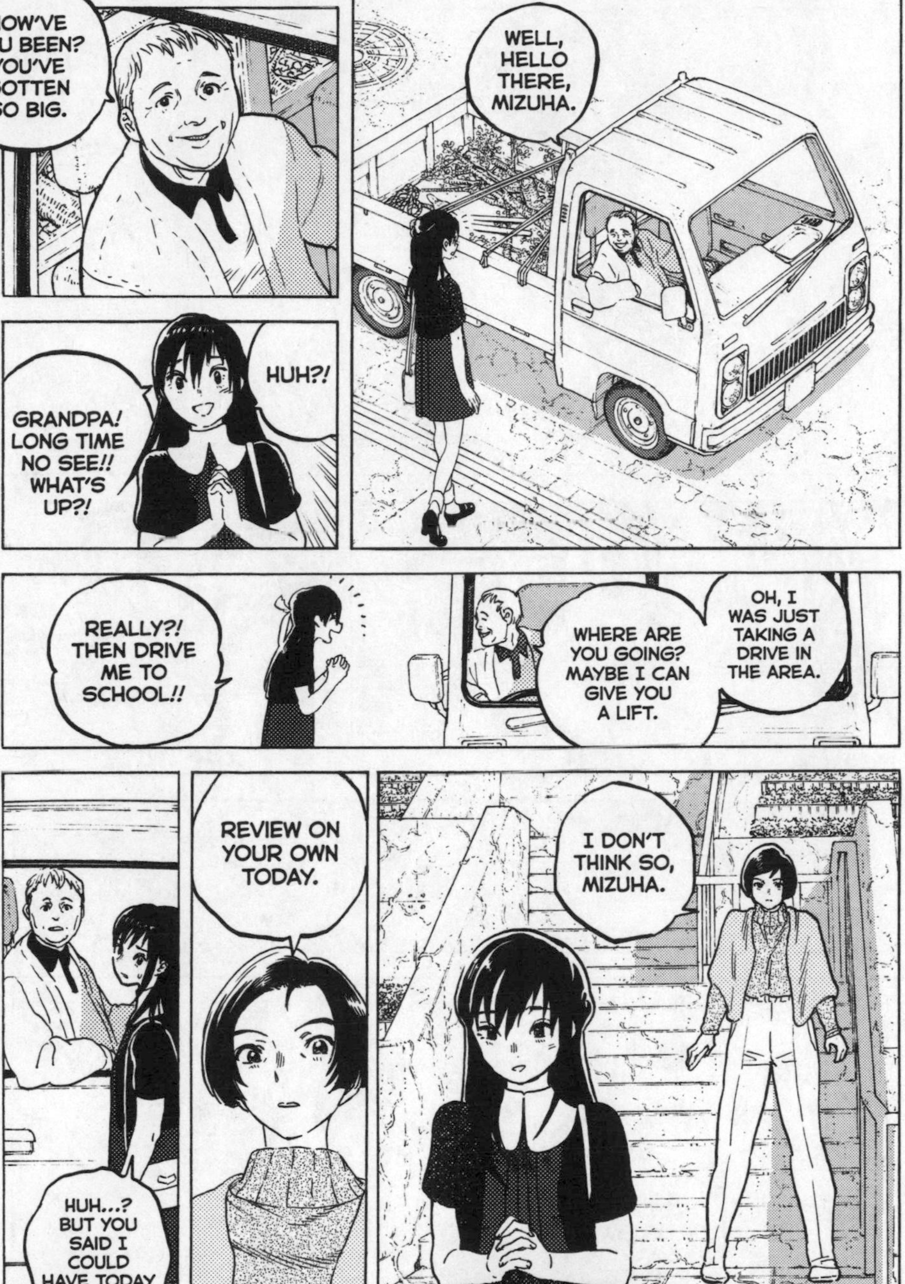
WELL, HELLO THERE, MIZUHA.
HOW'VE YOU BEEN? YOU'VE GOTTEN SO BIG.
HUH?!
GRANDPA! LONG TIME NO SEE!! WHAT'S UP?!
OH, I WAS JUST TAKING A DRIVE IN THE AREA.
WHERE ARE YOU GOING? MAYBE I CAN GIVE YOU A LIFT.
REALLY?! THEN DRIVE ME TO SCHOOL!!
I DON'T THINK SO, MIZUHA.
REVIEW ON YOUR OWN TODAY.
HUH...? BUT YOU SAID I COULD HAVE TODAY OFF...

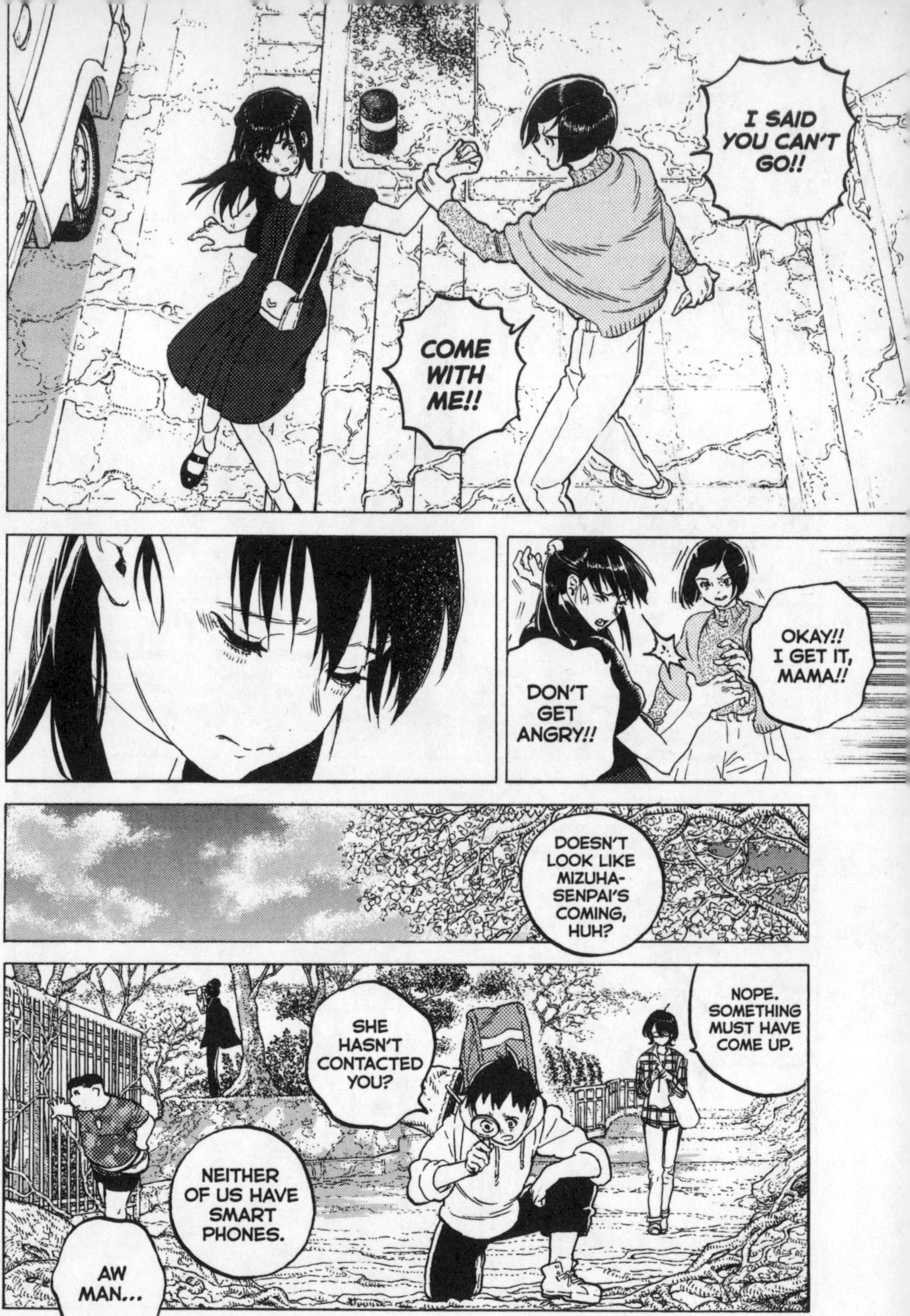
I SAID YOU CAN'T GO!!
COME WITH ME!!
OKAY!! I GET IT, MAMA!!
DON'T GET ANGRY!!
DOESN'T LOOK LIKE MIZUHA-SENPAI'S COMING, HUH?
NOPE. SOMETHING MUST HAVE COME UP.
SHE HASN'T CONTACTED YOU?
NEITHER OF US HAVE SMART PHONES.
AW MAN...

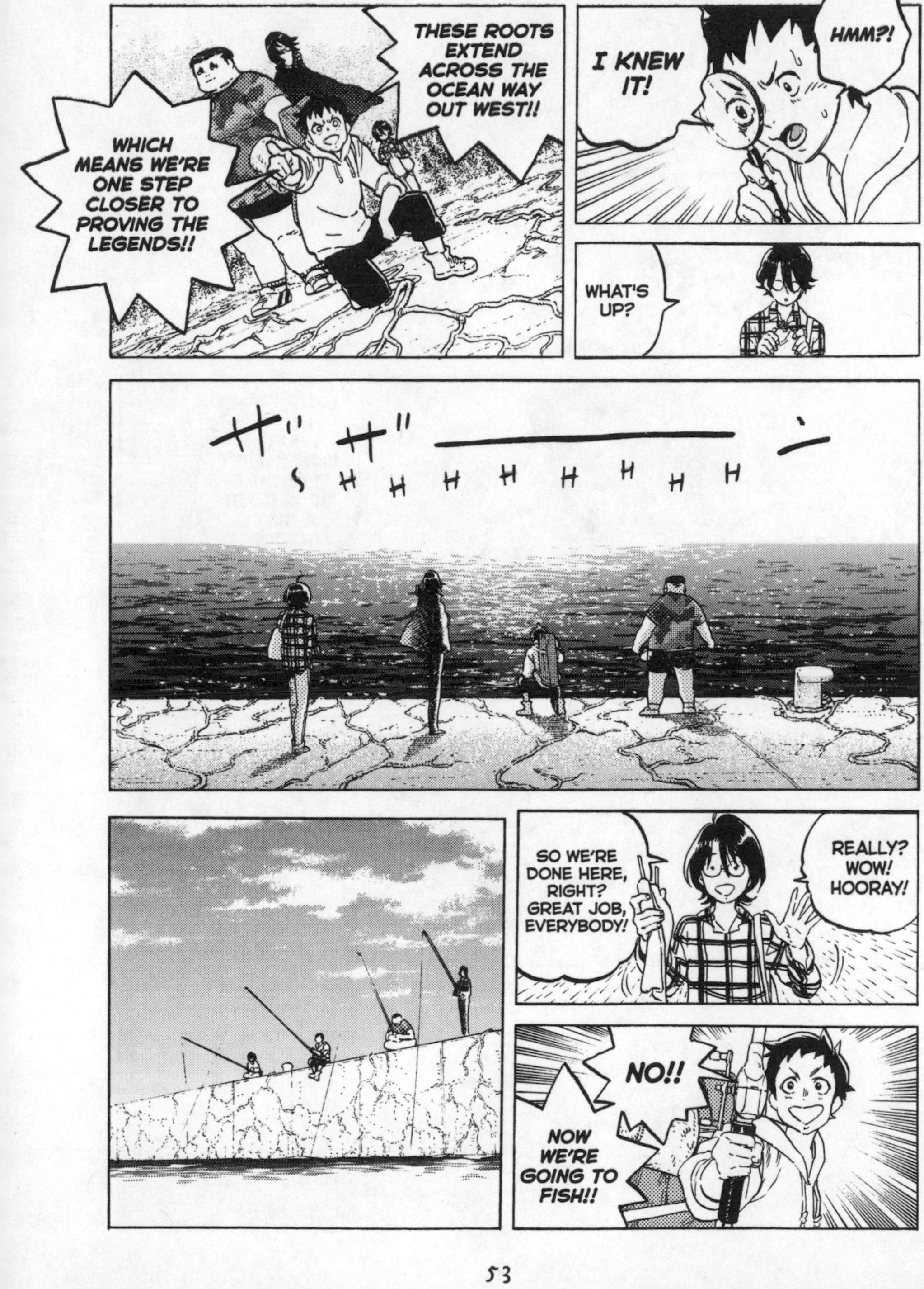
HMM?!
I KNEW IT!
WHAT'S UP?
THESE ROOTS EXTEND ACROSS THE OCEAN WAY OUT WEST!!
WHICH MEANS WE'RE ONE STEP CLOSER TO PROVING THE LEGENDS!!
SHHHHHHHH
REALLY? WOW! HOORAY!
SO WE'RE DONE HERE, RIGHT? GREAT JOB, EVERYBODY!
NO!!
NOW WE'RE GOING TO FISH!!

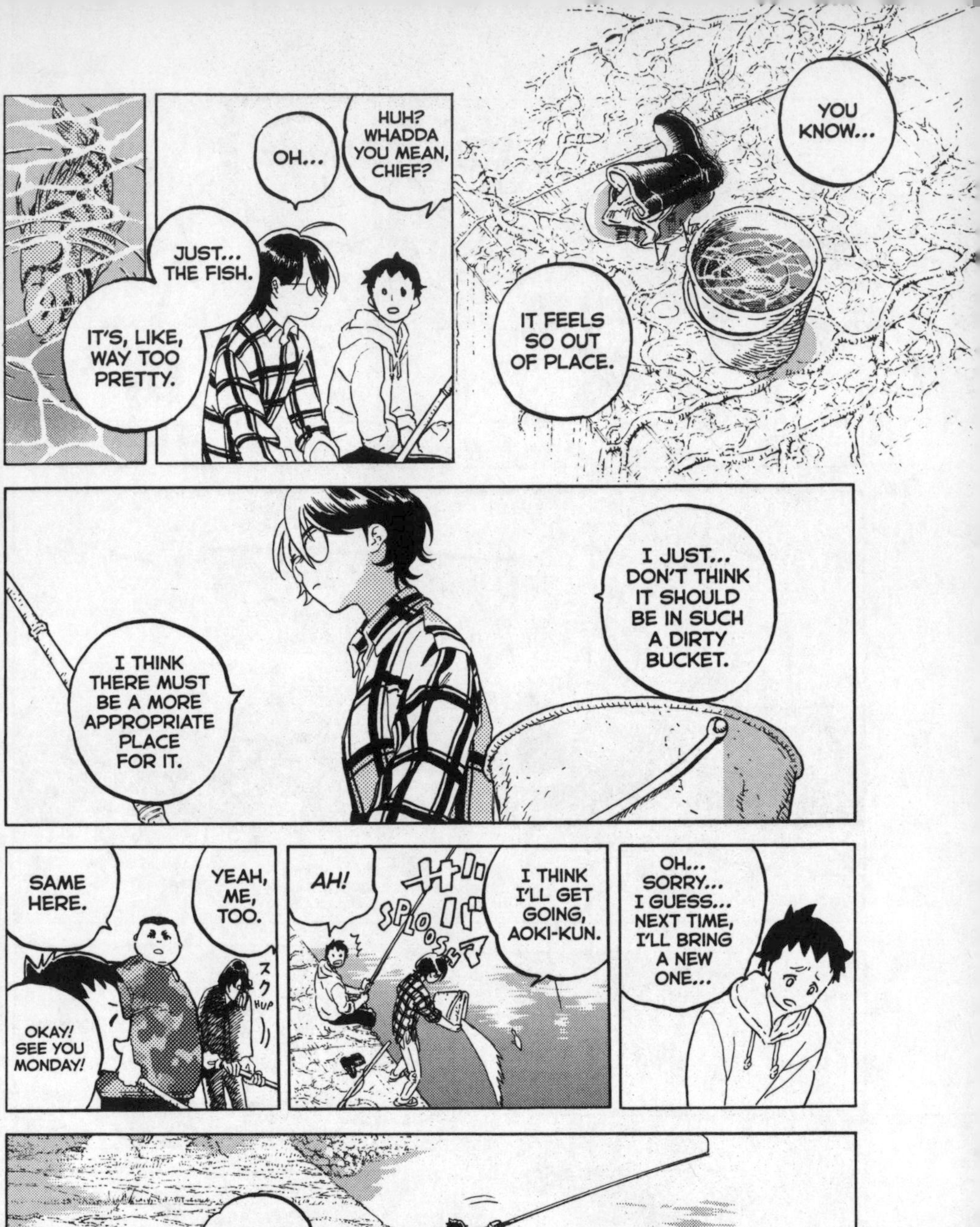
YOU KNOW...
IT FEELS SO OUT OF PLACE.
HUH? WHADDA YOU MEAN, CHIEF?
OH...
JUST... THE FISH.
IT'S, LIKE, WAY TOO PRETTY.
I JUST... DON'T THINK IT SHOULD BE IN SUCH A DIRTY BUCKET.
I THINK THERE MUST BE A MORE APPROPRIATE PLACE FOR IT.
OH... SORRY... I GUESS... NEXT TIME, I'LL BRING A NEW ONE...
I THINK I'LL GET GOING, AOKI-KUN.
SPLOOSH
AH!
YEAH, ME, TOO.
SAME HERE.
スク
HUP
OKAY! SEE YOU MONDAY!
TIME TO CATCH ME A WHOPPER!

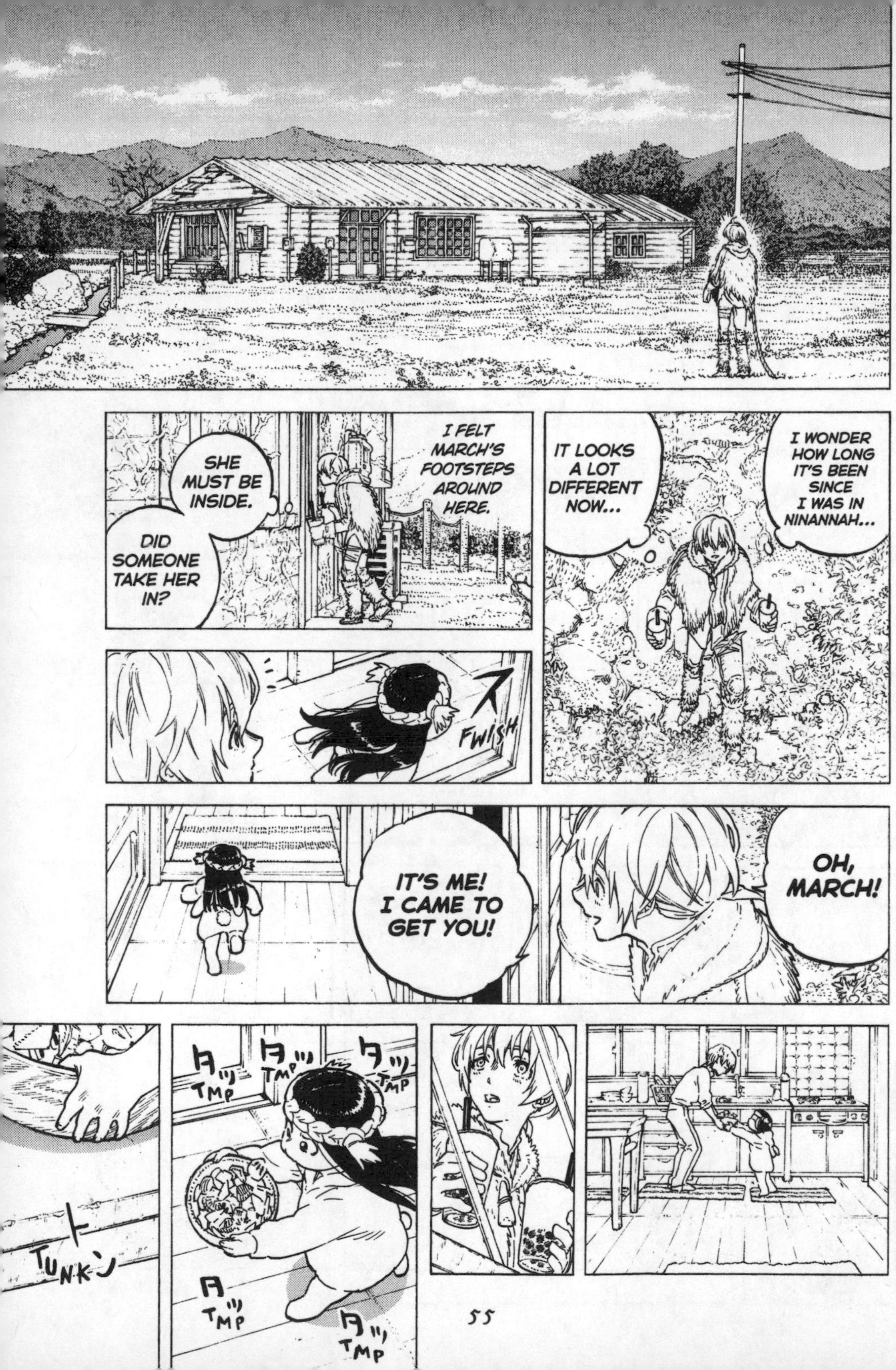
I WONDER HOW LONG IT'S BEEN SINCE I WAS IN NINANNAH...
IT LOOKS A LOT DIFFERENT NOW...
I FELT MARCH'S FOOTSTEPS AROUND HERE.
SHE MUST BE INSIDE.
DID SOMEONE TAKE HER IN?
FWISH
OH, MARCH!
IT'S ME! I CAME TO GET YOU!
TMP
TMP
TMP
TMP
TMP
TUNK

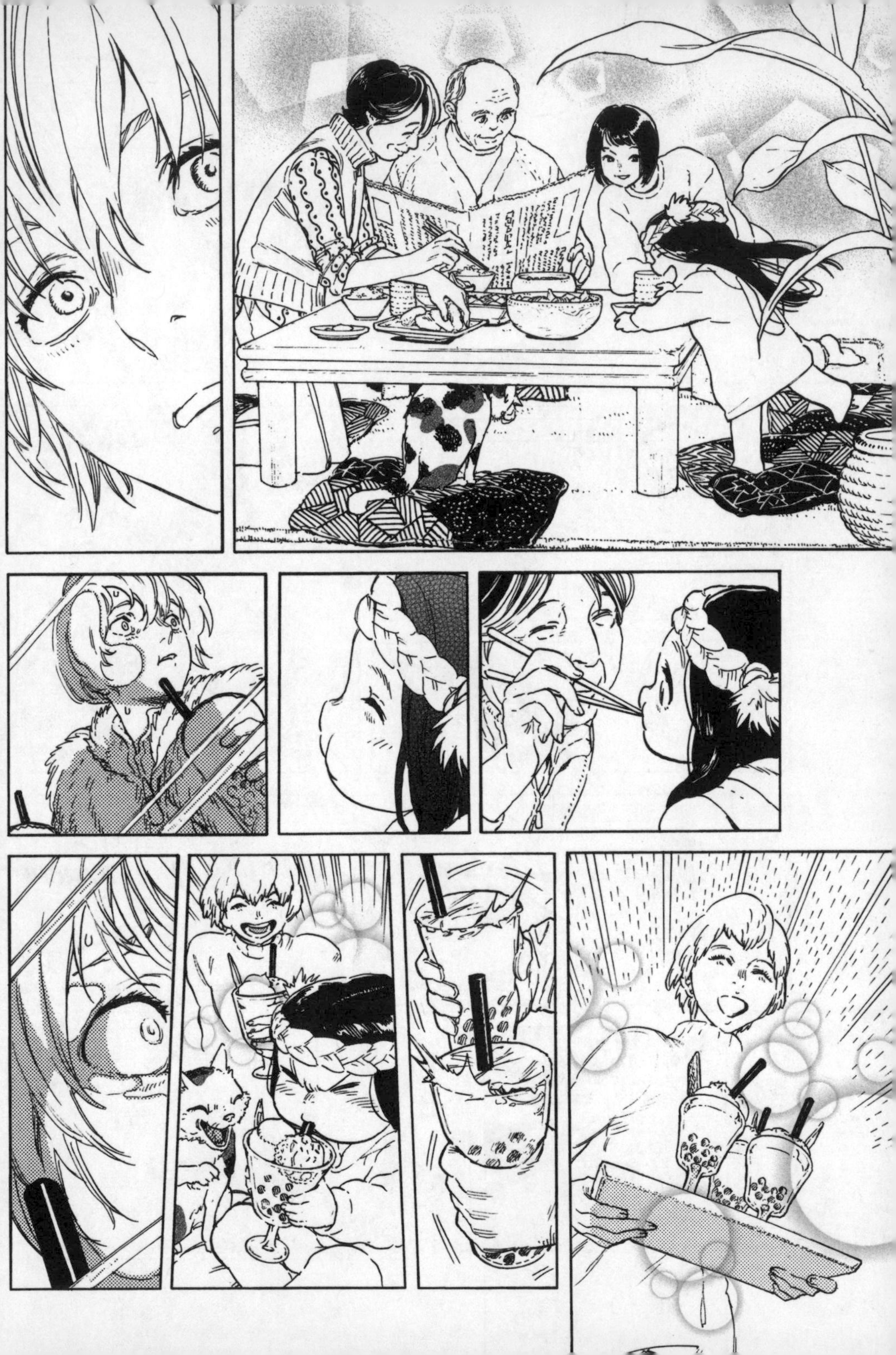

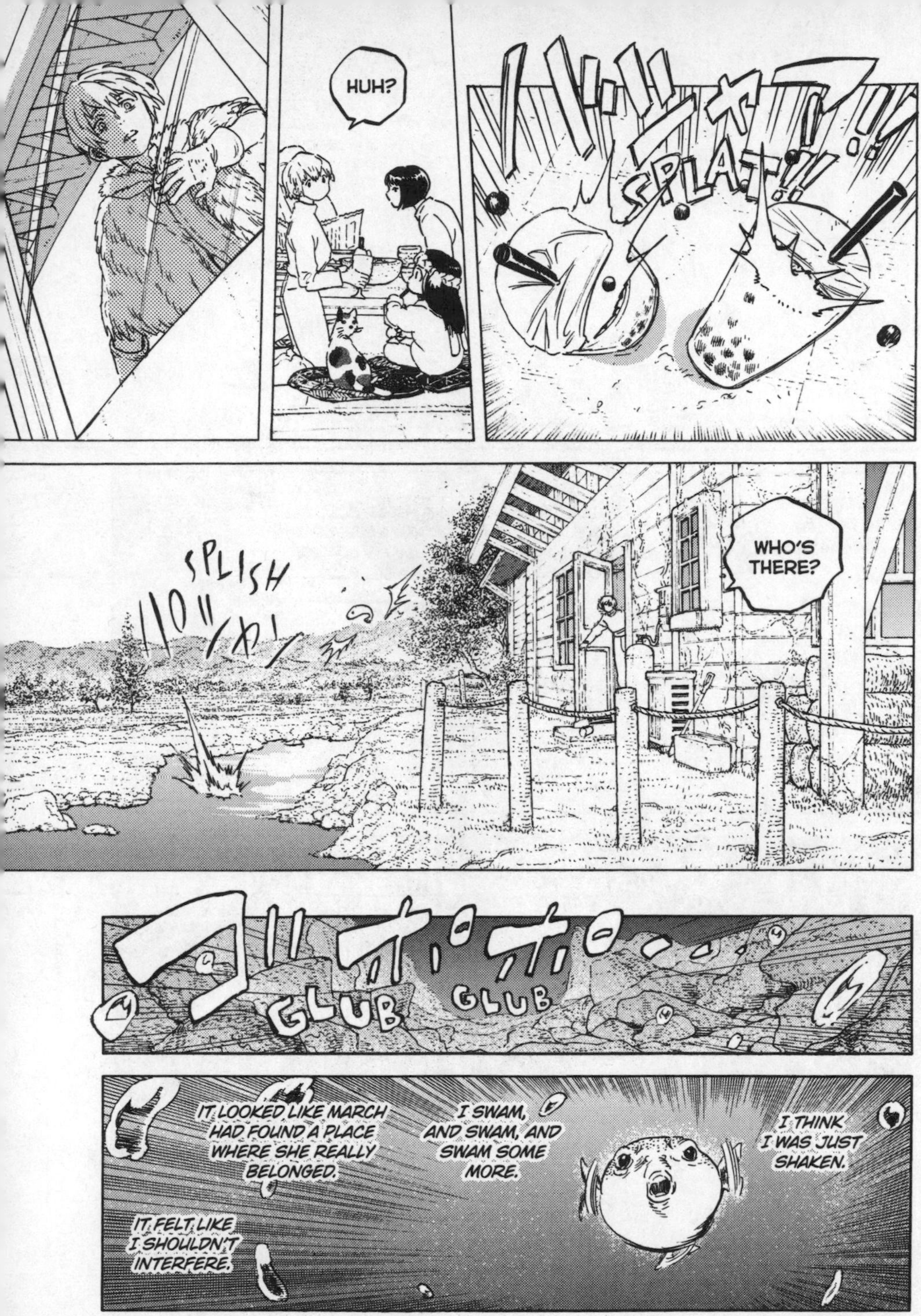
SPLAT!!
HUH?
WHO'S THERE?
SPLISH
GLUB GLUB
I THINK I WAS JUST SHAKEN.
I SWAM, AND SWAM, AND SWAM SOME MORE.
IT LOOKED LIKE MARCH HAD FOUND A PLACE WHERE SHE REALLY BELONGED.
IT FELT LIKE I SHOULDN'T INTERFERE.

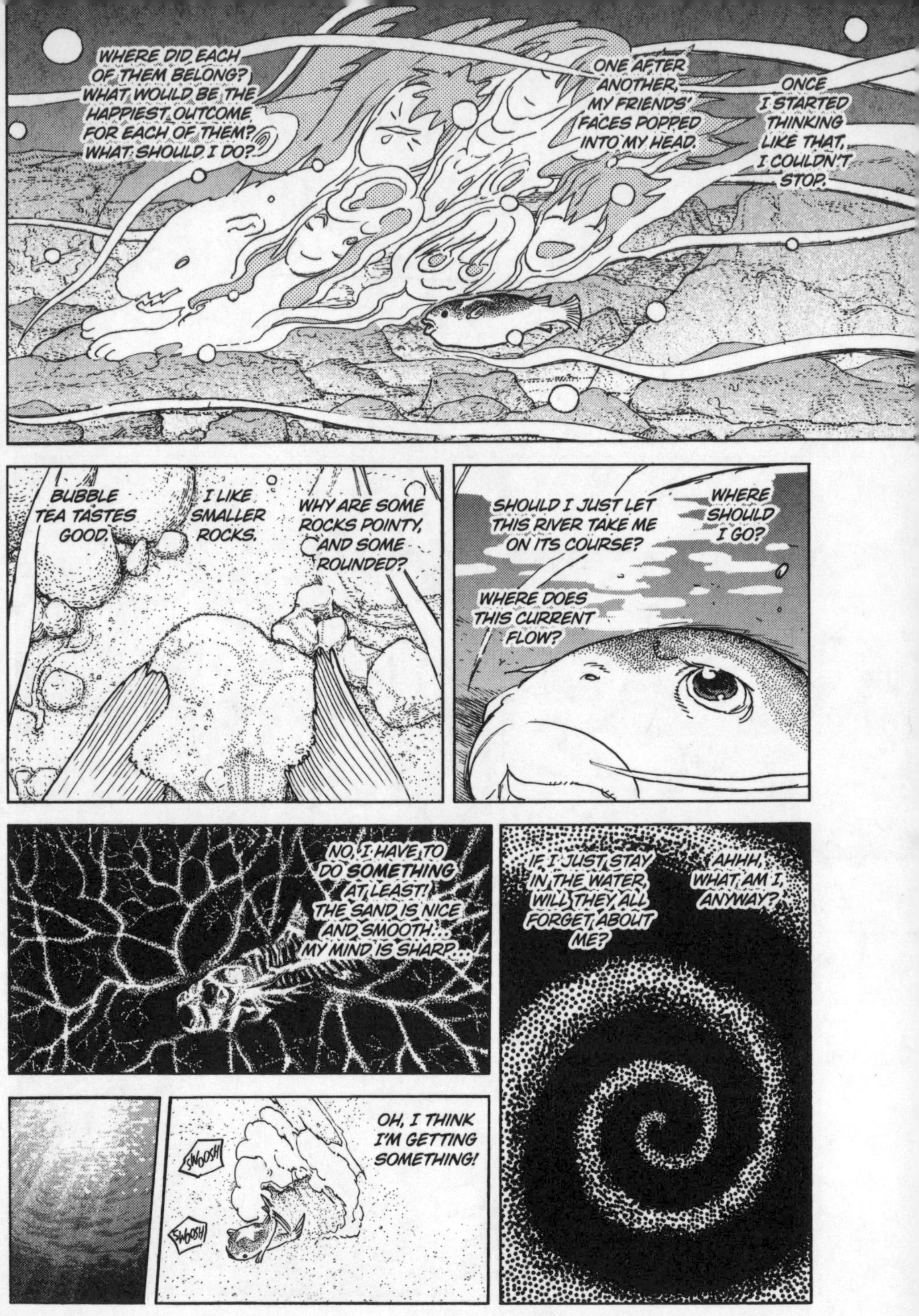
ONCE I STARTED THINKING LIKE THAT, I COULDN'T STOP.
ONE AFTER ANOTHER, MY FRIENDS' FACES POPPED INTO MY HEAD.
WHERE DID EACH OF THEM BELONG? WHAT WOULD BE THE HAPPIEST OUTCOME FOR EACH OF THEM? WHAT SHOULD I DO?
WHERE SHOULD I GO?
SHOULD I JUST LET THIS RIVER TAKE ME ON ITS COURSE?
WHERE DOES THIS CURRENT FLOW?
WHY ARE SOME ROCKS POINTY, AND SOME ROUNDED?
I LIKE SMALLER ROCKS.
BUBBLE TEA TASTES GOOD.
AHHH, WHAT AM I, ANYWAY?
IF I JUST STAY IN THE WATER, WILL THEY ALL FORGET ABOUT ME?
NO, I HAVE TO DO SOMETHING AT LEAST! THE SAND IS NICE AND SMOOTH... MY MIND IS SHARP...
OH, I THINK I'M GETTING SOMETHING!
SWOOSH
SWOOSH

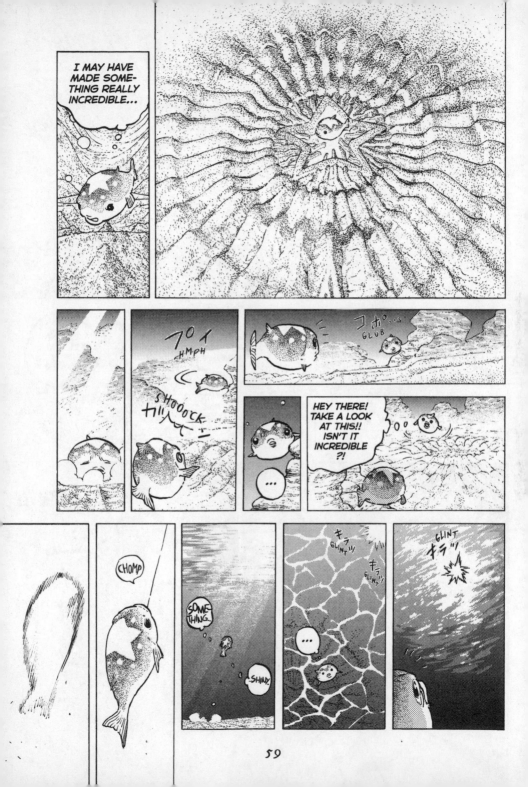

I MAY HAVE MADE SOMETHING REALLY INCREDIBLE...

HMPH

SHOOOCK

GLUB

HEY THERE! TAKE A LOOK AT THIS!! ISN'T IT INCREDIBLE ?!

...

CHOMP

SOMETHING

SHINY

...

GLINT

GLINT

GLINT

GLINT

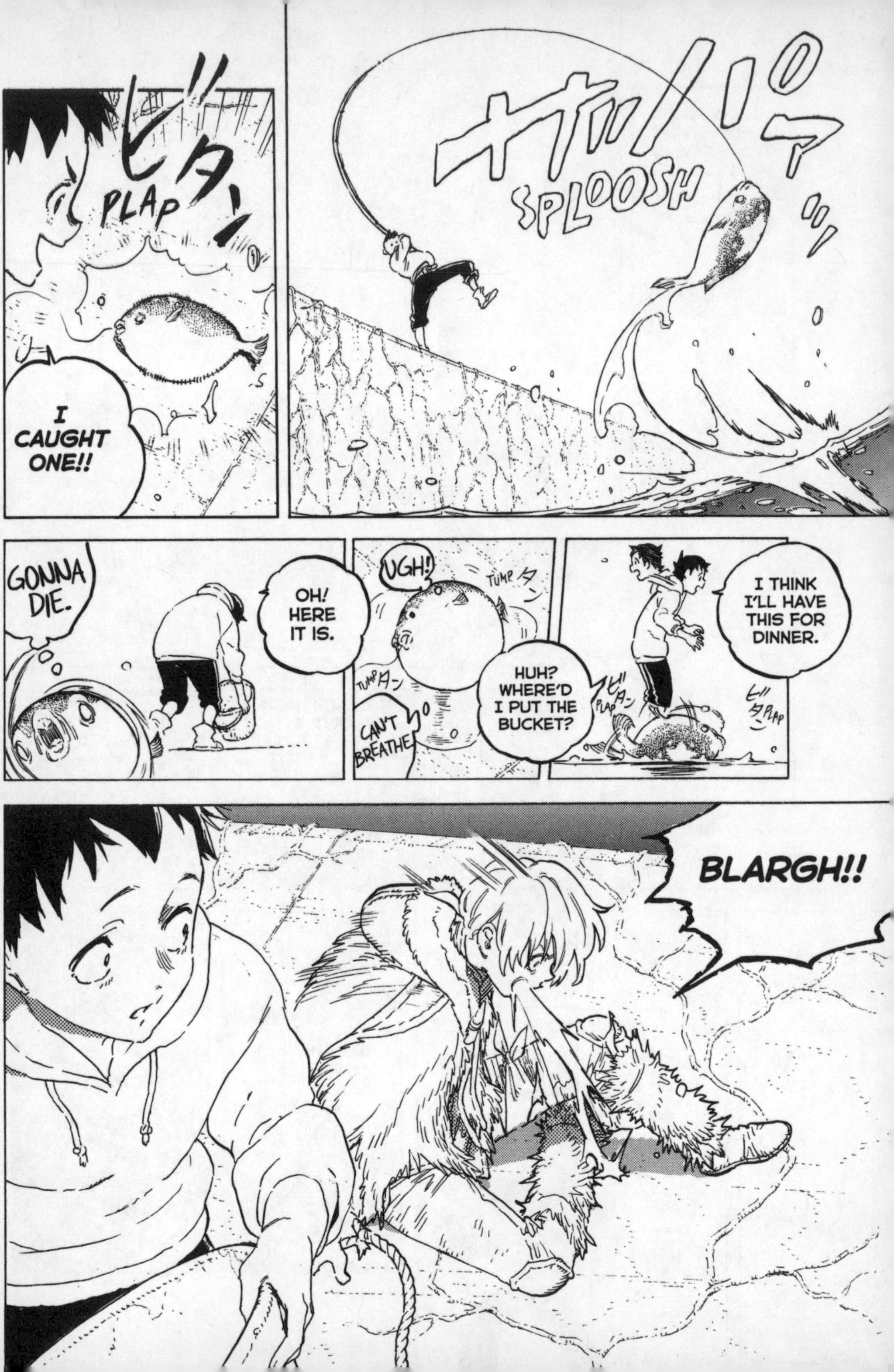
SPLOOSH
PLAP
I CAUGHT ONE!!
I THINK I'LL HAVE THIS FOR DINNER.
PLAP
PLAP
UGH!
TUMP
TUMP
HUH? WHERE'D I PUT THE BUCKET?
CAN'T BREATHE
OH! HERE IT IS.
GONNA DIE.
BLARGH!!

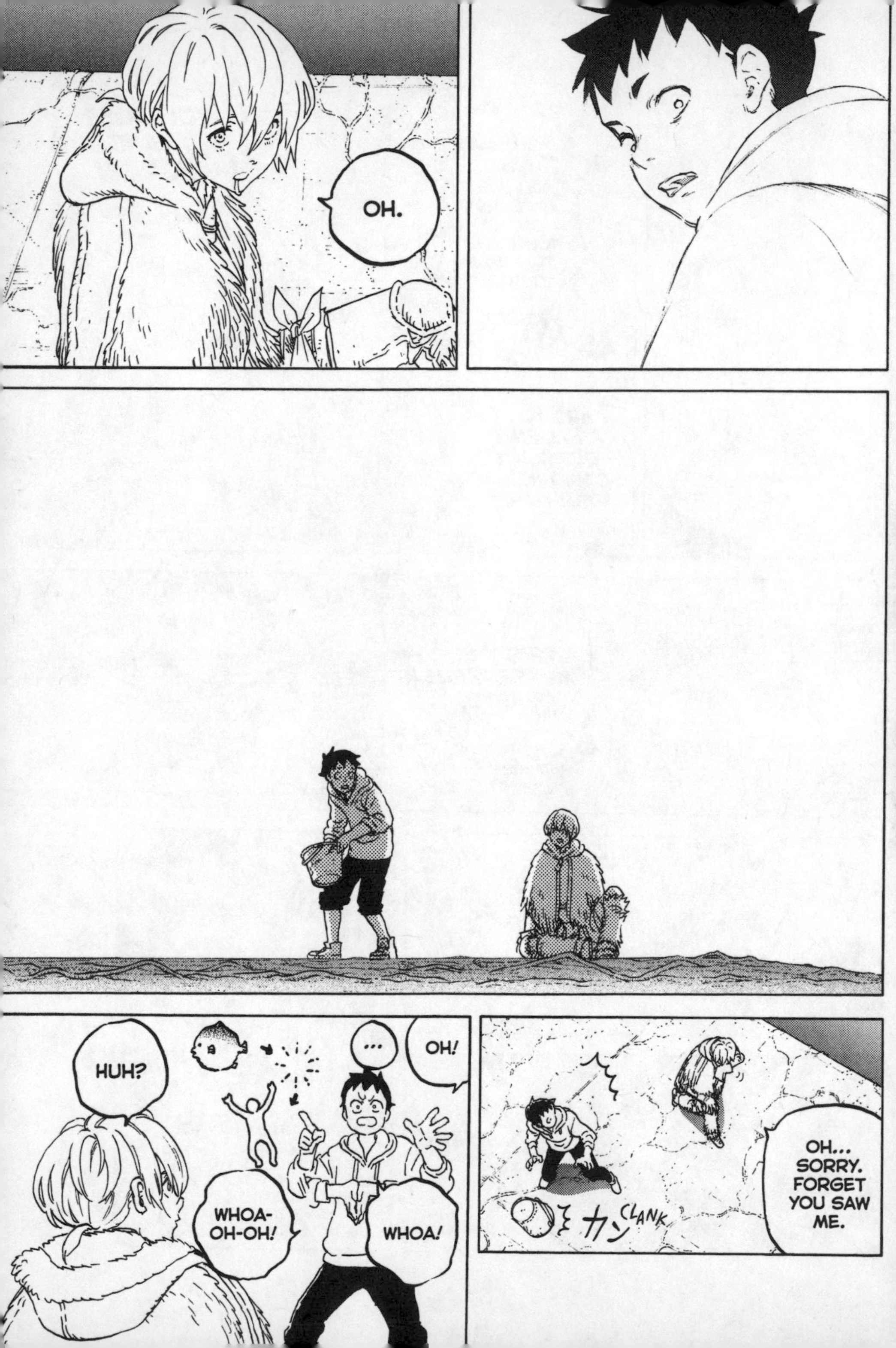
OH.
OH... SORRY. FORGET YOU SAW ME.
カン CLANK
OH!
...
HUH?
WHOA!
WHOA-OH-OH!

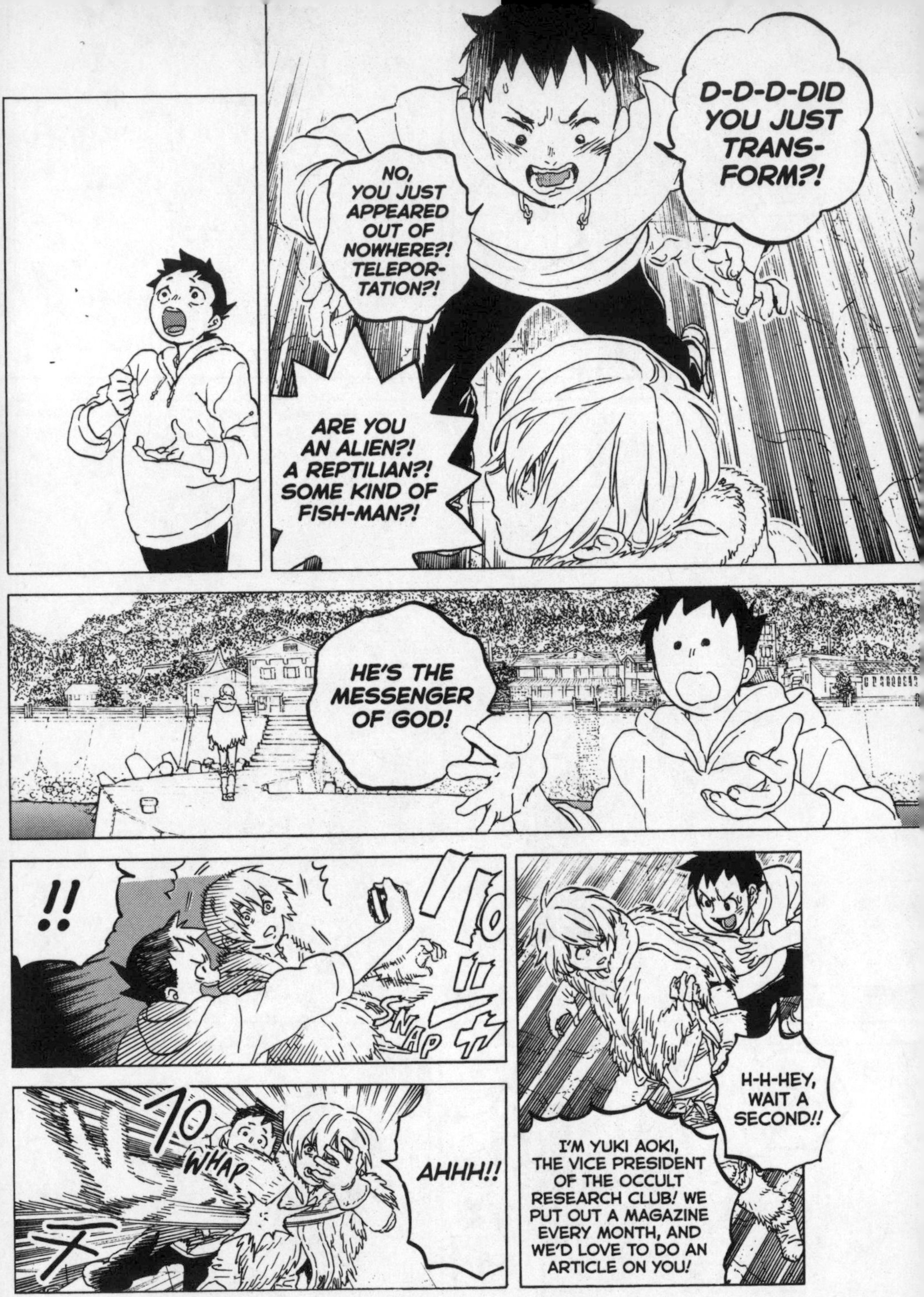
D-D-D-DID YOU JUST TRANS-FORM?!
NO, YOU JUST APPEARED OUT OF NOWHERE?! TELEPOR-TATION?!
ARE YOU AN ALIEN?! A REPTILIAN?! SOME KIND OF FISH-MAN?!
HE'S THE MESSENGER OF GOD!
H-H-HEY, WAIT A SECOND!!
I'M YUKI AOKI, THE VICE PRESIDENT OF THE OCCULT RESEARCH CLUB! WE PUT OUT A MAGAZINE EVERY MONTH, AND WE'D LOVE TO DO AN ARTICLE ON YOU!
!!
SNAP
WHAP
AHHH!!

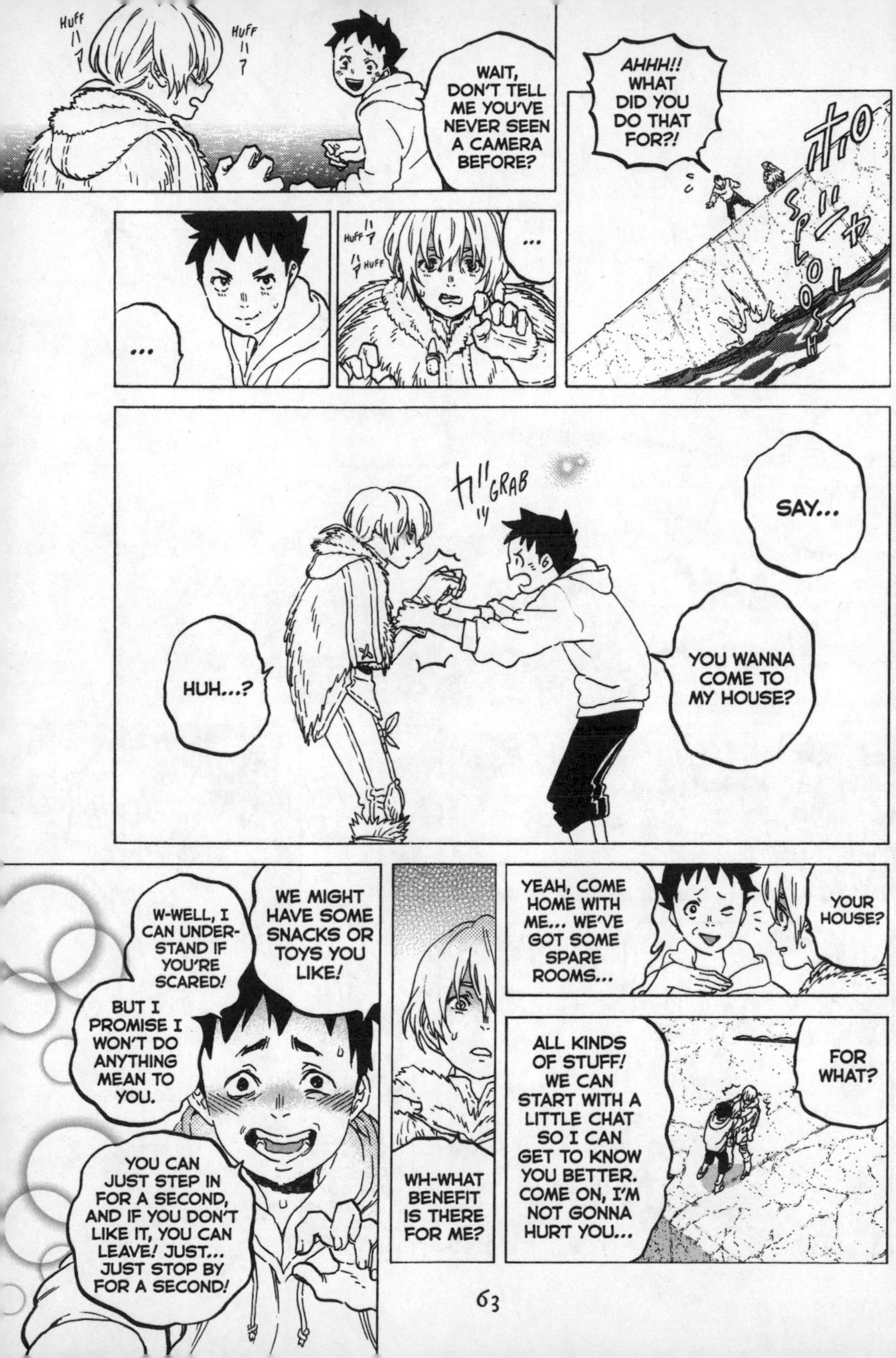
AHHH!! WHAT DID YOU DO THAT FOR?!
SPLOOSH
HUFF
HUFF
WAIT, DON'T TELL ME YOU'VE NEVER SEEN A CAMERA BEFORE?
HUFF
HUFF
...
...
SAY...
YOU WANNA COME TO MY HOUSE?
GRAB
HUH...?
YOUR HOUSE?
YEAH, COME HOME WITH ME... WE'VE GOT SOME SPARE ROOMS...
FOR WHAT?
ALL KINDS OF STUFF! WE CAN START WITH A LITTLE CHAT SO I CAN GET TO KNOW YOU BETTER. COME ON, I'M NOT GONNA HURT YOU...
WH-WHAT BENEFIT IS THERE FOR ME?
WE MIGHT HAVE SOME SNACKS OR TOYS YOU LIKE!
W-WELL, I CAN UNDERSTAND IF YOU'RE SCARED!
BUT I PROMISE I WON'T DO ANYTHING MEAN TO YOU.
YOU CAN JUST STEP IN FOR A SECOND, AND IF YOU DON'T LIKE IT, YOU CAN LEAVE! JUST... JUST STOP BY FOR A SECOND!

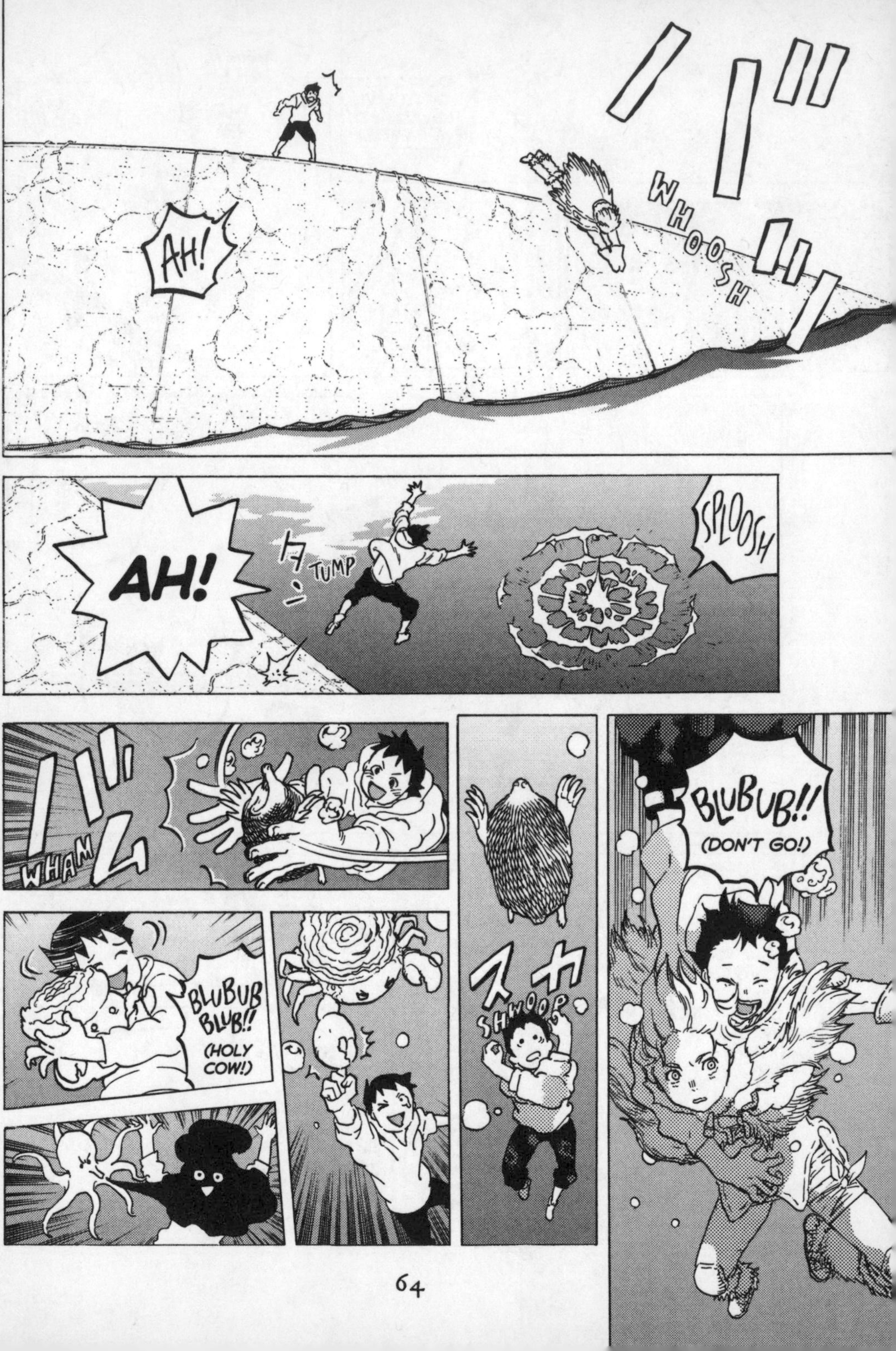
WHOOSH
AH!
SPLOOSH
TUMP
AH!
BLUBUB!!
(DON'T GO!)
SHWOOP
WHAM
BLUBUB BLUB!!
(HOLY COW!)

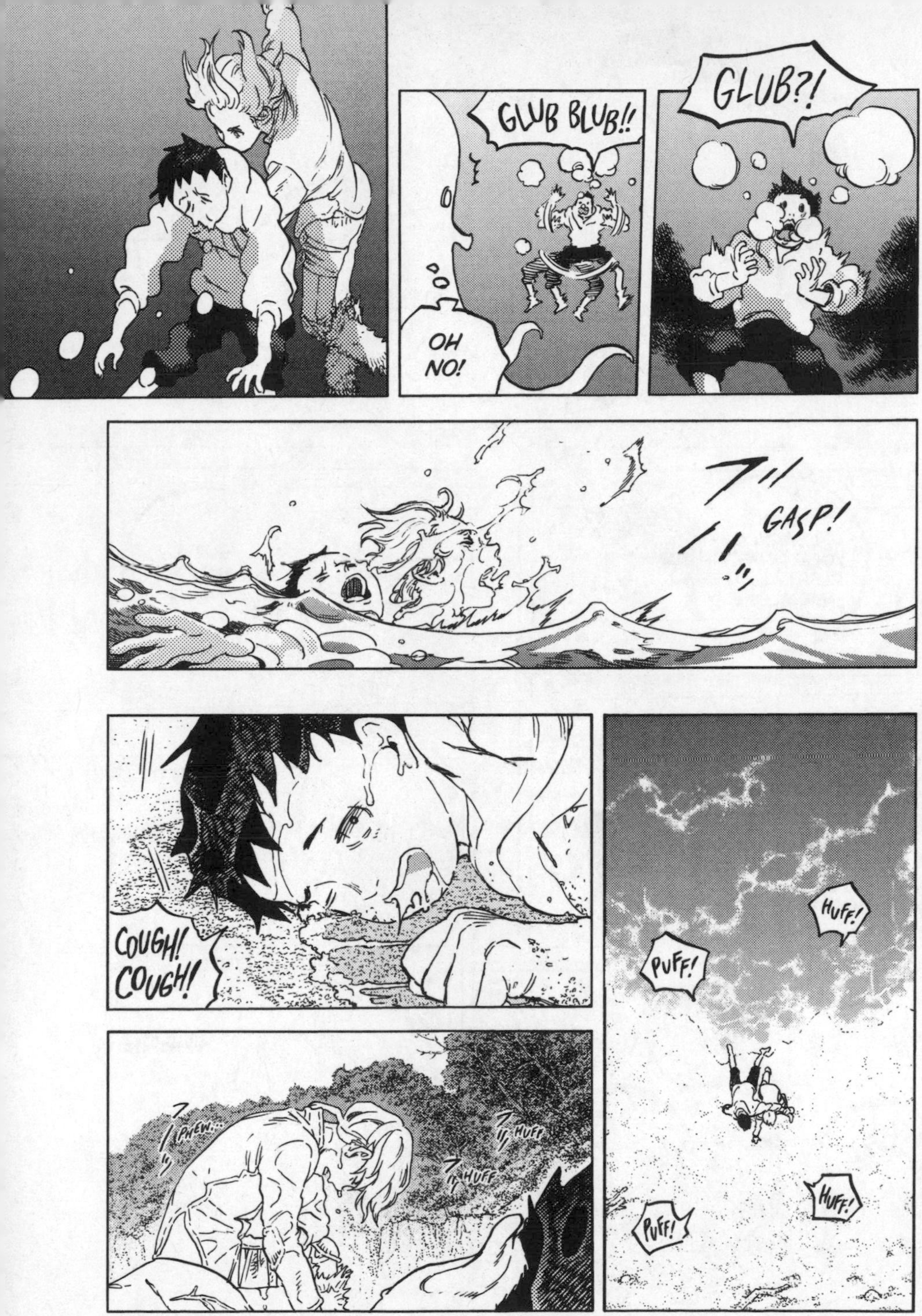
GLUB?!
GLUB BLUB!!
OH NO!
GASP!
HUFF!
PUFF!
HUFF!
PUFF!
COUGH! COUGH!
HUFF
HUFF
PHEW...

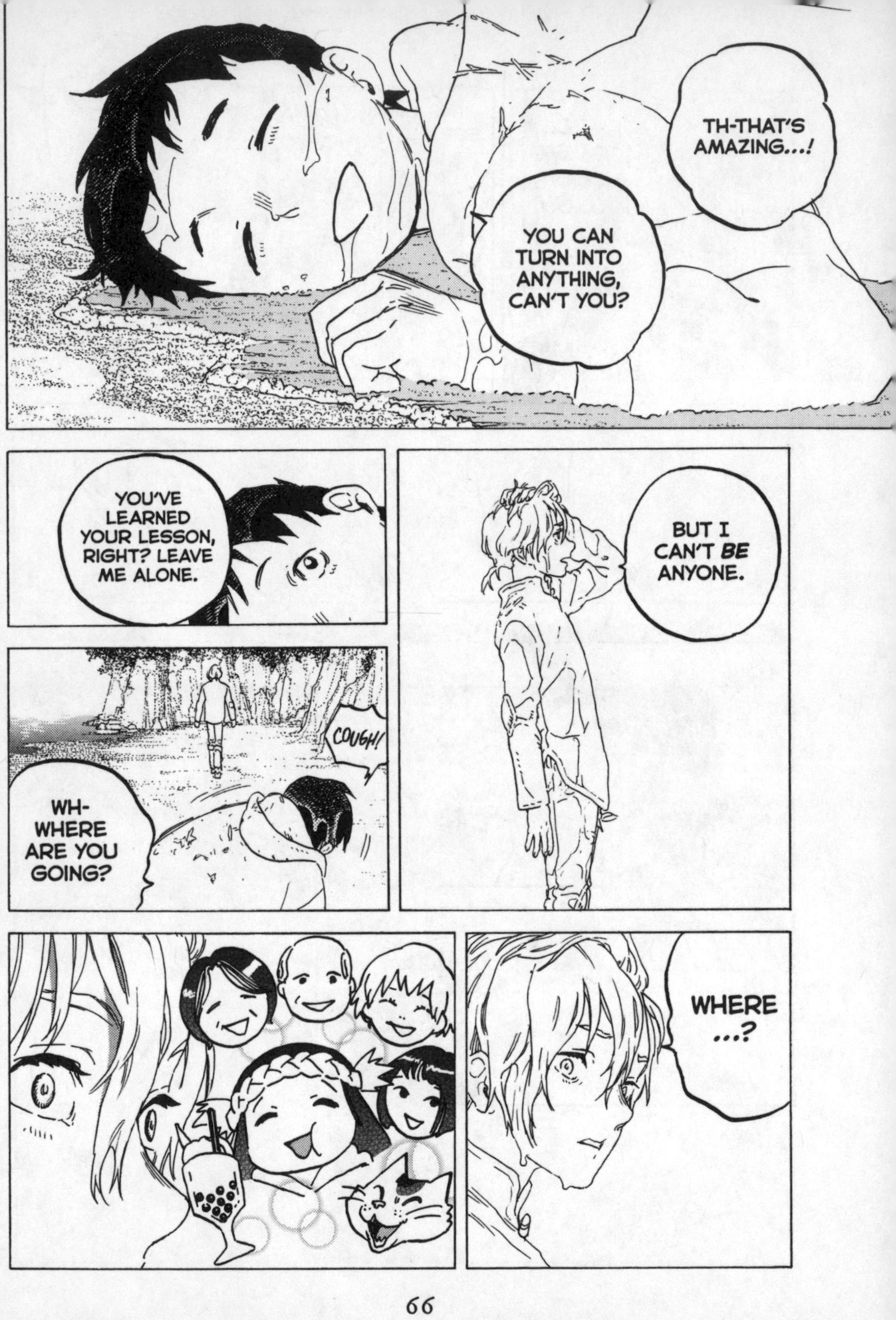
TH-THAT'S AMAZING...!
YOU CAN TURN INTO ANYTHING, CAN'T YOU?
BUT I CAN'T *BE* ANYONE.
YOU'VE LEARNED YOUR LESSON, RIGHT? LEAVE ME ALONE.
COUGH!
WH- WHERE ARE YOU GOING?
WHERE ...?

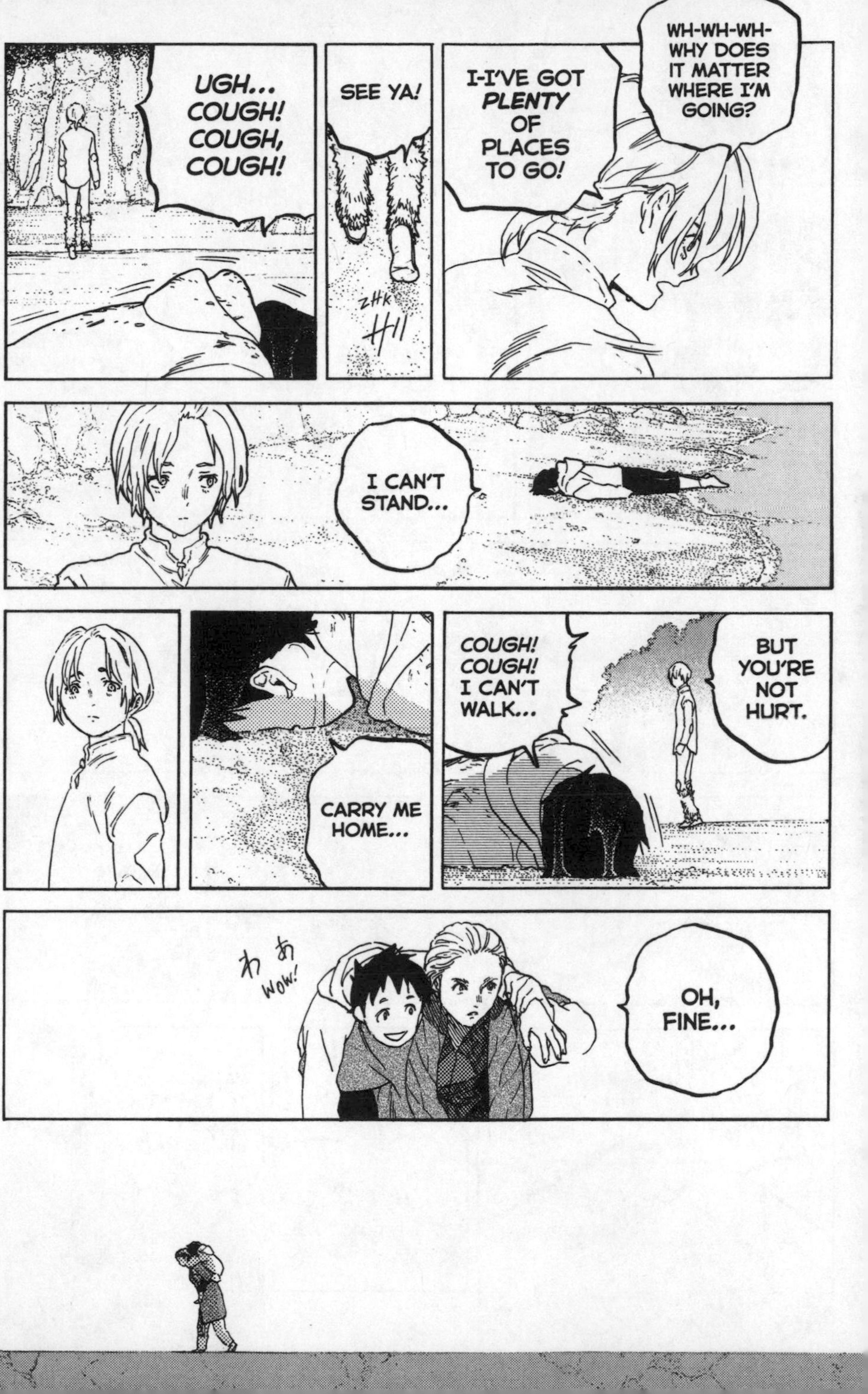
WH-WH-WH-WHY DOES IT MATTER WHERE I'M GOING?
I-I'VE GOT *PLENTY* OF PLACES TO GO!
SEE YA!
ZHK
UGH... COUGH! COUGH, COUGH!
I CAN'T STAND...
BUT YOU'RE NOT HURT.
COUGH! COUGH! I CAN'T WALK...
CARRY ME HOME...
OH, FINE...
わあ
WOW!

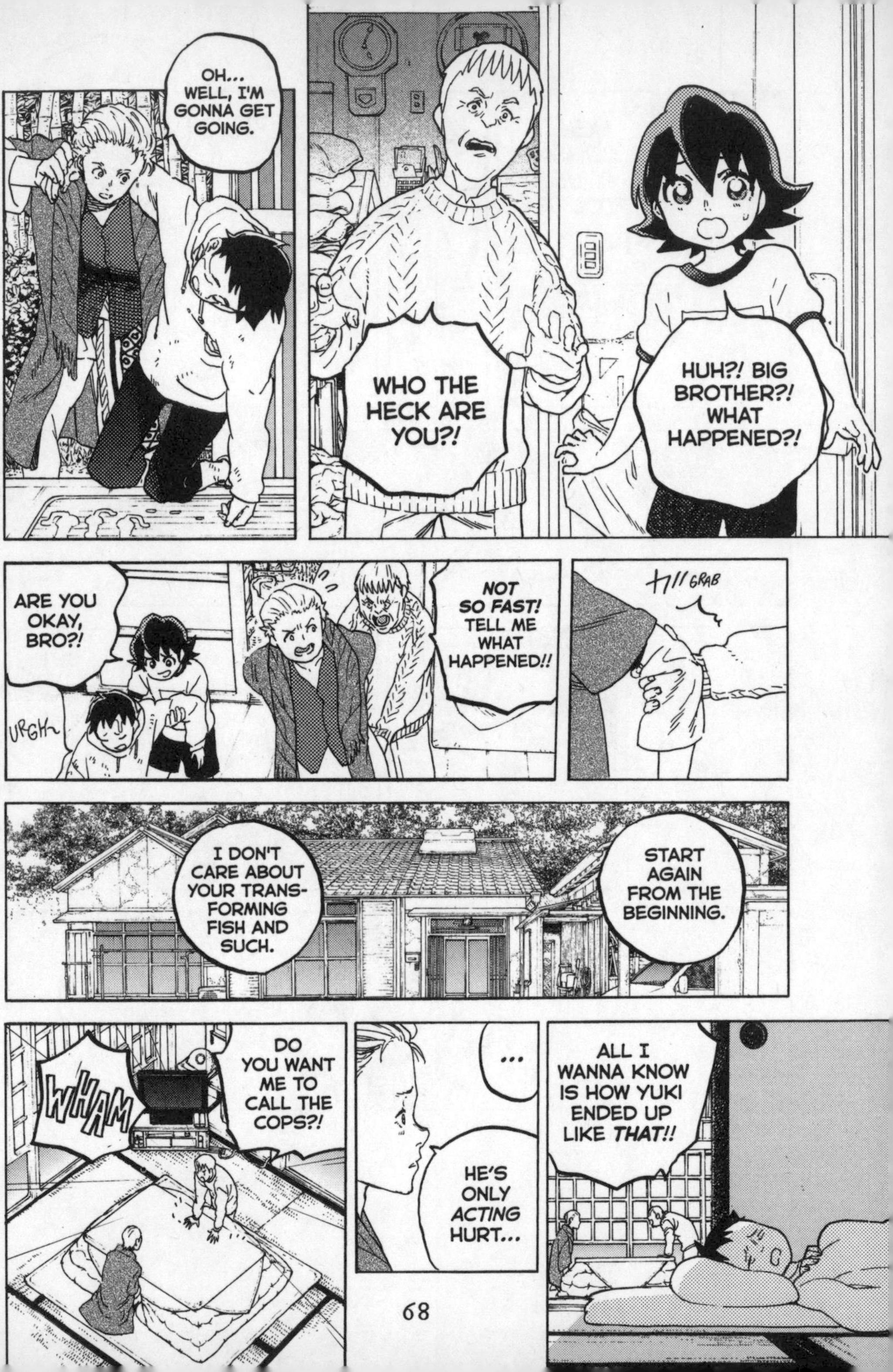
HUH?! BIG BROTHER?! WHAT HAPPENED?!
WHO THE HECK ARE YOU?!
OH... WELL, I'M GONNA GET GOING.
ガッ GRAB
NOT SO FAST! TELL ME WHAT HAPPENED!!
ARE YOU OKAY, BRO?!
URGH~
START AGAIN FROM THE BEGINNING.
I DON'T CARE ABOUT YOUR TRANS-FORMING FISH AND SUCH.
ALL I WANNA KNOW IS HOW YUKI ENDED UP LIKE THAT!!
...
HE'S ONLY ACTING HURT...
DO YOU WANT ME TO CALL THE COPS?!
WHAM

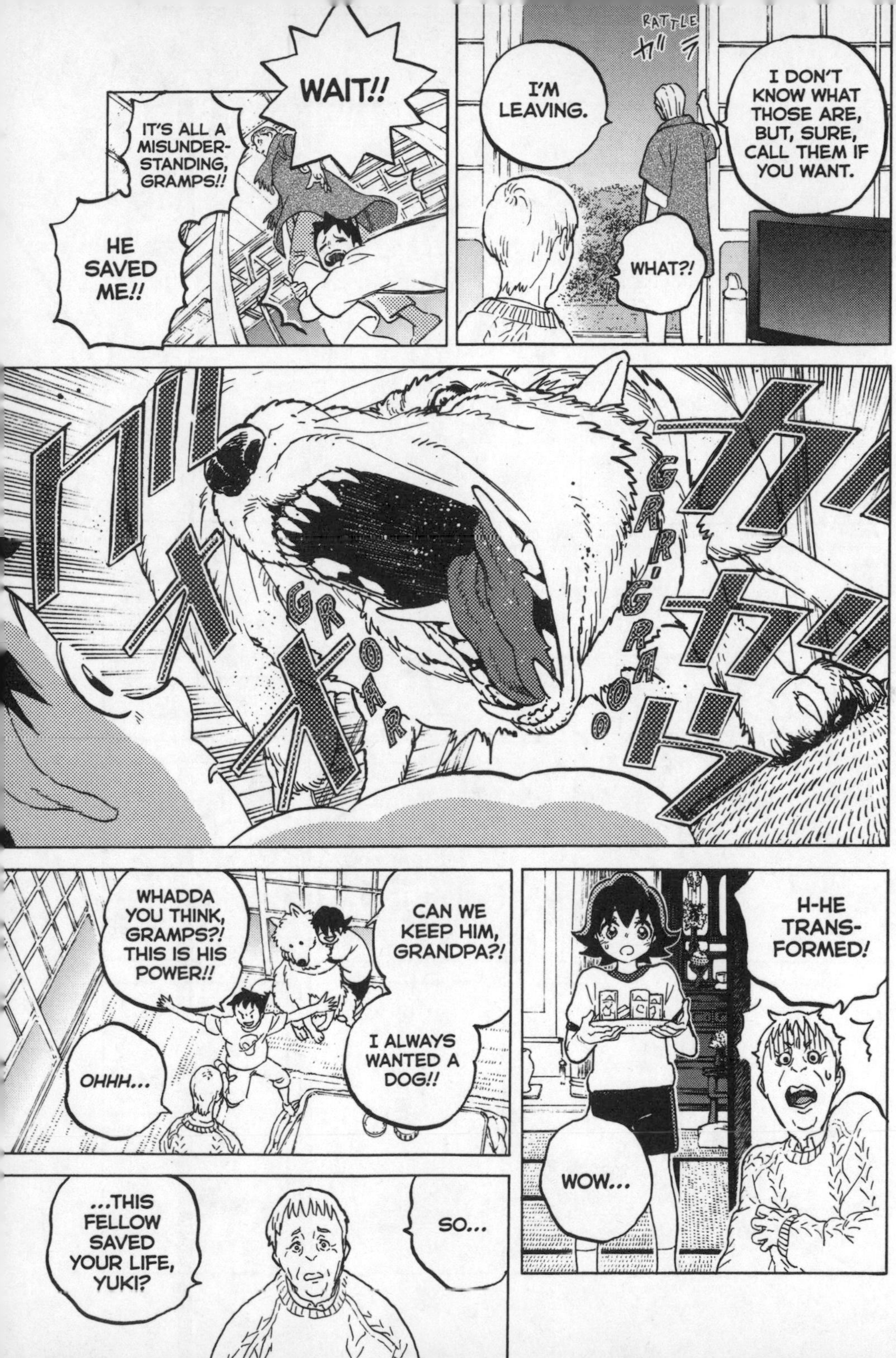
RATTLE
I DON'T KNOW WHAT THOSE ARE, BUT, SURE, CALL THEM IF YOU WANT.
I'M LEAVING.
WHAT?!
WAIT!!
IT'S ALL A MISUNDER-STANDING, GRAMPS!!
HE SAVED ME!!
GRR-GRAOO
GROOARR
H-HE TRANS-FORMED!
WOW...
CAN WE KEEP HIM, GRANDPA?!
WHADDA YOU THINK, GRAMPS?! THIS IS HIS POWER!!
I ALWAYS WANTED A DOG!!
OHHH...
SO...
...THIS FELLOW SAVED YOUR LIFE, YUKI?

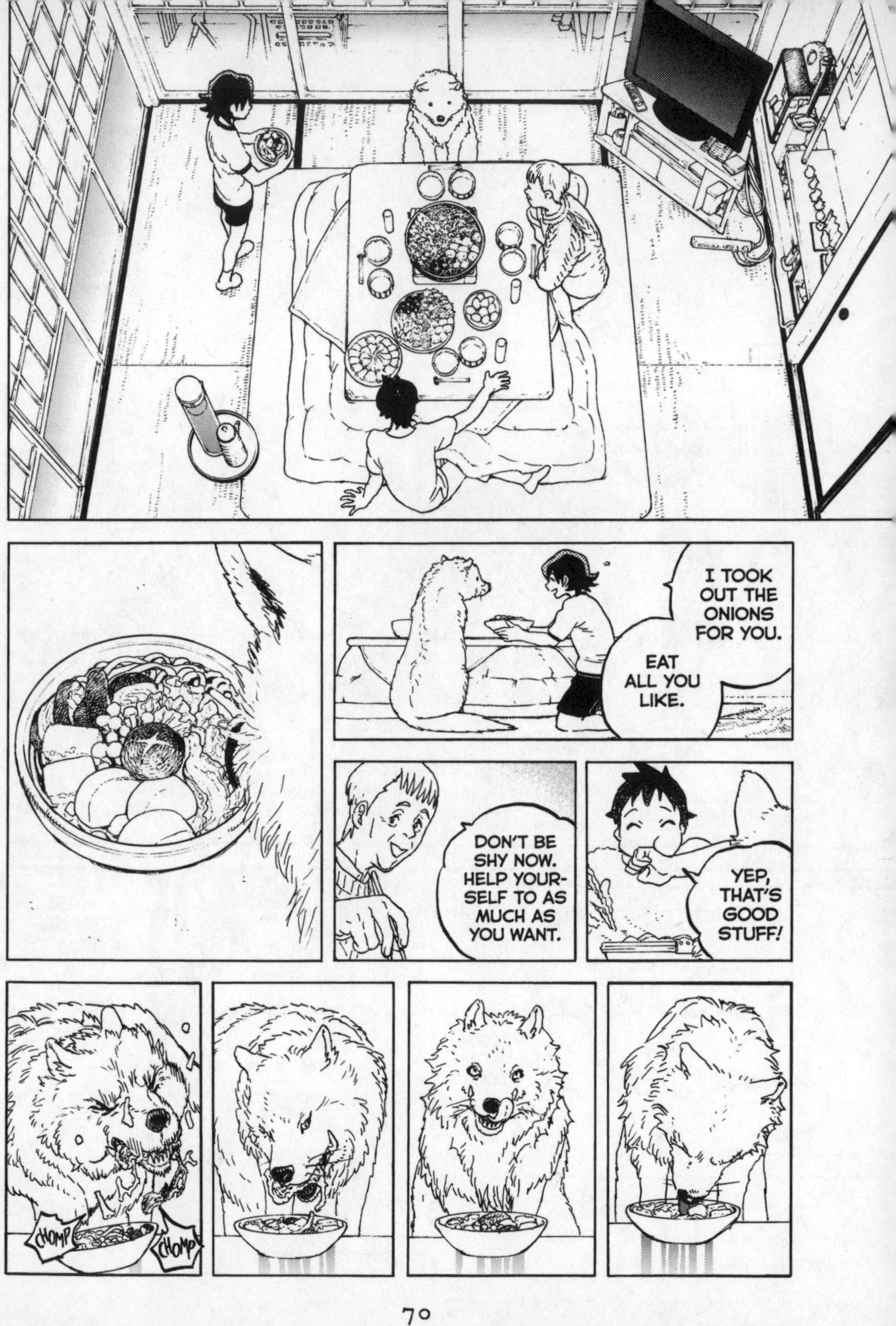
I TOOK OUT THE ONIONS FOR YOU.
EAT ALL YOU LIKE.
YEP, THAT'S GOOD STUFF!
DON'T BE SHY NOW. HELP YOURSELF TO AS MUCH AS YOU WANT.
CHOMP
CHOMP

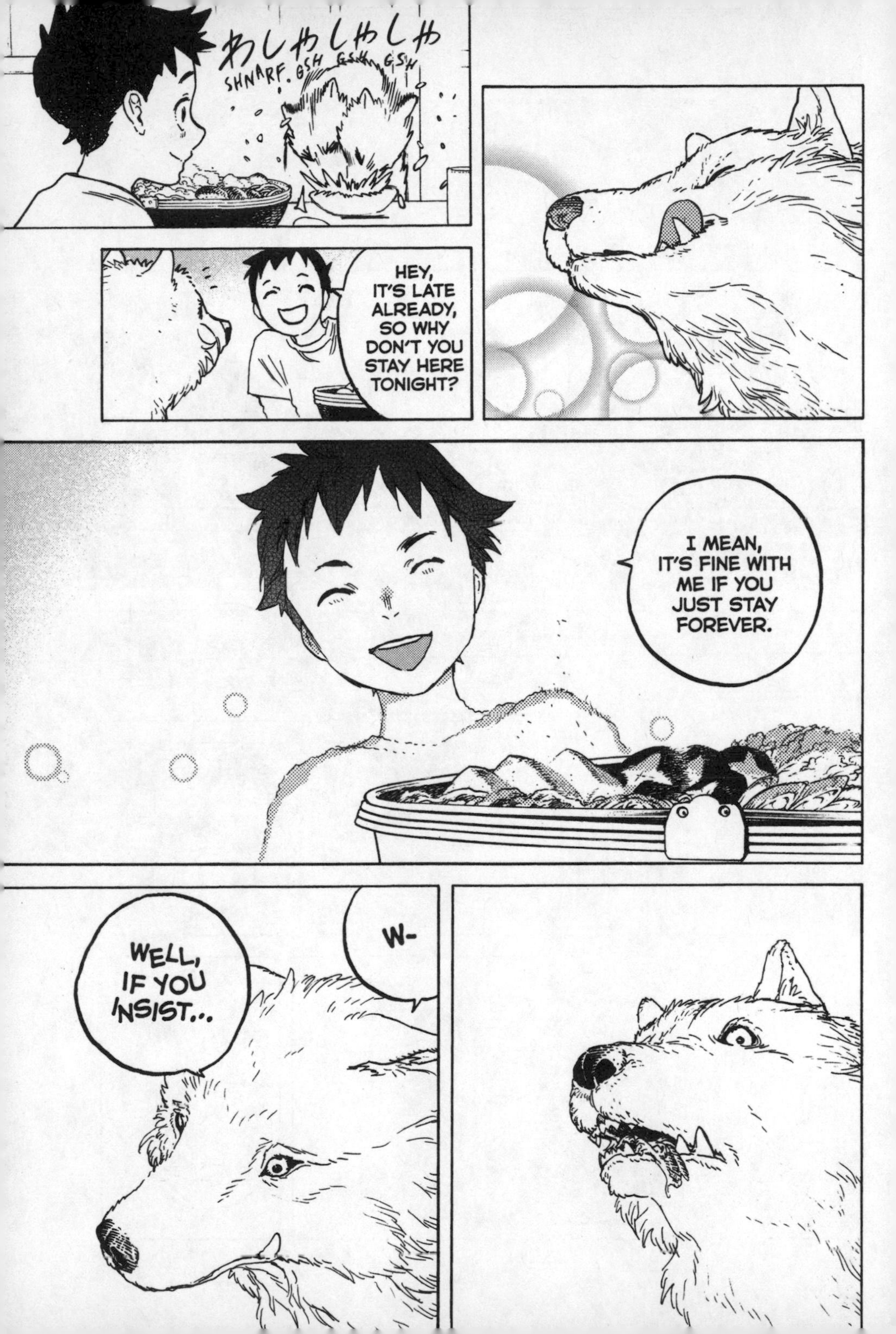

わしゃしゃしゃ
SHNARF. GSH GSH GSH
HEY, IT'S LATE ALREADY, SO WHY DON'T YOU STAY HERE TONIGHT?
I MEAN, IT'S FINE WITH ME IF YOU JUST STAY FOREVER.
W-
WELL, IF YOU INSIST...

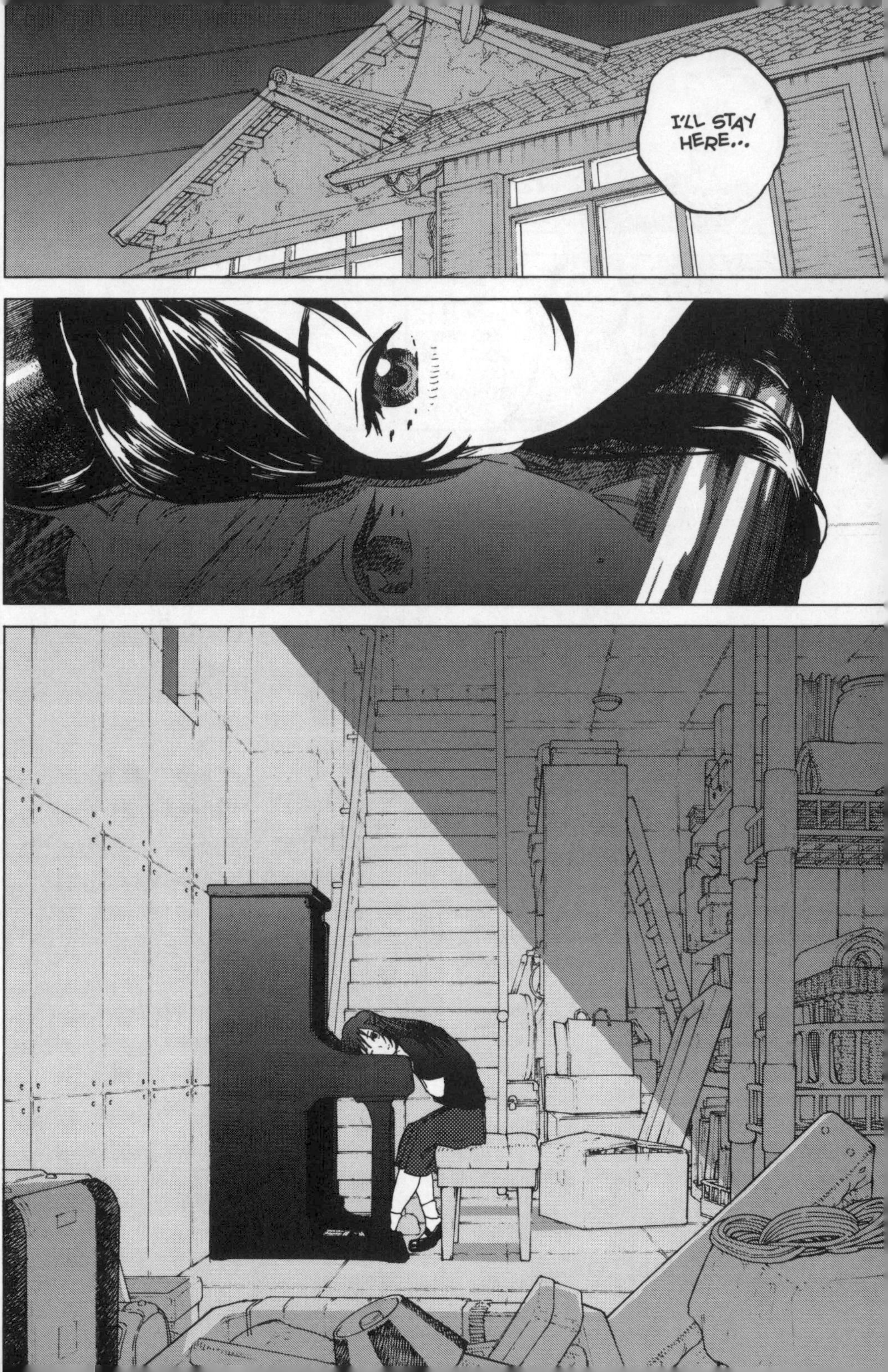
I'LL STAY HERE...

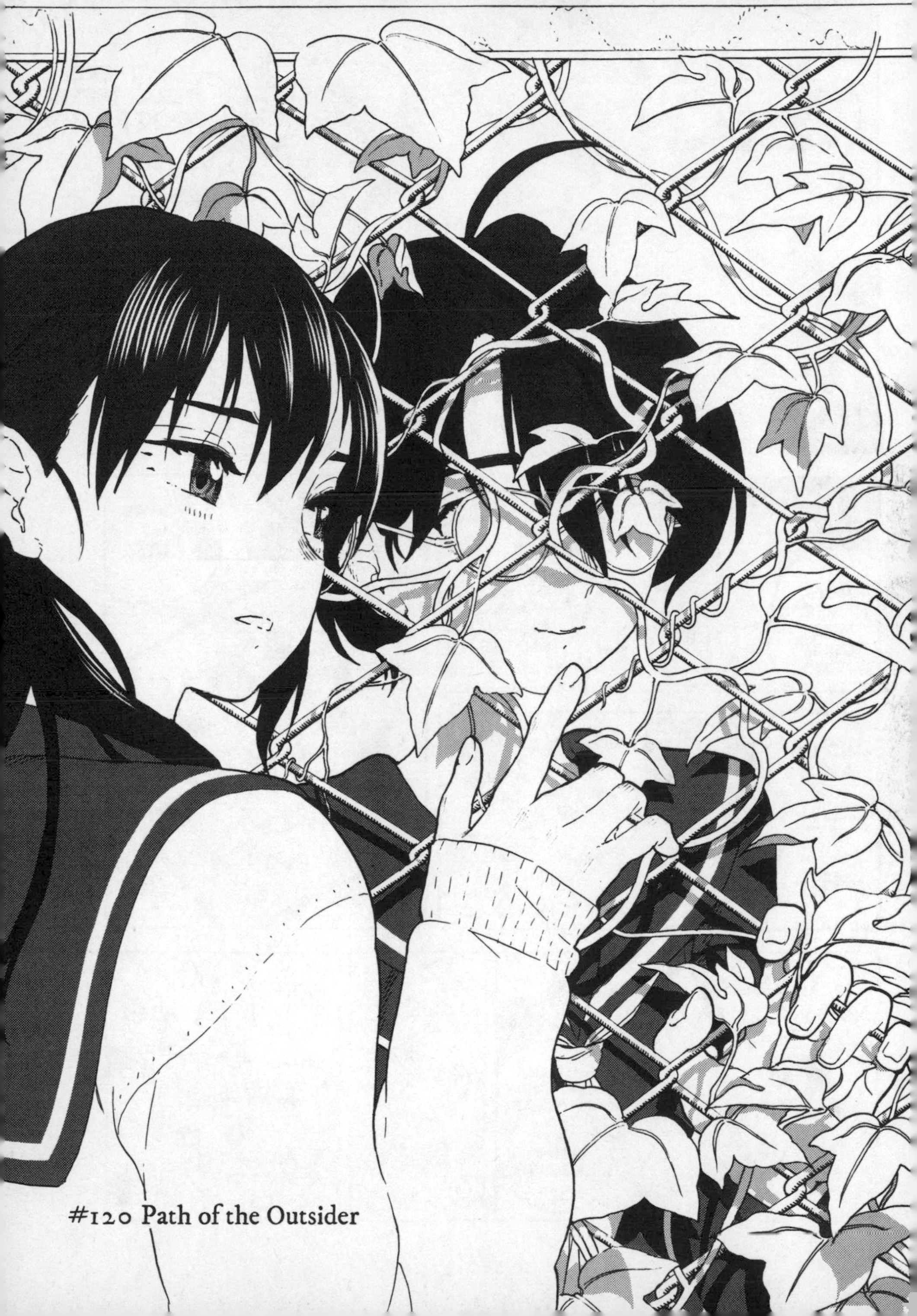
#120 Path of the Outsider

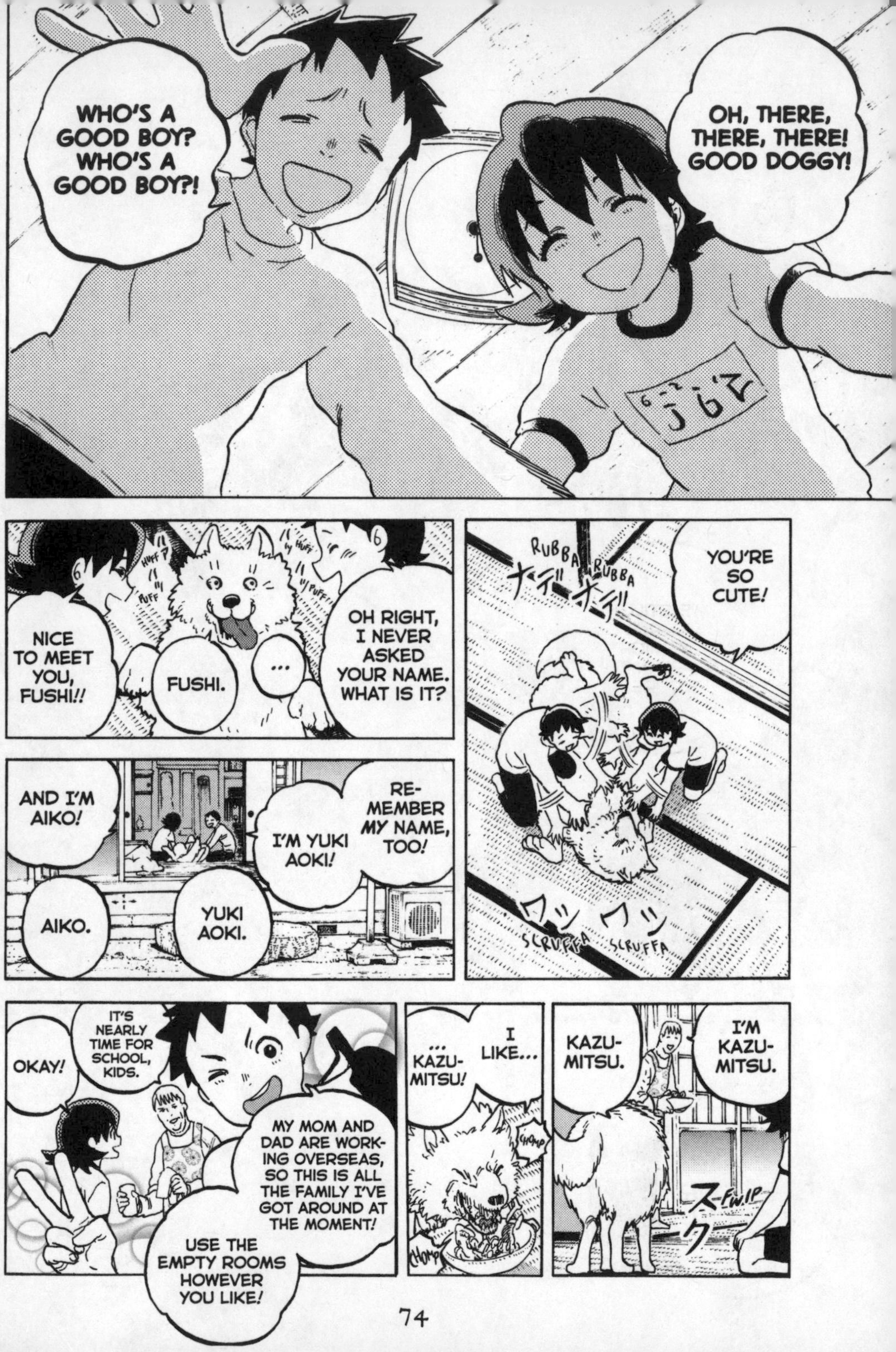
OH, THERE, THERE, THERE! GOOD DOGGY!
WHO'S A GOOD BOY? WHO'S A GOOD BOY?!
RUBBA RUBBA
ナデ ナデ
YOU'RE SO CUTE!
ワッ ワッ
SCRUFFA SCRUFFA
HUFF HUFF PUFF PUFF
OH RIGHT, I NEVER ASKED YOUR NAME. WHAT IS IT?
...
FUSHI.
NICE TO MEET YOU, FUSHI!!
RE-MEMBER MY NAME, TOO!
I'M YUKI AOKI!
AND I'M AIKO!
YUKI AOKI.
AIKO.
I'M KAZU-MITSU.
KAZU-MITSU.
スーッ
FWIP
I LIKE...
...KAZU-MITSU!
CHOMP
CHOMP
IT'S NEARLY TIME FOR SCHOOL, KIDS.
OKAY!
MY MOM AND DAD ARE WORK-ING OVERSEAS, SO THIS IS ALL THE FAMILY I'VE GOT AROUND AT THE MOMENT!
USE THE EMPTY ROOMS HOWEVER YOU LIKE!

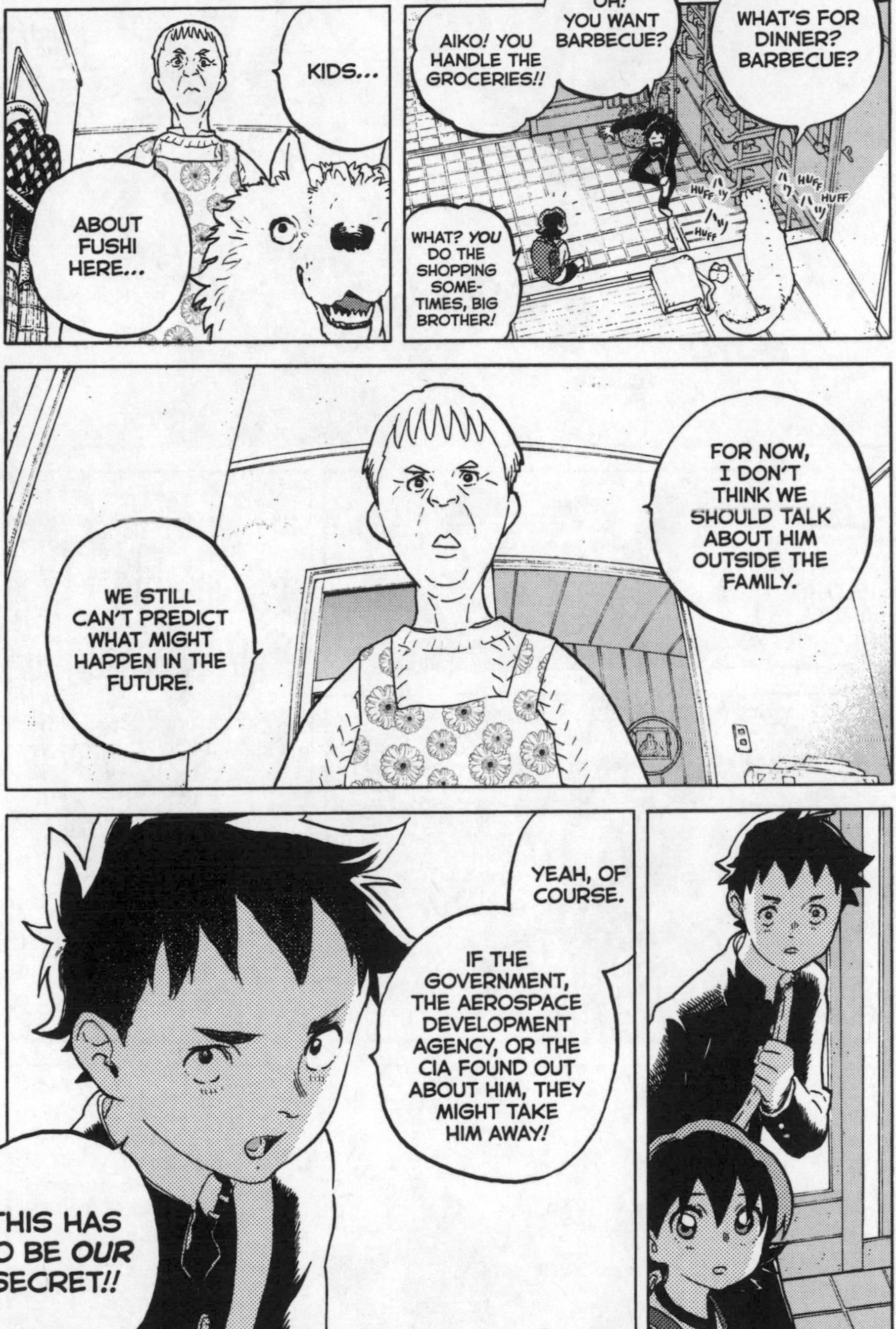
WHAT'S FOR DINNER? BARBECUE?
HUFF HUFF
HUFF HUFF
OH! YOU WANT BARBECUE?
AIKO! YOU HANDLE THE GROCERIES!!
WHAT? *YOU* DO THE SHOPPING SOME-TIMES, BIG BROTHER!
KIDS...
ABOUT FUSHI HERE...
FOR NOW, I DON'T THINK WE SHOULD TALK ABOUT HIM OUTSIDE THE FAMILY.
WE STILL CAN'T PREDICT WHAT MIGHT HAPPEN IN THE FUTURE.
YEAH, OF COURSE.
IF THE GOVERNMENT, THE AEROSPACE DEVELOPMENT AGENCY, OR THE CIA FOUND OUT ABOUT HIM, THEY MIGHT TAKE HIM AWAY!
THIS HAS TO BE *OUR* SECRET!!

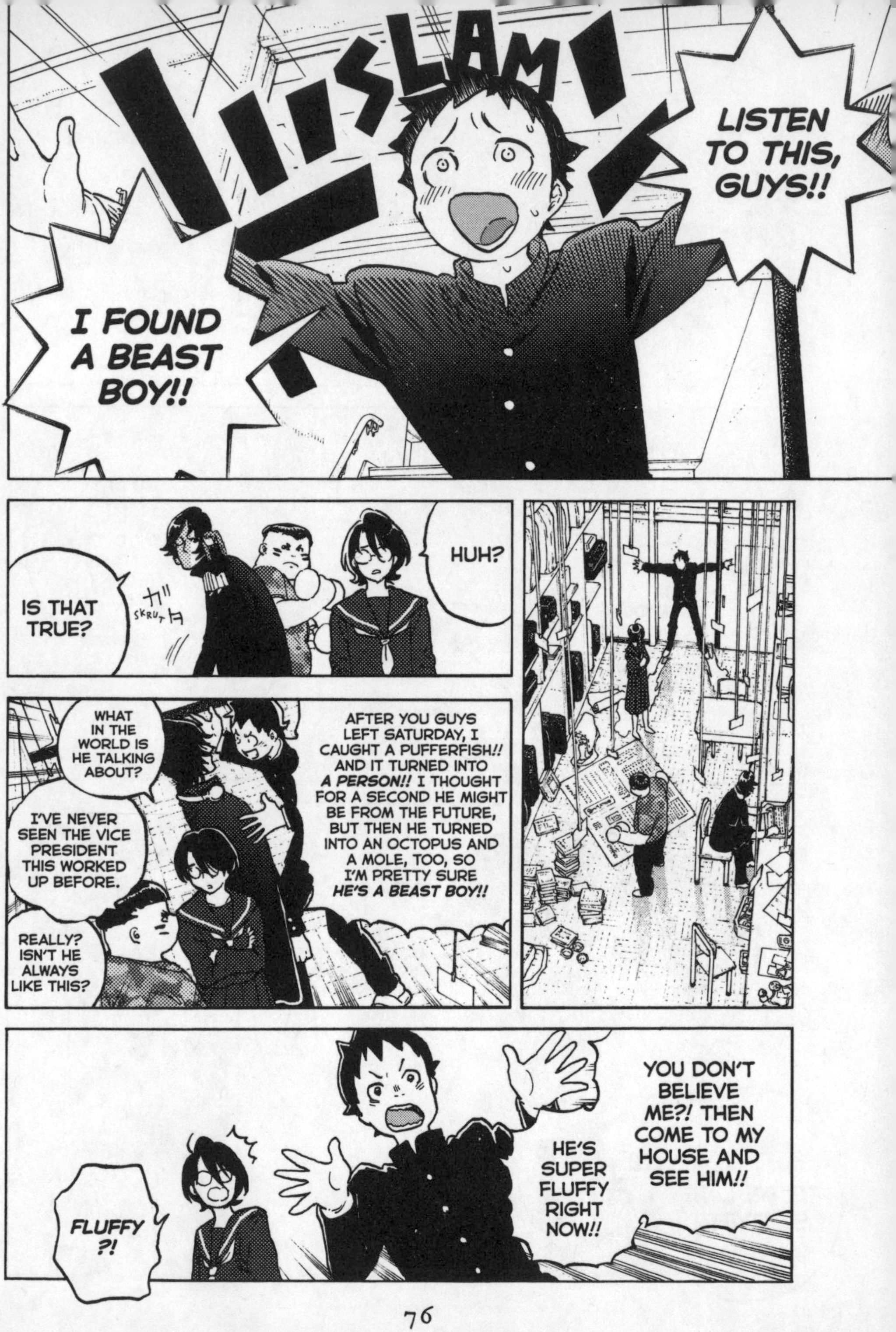
SLAM!
LISTEN TO THIS, GUYS!!
I FOUND A BEAST BOY!!
HUH?
IS THAT TRUE?
SKRUT
AFTER YOU GUYS LEFT SATURDAY, I CAUGHT A PUFFERFISH!! AND IT TURNED INTO *A PERSON!!* I THOUGHT FOR A SECOND HE MIGHT BE FROM THE FUTURE, BUT THEN HE TURNED INTO AN OCTOPUS AND A MOLE, TOO, SO I'M PRETTY SURE *HE'S A BEAST BOY!!*
WHAT IN THE WORLD IS HE TALKING ABOUT?
I'VE NEVER SEEN THE VICE PRESIDENT THIS WORKED UP BEFORE.
REALLY? ISN'T HE ALWAYS LIKE THIS?
YOU DON'T BELIEVE ME?! THEN COME TO MY HOUSE AND SEE HIM!!
HE'S SUPER FLUFFY RIGHT NOW!!
FLUFFY?!

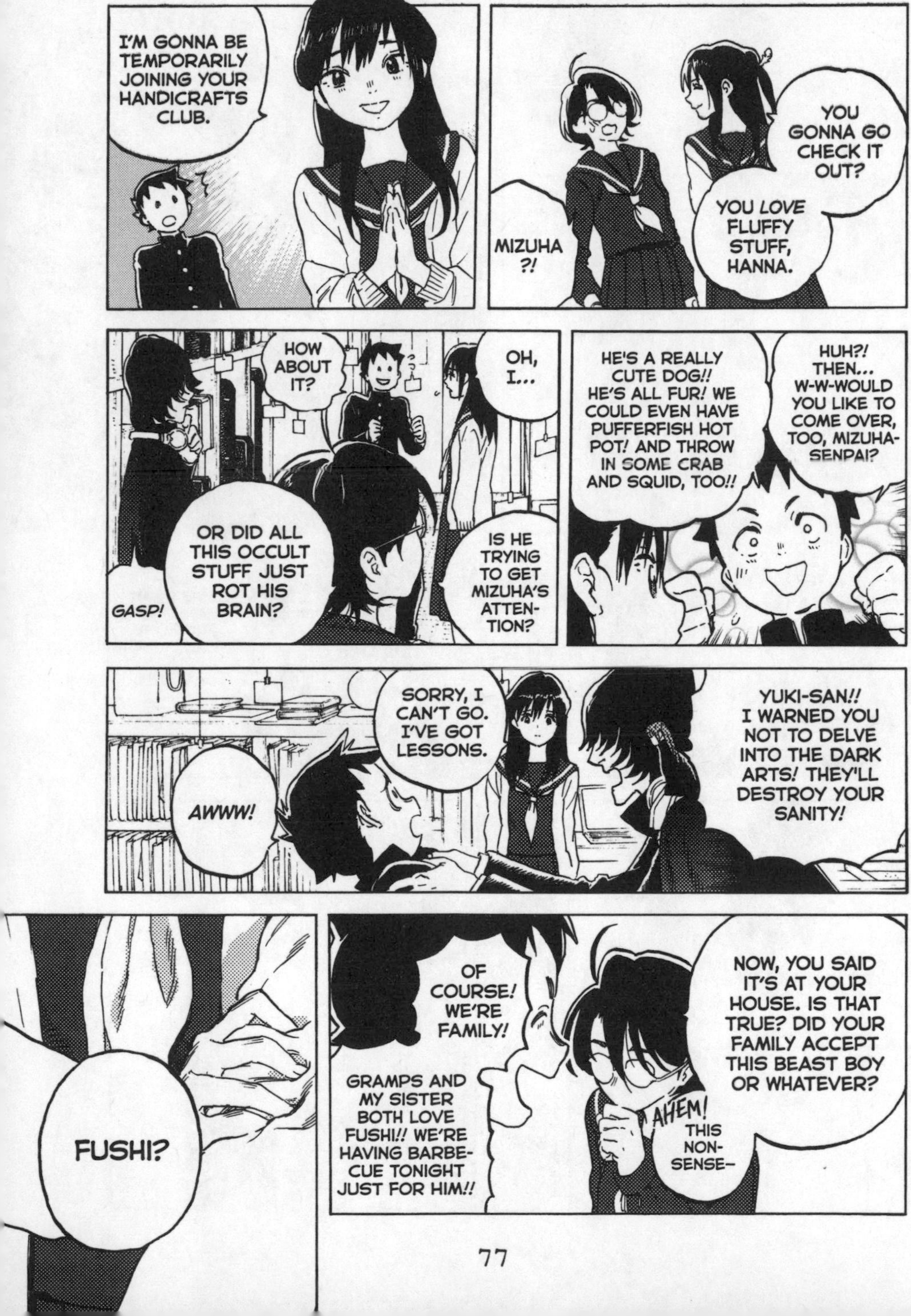
YOU GONNA GO CHECK IT OUT?
YOU LOVE FLUFFY STUFF, HANNA.
MIZUHA ?!
I'M GONNA BE TEMPORARILY JOINING YOUR HANDICRAFTS CLUB.
HUH?! THEN... W-W-WOULD YOU LIKE TO COME OVER, TOO, MIZUHA-SENPAI?
HE'S A REALLY CUTE DOG!! HE'S ALL FUR! WE COULD EVEN HAVE PUFFERFISH HOT POT! AND THROW IN SOME CRAB AND SQUID, TOO!!
OH, I...
HOW ABOUT IT?
IS HE TRYING TO GET MIZUHA'S ATTEN-TION?
OR DID ALL THIS OCCULT STUFF JUST ROT HIS BRAIN?
GASP!
YUKI-SAN!! I WARNED YOU NOT TO DELVE INTO THE DARK ARTS! THEY'LL DESTROY YOUR SANITY!
SORRY, I CAN'T GO. I'VE GOT LESSONS.
AWWW!
NOW, YOU SAID IT'S AT YOUR HOUSE. IS THAT TRUE? DID YOUR FAMILY ACCEPT THIS BEAST BOY OR WHATEVER?
AHEM!
THIS NON-SENSE–
OF COURSE! WE'RE FAMILY!
GRAMPS AND MY SISTER BOTH LOVE FUSHI!! WE'RE HAVING BARBE-CUE TONIGHT JUST FOR HIM!!
FUSHI?

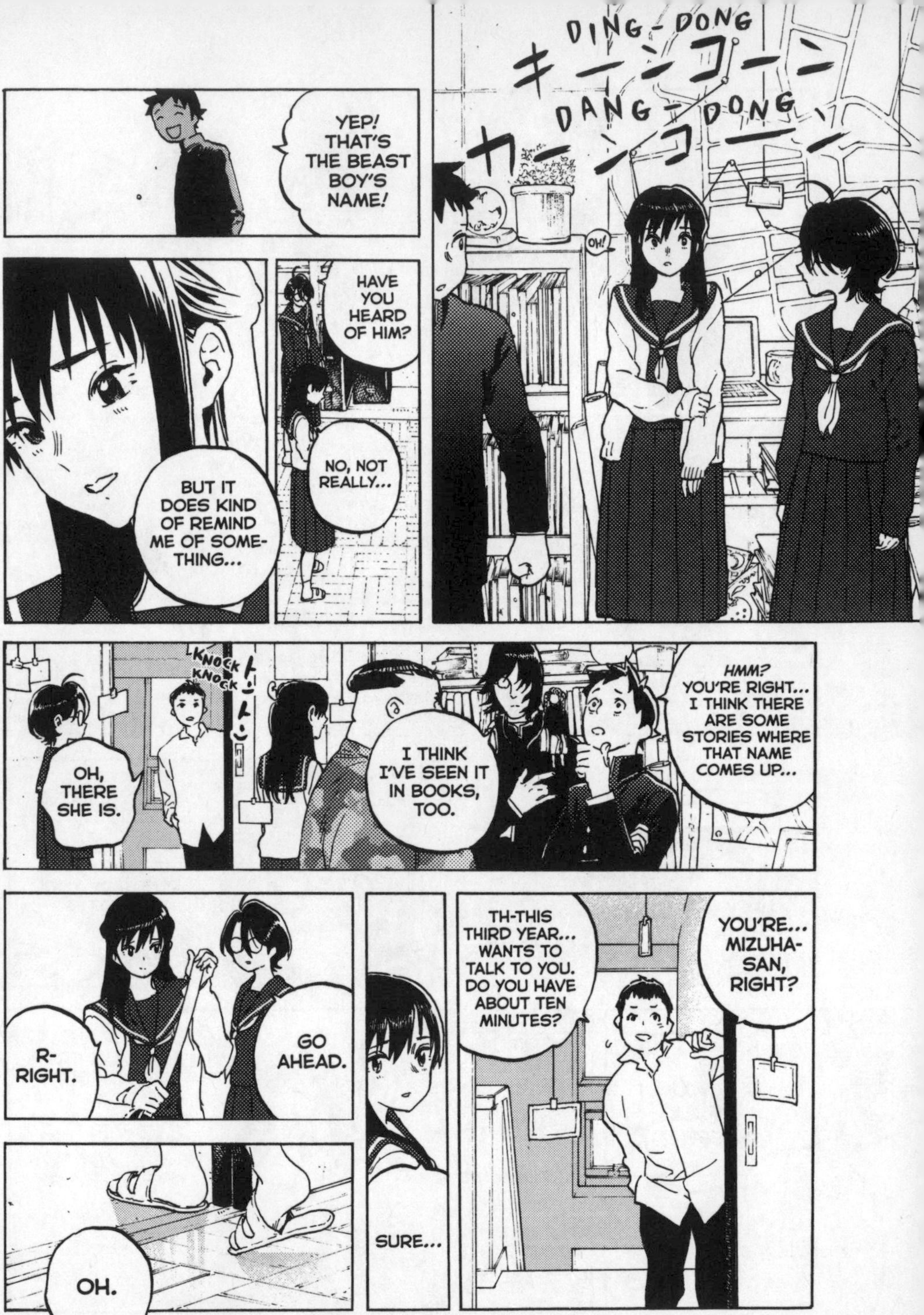
DING-DONG
DANG-DONG
OH!
YEP! THAT'S THE BEAST BOY'S NAME!
HAVE YOU HEARD OF HIM?
NO, NOT REALLY...
BUT IT DOES KIND OF REMIND ME OF SOME-THING...
HMM? YOU'RE RIGHT... I THINK THERE ARE SOME STORIES WHERE THAT NAME COMES UP...
I THINK I'VE SEEN IT IN BOOKS, TOO.
KNOCK KNOCK
OH, THERE SHE IS.
YOU'RE... MIZUHA-SAN, RIGHT?
TH-THIS THIRD YEAR... WANTS TO TALK TO YOU. DO YOU HAVE ABOUT TEN MINUTES?
SURE...
GO AHEAD.
R-RIGHT.
OH.

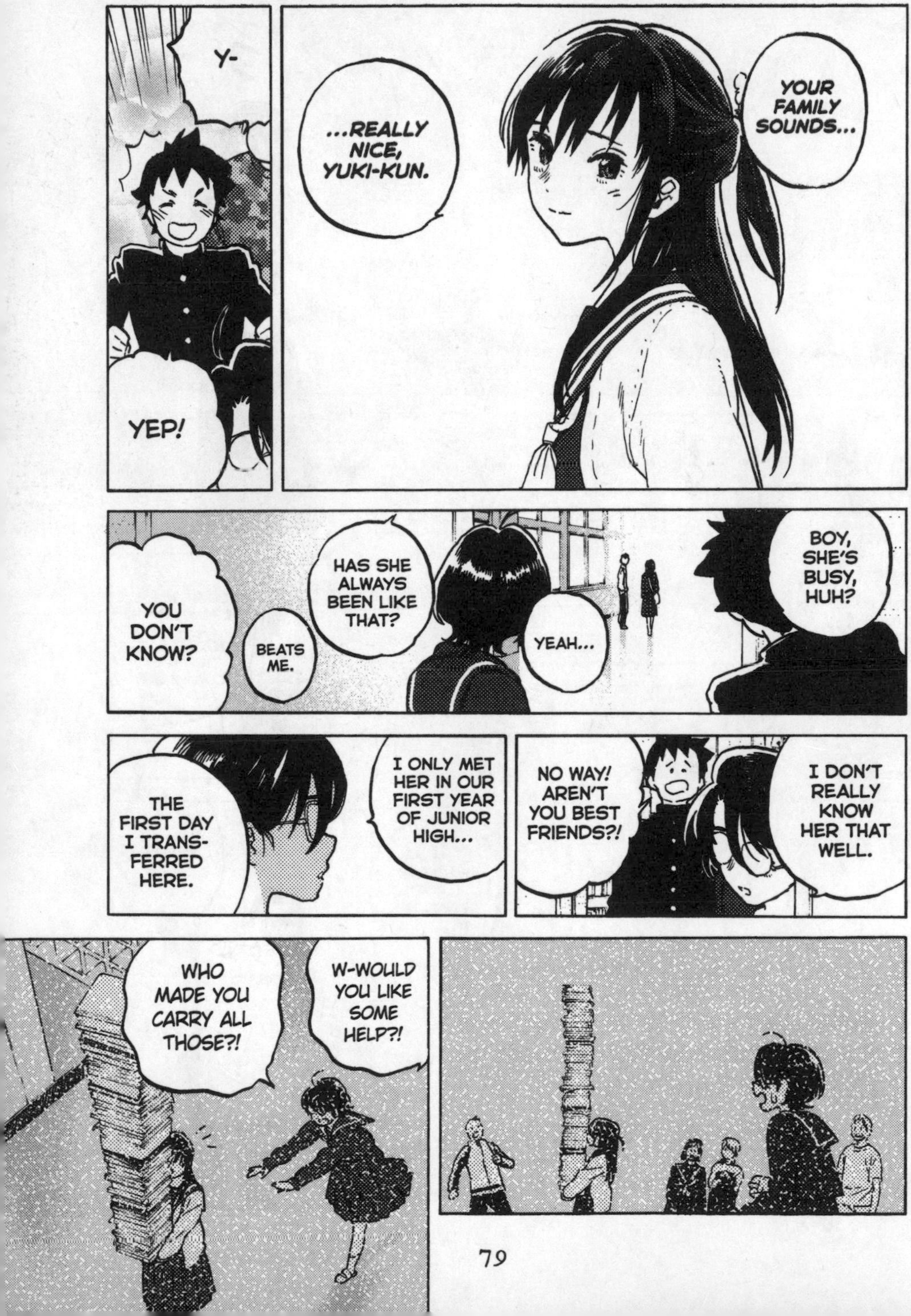
YOUR FAMILY SOUNDS...
...REALLY NICE, YUKI-KUN.
Y-
YEP!
BOY, SHE'S BUSY, HUH?
YEAH...
HAS SHE ALWAYS BEEN LIKE THAT?
BEATS ME.
YOU DON'T KNOW?
I DON'T REALLY KNOW HER THAT WELL.
NO WAY! AREN'T YOU BEST FRIENDS?!
I ONLY MET HER IN OUR FIRST YEAR OF JUNIOR HIGH...
THE FIRST DAY I TRANS-FERRED HERE.
W-WOULD YOU LIKE SOME HELP?!
WHO MADE YOU CARRY ALL THOSE?!

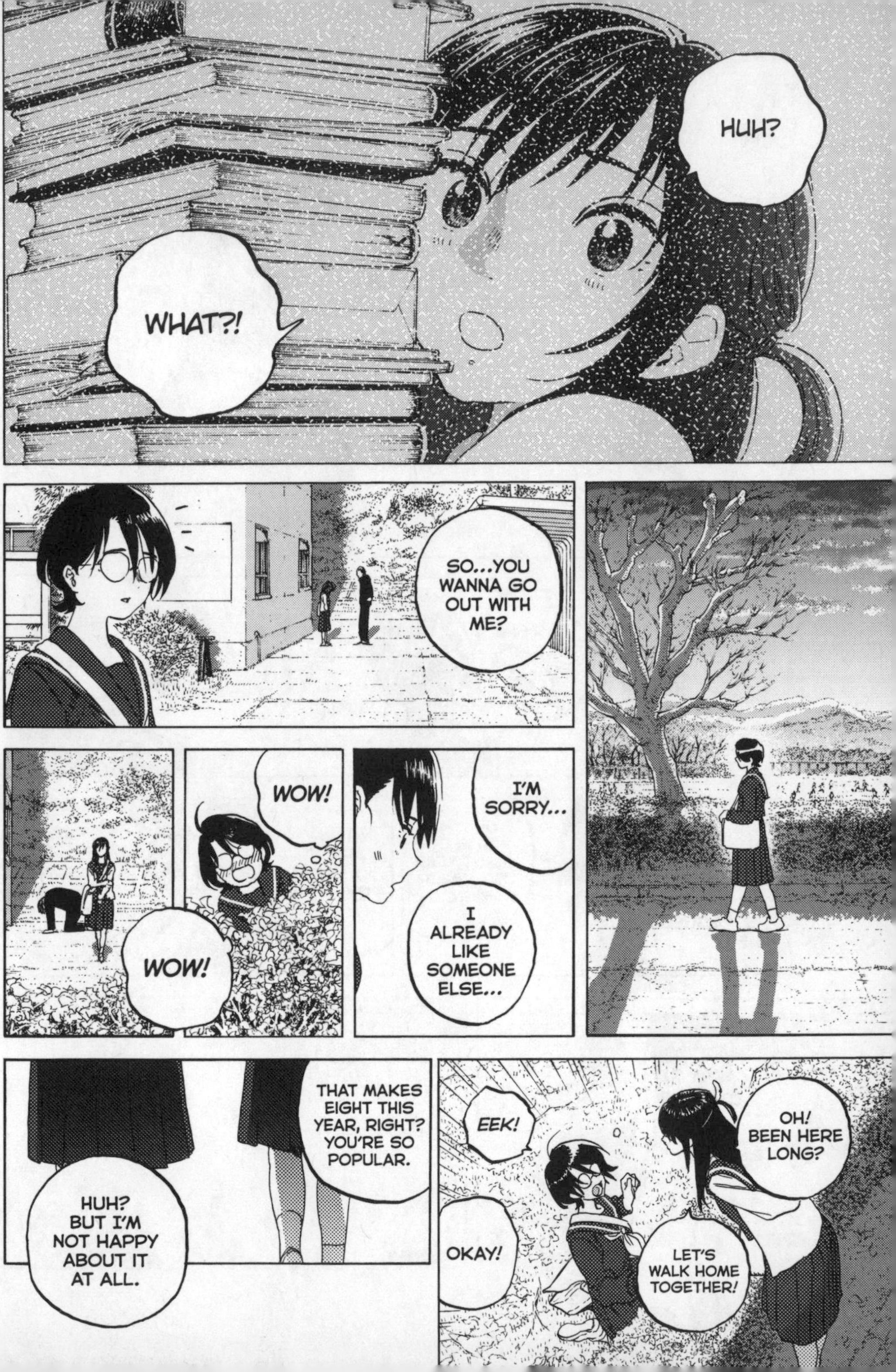
HUH?
WHAT?!
SO...YOU WANNA GO OUT WITH ME?
I'M SORRY...
I ALREADY LIKE SOMEONE ELSE...
WOW!
WOW!
OH! BEEN HERE LONG?
EEK!
LET'S WALK HOME TOGETHER!
OKAY!
THAT MAKES EIGHT THIS YEAR, RIGHT? YOU'RE SO POPULAR.
HUH? BUT I'M NOT HAPPY ABOUT IT AT ALL.

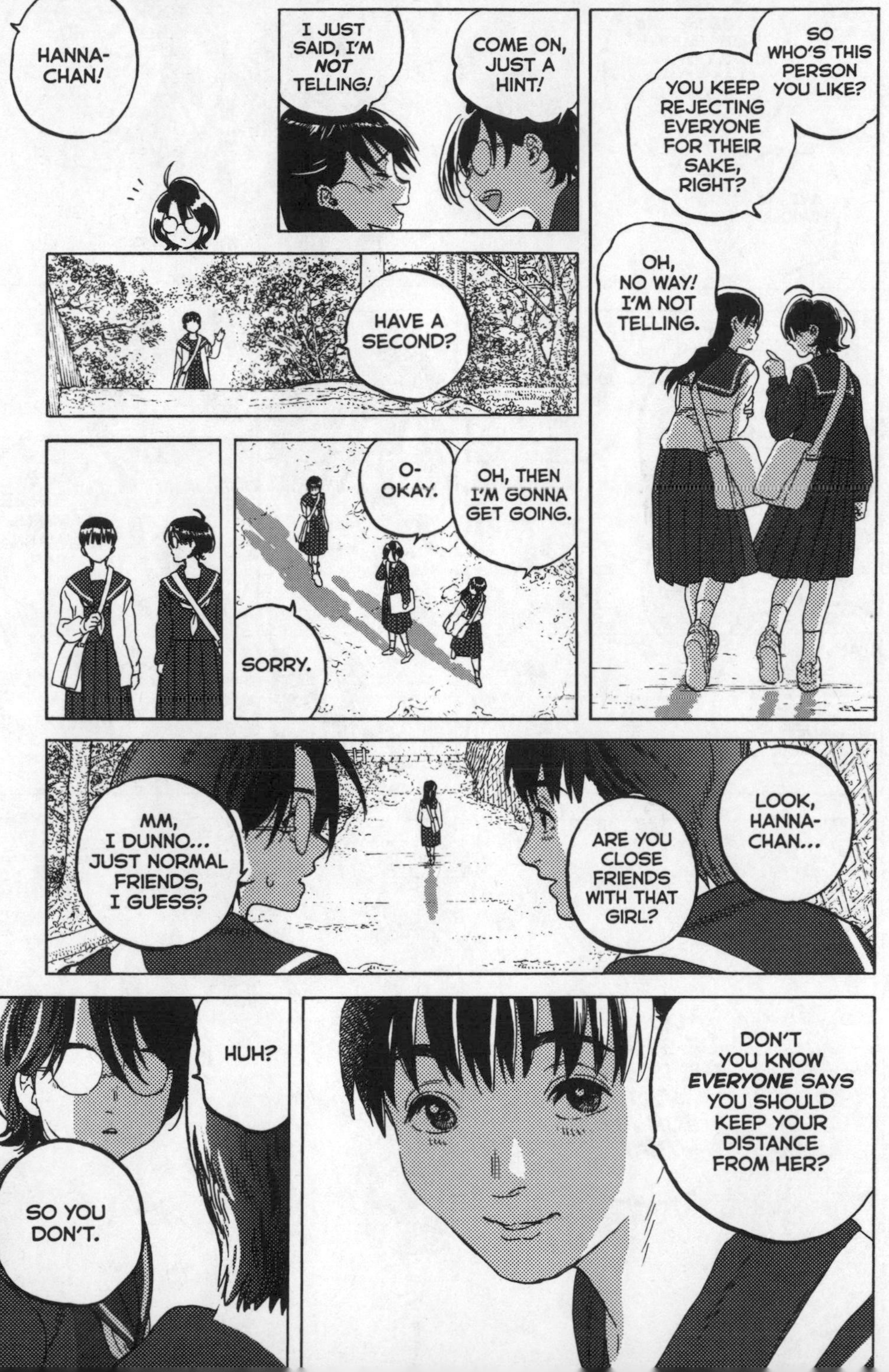
SO WHO'S THIS PERSON YOU LIKE?
YOU KEEP REJECTING EVERYONE FOR THEIR SAKE, RIGHT?
OH, NO WAY! I'M NOT TELLING.
COME ON, JUST A HINT!
I JUST SAID, I'M *NOT* TELLING!
HANNA-CHAN!
HAVE A SECOND?
OH, THEN I'M GONNA GET GOING.
O-OKAY.
SORRY.
LOOK, HANNA-CHAN...
ARE YOU CLOSE FRIENDS WITH THAT GIRL?
MM, I DUNNO... JUST NORMAL FRIENDS, I GUESS?
DON'T YOU KNOW *EVERYONE* SAYS YOU SHOULD KEEP YOUR DISTANCE FROM HER?
HUH?
SO YOU DON'T.

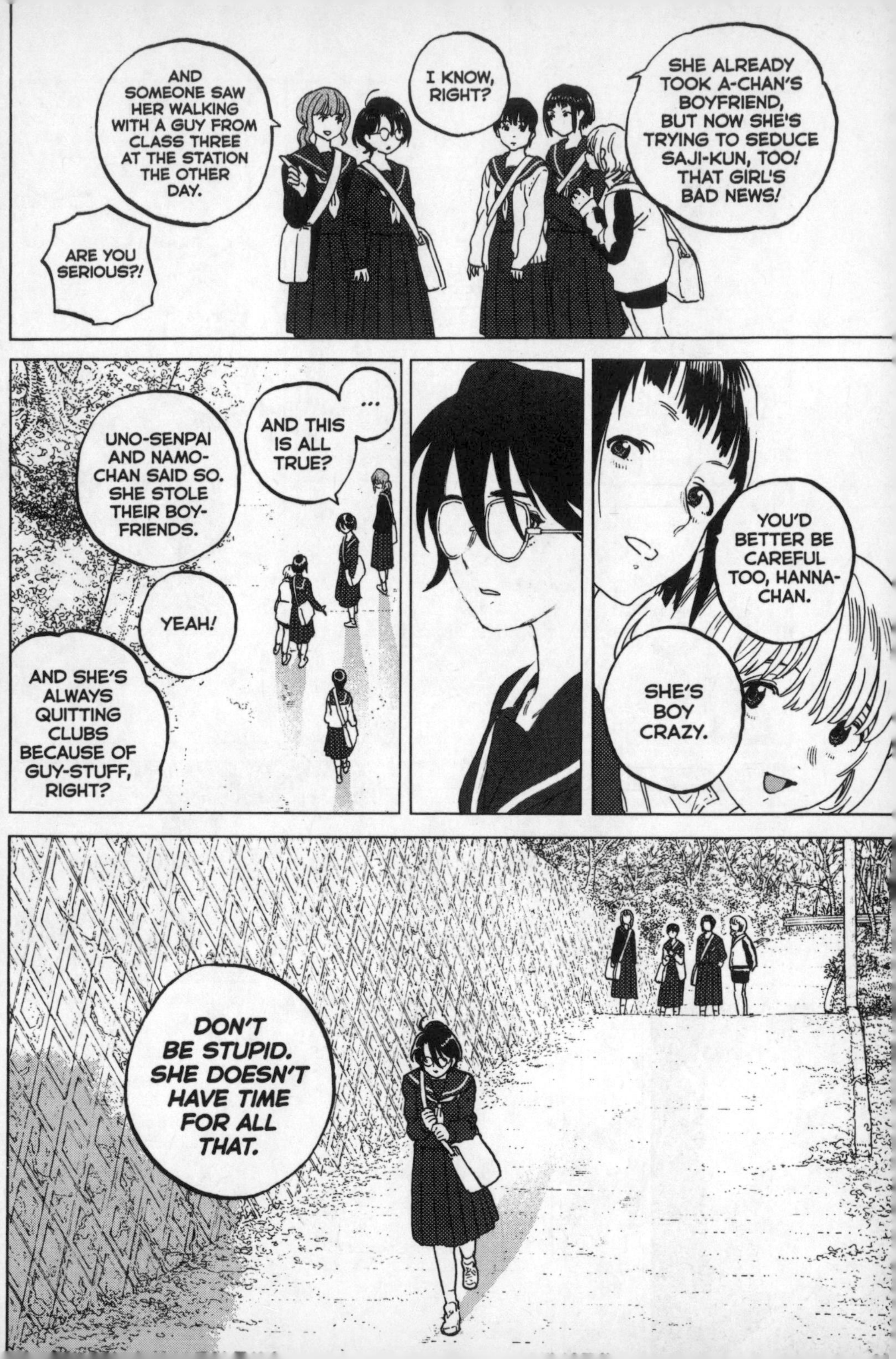
SHE ALREADY TOOK A-CHAN'S BOYFRIEND, BUT NOW SHE'S TRYING TO SEDUCE SAJI-KUN, TOO! THAT GIRL'S BAD NEWS!
I KNOW, RIGHT?
AND SOMEONE SAW HER WALKING WITH A GUY FROM CLASS THREE AT THE STATION THE OTHER DAY.
ARE YOU SERIOUS?!
YOU'D BETTER BE CAREFUL TOO, HANNA-CHAN.
SHE'S BOY CRAZY.
...
AND THIS IS ALL TRUE?
UNO-SENPAI AND NAMO-CHAN SAID SO. SHE STOLE THEIR BOY-FRIENDS.
YEAH!
AND SHE'S ALWAYS QUITTING CLUBS BECAUSE OF GUY-STUFF, RIGHT?
DON'T BE STUPID. SHE DOESN'T HAVE TIME FOR ALL THAT.

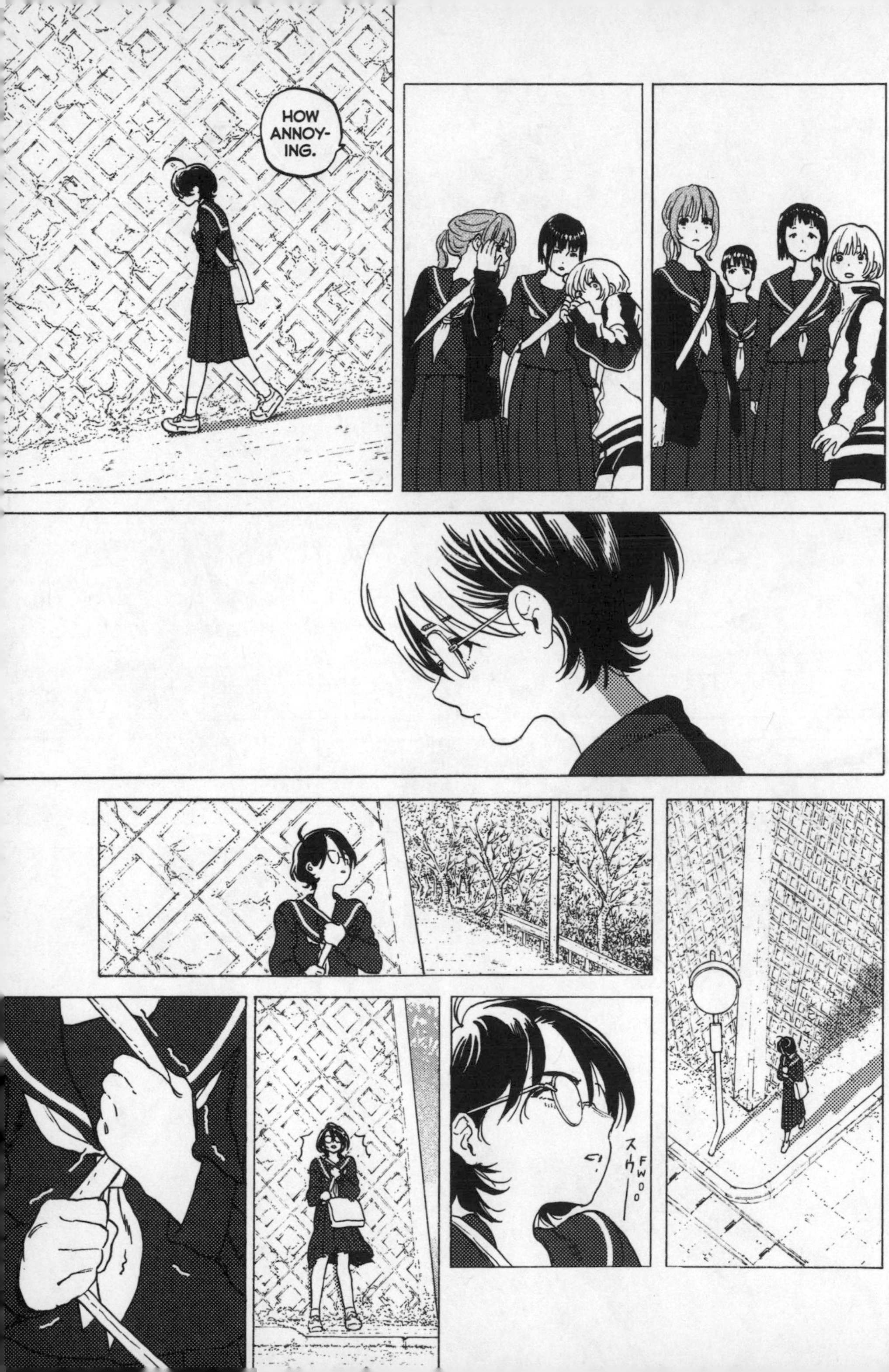
HOW ANNOY-ING.
スウー
FWOO

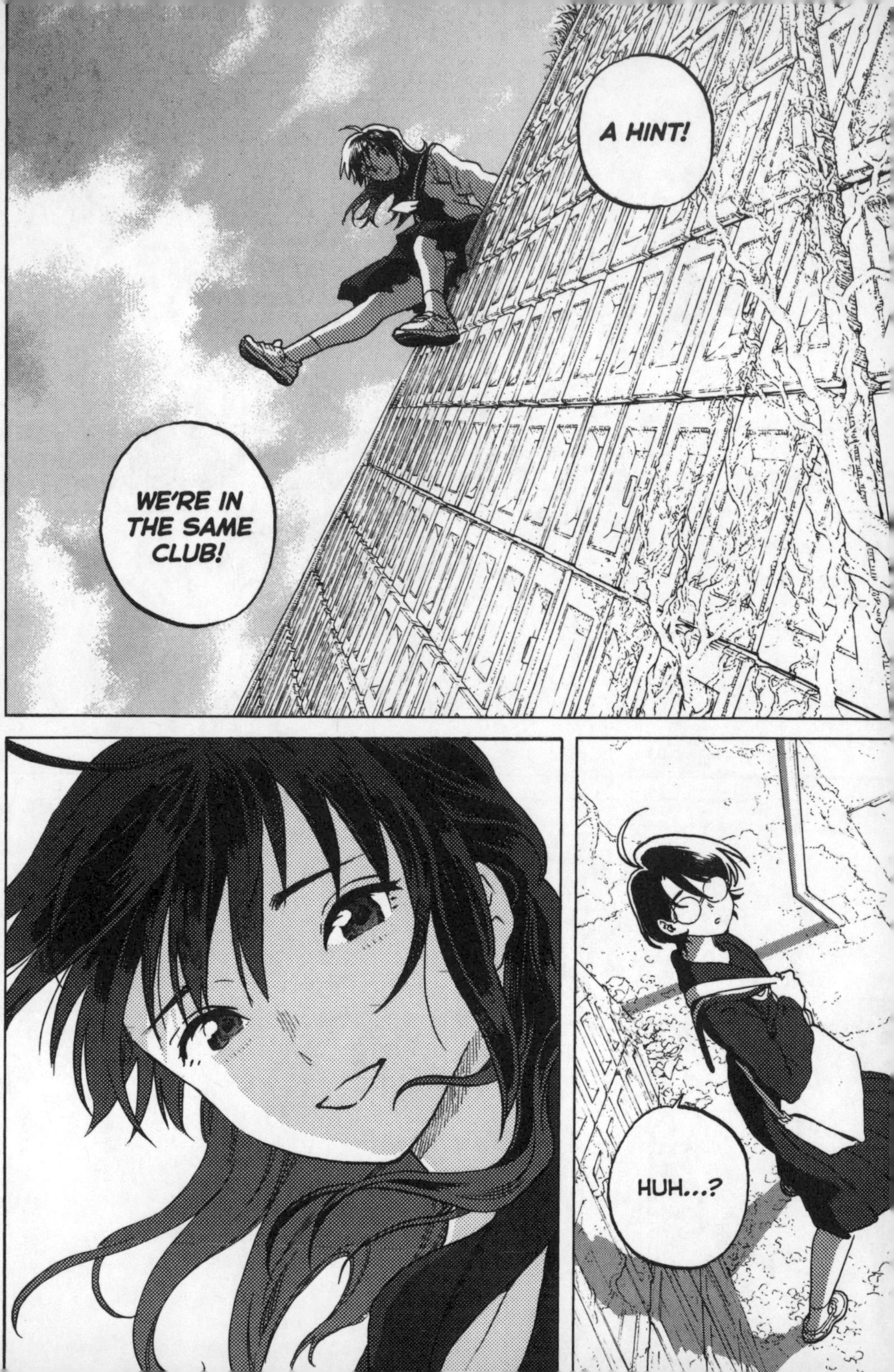
A HINT!
WE'RE IN THE SAME CLUB!
HUH...?

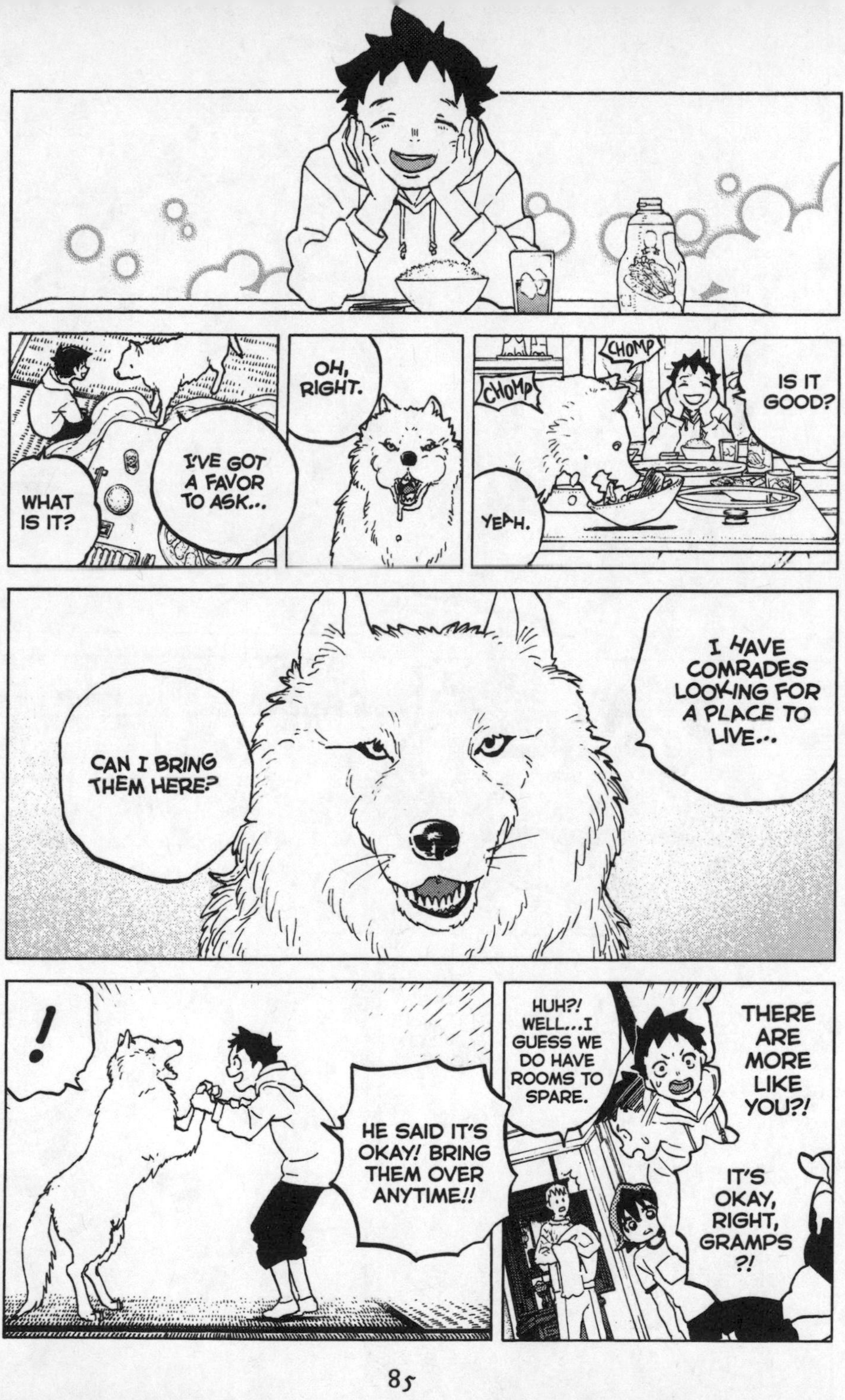
CHOMP
CHOMP
IS IT GOOD?
YEAH.
OH, RIGHT.
I'VE GOT A FAVOR TO ASK...
WHAT IS IT?
I HAVE COMRADES LOOKING FOR A PLACE TO LIVE...
CAN I BRING THEM HERE?
THERE ARE MORE LIKE YOU?!
IT'S OKAY, RIGHT, GRAMPS?!
HUH?! WELL...I GUESS WE DO HAVE ROOMS TO SPARE.
HE SAID IT'S OKAY! BRING THEM OVER ANYTIME!!
!

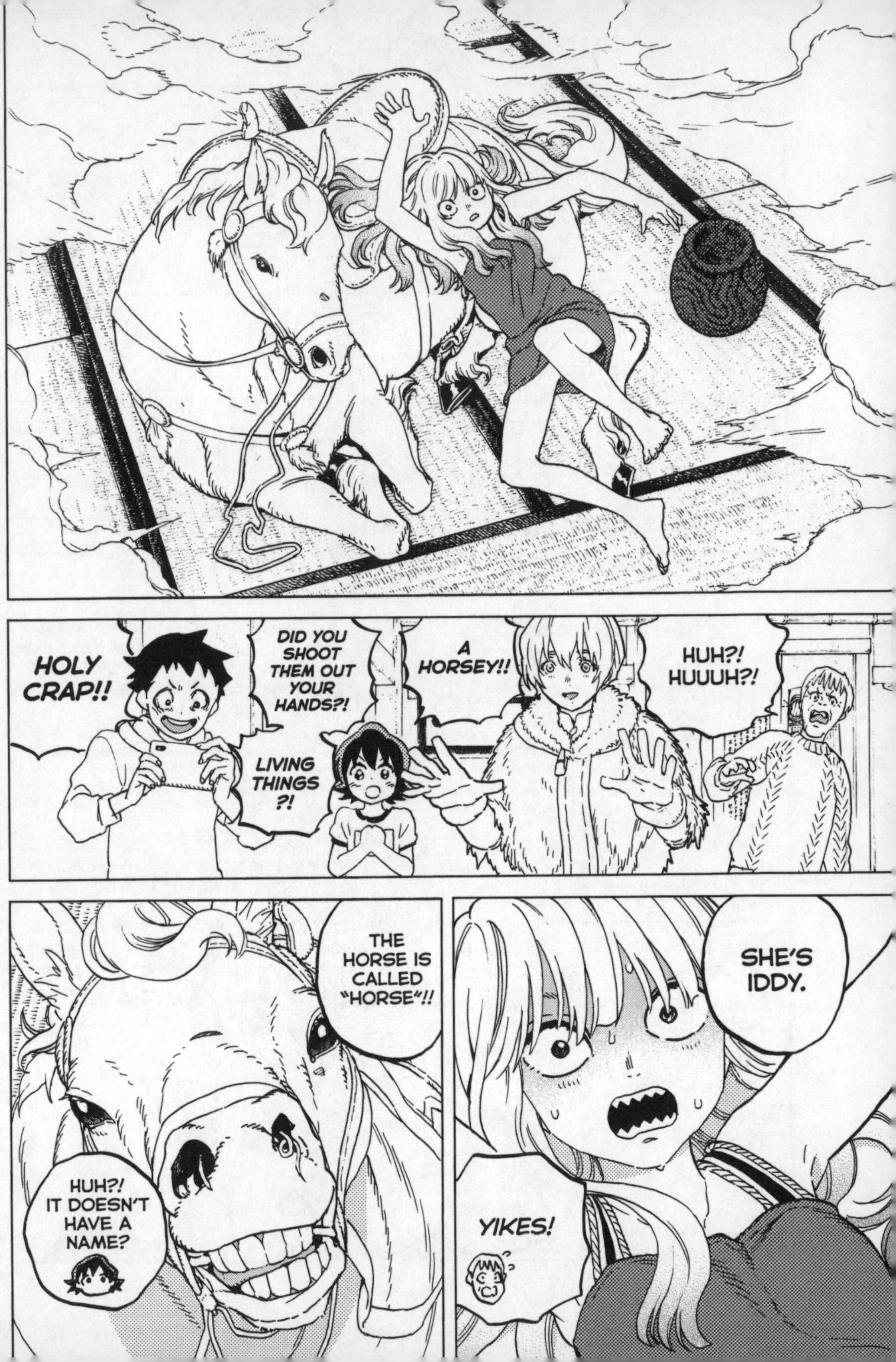
HUH?! HUUUH?!
A HORSEY!!
DID YOU SHOOT THEM OUT YOUR HANDS?!
LIVING THINGS ?!
HOLY CRAP!!
SHE'S IDDY.
YIKES!
THE HORSE IS CALLED "HORSE"!!
HUH?! IT DOESN'T HAVE A NAME?

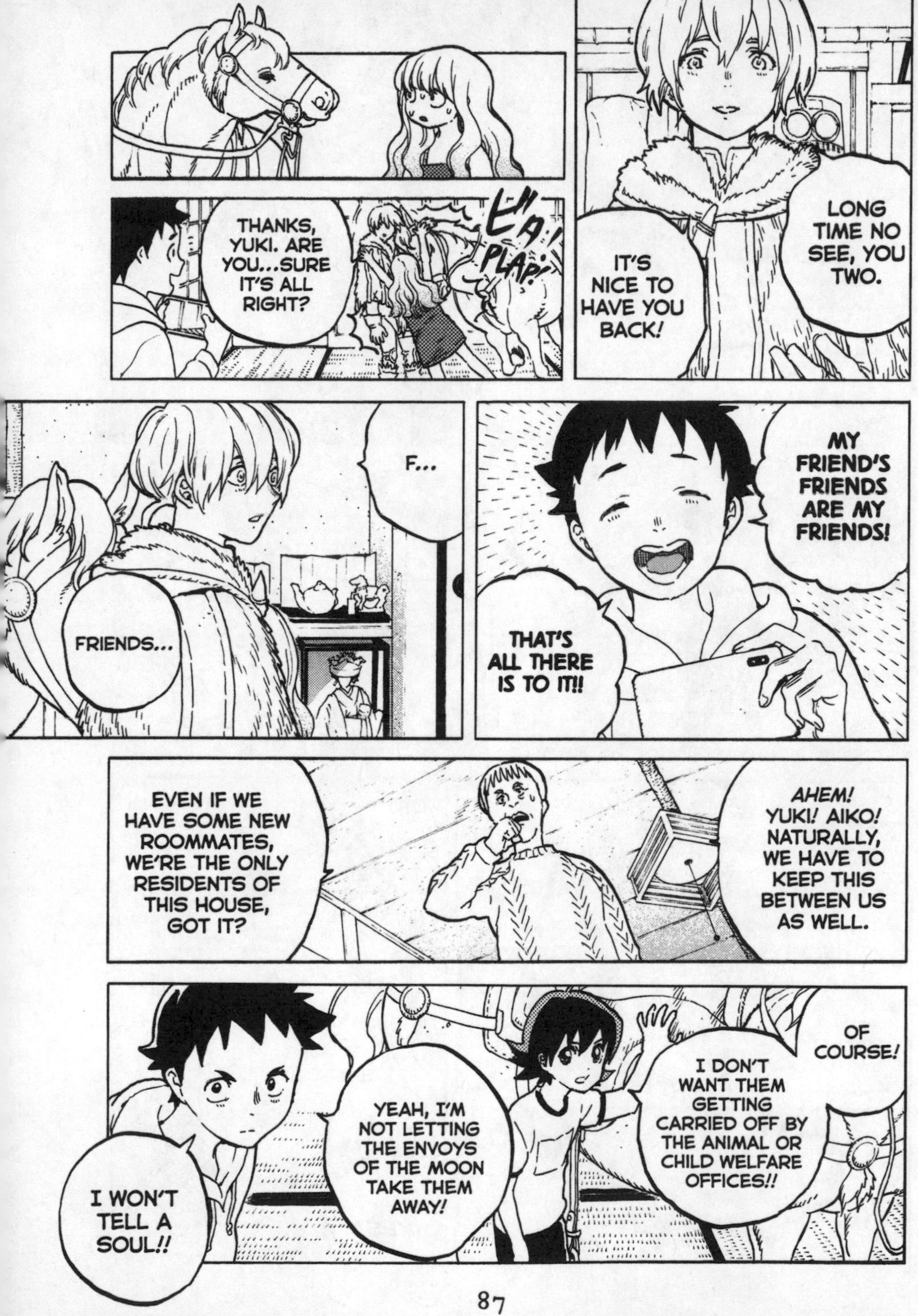
LONG TIME NO SEE, YOU TWO.
IT'S NICE TO HAVE YOU BACK!
PLAP!
THANKS, YUKI. ARE YOU...SURE IT'S ALL RIGHT?
MY FRIEND'S FRIENDS ARE MY FRIENDS!
THAT'S ALL THERE IS TO IT!!
F...
FRIENDS...
AHEM! YUKI! AIKO! NATURALLY, WE HAVE TO KEEP THIS BETWEEN US AS WELL.
EVEN IF WE HAVE SOME NEW ROOMMATES, WE'RE THE ONLY RESIDENTS OF THIS HOUSE, GOT IT?
OF COURSE!
I DON'T WANT THEM GETTING CARRIED OFF BY THE ANIMAL OR CHILD WELFARE OFFICES!!
YEAH, I'M NOT LETTING THE ENVOYS OF THE MOON TAKE THEM AWAY!
I WON'T TELL A SOUL!!

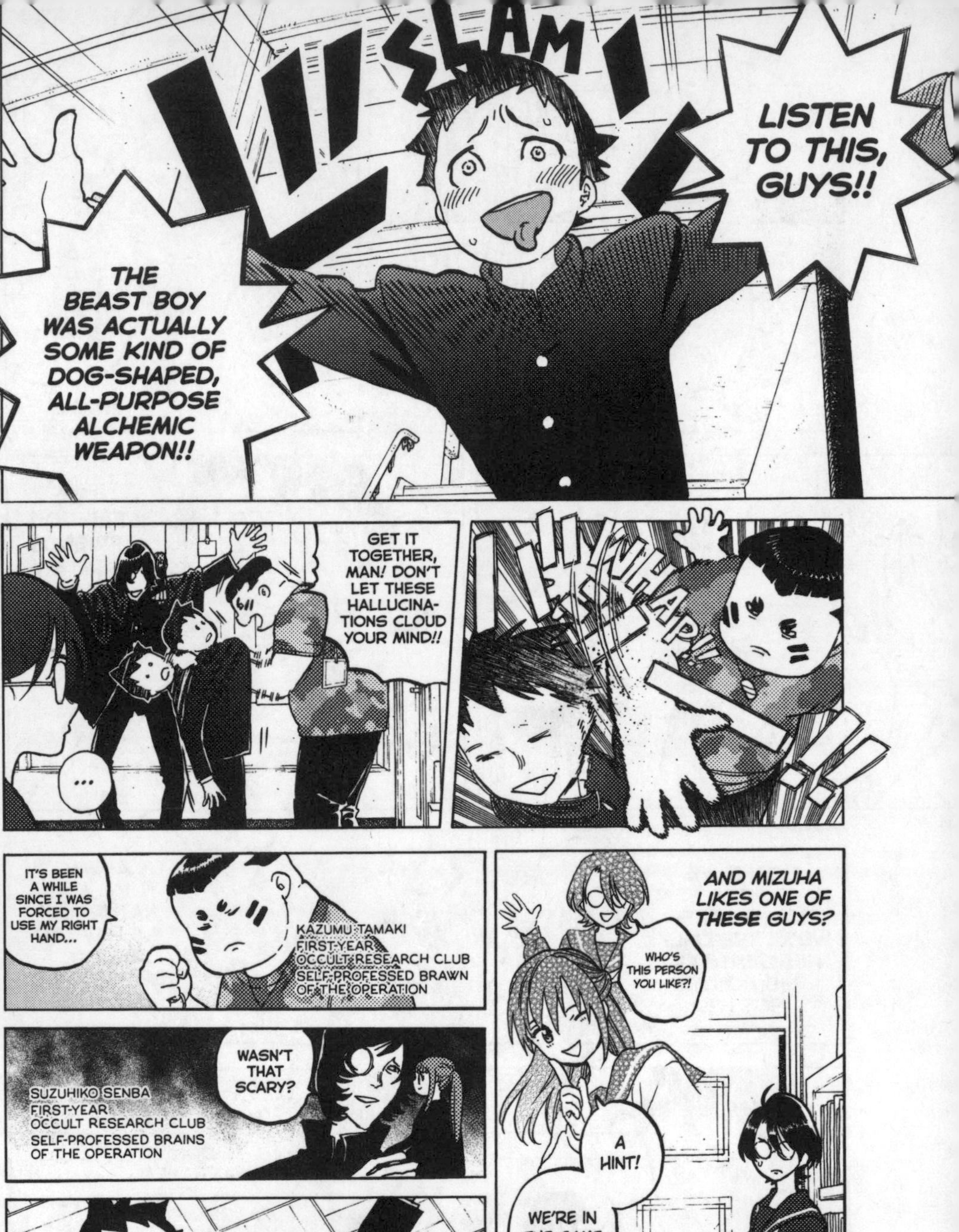

SLAM!
LISTEN TO THIS, GUYS!!
THE BEAST BOY WAS ACTUALLY SOME KIND OF DOG-SHAPED, ALL-PURPOSE ALCHEMIC WEAPON!!
WHAP!!
GET IT TOGETHER, MAN! DON'T LET THESE HALLUCINATIONS CLOUD YOUR MIND!!
...
AND MIZUHA LIKES ONE OF THESE GUYS?
WHO'S THIS PERSON YOU LIKE?!
A HINT!
WE'RE IN THE SAME CLUB!
IT'S BEEN A WHILE SINCE I WAS FORCED TO USE MY RIGHT HAND...
KAZUMU TAMAKI
FIRST-YEAR
OCCULT RESEARCH CLUB
SELF-PROFESSED BRAWN OF THE OPERATION
WASN'T THAT SCARY?
SUZUHIKO SENBA
FIRST-YEAR
OCCULT RESEARCH CLUB
SELF-PROFESSED BRAINS OF THE OPERATION
YUKI AOKI
FIRST-YEAR
OCCULT RESEARCH CLUB
VICE PRESIDENT

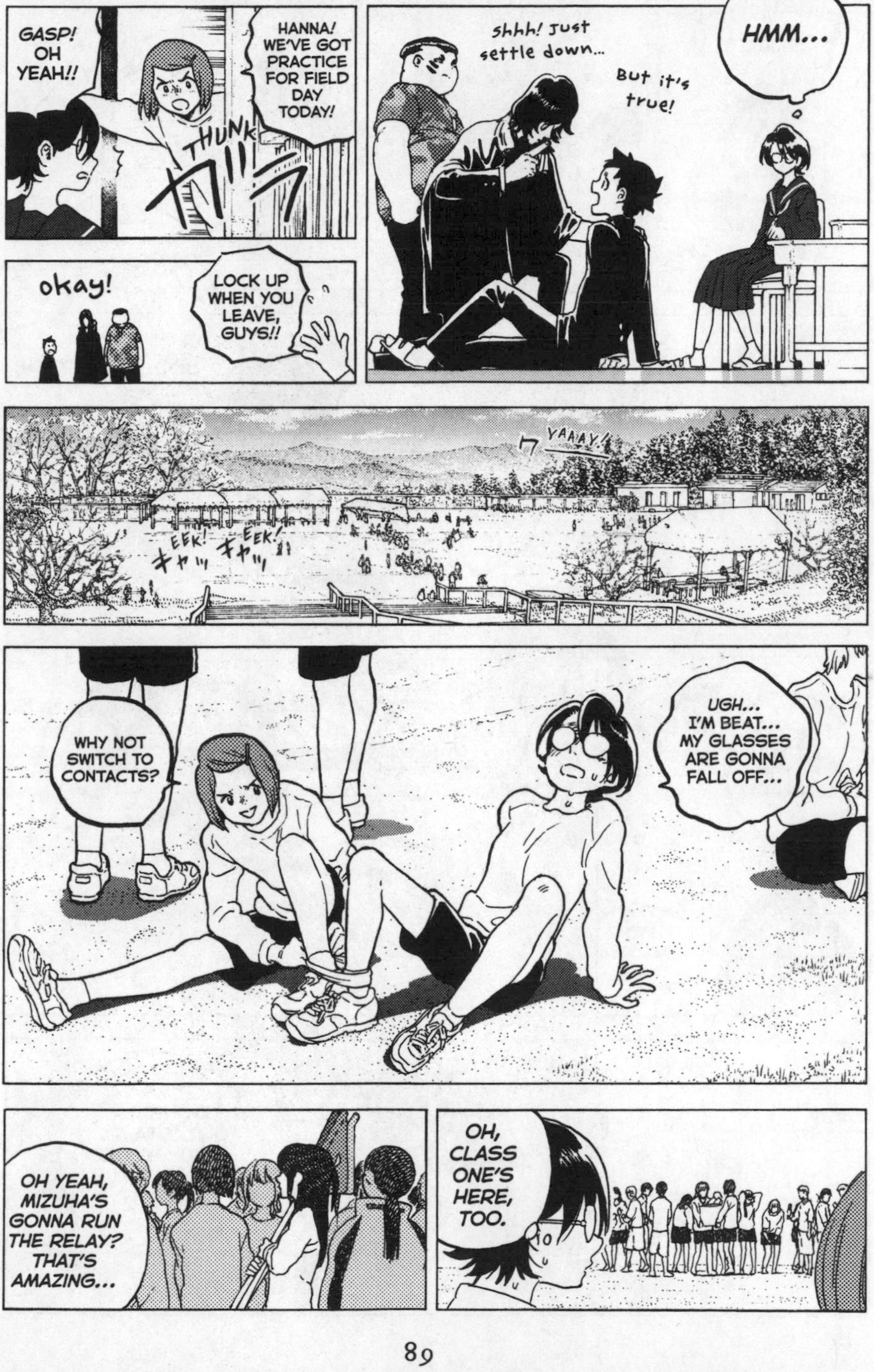
HMM...
But it's true!
shhh! Just settle down...
HANNA! WE'VE GOT PRACTICE FOR FIELD DAY TODAY!
THUNK
GASP! OH YEAH!!
LOCK UP WHEN YOU LEAVE, GUYS!!
okay!
YAAAY!
EEK! EEK!
UGH... I'M BEAT... MY GLASSES ARE GONNA FALL OFF...
WHY NOT SWITCH TO CONTACTS?
OH, CLASS ONE'S HERE, TOO.
OH YEAH, MIZUHA'S GONNA RUN THE RELAY? THAT'S AMAZING...

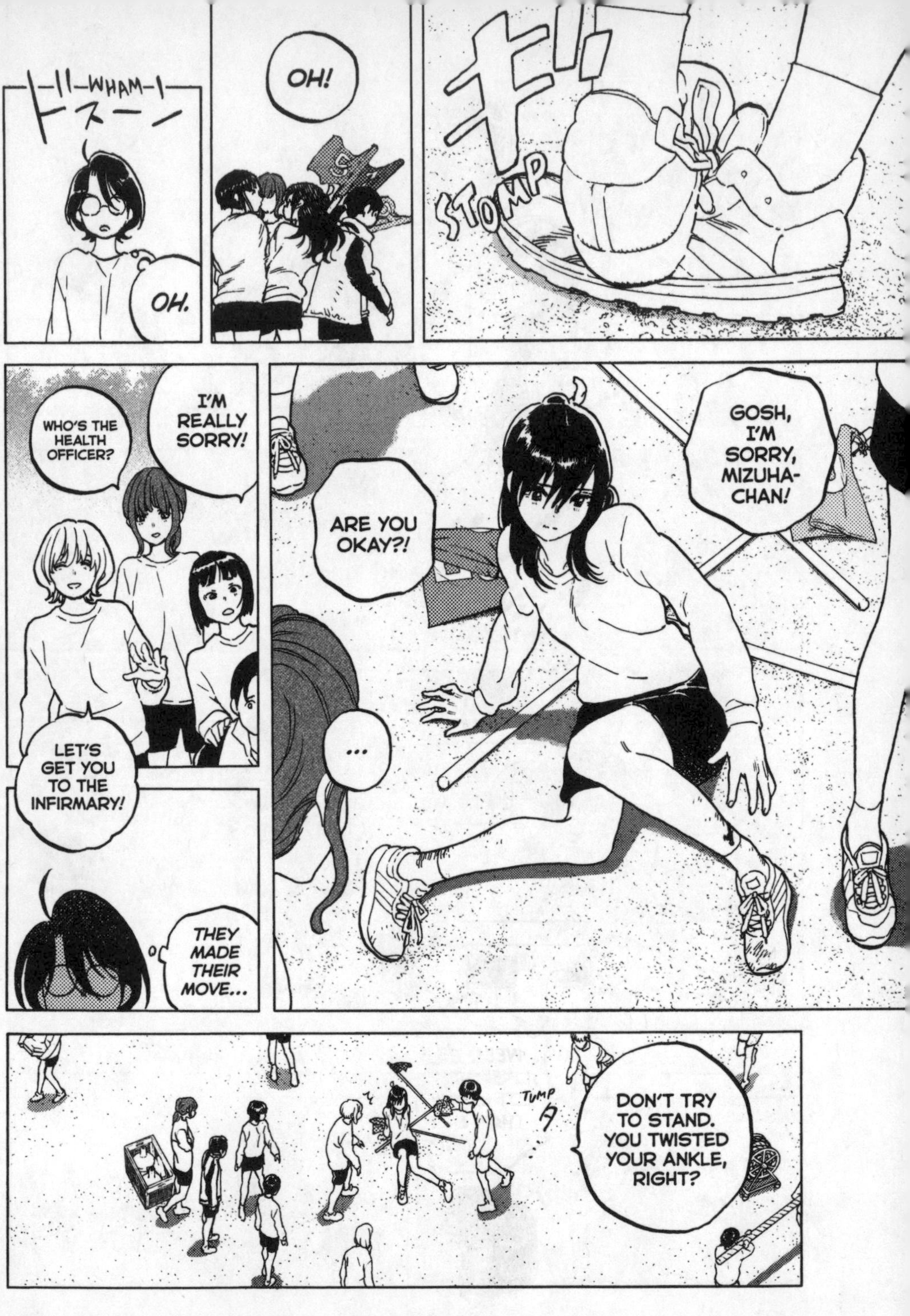
STOMP
OH!
WHAM
OH.
GOSH, I'M SORRY, MIZUHA-CHAN!
ARE YOU OKAY?!
...
I'M REALLY SORRY!
WHO'S THE HEALTH OFFICER?
LET'S GET YOU TO THE INFIRMARY!
THEY MADE THEIR MOVE...
TUMP
DON'T TRY TO STAND. YOU TWISTED YOUR ANKLE, RIGHT?

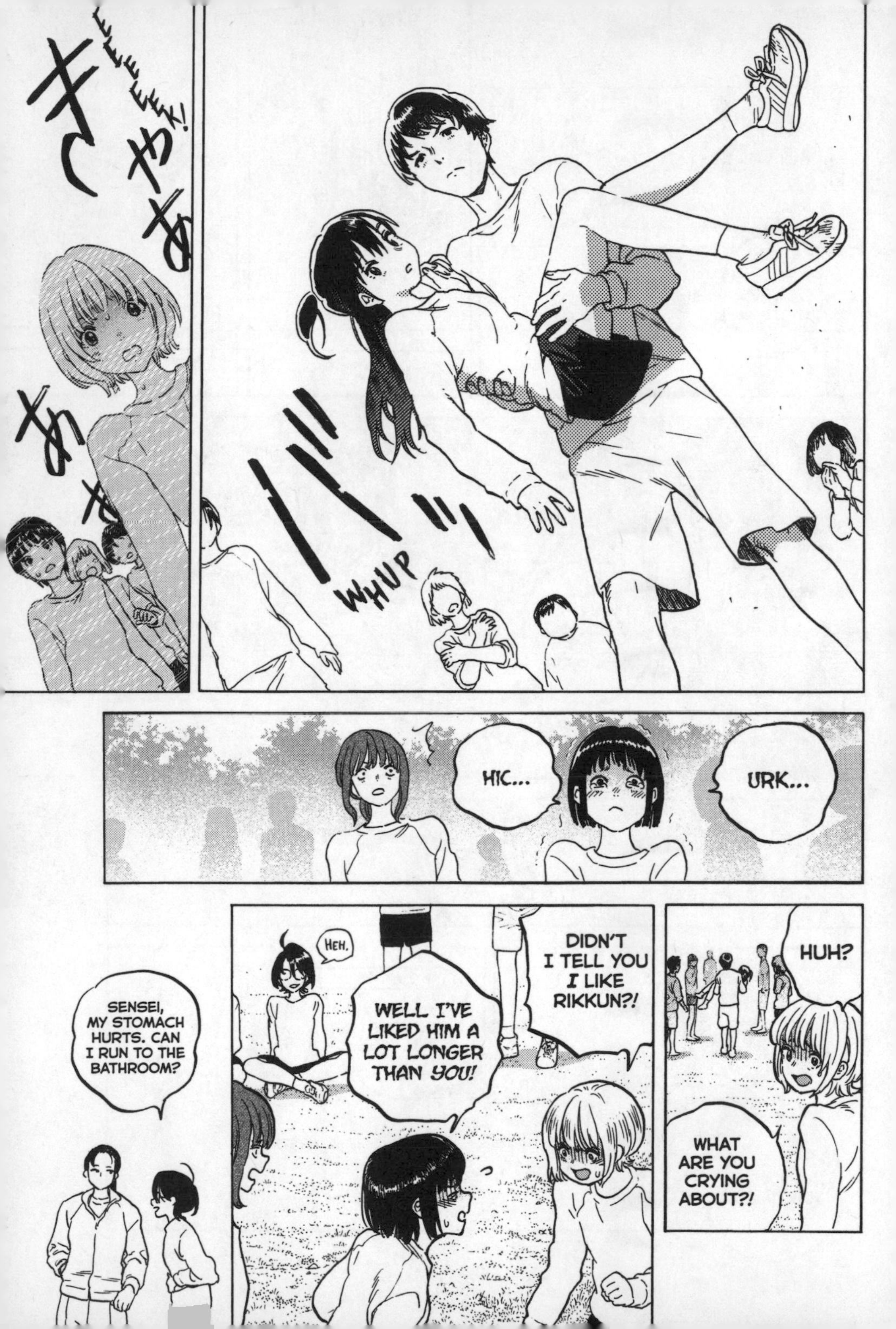
WHUP
きゃあああ
EEEEEEK!
URK...
HIC...
HUH?
WHAT ARE YOU CRYING ABOUT?!
DIDN'T I TELL YOU I LIKE RIKKUN?!
WELL I'VE LIKED HIM A LOT LONGER THAN YOU!
HEH.
SENSEI, MY STOMACH HURTS. CAN I RUN TO THE BATHROOM?

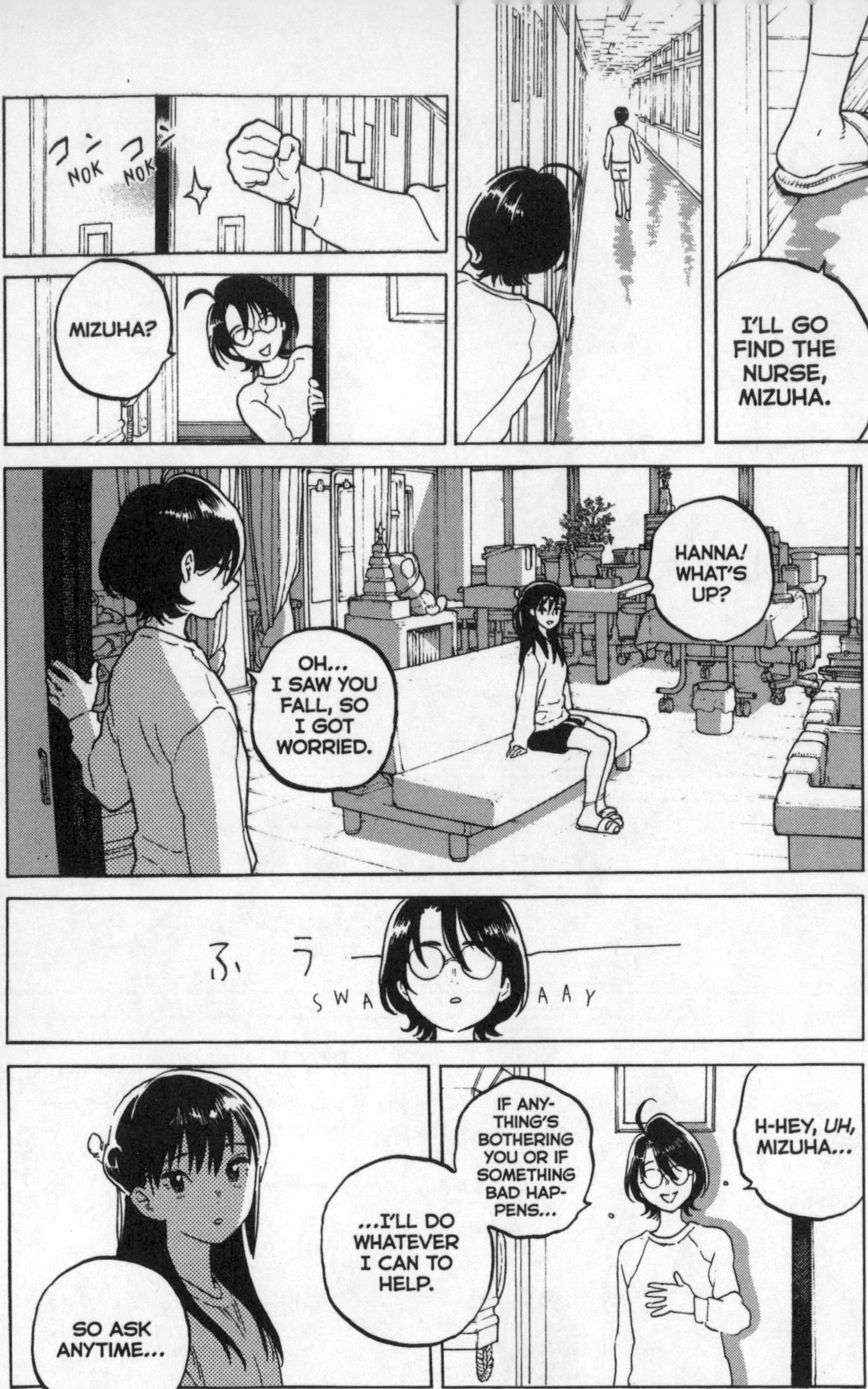
ガラ
RATTLE
I'LL GO FIND THE NURSE, MIZUHA.
コンコン
NOK NOK
MIZUHA?
HANNA! WHAT'S UP?
OH... I SAW YOU FALL, SO I GOT WORRIED.
ふラ
SWAAAY
H-HEY, UH, MIZUHA...
IF ANYTHING'S BOTHERING YOU OR IF SOMETHING BAD HAPPENS...
...I'LL DO WHATEVER I CAN TO HELP.
SO ASK ANYTIME...

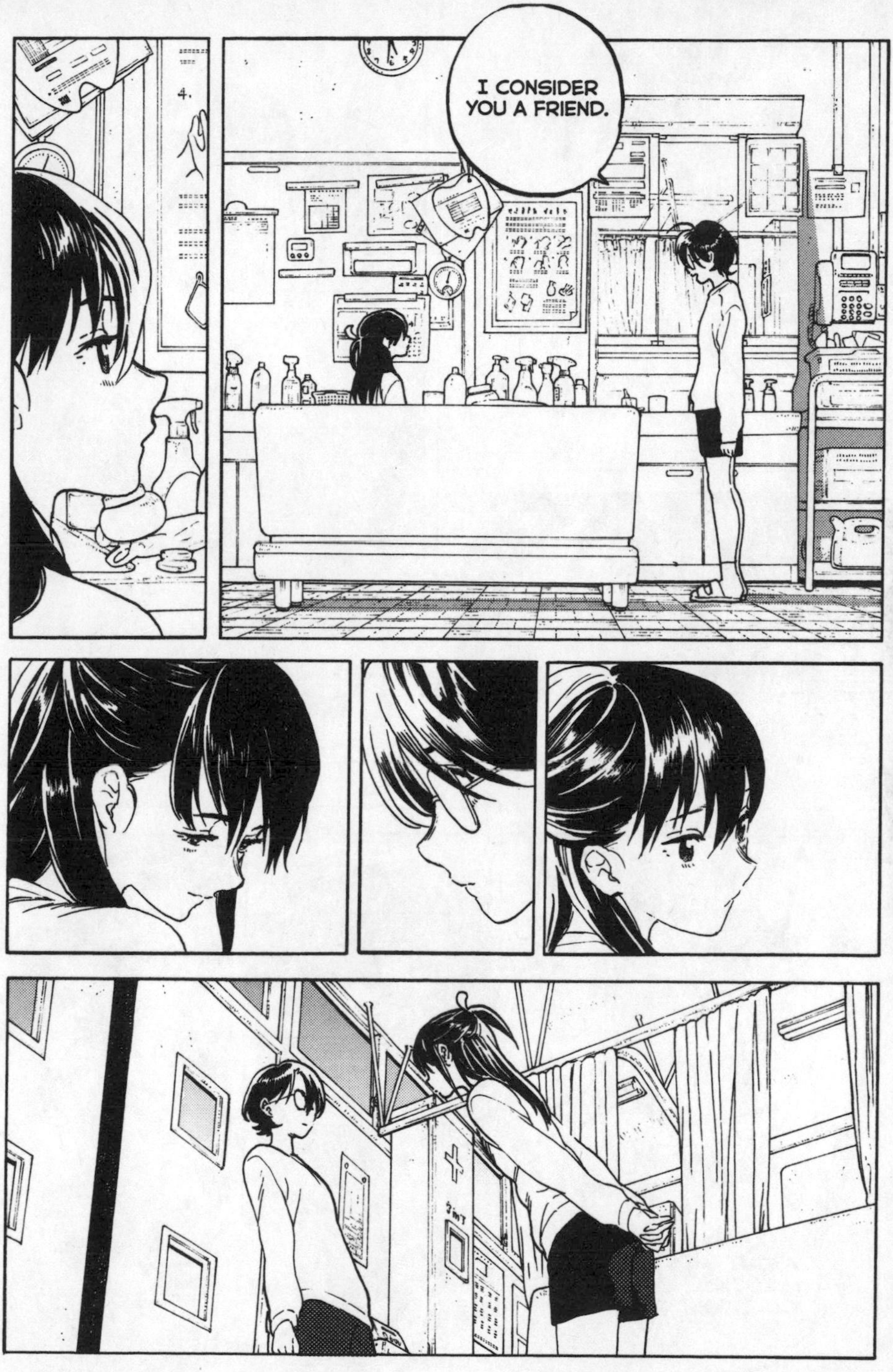
I CONSIDER YOU A FRIEND.

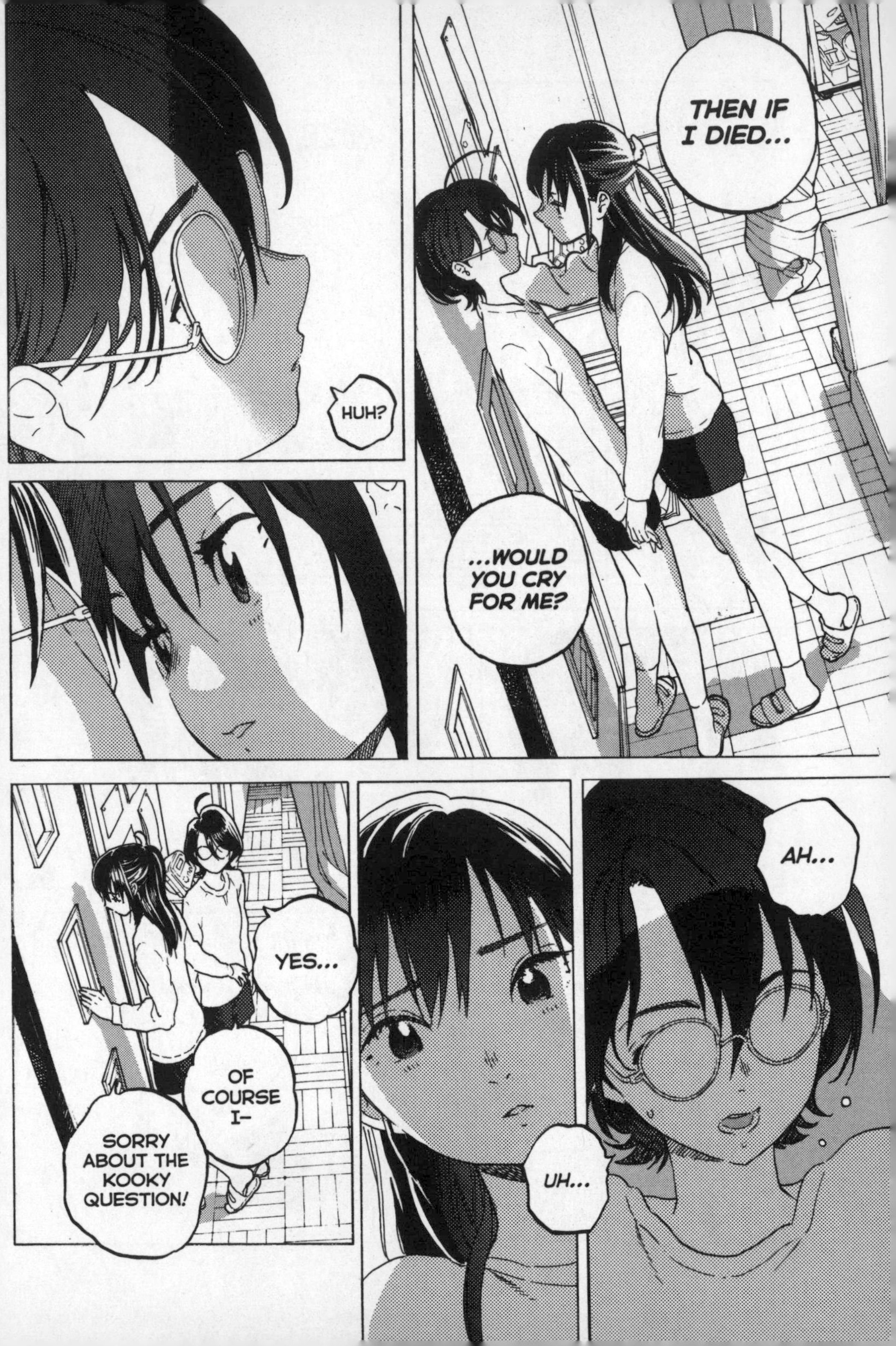
THEN IF I DIED...
...WOULD YOU CRY FOR ME?
HUH?
AH...
UH...
YES...
OF COURSE I–
SORRY ABOUT THE KOOKY QUESTION!

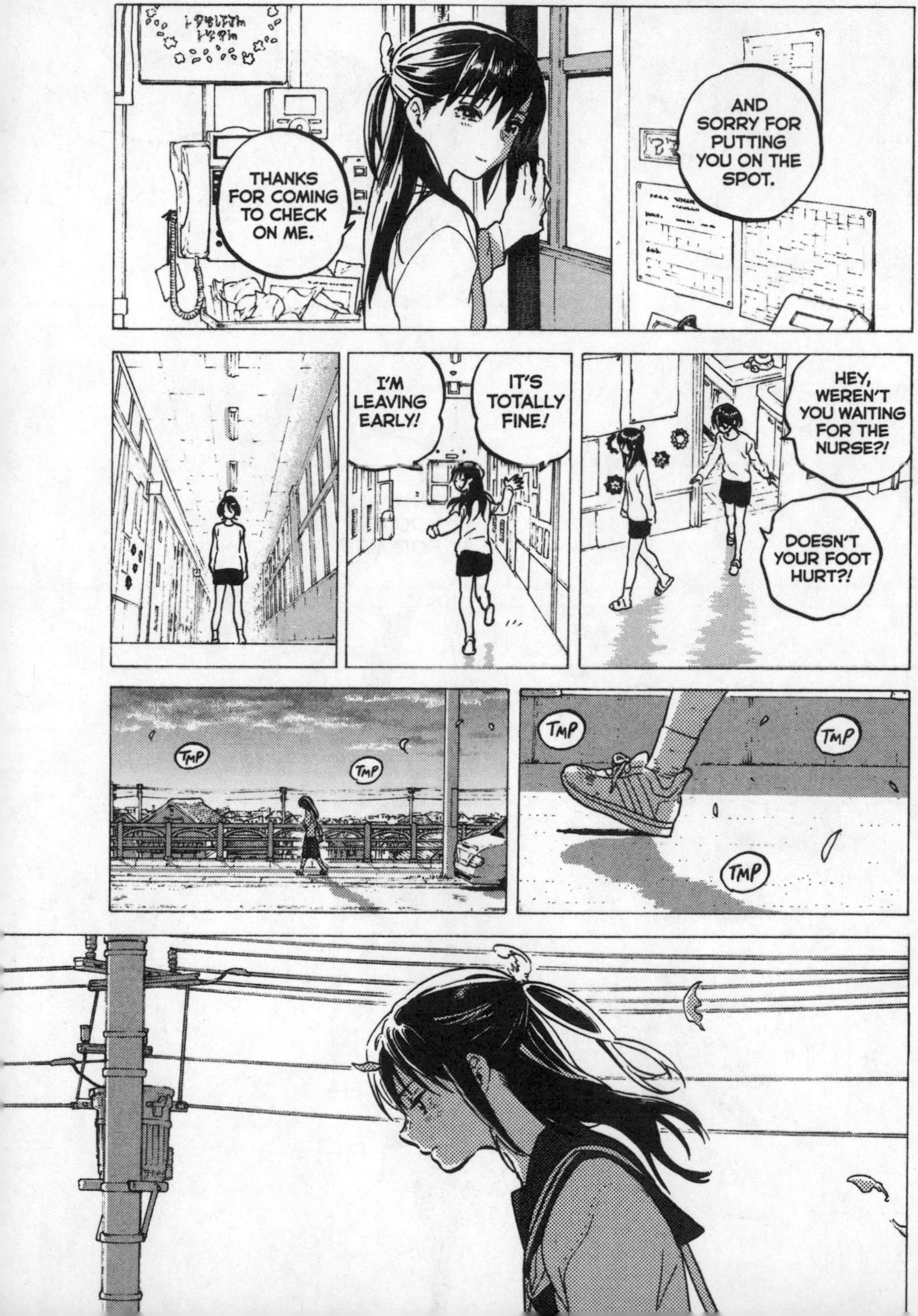
AND SORRY FOR PUTTING YOU ON THE SPOT.
THANKS FOR COMING TO CHECK ON ME.
HEY, WEREN'T YOU WAITING FOR THE NURSE?!
DOESN'T YOUR FOOT HURT?!
IT'S TOTALLY FINE!
I'M LEAVING EARLY!
TMP
TMP
TMP
TMP
TMP

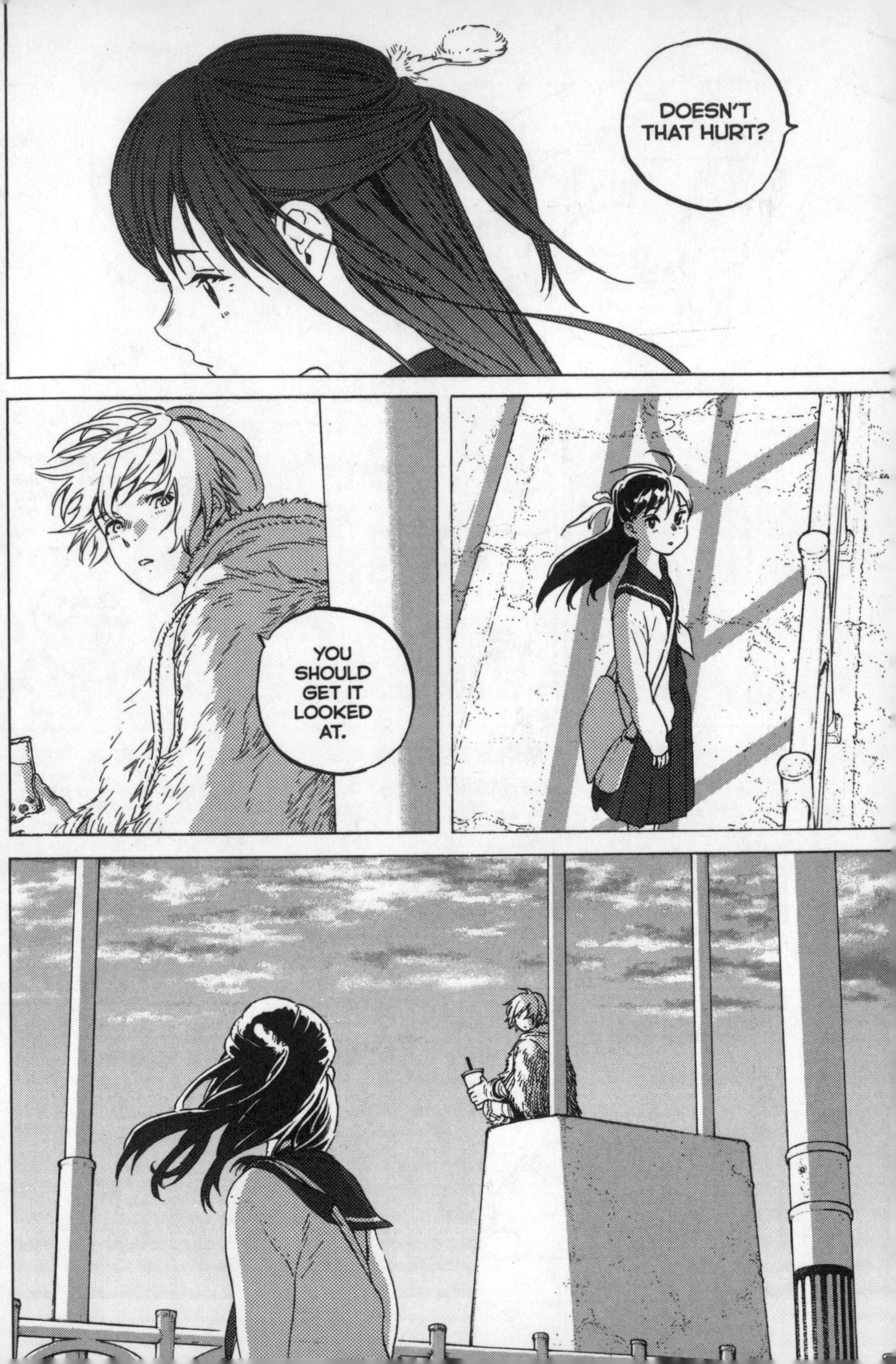
DOESN'T THAT HURT?
YOU SHOULD GET IT LOOKED AT.

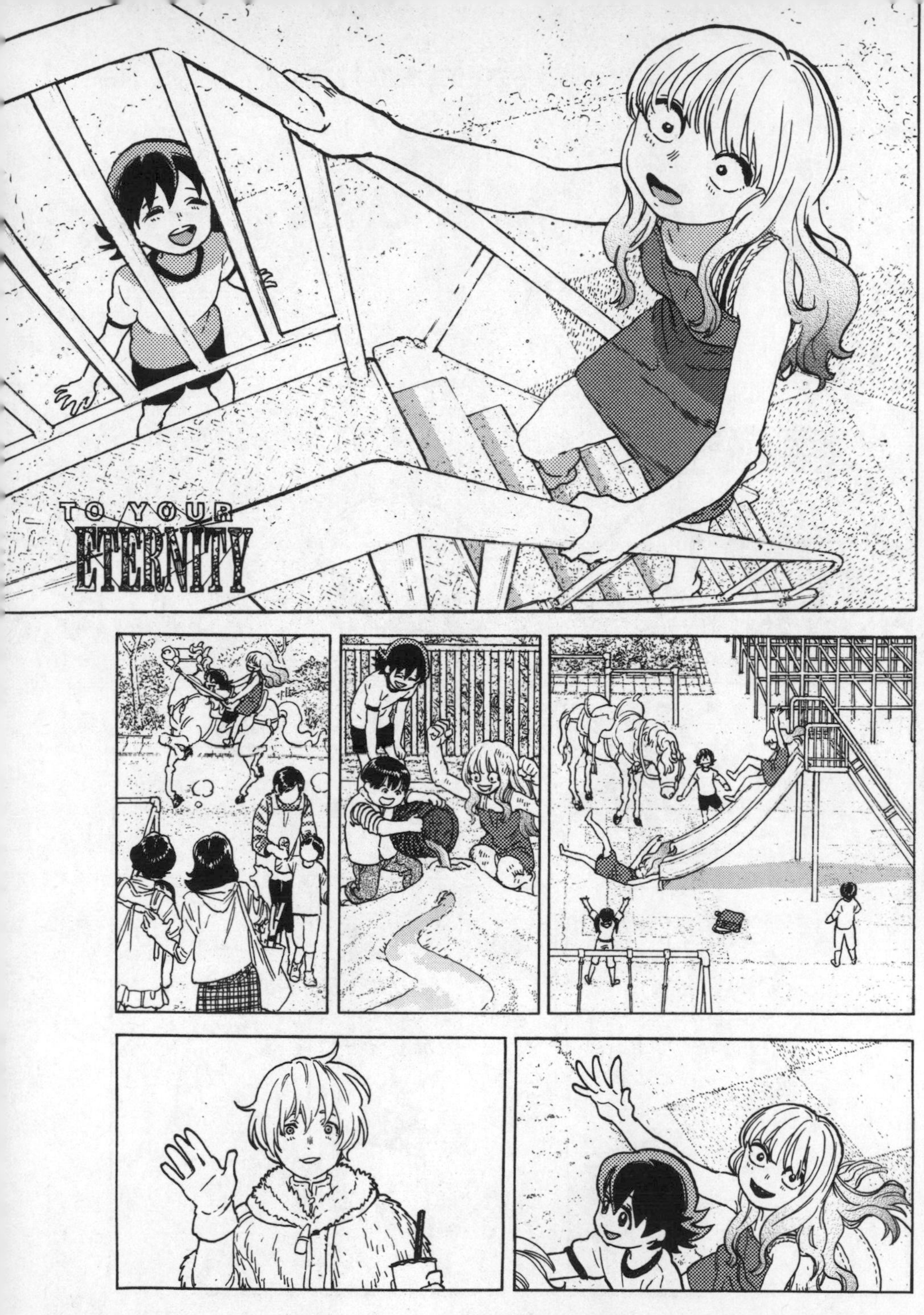
TO YOUR
ETERNITY

#121 Long-Sought Home

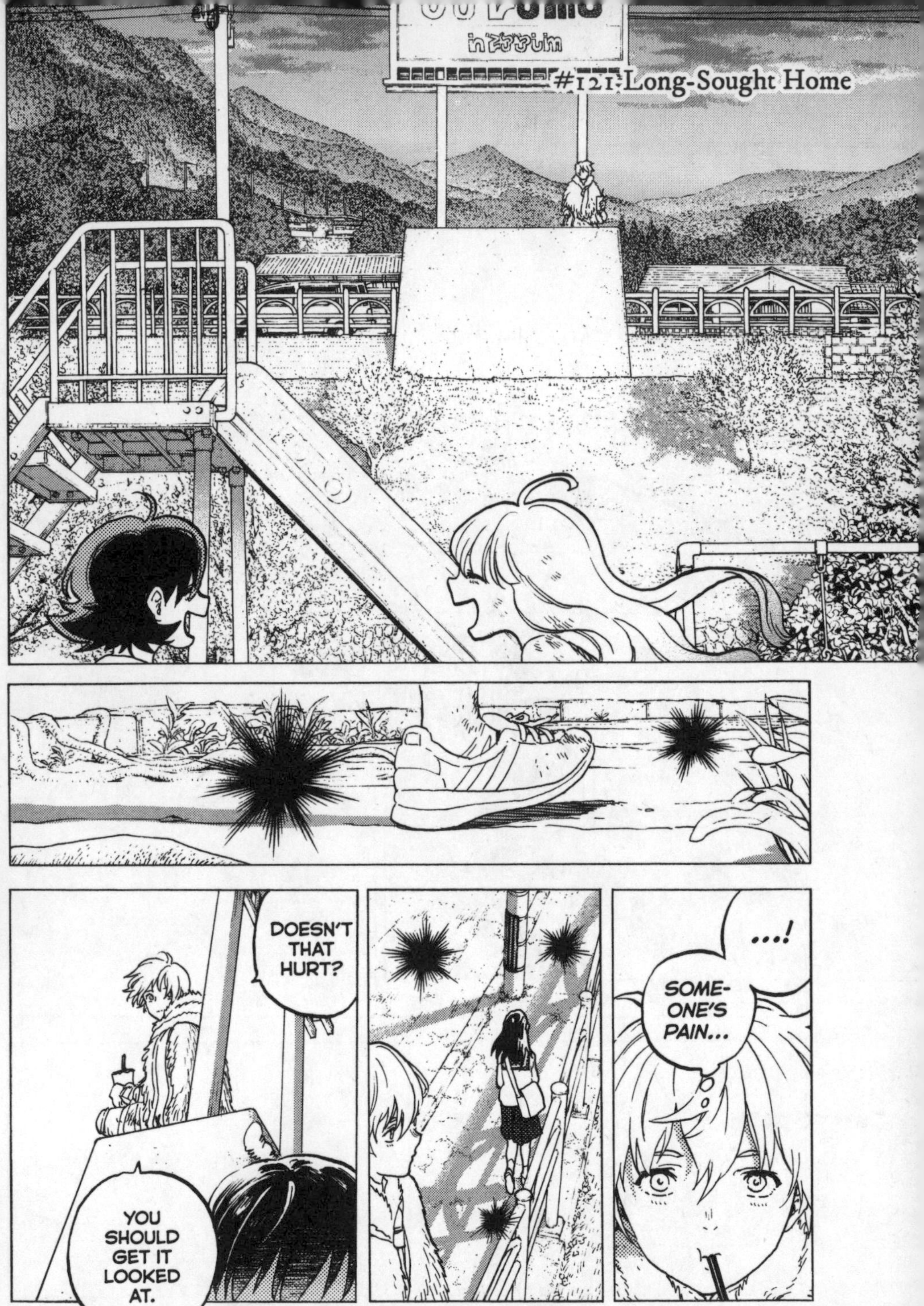

...!
SOME-ONE'S PAIN...
DOESN'T THAT HURT?
YOU SHOULD GET IT LOOKED AT.

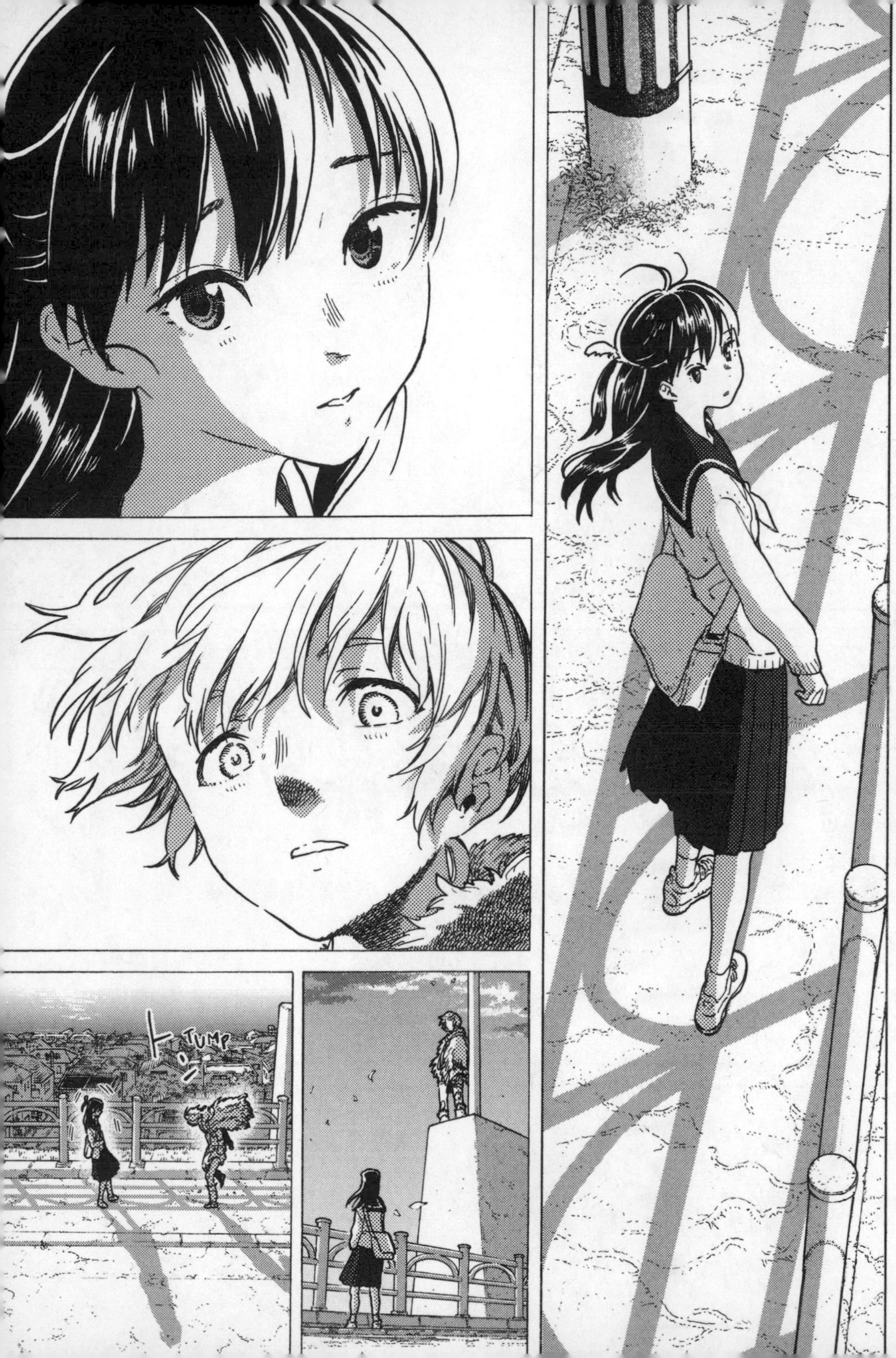
TUMP

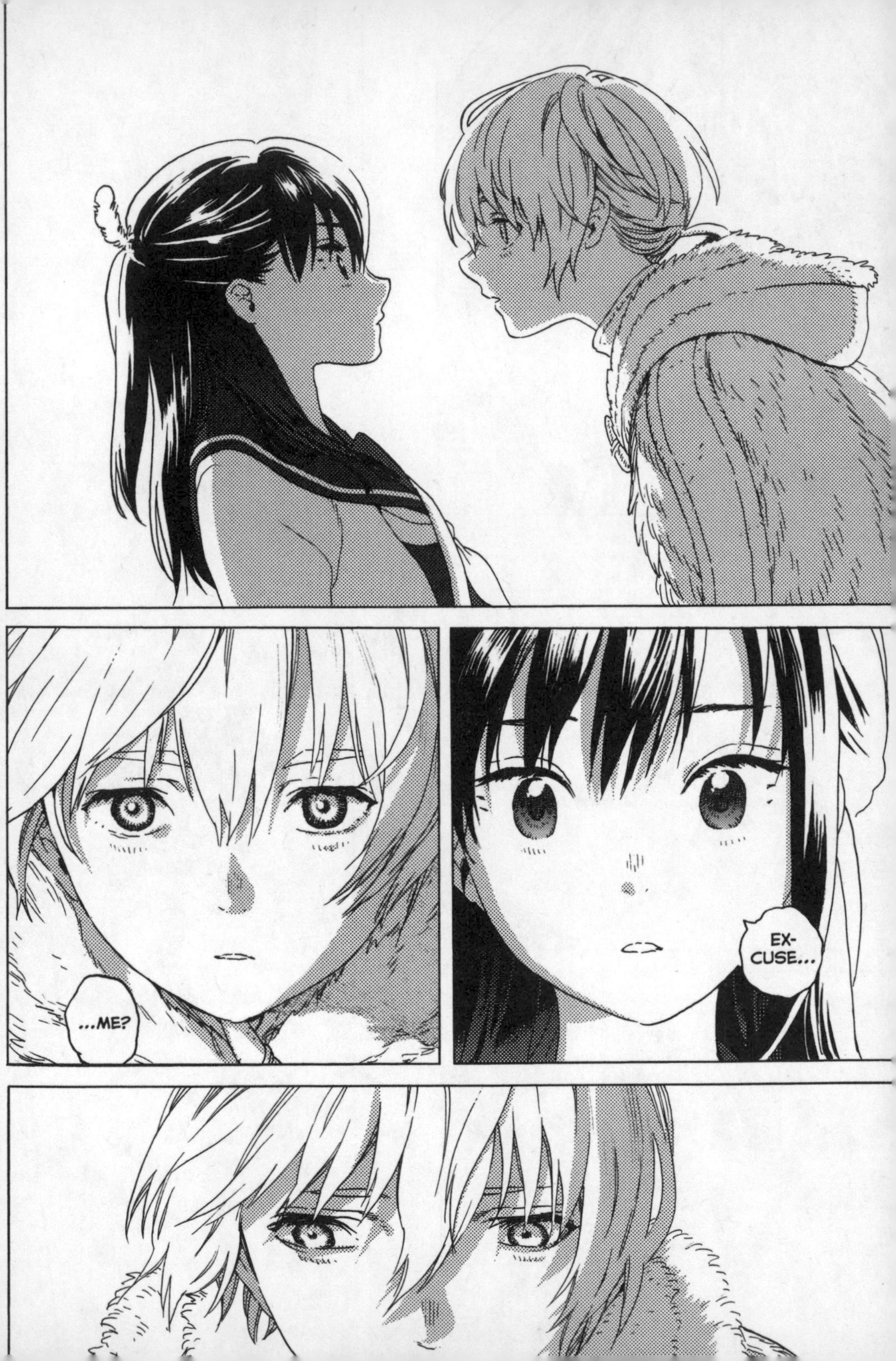
EX-CUSE...
...ME?

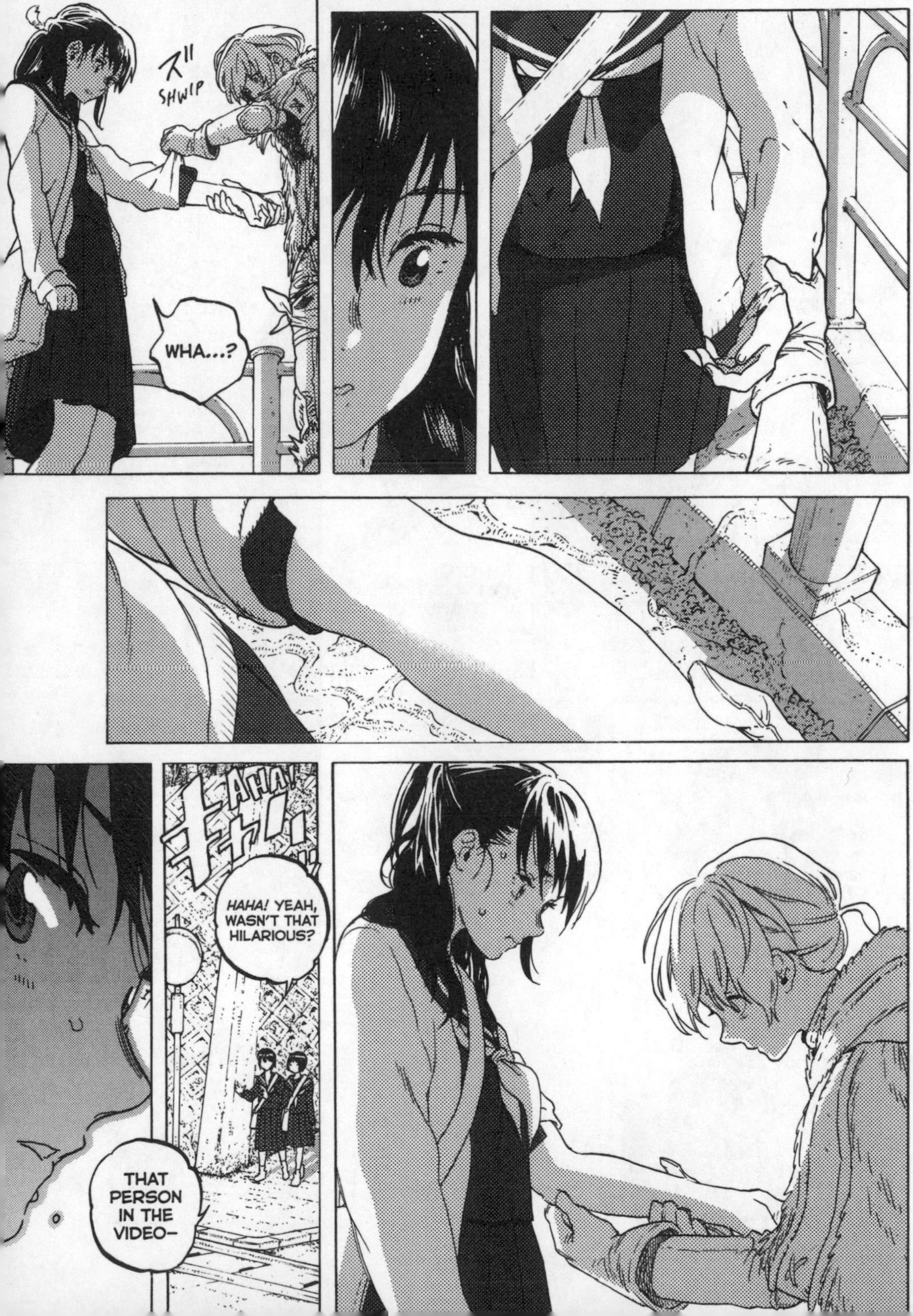
ズ
SHWIP
WHA...?
AHA!
HAHA! YEAH, WASN'T THAT HILARIOUS?
THAT PERSON IN THE VIDEO—

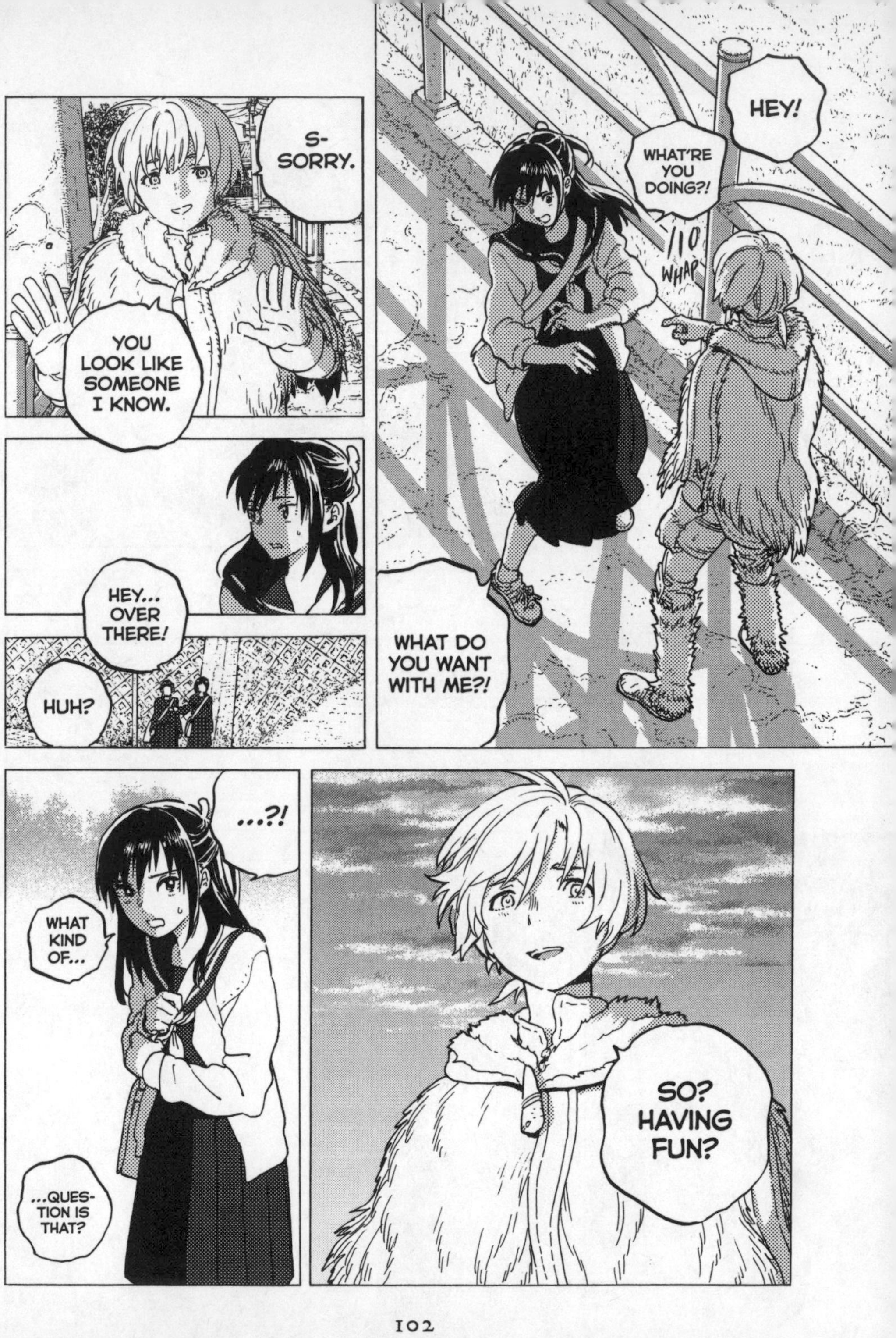
HEY!
WHAT'RE YOU DOING?!
WHAP
WHAT DO YOU WANT WITH ME?!
S-SORRY.
YOU LOOK LIKE SOMEONE I KNOW.
HEY... OVER THERE!
HUH?
SO? HAVING FUN?
...?!
WHAT KIND OF...
...QUES-TION IS THAT?

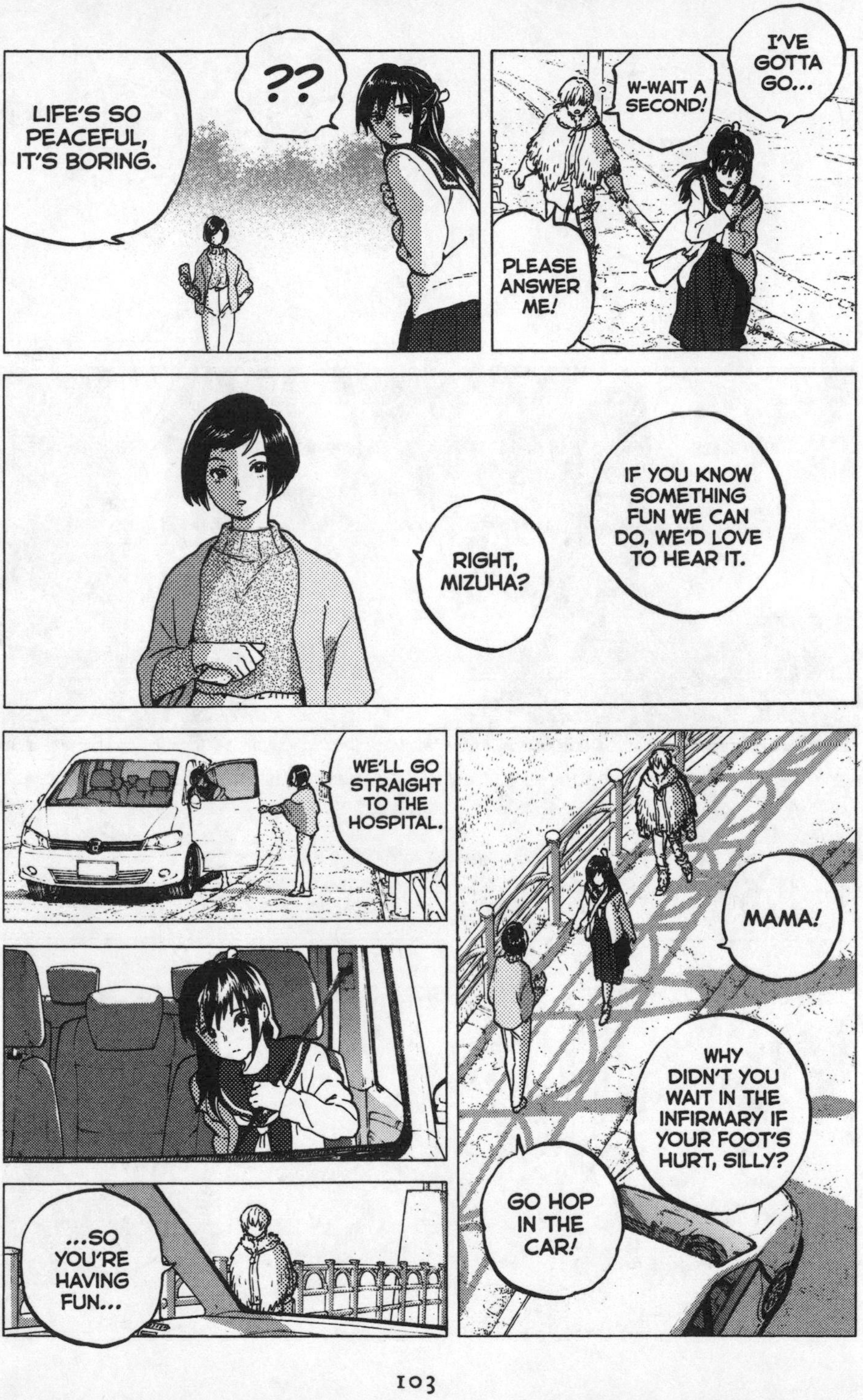
I'VE GOTTA GO...
W-WAIT A SECOND!
PLEASE ANSWER ME!
??
LIFE'S SO PEACEFUL, IT'S BORING.
IF YOU KNOW SOMETHING FUN WE CAN DO, WE'D LOVE TO HEAR IT.
RIGHT, MIZUHA?
MAMA!
WHY DIDN'T YOU WAIT IN THE INFIRMARY IF YOUR FOOT'S HURT, SILLY?
GO HOP IN THE CAR!
WE'LL GO STRAIGHT TO THE HOSPITAL.
...SO YOU'RE HAVING FUN...

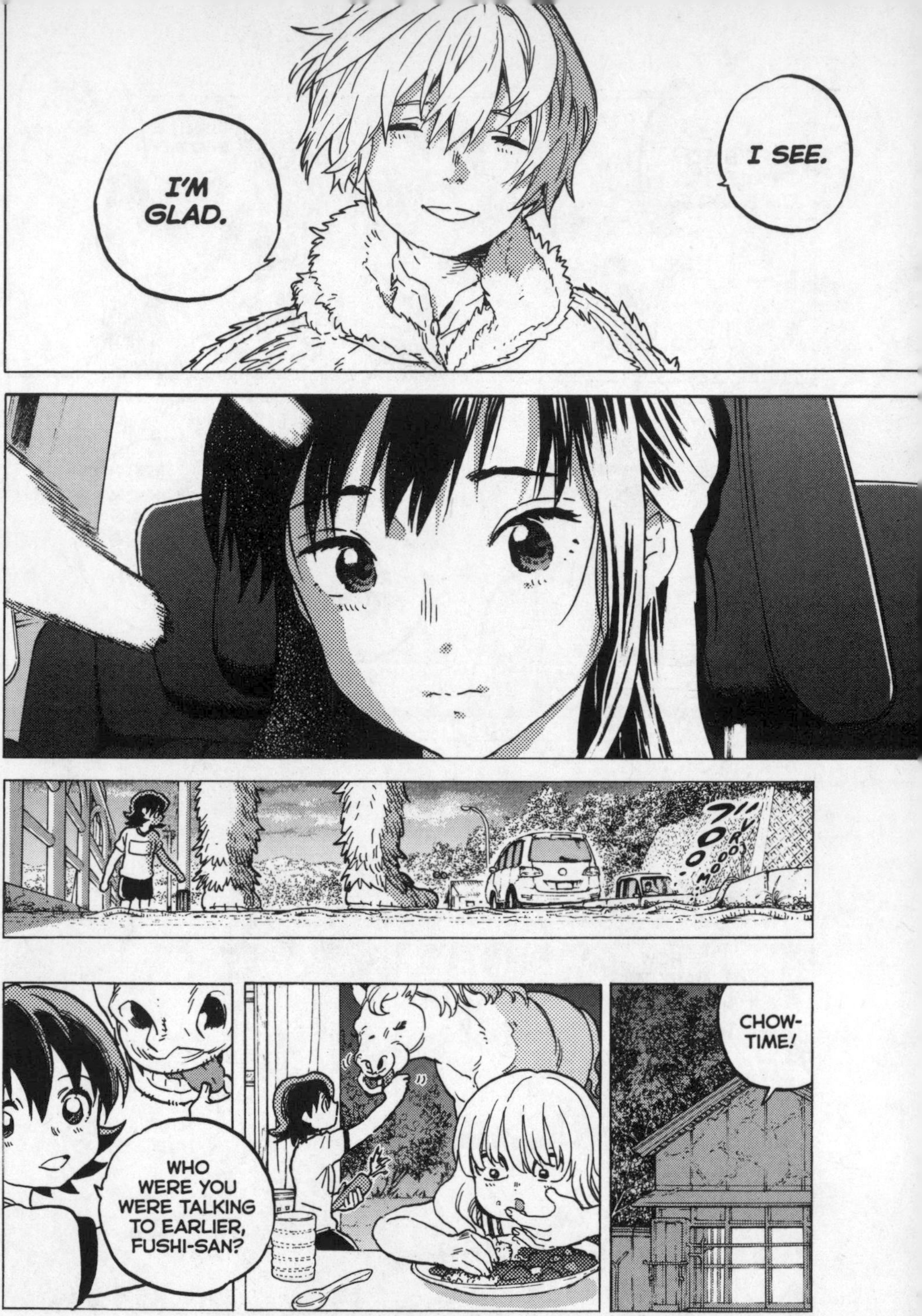
I SEE.
I'M GLAD.
VROOOM
CHOW-TIME!
WHO WERE YOU WERE TALKING TO EARLIER, FUSHI-SAN?

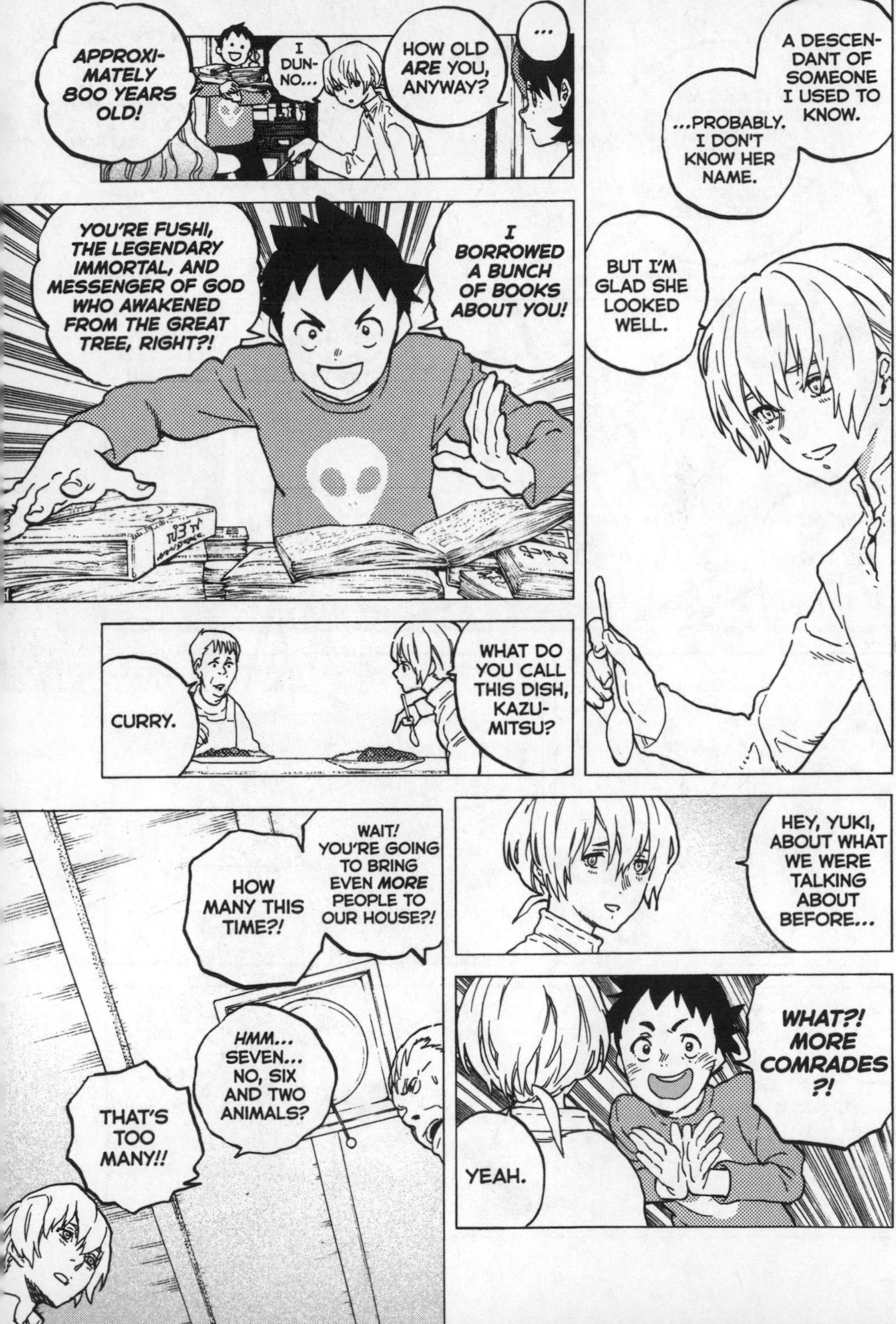
A DESCENDANT OF SOMEONE I USED TO KNOW.
...PROBABLY. I DON'T KNOW HER NAME.
BUT I'M GLAD SHE LOOKED WELL.
...
HOW OLD ARE YOU, ANYWAY?
I DUNNO...
APPROXIMATELY 800 YEARS OLD!
I BORROWED A BUNCH OF BOOKS ABOUT YOU!
YOU'RE FUSHI, THE LEGENDARY IMMORTAL, AND MESSENGER OF GOD WHO AWAKENED FROM THE GREAT TREE, RIGHT?!
WHAT DO YOU CALL THIS DISH, KAZUMITSU?
CURRY.
HEY, YUKI, ABOUT WHAT WE WERE TALKING ABOUT BEFORE...
WHAT?! MORE COMRADES?!
YEAH.
WAIT! YOU'RE GOING TO BRING EVEN MORE PEOPLE TO OUR HOUSE?!
HOW MANY THIS TIME?!
HMM... SEVEN... NO, SIX AND TWO ANIMALS?
THAT'S TOO MANY!!

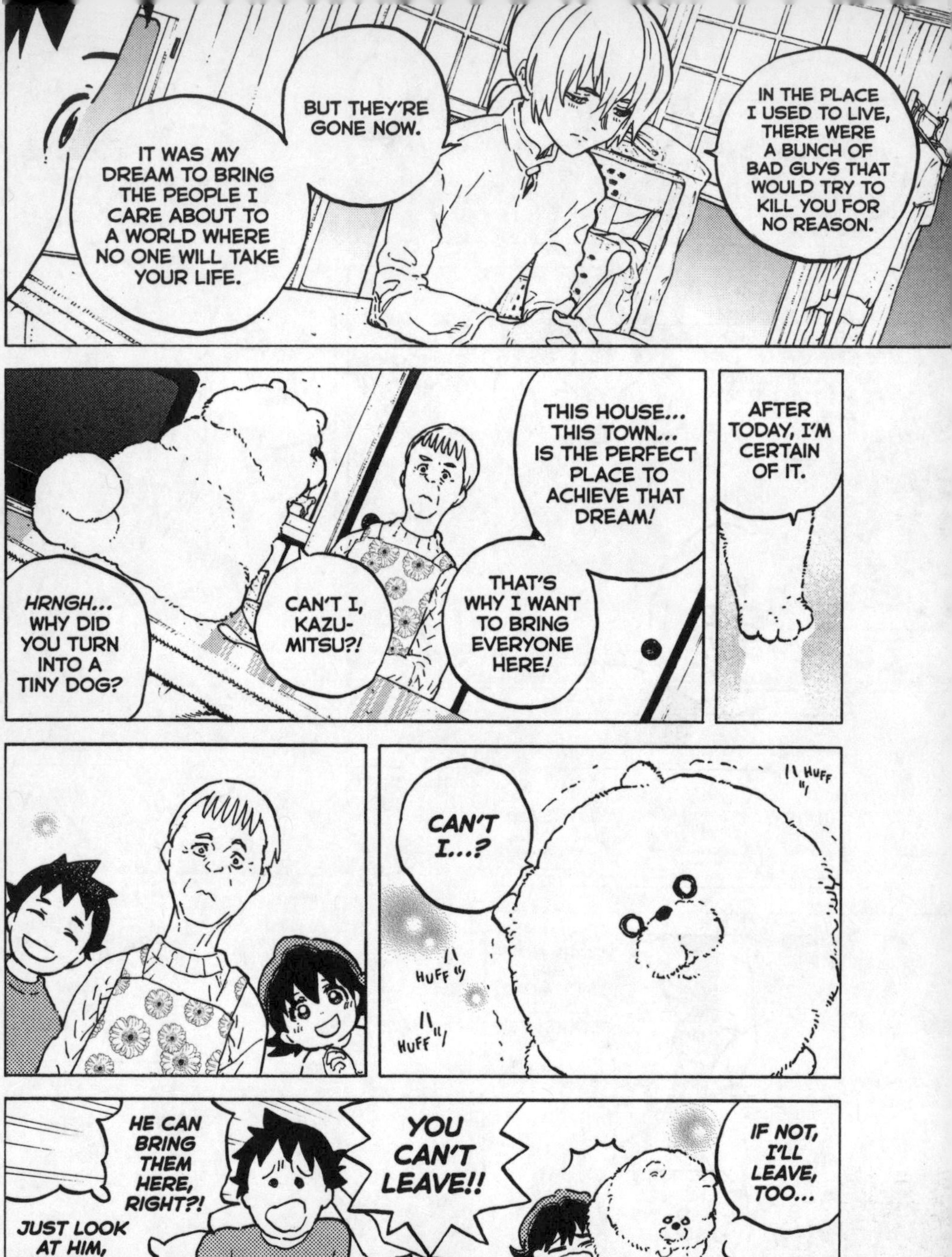
IN THE PLACE I USED TO LIVE, THERE WERE A BUNCH OF BAD GUYS THAT WOULD TRY TO KILL YOU FOR NO REASON.
BUT THEY'RE GONE NOW.
IT WAS MY DREAM TO BRING THE PEOPLE I CARE ABOUT TO A WORLD WHERE NO ONE WILL TAKE YOUR LIFE.
AFTER TODAY, I'M CERTAIN OF IT.
THIS HOUSE... THIS TOWN... IS THE PERFECT PLACE TO ACHIEVE THAT DREAM!
THAT'S WHY I WANT TO BRING EVERYONE HERE!
CAN'T I, KAZU-MITSU?!
HRNGH... WHY DID YOU TURN INTO A TINY DOG?
HUFF
CAN'T I...?
HUFF
HUFF
IF NOT, I'LL LEAVE, TOO...
YOU CAN'T LEAVE!!
HE CAN BRING THEM HERE, RIGHT?!
JUST LOOK AT HIM, GRAMPS!! DON'T YOU SEE HOW POOFY HE IS?!

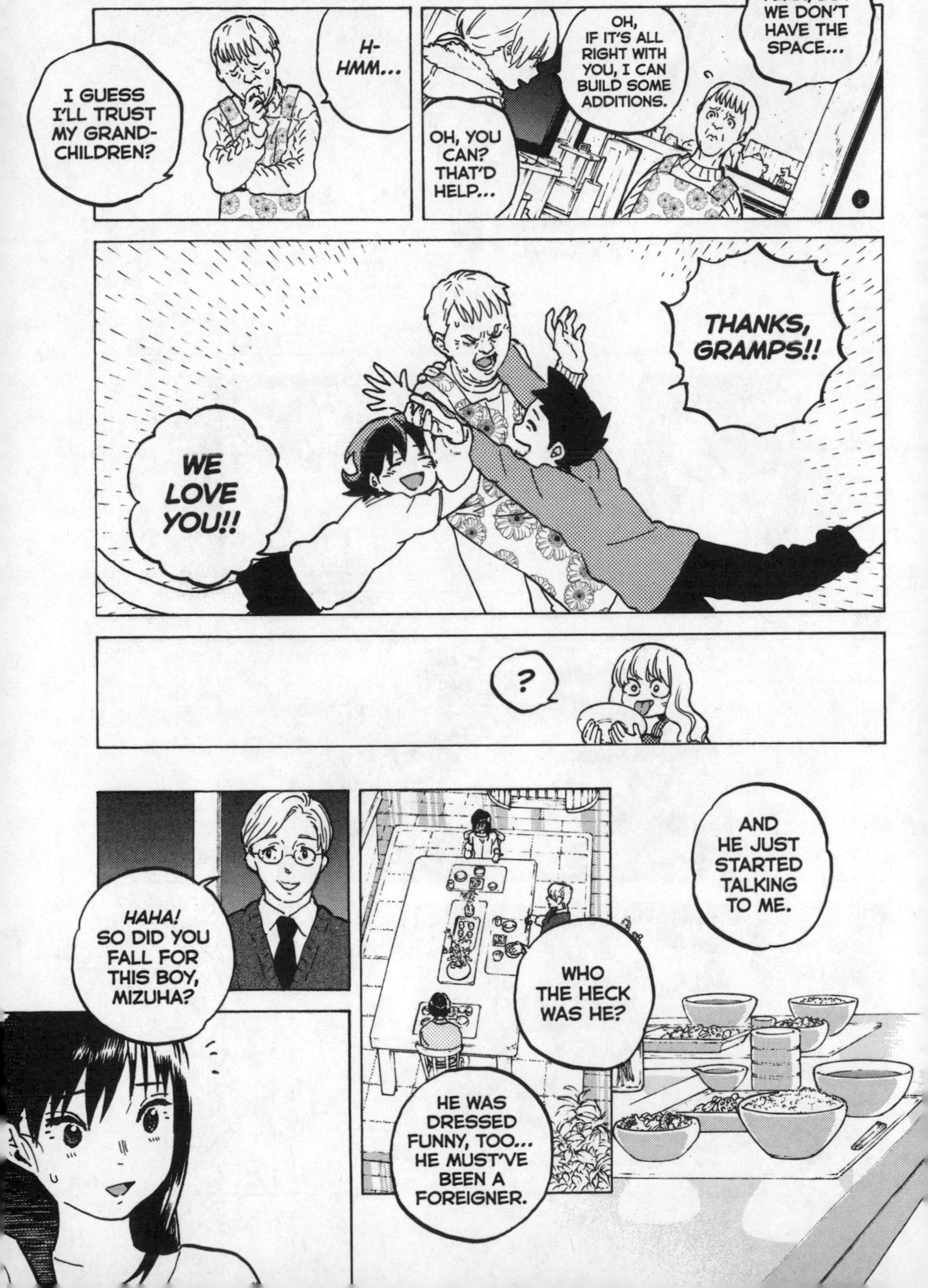
YEAH, BUT WE DON'T HAVE THE SPACE...
OH, IF IT'S ALL RIGHT WITH YOU, I CAN BUILD SOME ADDITIONS.
OH, YOU CAN? THAT'D HELP...
H-HMM...
I GUESS I'LL TRUST MY GRAND-CHILDREN?
THANKS, GRAMPS!!
WE LOVE YOU!!
?
AND HE JUST STARTED TALKING TO ME.
WHO THE HECK WAS HE?
HE WAS DRESSED FUNNY, TOO... HE MUST'VE BEEN A FOREIGNER.
HAHA! SO DID YOU FALL FOR THIS BOY, MIZUHA?

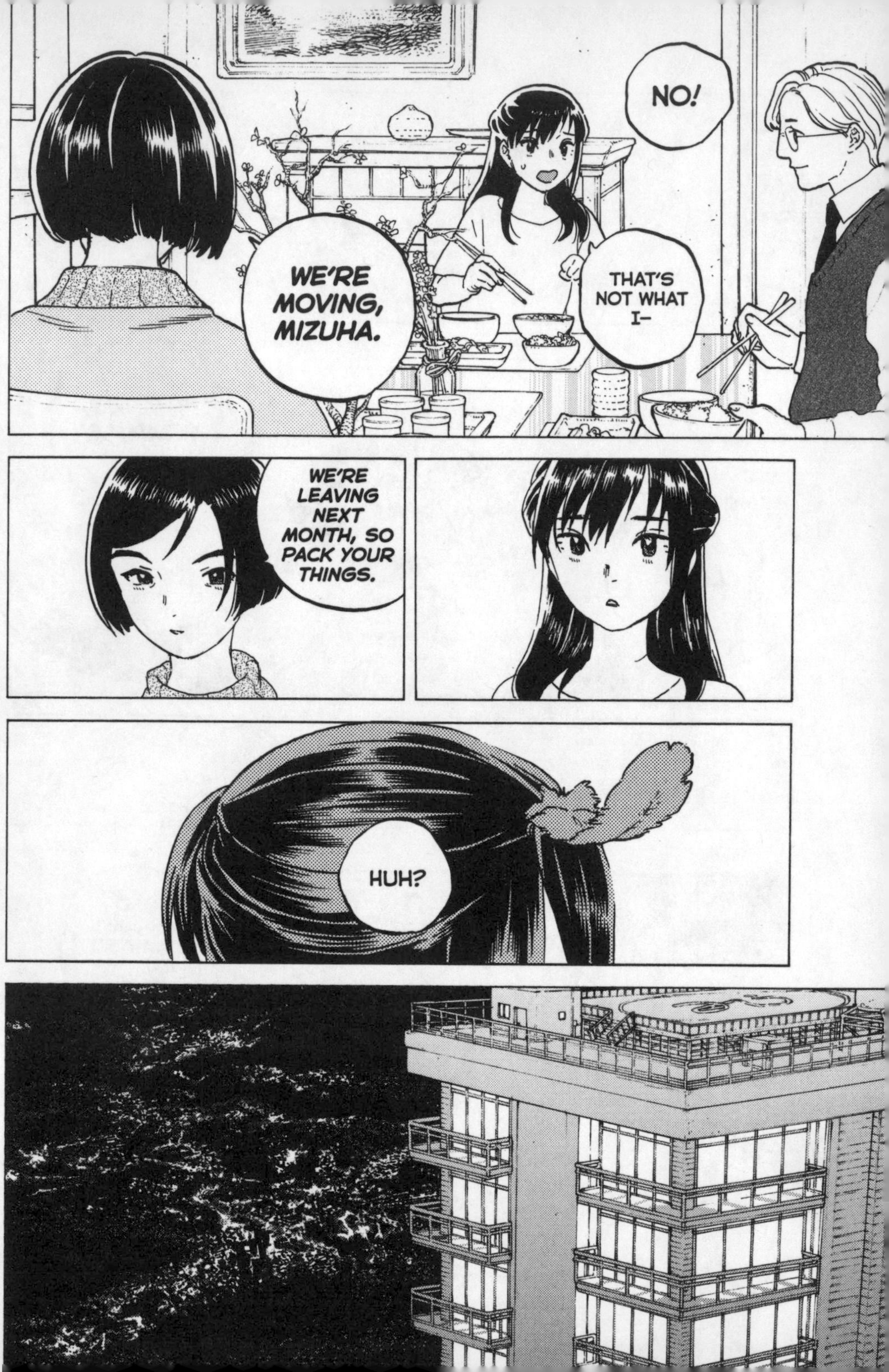
NO!
THAT'S NOT WHAT I–
WE'RE MOVING, MIZUHA.
WE'RE LEAVING NEXT MONTH, SO PACK YOUR THINGS.
HUH?

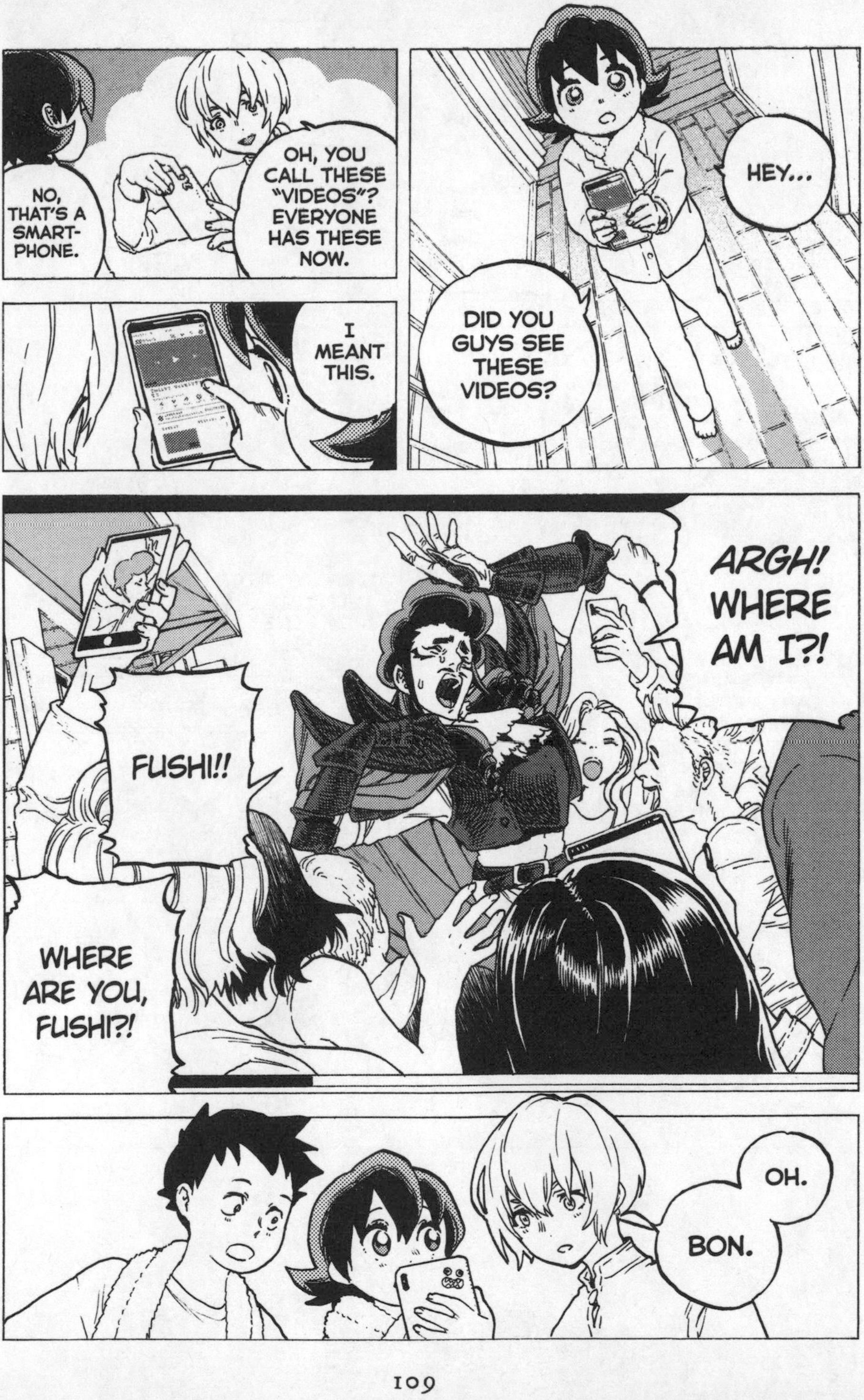
HEY...
DID YOU GUYS SEE THESE VIDEOS?
OH, YOU CALL THESE "VIDEOS"? EVERYONE HAS THESE NOW.
NO, THAT'S A SMARTPHONE.
I MEANT THIS.
ARGH! WHERE AM I?!
FUSHI!!
WHERE ARE YOU, FUSHI?!
OH.
BON.

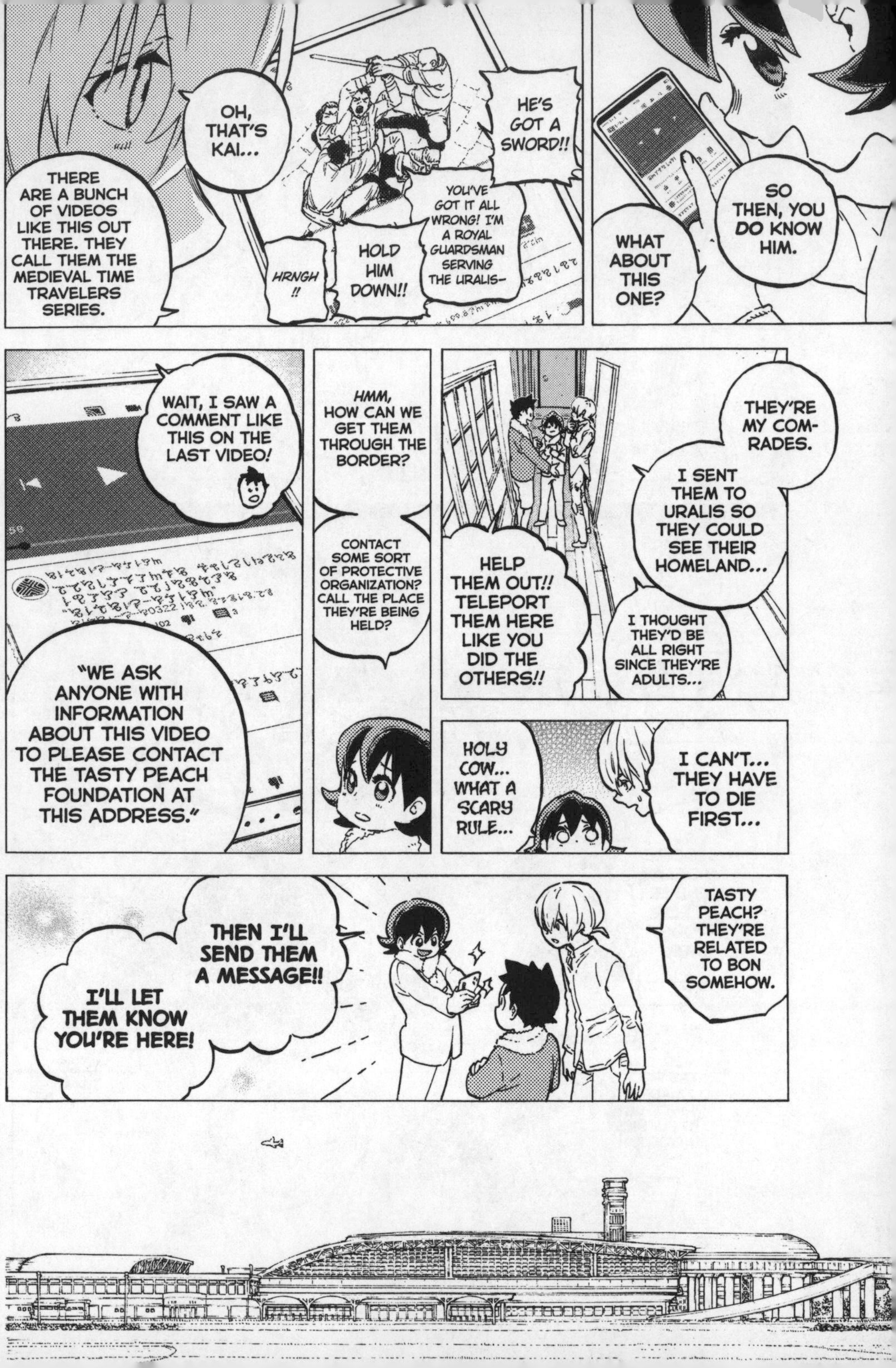
SO THEN, YOU DO KNOW HIM.
WHAT ABOUT THIS ONE?
HE'S GOT A SWORD!!
OH, THAT'S KAI...
YOU'VE GOT IT ALL WRONG! I'M A ROYAL GUARDSMAN SERVING THE URALIS-
HOLD HIM DOWN!!
HRNGH!!
THERE ARE A BUNCH OF VIDEOS LIKE THIS OUT THERE. THEY CALL THEM THE MEDIEVAL TIME TRAVELERS SERIES.
THEY'RE MY COMRADES.
I SENT THEM TO URALIS SO THEY COULD SEE THEIR HOMELAND...
I THOUGHT THEY'D BE ALL RIGHT SINCE THEY'RE ADULTS...
HELP THEM OUT!! TELEPORT THEM HERE LIKE YOU DID THE OTHERS!!
I CAN'T... THEY HAVE TO DIE FIRST...
HOLY COW... WHAT A SCARY RULE...
HMM, HOW CAN WE GET THEM THROUGH THE BORDER?
CONTACT SOME SORT OF PROTECTIVE ORGANIZATION? CALL THE PLACE THEY'RE BEING HELD?
WAIT, I SAW A COMMENT LIKE THIS ON THE LAST VIDEO!
"WE ASK ANYONE WITH INFORMATION ABOUT THIS VIDEO TO PLEASE CONTACT THE TASTY PEACH FOUNDATION AT THIS ADDRESS."
TASTY PEACH? THEY'RE RELATED TO BON SOMEHOW.
THEN I'LL SEND THEM A MESSAGE!!
I'LL LET THEM KNOW YOU'RE HERE!

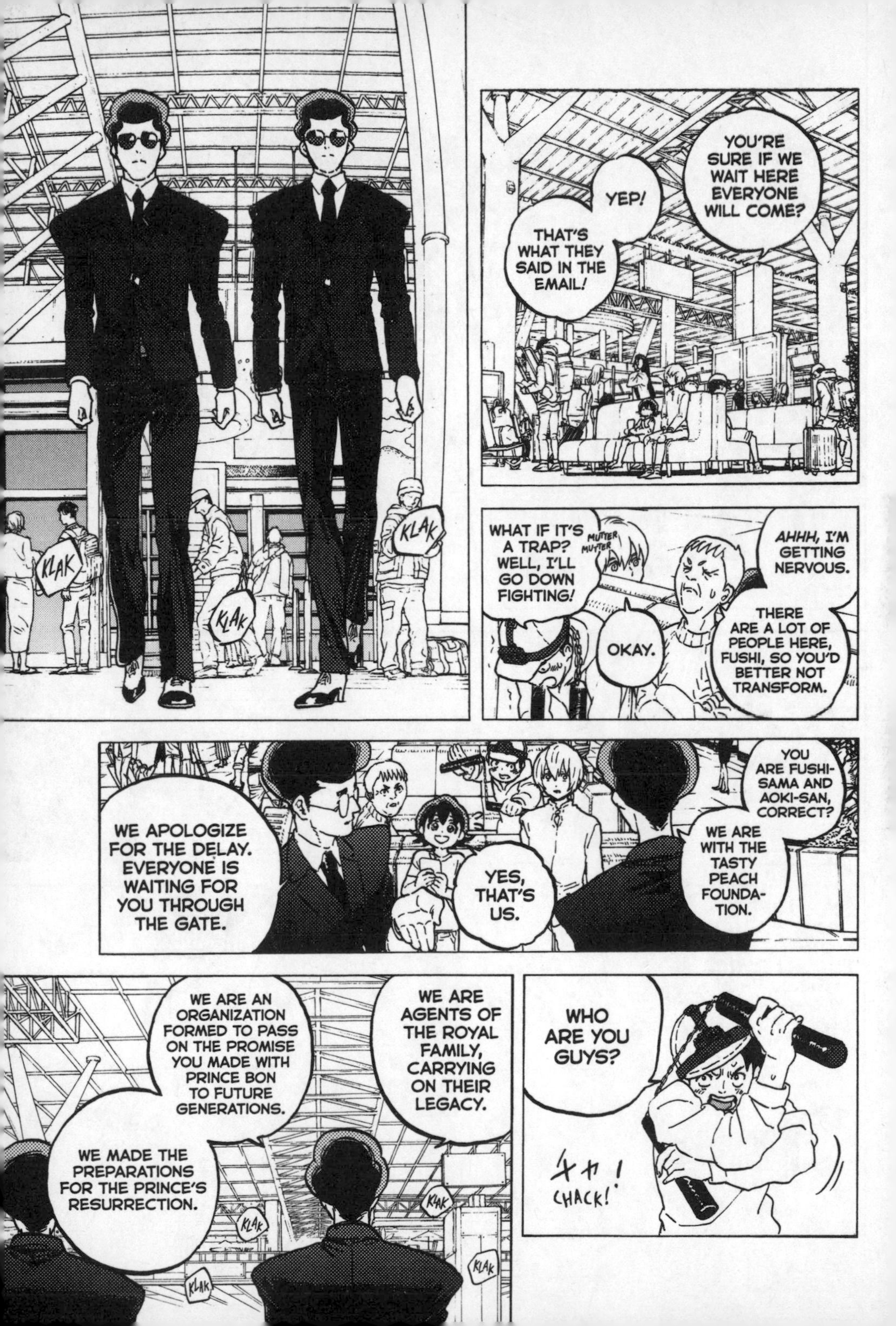
YOU'RE SURE IF WE WAIT HERE EVERYONE WILL COME?
YEP!
THAT'S WHAT THEY SAID IN THE EMAIL!
AHHH, I'M GETTING NERVOUS.
THERE ARE A LOT OF PEOPLE HERE, FUSHI, SO YOU'D BETTER NOT TRANSFORM.
OKAY.
WHAT IF IT'S A TRAP? WELL, I'LL GO DOWN FIGHTING!
MUTTER MUTTER
KLAK
KLAK
KLAK
KLAK
YOU ARE FUSHI-SAMA AND AOKI-SAN, CORRECT?
WE ARE WITH THE TASTY PEACH FOUNDATION.
YES, THAT'S US.
WE APOLOGIZE FOR THE DELAY. EVERYONE IS WAITING FOR YOU THROUGH THE GATE.
WHO ARE YOU GUYS?
CHACK!
WE ARE AGENTS OF THE ROYAL FAMILY, CARRYING ON THEIR LEGACY.
WE ARE AN ORGANIZATION FORMED TO PASS ON THE PROMISE YOU MADE WITH PRINCE BON TO FUTURE GENERATIONS.
WE MADE THE PREPARATIONS FOR THE PRINCE'S RESURRECTION.
KLAK
KLAK
KLAK
KLAK

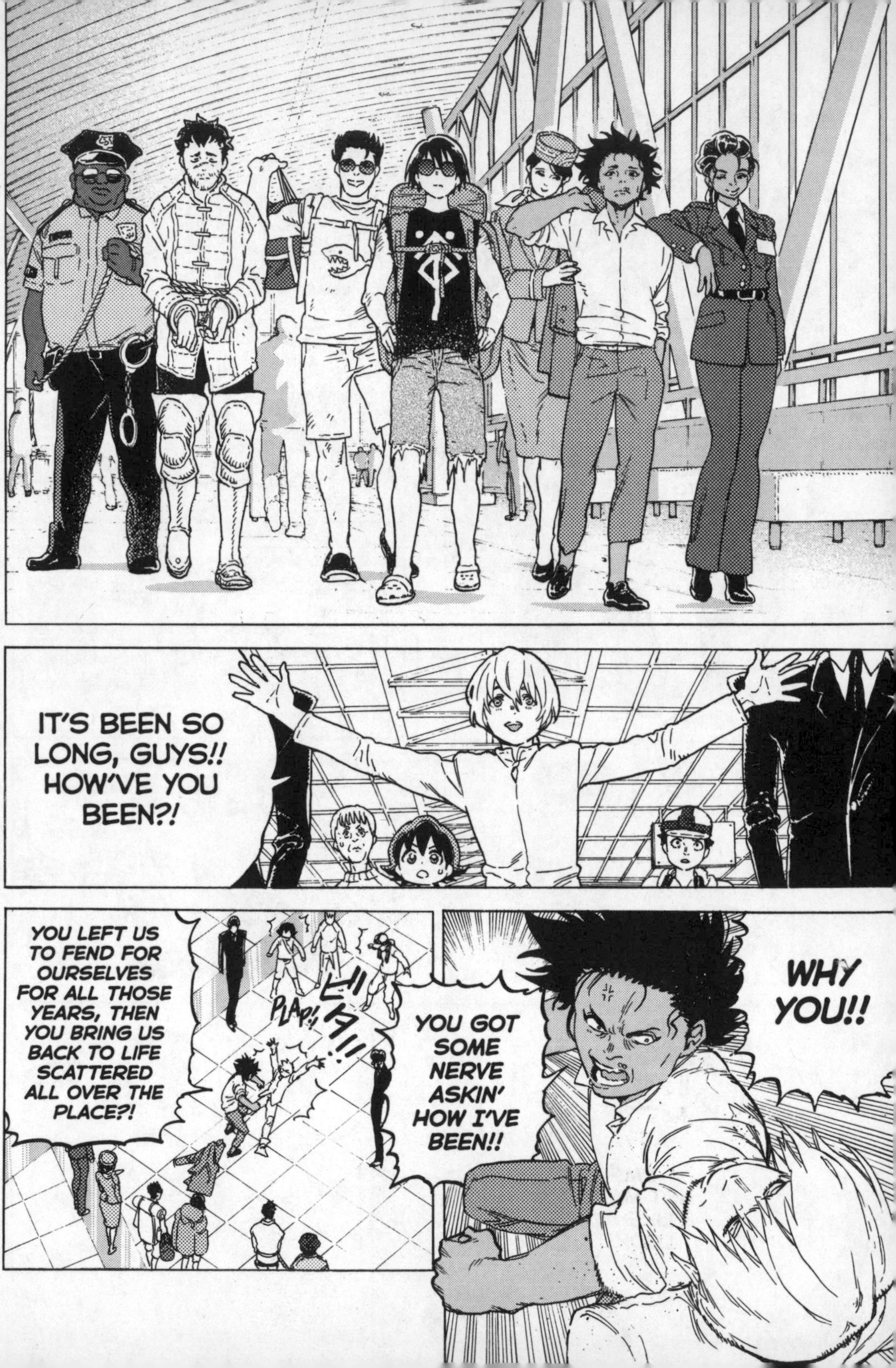
IT'S BEEN SO LONG, GUYS!! HOW'VE YOU BEEN?!
WHY YOU!!
YOU GOT SOME NERVE ASKIN' HOW I'VE BEEN!!
YOU LEFT US TO FEND FOR OURSELVES FOR ALL THOSE YEARS, THEN YOU BRING US BACK TO LIFE SCATTERED ALL OVER THE PLACE?!
PLAP!

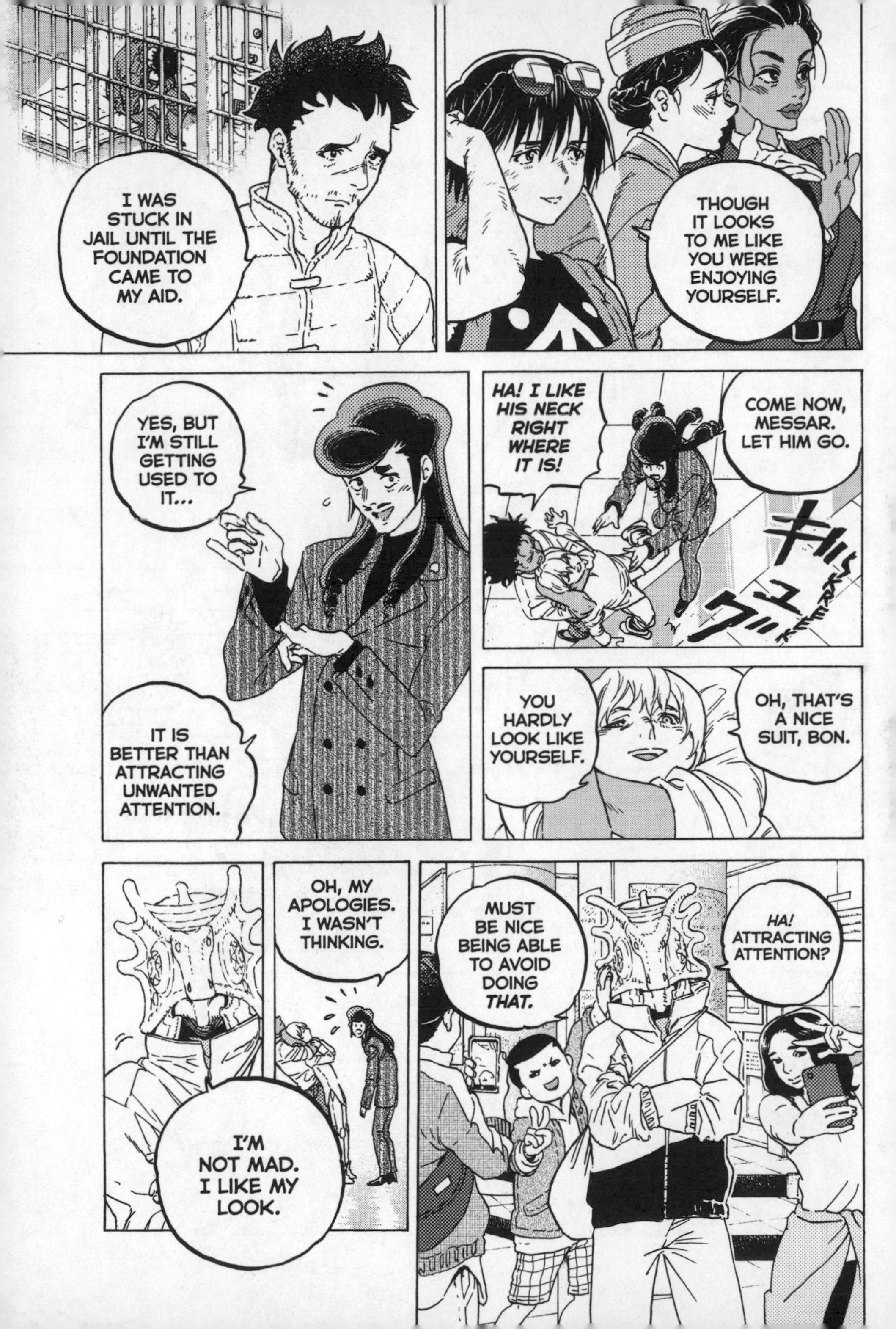
THOUGH IT LOOKS TO ME LIKE YOU WERE ENJOYING YOURSELF.
I WAS STUCK IN JAIL UNTIL THE FOUNDATION CAME TO MY AID.
COME NOW, MESSAR. LET HIM GO.
HA! I LIKE HIS NECK RIGHT WHERE IT IS!
SKREEK
OH, THAT'S A NICE SUIT, BON.
YOU HARDLY LOOK LIKE YOURSELF.
YES, BUT I'M STILL GETTING USED TO IT...
IT IS BETTER THAN ATTRACTING UNWANTED ATTENTION.
HA! ATTRACTING ATTENTION?
MUST BE NICE BEING ABLE TO AVOID DOING *THAT.*
OH, MY APOLOGIES. I WASN'T THINKING.
I'M NOT MAD. I LIKE MY LOOK.

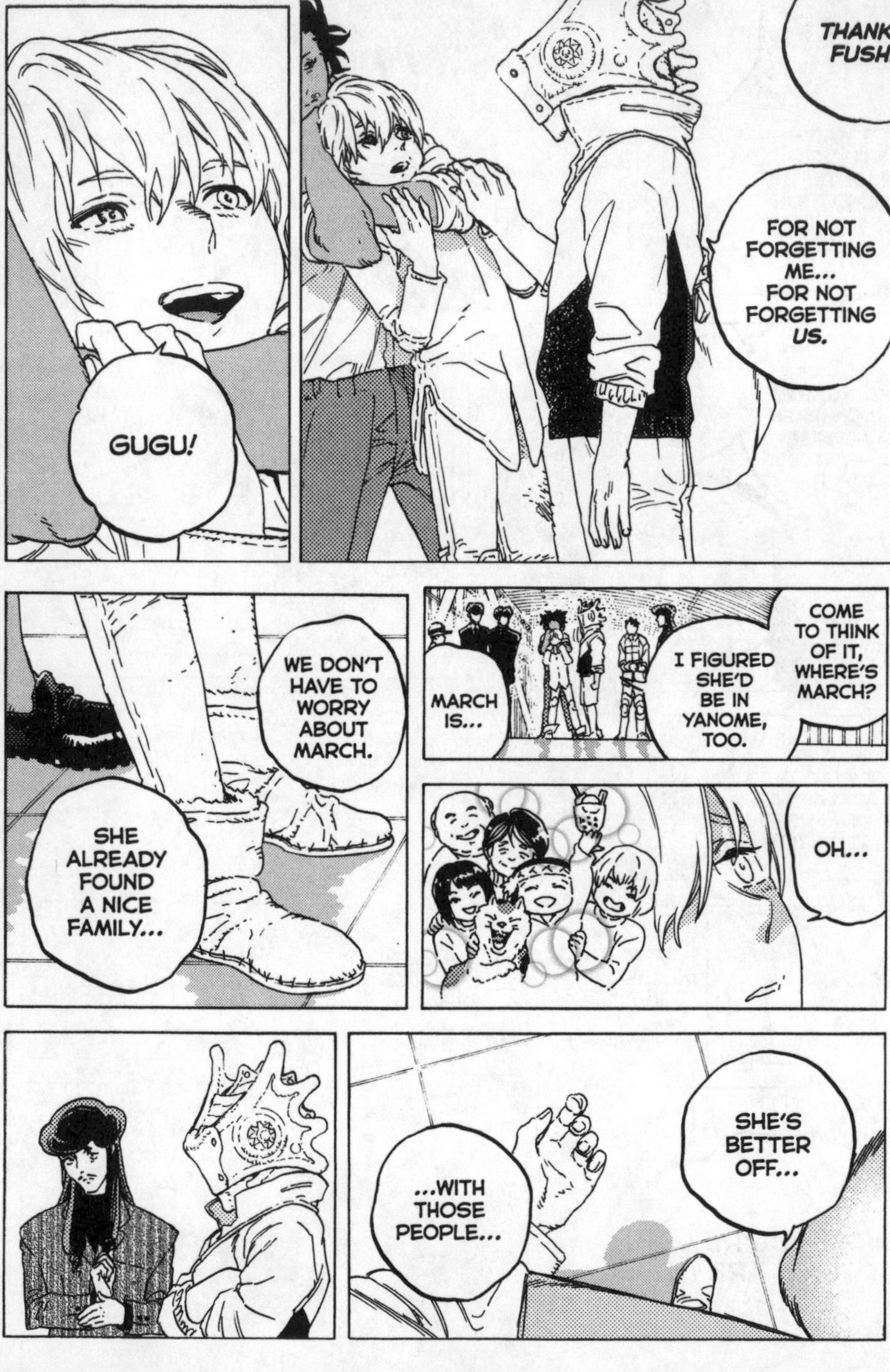
THANKS, FUSHI.
FOR NOT FORGETTING ME... FOR NOT FORGETTING US.
GUGU!
COME TO THINK OF IT, WHERE'S MARCH?
I FIGURED SHE'D BE IN YANOME, TOO.
MARCH IS...
OH...
WE DON'T HAVE TO WORRY ABOUT MARCH.
SHE ALREADY FOUND A NICE FAMILY...
SHE'S BETTER OFF...
...WITH THOSE PEOPLE...

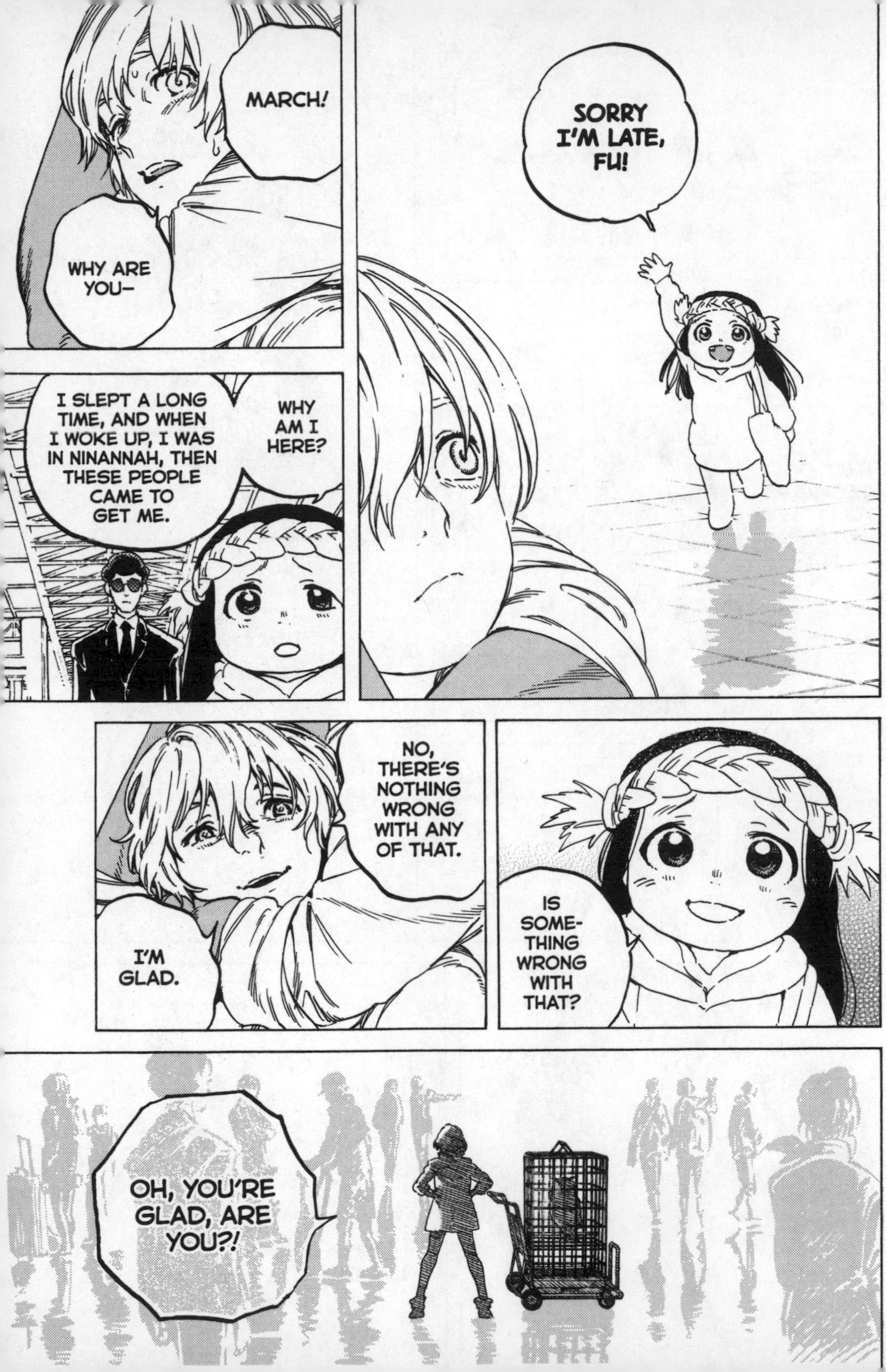
SORRY I'M LATE, FU!
MARCH!
WHY ARE YOU—
WHY AM I HERE?
I SLEPT A LONG TIME, AND WHEN I WOKE UP, I WAS IN NINANNAH, THEN THESE PEOPLE CAME TO GET ME.
IS SOME-THING WRONG WITH THAT?
NO, THERE'S NOTHING WRONG WITH ANY OF THAT.
I'M GLAD.
OH, YOU'RE GLAD, ARE YOU?!

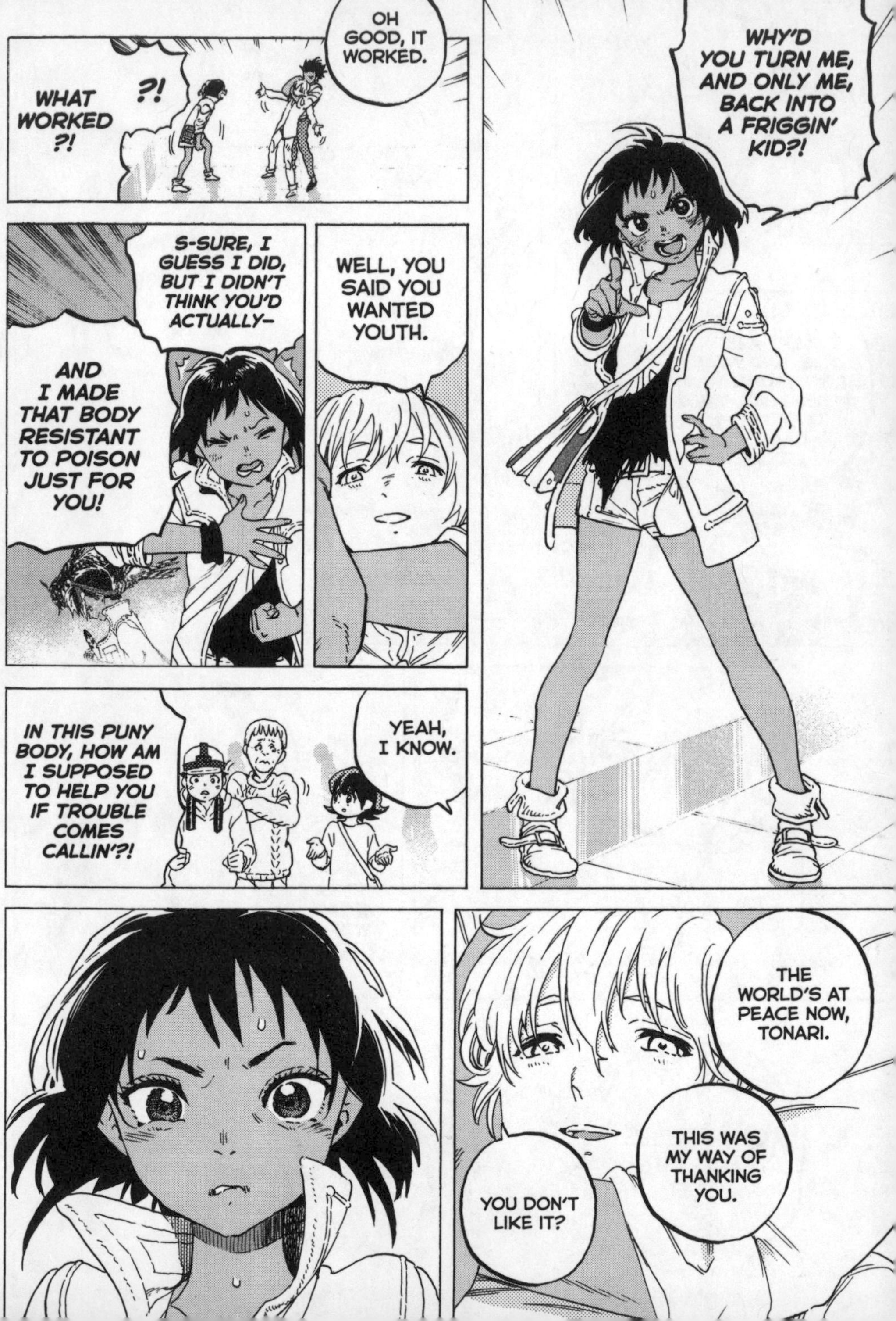
WHY'D YOU TURN ME, AND ONLY ME, BACK INTO A FRIGGIN' KID?!
OH GOOD, IT WORKED.
?!
WHAT WORKED ?!
WELL, YOU SAID YOU WANTED YOUTH.
S-SURE, I GUESS I DID, BUT I DIDN'T THINK YOU'D ACTUALLY–
AND I MADE THAT BODY RESISTANT TO POISON JUST FOR YOU!
IN THIS PUNY BODY, HOW AM I SUPPOSED TO HELP YOU IF TROUBLE COMES CALLIN'?!
YEAH, I KNOW.
THE WORLD'S AT PEACE NOW, TONARI.
THIS WAS MY WAY OF THANKING YOU.
YOU DON'T LIKE IT?

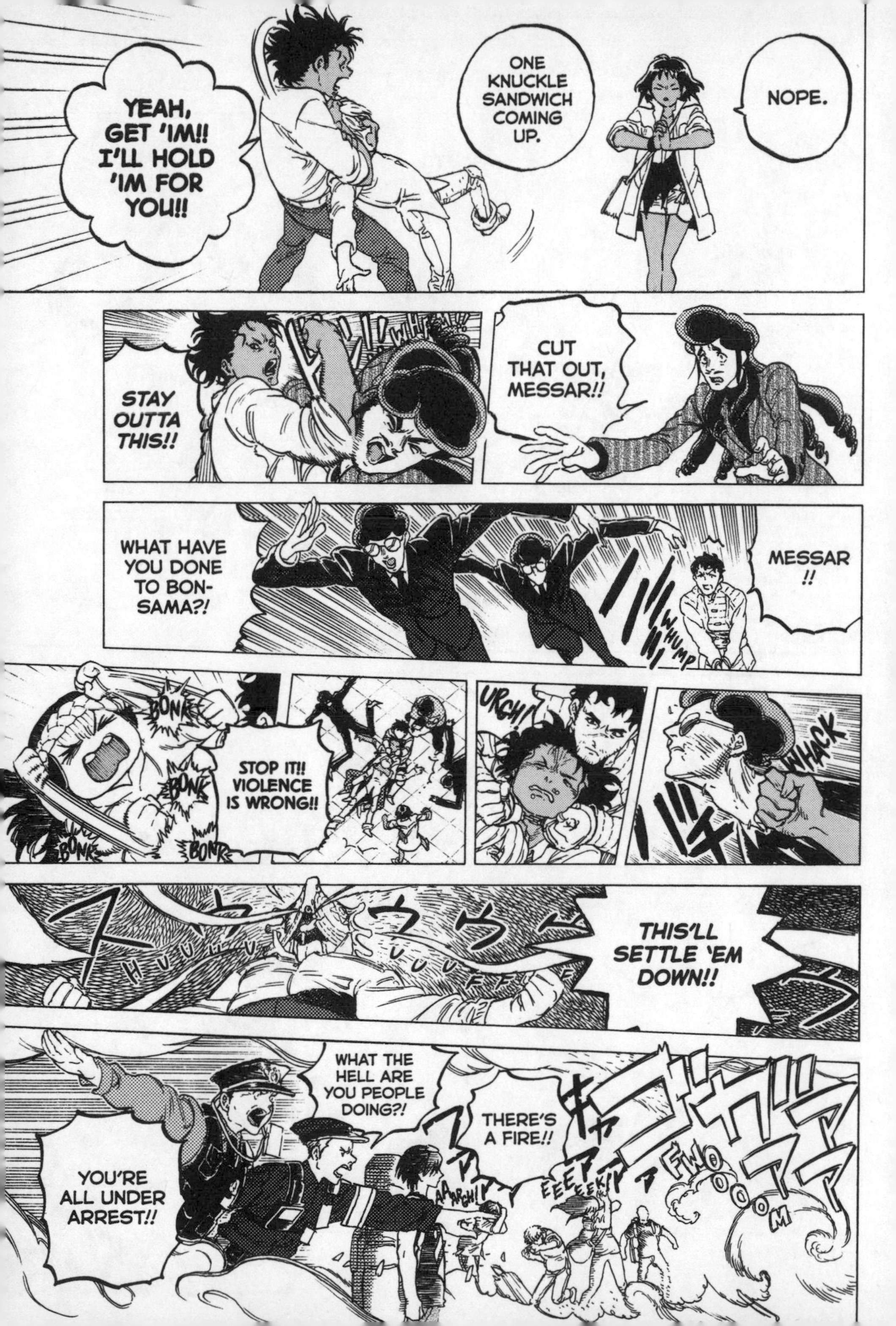
NOPE.
ONE KNUCKLE SANDWICH COMING UP.
YEAH, GET 'IM!! I'LL HOLD 'IM FOR YOU!!
CUT THAT OUT, MESSAR!!
STAY OUTTA THIS!!
MESSAR !!
WHUMP
WHAT HAVE YOU DONE TO BON-SAMA?!
WHACK
URCH!
STOP IT!! VIOLENCE IS WRONG!!
BONK
BONK
BONK
BONK
THIS'LL SETTLE 'EM DOWN!!
FWOOOOOM
EEEK
EEEE
THERE'S A FIRE!!
WHAT THE HELL ARE YOU PEOPLE DOING?!
AAARGH!!
YOU'RE ALL UNDER ARREST!!

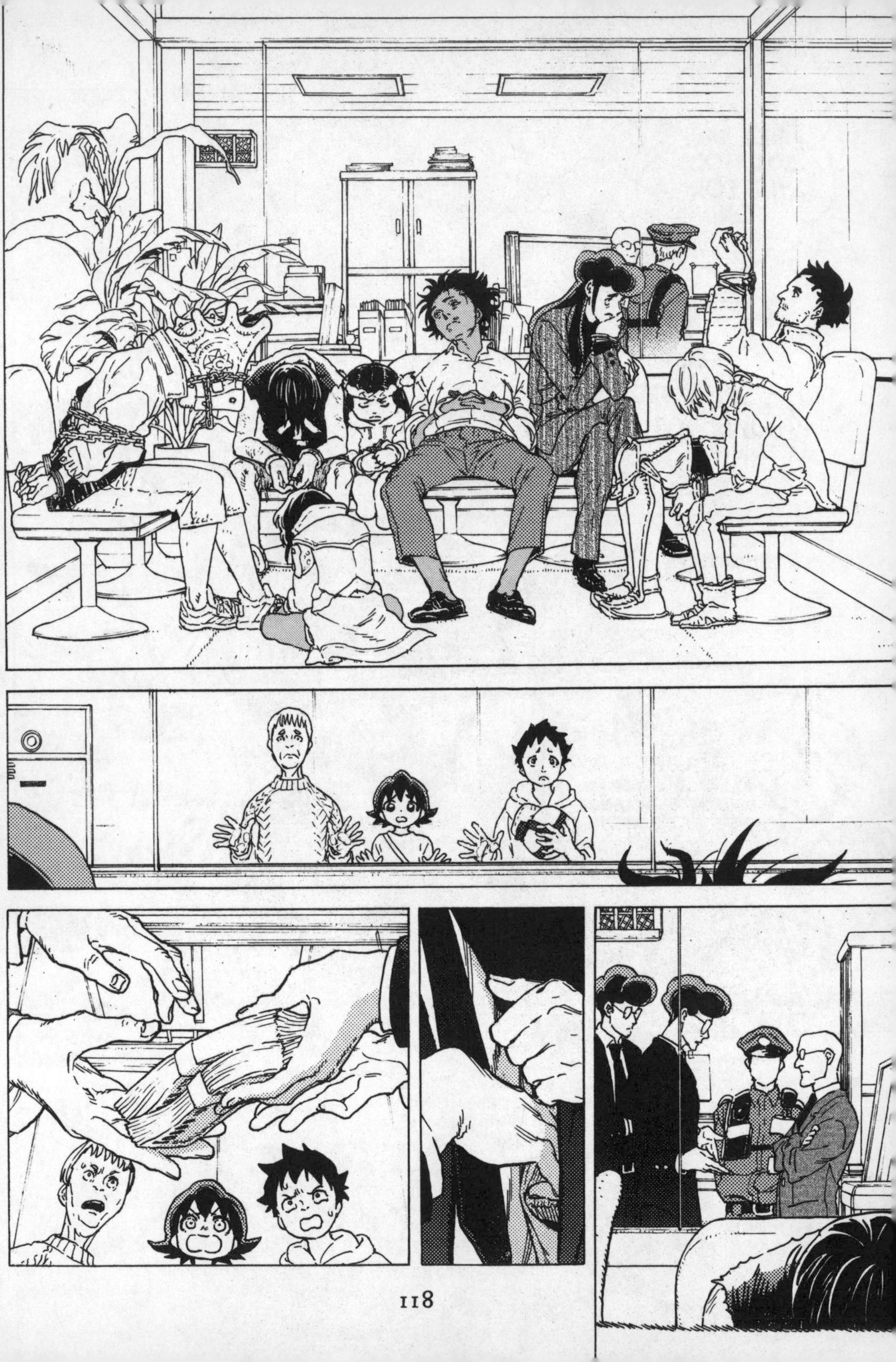

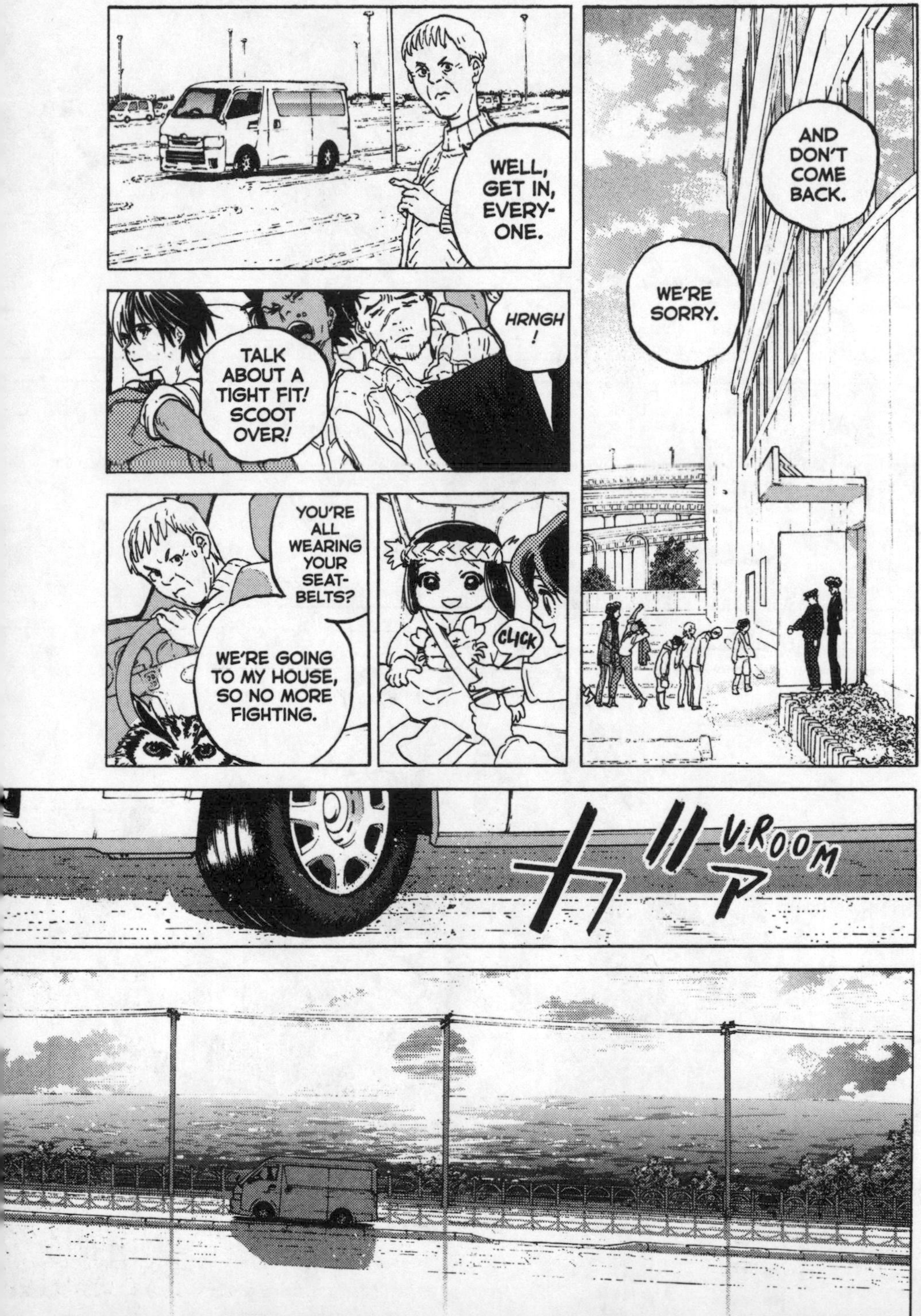
AND DON'T COME BACK.
WE'RE SORRY.
WELL, GET IN, EVERY-ONE.
HRNGH!
TALK ABOUT A TIGHT FIT! SCOOT OVER!
CLICK
YOU'RE ALL WEARING YOUR SEAT-BELTS?
WE'RE GOING TO MY HOUSE, SO NO MORE FIGHTING.
VROOM

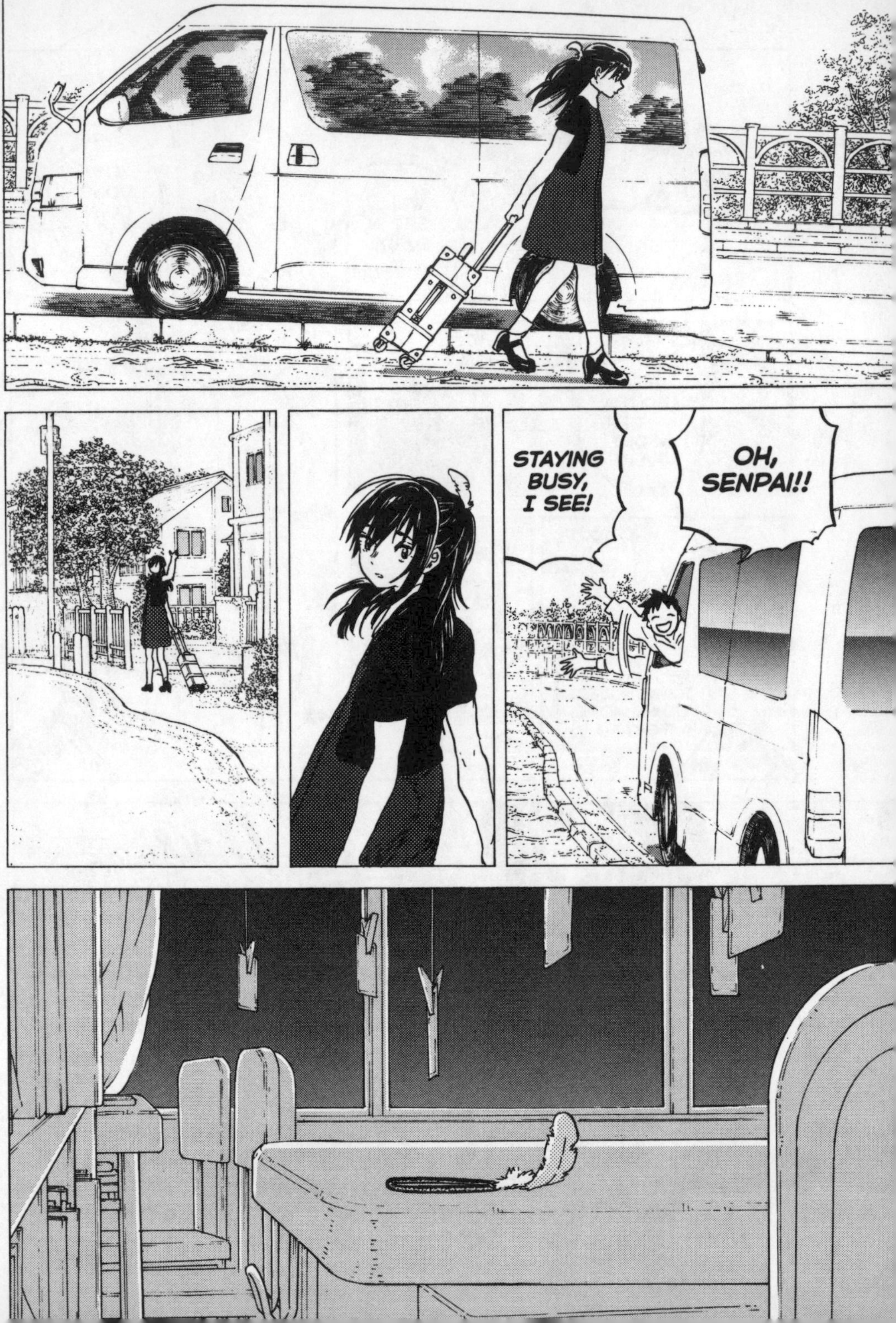
OH, SENPAI!!
STAYING BUSY, I SEE!

#122 Bound Hearts

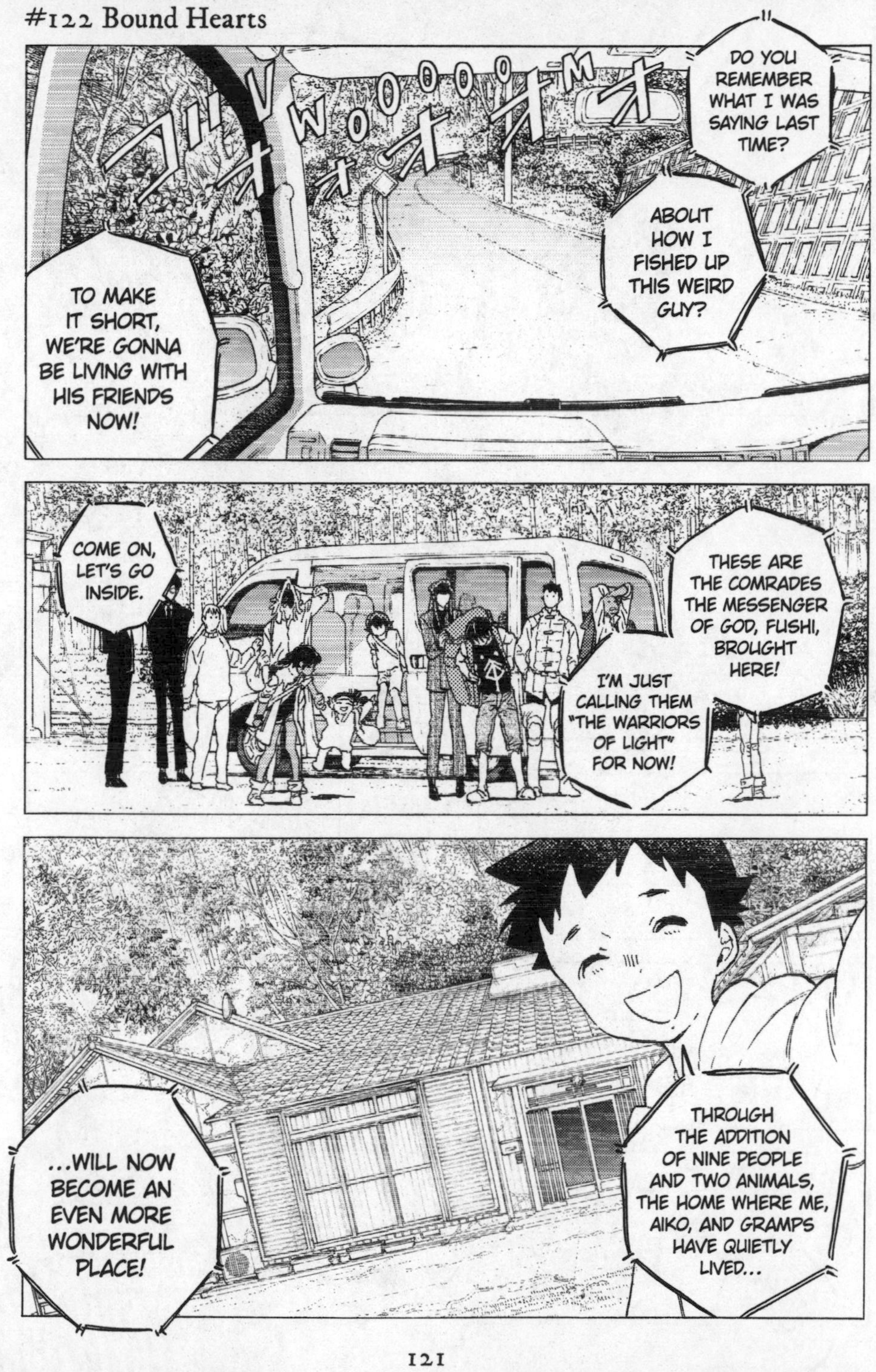
VWOOOOOM
DO YOU REMEMBER WHAT I WAS SAYING LAST TIME?
ABOUT HOW I FISHED UP THIS WEIRD GUY?
TO MAKE IT SHORT, WE'RE GONNA BE LIVING WITH HIS FRIENDS NOW!
THESE ARE THE COMRADES THE MESSENGER OF GOD, FUSHI, BROUGHT HERE!
I'M JUST CALLING THEM "THE WARRIORS OF LIGHT" FOR NOW!
COME ON, LET'S GO INSIDE.
THROUGH THE ADDITION OF NINE PEOPLE AND TWO ANIMALS, THE HOME WHERE ME, AIKO, AND GRAMPS HAVE QUIETLY LIVED...
...WILL NOW BECOME AN EVEN MORE WONDERFUL PLACE!

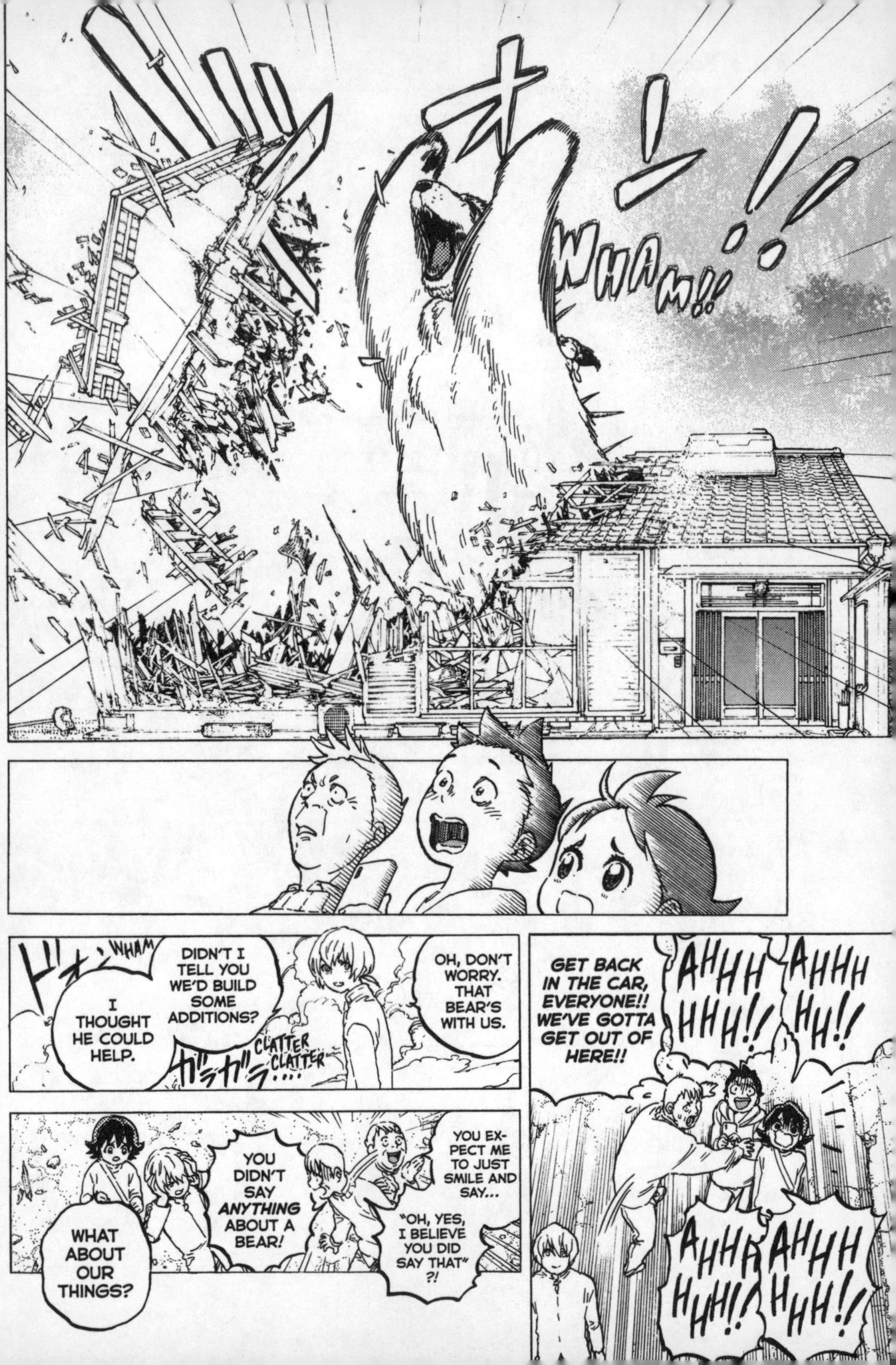
WHAM!!
GET BACK IN THE CAR, EVERYONE!! WE'VE GOTTA GET OUT OF HERE!!
AHHHHHH!!
AHHHHH!!
AHHHHHH!!
AHHHHHH!!
OH, DON'T WORRY. THAT BEAR'S WITH US.
DIDN'T I TELL YOU WE'D BUILD SOME ADDITIONS?
WHAM
I THOUGHT HE COULD HELP.
CLATTER CLATTER....
YOU EXPECT ME TO JUST SMILE AND SAY...
"OH, YES, I BELIEVE YOU DID SAY THAT"?!
YOU DIDN'T SAY *ANYTHING* ABOUT A BEAR!
WHAT ABOUT OUR THINGS?

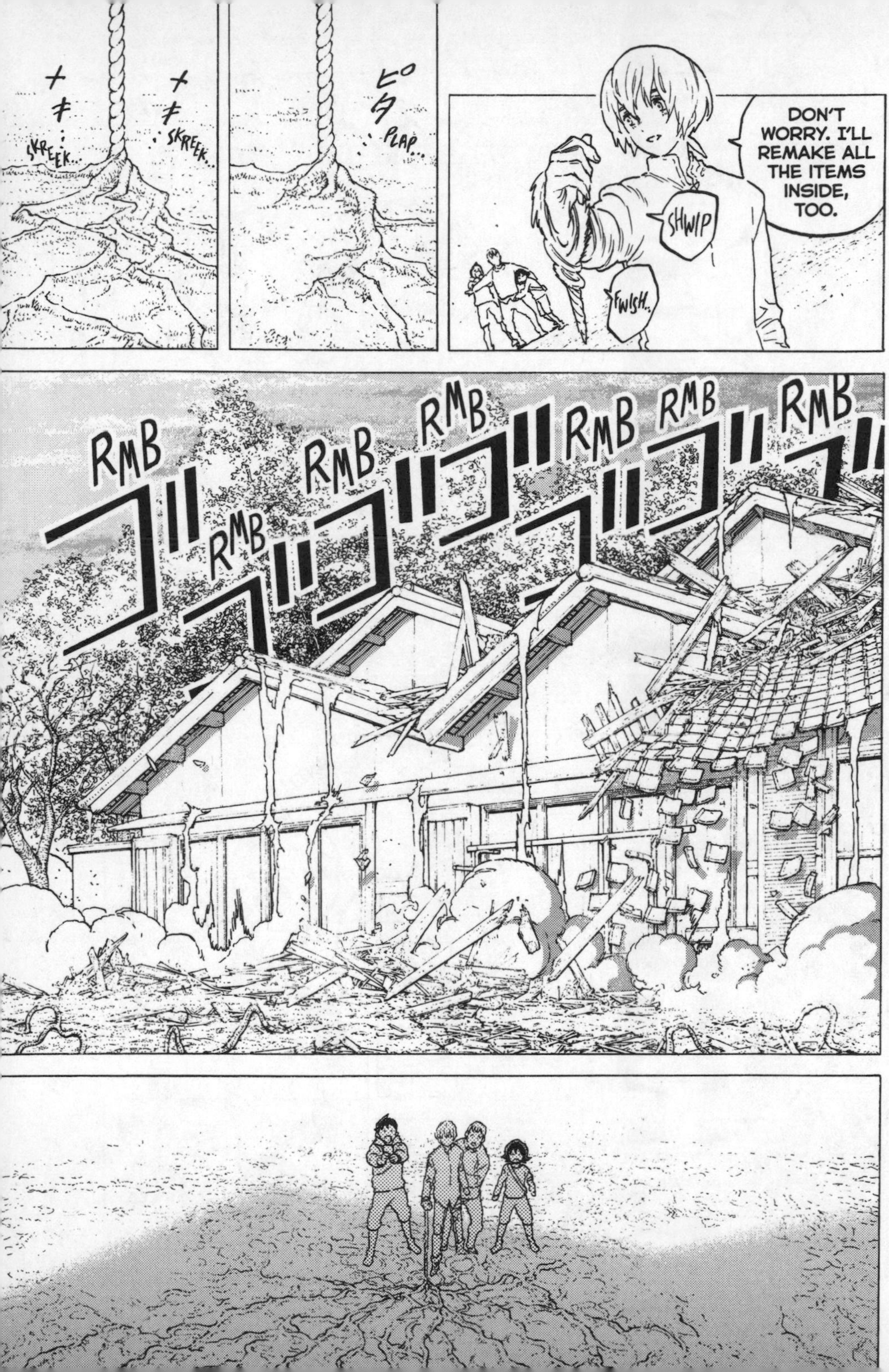

DON'T WORRY. I'LL REMAKE ALL THE ITEMS INSIDE, TOO.
SHWIP
FWISH...
ピタ
PLAP...
SKREEK...
SKREEK...
RMB RMB RMB RMB RMB RMB RMB

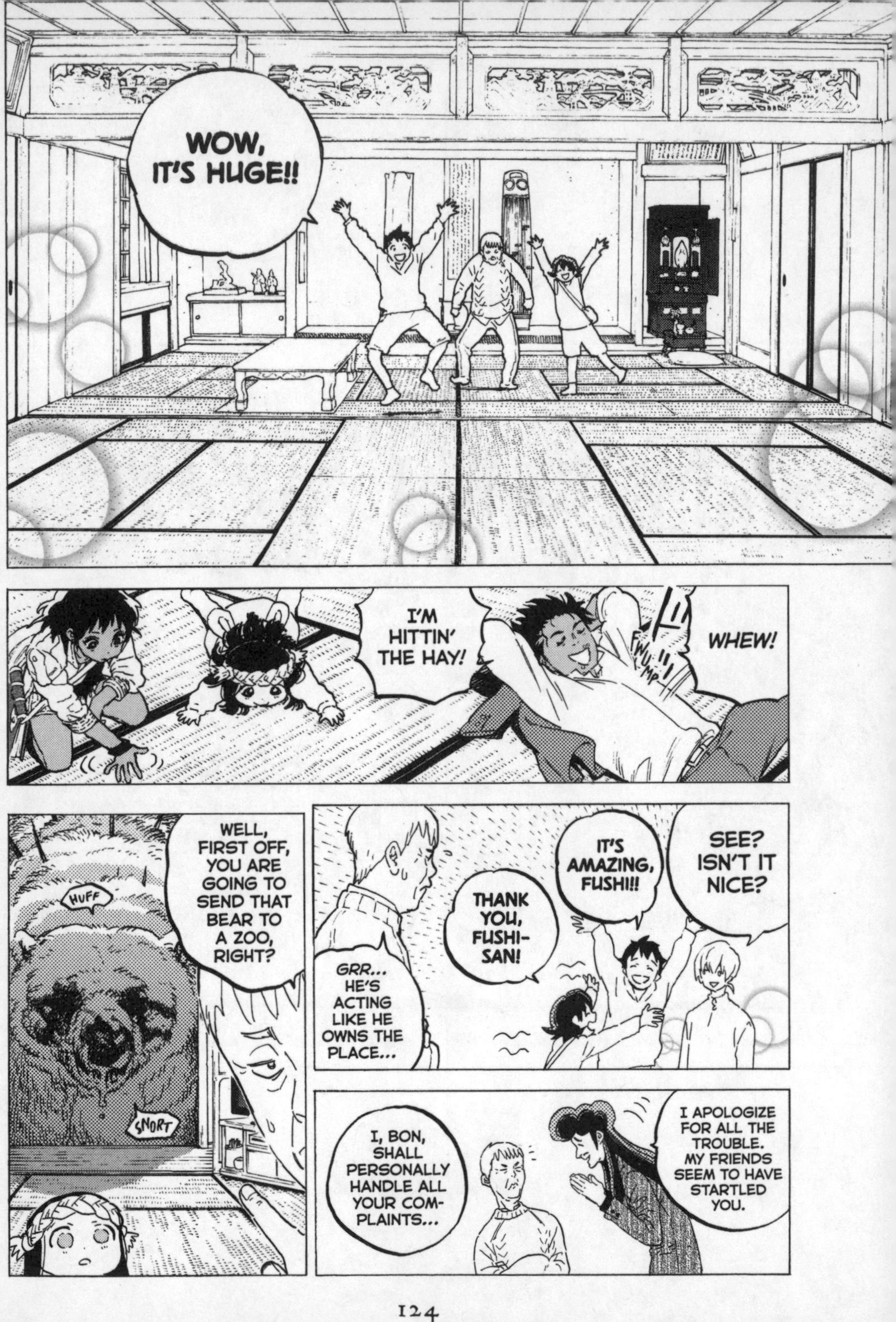
WOW, IT'S HUGE!!
WHEW!
FWUMP
I'M HITTIN' THE HAY!
SEE? ISN'T IT NICE?
IT'S AMAZING, FUSHI!!!
THANK YOU, FUSHI-SAN!
GRR... HE'S ACTING LIKE HE OWNS THE PLACE...
I APOLOGIZE FOR ALL THE TROUBLE. MY FRIENDS SEEM TO HAVE STARTLED YOU.
I, BON, SHALL PERSONALLY HANDLE ALL YOUR COM-PLAINTS...
WELL, FIRST OFF, YOU ARE GOING TO SEND THAT BEAR TO A ZOO, RIGHT?
HUFF
SNORT

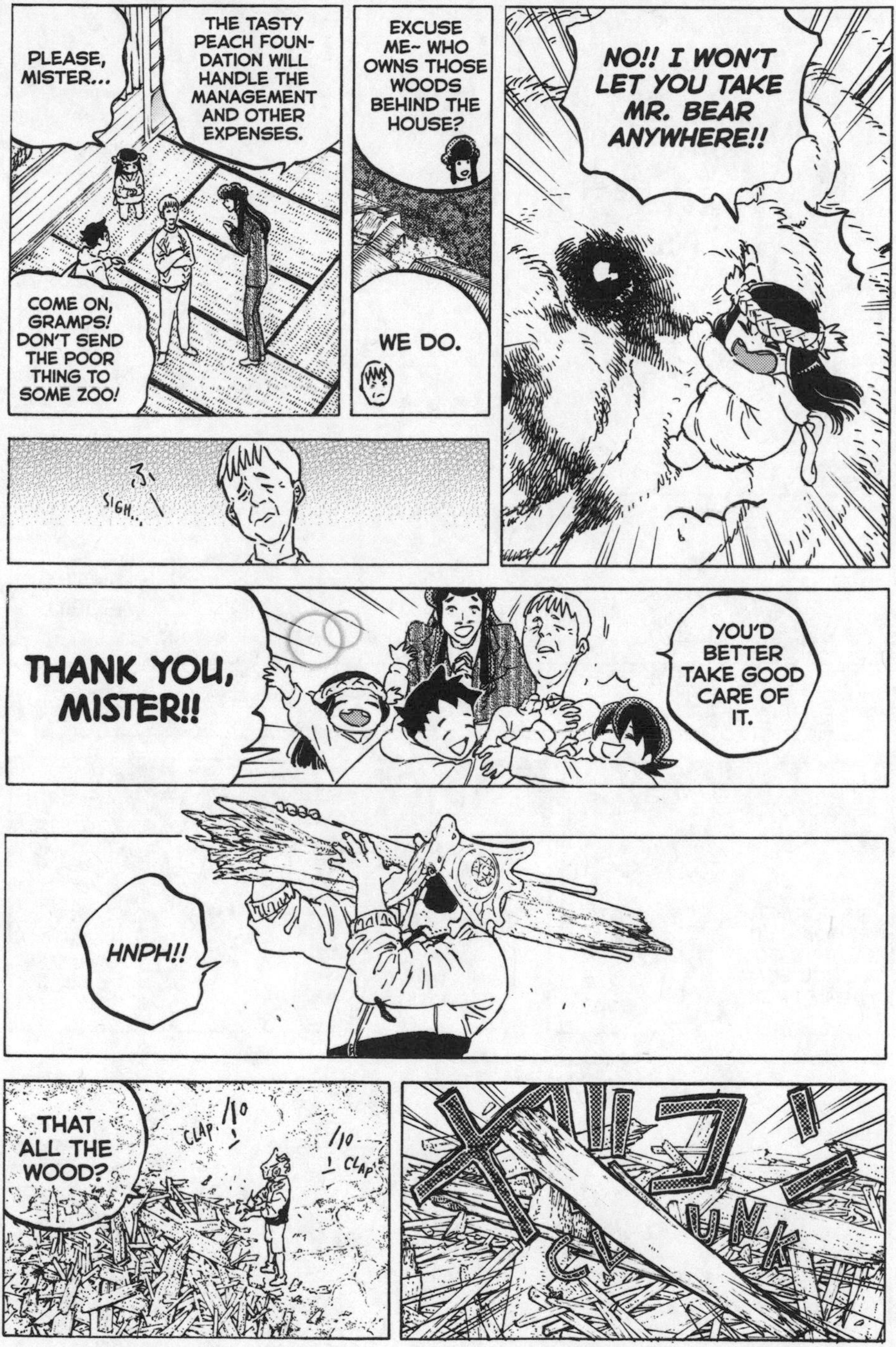
NO!! I WON'T LET YOU TAKE MR. BEAR ANYWHERE!!
EXCUSE ME~ WHO OWNS THOSE WOODS BEHIND THE HOUSE?
WE DO.
THE TASTY PEACH FOUNDATION WILL HANDLE THE MANAGEMENT AND OTHER EXPENSES.
PLEASE, MISTER...
COME ON, GRAMPS! DON'T SEND THE POOR THING TO SOME ZOO!
SIGH...
YOU'D BETTER TAKE GOOD CARE OF IT.
THANK YOU, MISTER!!
HNPH!!
CLUNK
CLAP
CLAP
THAT ALL THE WOOD?

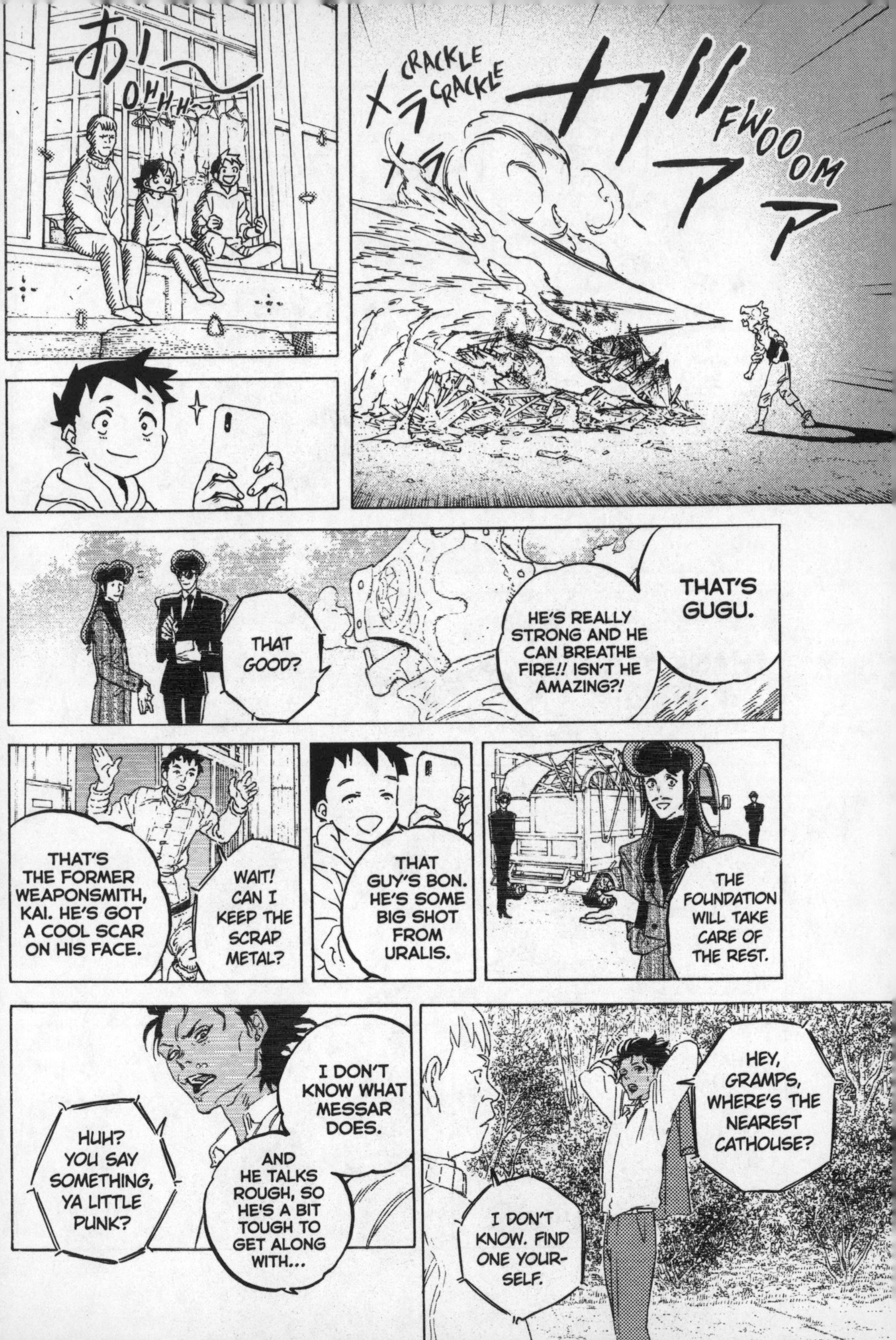
CRACKLE CRACKLE
メラメラ
カアア
FWOOOOM
おー
OHHH
THAT'S GUGU.
HE'S REALLY STRONG AND HE CAN BREATHE FIRE!! ISN'T HE AMAZING?!
THAT GOOD?
THE FOUNDATION WILL TAKE CARE OF THE REST.
THAT GUY'S BON. HE'S SOME BIG SHOT FROM URALIS.
WAIT! CAN I KEEP THE SCRAP METAL?
THAT'S THE FORMER WEAPONSMITH, KAI. HE'S GOT A COOL SCAR ON HIS FACE.
HEY, GRAMPS, WHERE'S THE NEAREST CATHOUSE?
I DON'T KNOW. FIND ONE YOURSELF.
I DON'T KNOW WHAT MESSAR DOES.
AND HE TALKS ROUGH, SO HE'S A BIT TOUGH TO GET ALONG WITH...
HUH? YOU SAY SOMETHING, YA LITTLE PUNK?

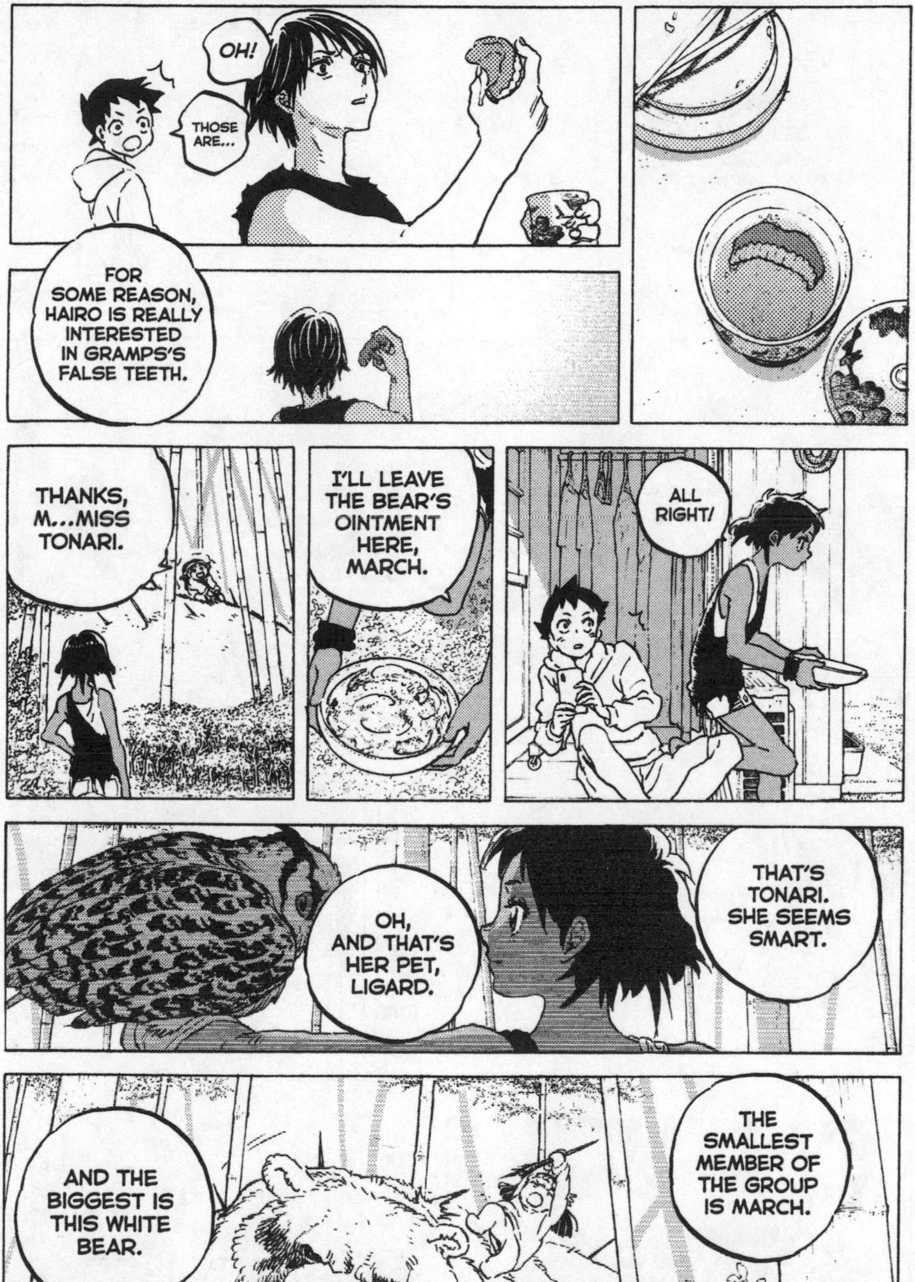
OH!
THOSE ARE...
FOR SOME REASON, HAIRO IS REALLY INTERESTED IN GRAMPS'S FALSE TEETH.
ALL RIGHT!
I'LL LEAVE THE BEAR'S OINTMENT HERE, MARCH.
THANKS, M...MISS TONARI.
THAT'S TONARI. SHE SEEMS SMART.
OH, AND THAT'S HER PET, LIGARD.
THE SMALLEST MEMBER OF THE GROUP IS MARCH.
AND THE BIGGEST IS THIS WHITE BEAR.

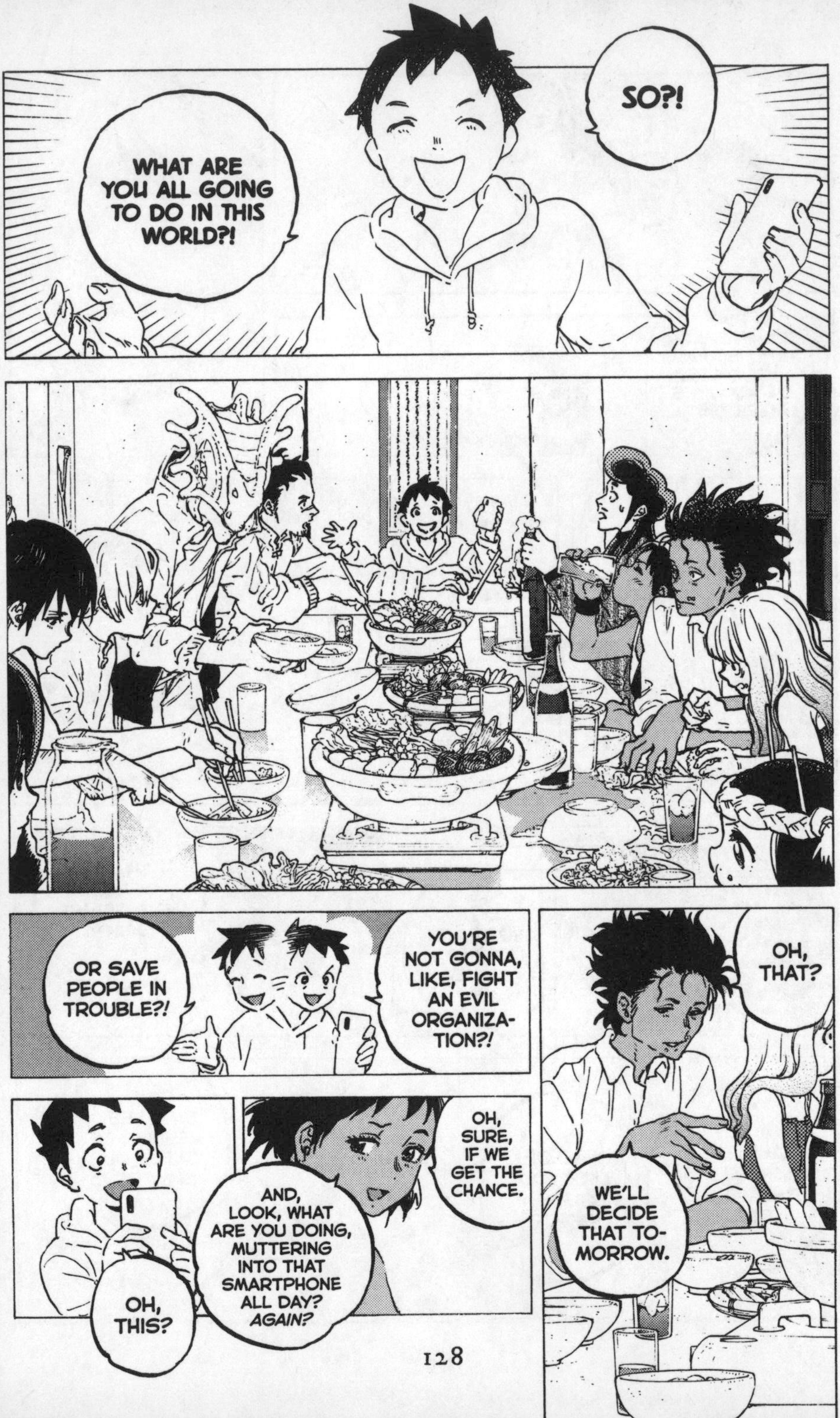
SO?!
WHAT ARE YOU ALL GOING TO DO IN THIS WORLD?!
OH, THAT?
WE'LL DECIDE THAT TO-MORROW.
YOU'RE NOT GONNA, LIKE, FIGHT AN EVIL ORGANIZA-TION?!
OR SAVE PEOPLE IN TROUBLE?!
OH, SURE, IF WE GET THE CHANCE.
AND, LOOK, WHAT ARE YOU DOING, MUTTERING INTO THAT SMARTPHONE ALL DAY? *AGAIN?*
OH, THIS?

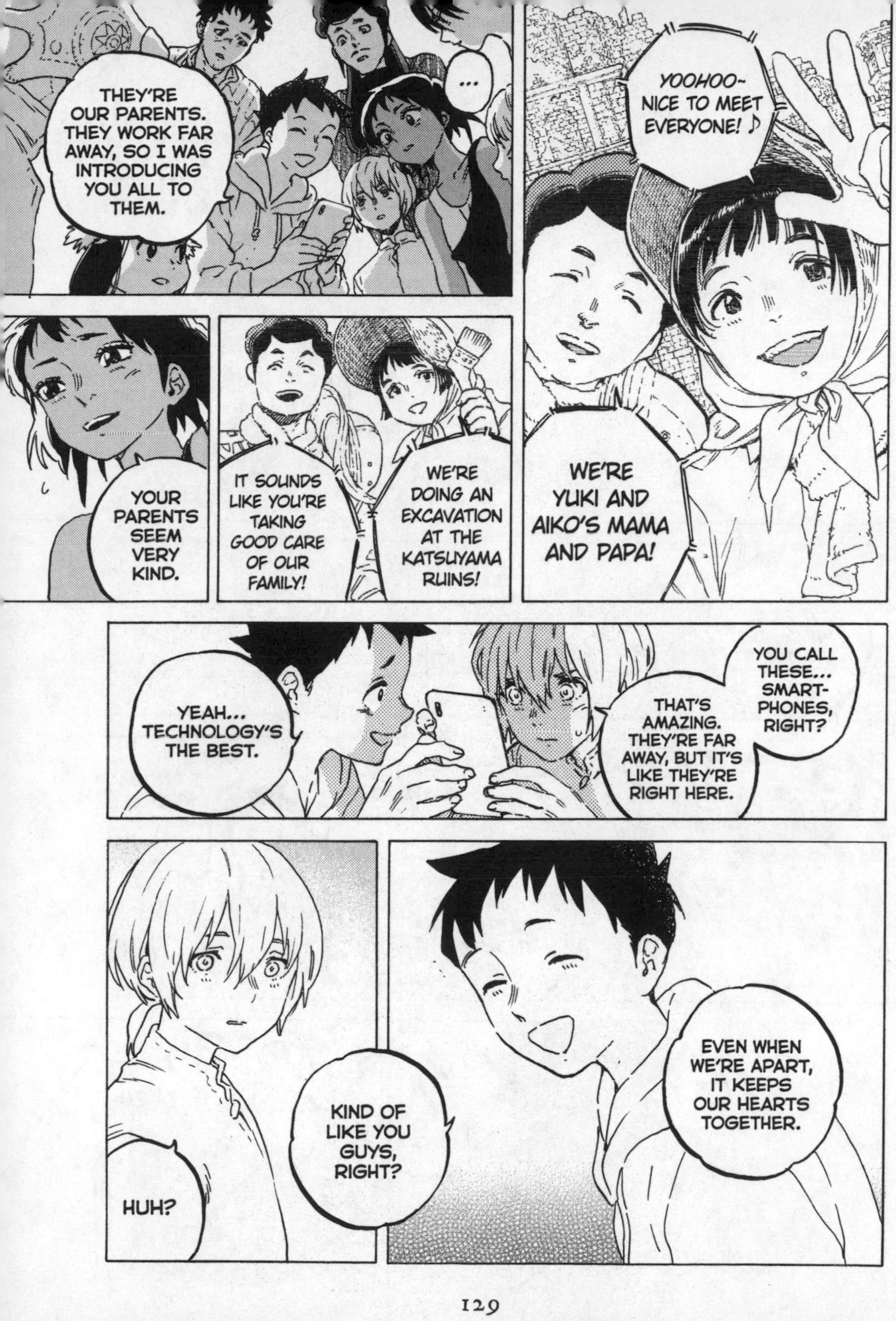
YOOHOO~ NICE TO MEET EVERYONE! ♪
WE'RE YUKI AND AIKO'S MAMA AND PAPA!
...
THEY'RE OUR PARENTS. THEY WORK FAR AWAY, SO I WAS INTRODUCING YOU ALL TO THEM.
WE'RE DOING AN EXCAVATION AT THE KATSUYAMA RUINS!
IT SOUNDS LIKE YOU'RE TAKING GOOD CARE OF OUR FAMILY!
YOUR PARENTS SEEM VERY KIND.
YOU CALL THESE... SMART-PHONES, RIGHT?
THAT'S AMAZING. THEY'RE FAR AWAY, BUT IT'S LIKE THEY'RE RIGHT HERE.
YEAH... TECHNOLOGY'S THE BEST.
EVEN WHEN WE'RE APART, IT KEEPS OUR HEARTS TOGETHER.
KIND OF LIKE YOU GUYS, RIGHT?
HUH?

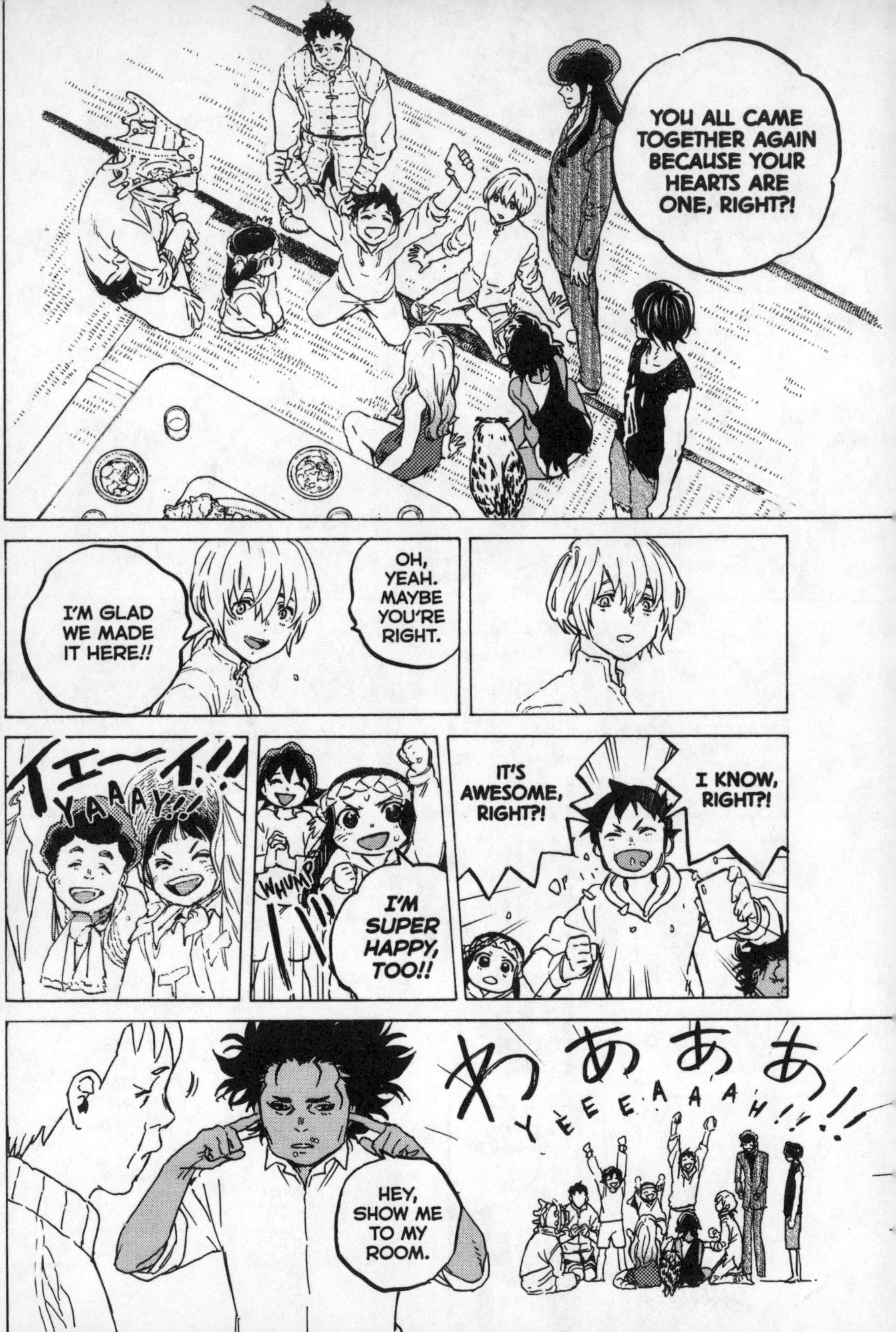
YOU ALL CAME TOGETHER AGAIN BECAUSE YOUR HEARTS ARE ONE, RIGHT?!
OH, YEAH. MAYBE YOU'RE RIGHT.
I'M GLAD WE MADE IT HERE!!
I KNOW, RIGHT?!
IT'S AWESOME, RIGHT?!
WHUMP
I'M SUPER HAPPY, TOO!!
イエ～イ!!
YAAAY!!
わあああ
YEEEAAAAH!!!!
HEY, SHOW ME TO MY ROOM.

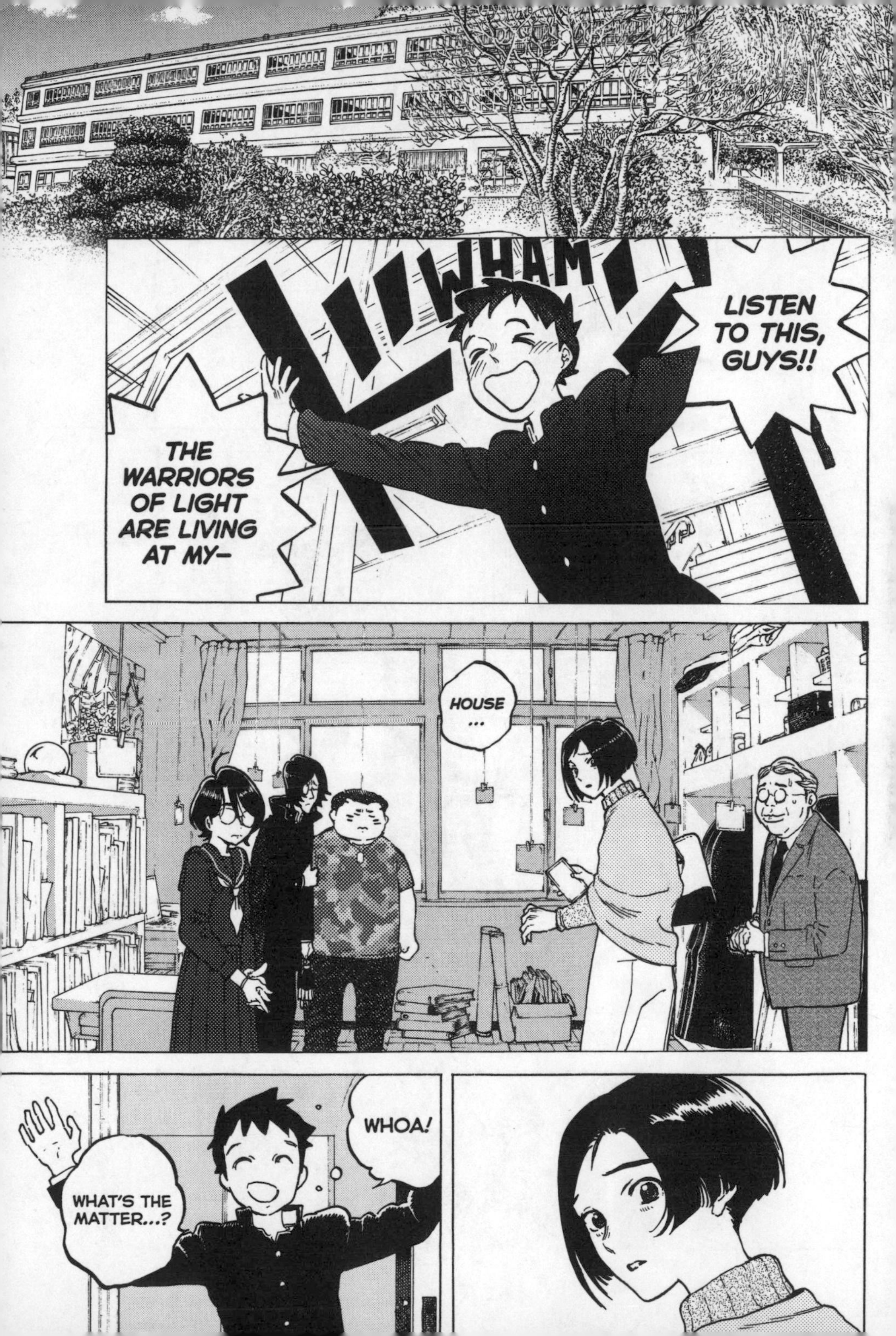
WHAM
LISTEN TO THIS, GUYS!!
THE WARRIORS OF LIGHT ARE LIVING AT MY–
HOUSE ...
WHOA!
WHAT'S THE MATTER...?

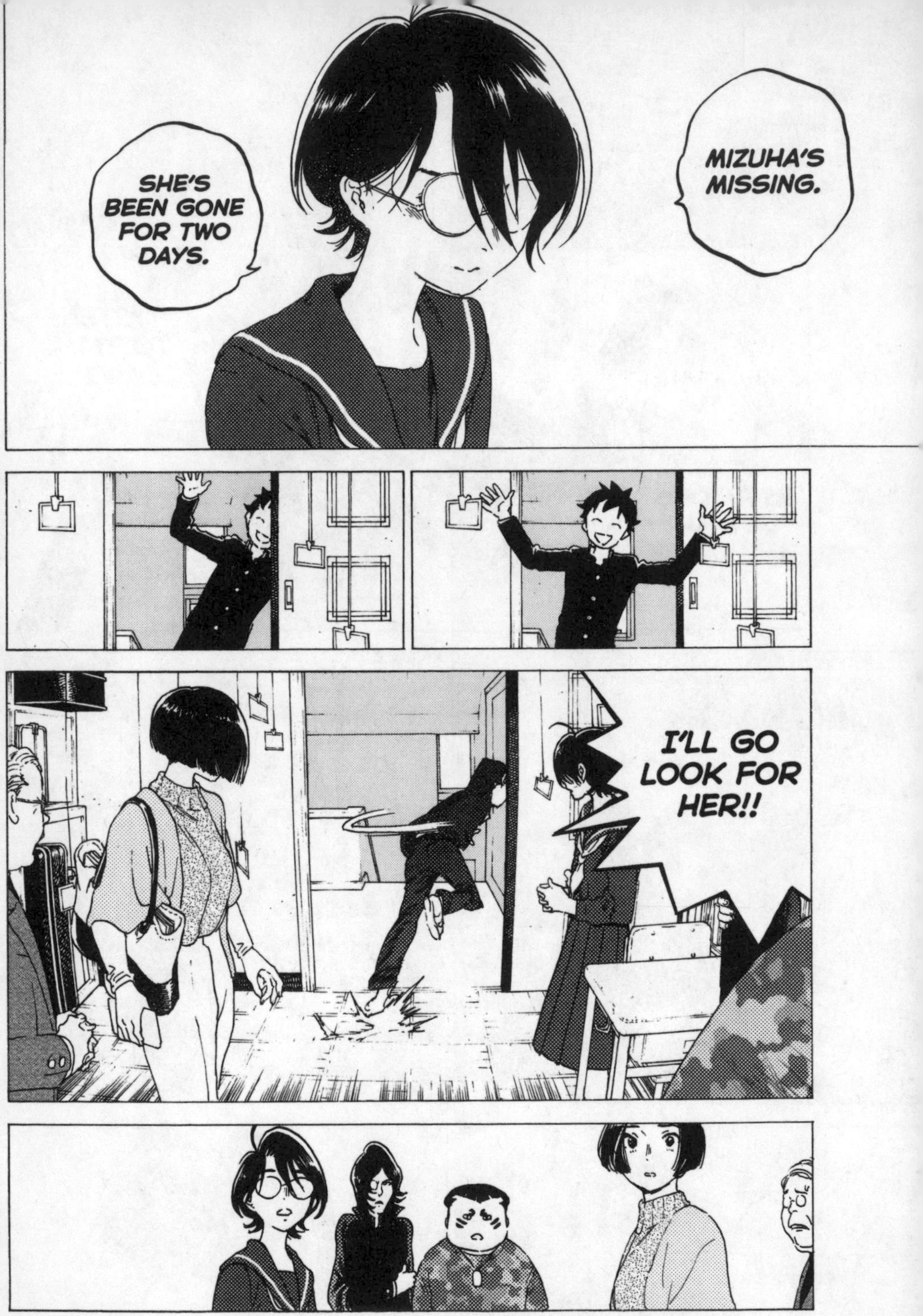
MIZUHA'S MISSING.
SHE'S BEEN GONE FOR TWO DAYS.
I'LL GO LOOK FOR HER!!

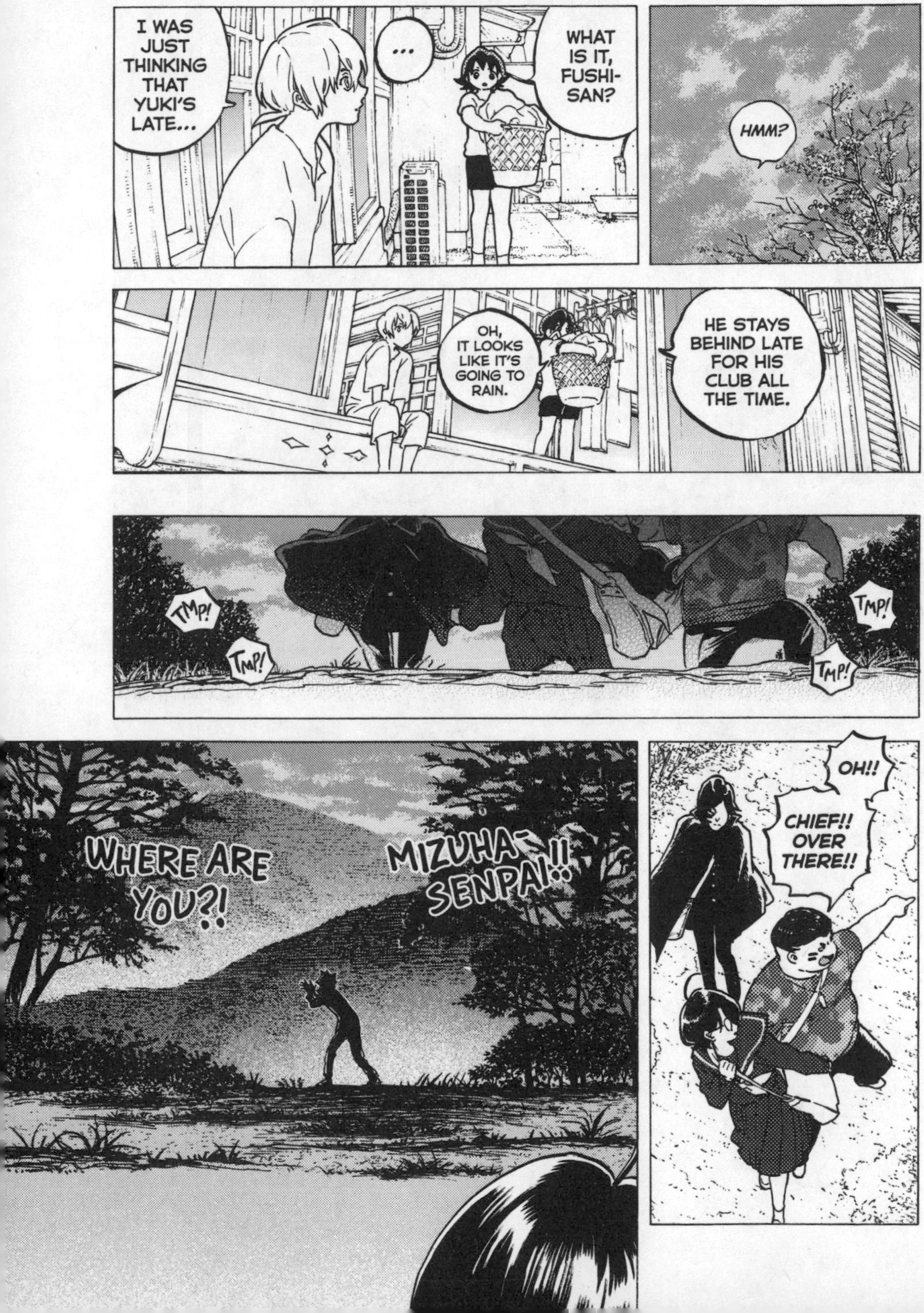
HMM?
WHAT IS IT, FUSHI-SAN?
...
I WAS JUST THINKING THAT YUKI'S LATE...
HE STAYS BEHIND LATE FOR HIS CLUB ALL THE TIME.
OH, IT LOOKS LIKE IT'S GOING TO RAIN.
TMP!
TMP!
TMP!
TMP!
OH!!
CHIEF!! OVER THERE!!
MIZUHA-SENPAI!!
WHERE ARE YOU?!

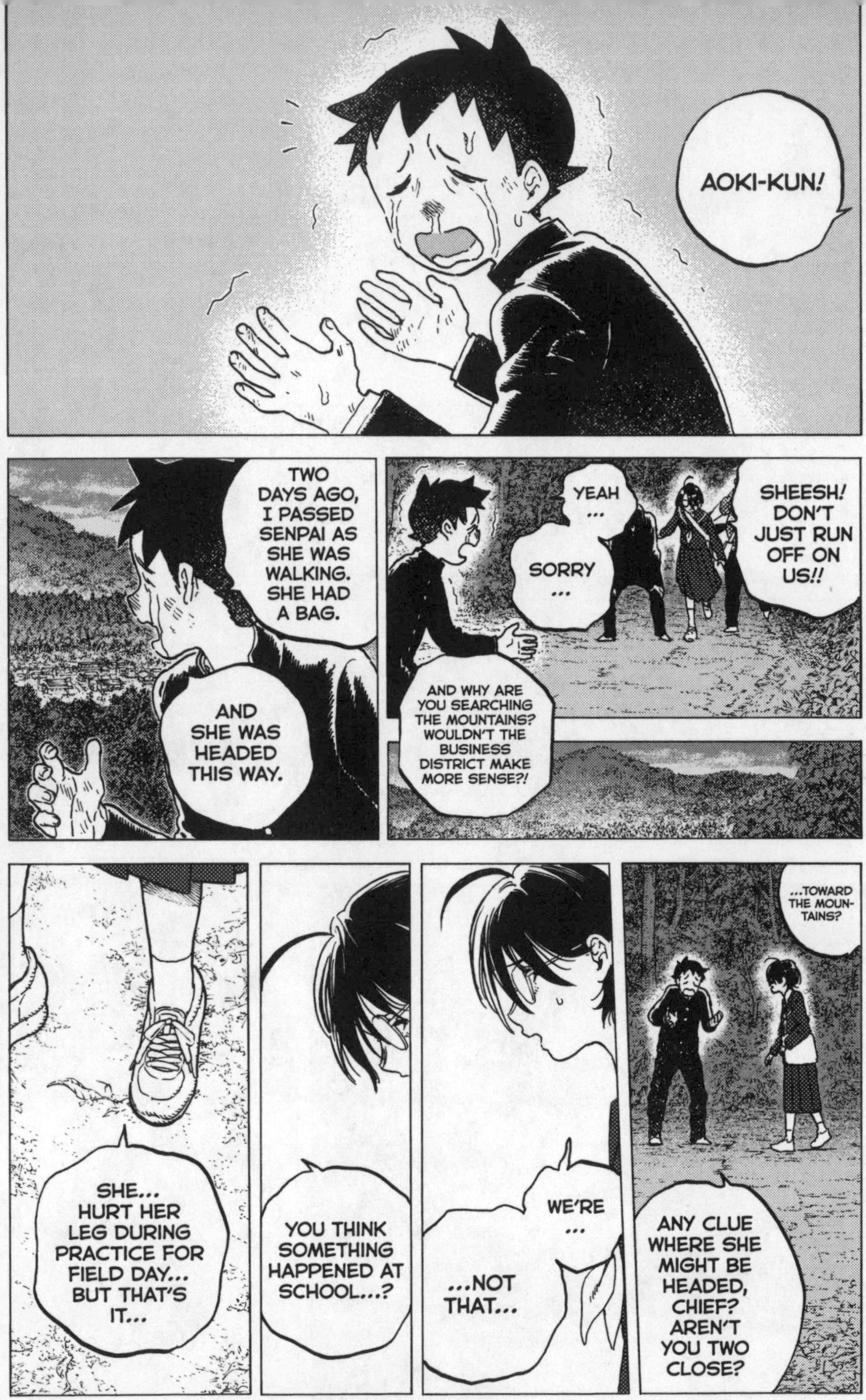
AOKI-KUN!
SHEESH! DON'T JUST RUN OFF ON US!!
YEAH ...
SORRY ...
AND WHY ARE YOU SEARCHING THE MOUNTAINS? WOULDN'T THE BUSINESS DISTRICT MAKE MORE SENSE?!
TWO DAYS AGO, I PASSED SENPAI AS SHE WAS WALKING. SHE HAD A BAG.
AND SHE WAS HEADED THIS WAY.
...TOWARD THE MOUN-TAINS?
ANY CLUE WHERE SHE MIGHT BE HEADED, CHIEF? AREN'T YOU TWO CLOSE?
WE'RE ...
...NOT THAT...
YOU THINK SOMETHING HAPPENED AT SCHOOL...?
SHE... HURT HER LEG DURING PRACTICE FOR FIELD DAY... BUT THAT'S IT...

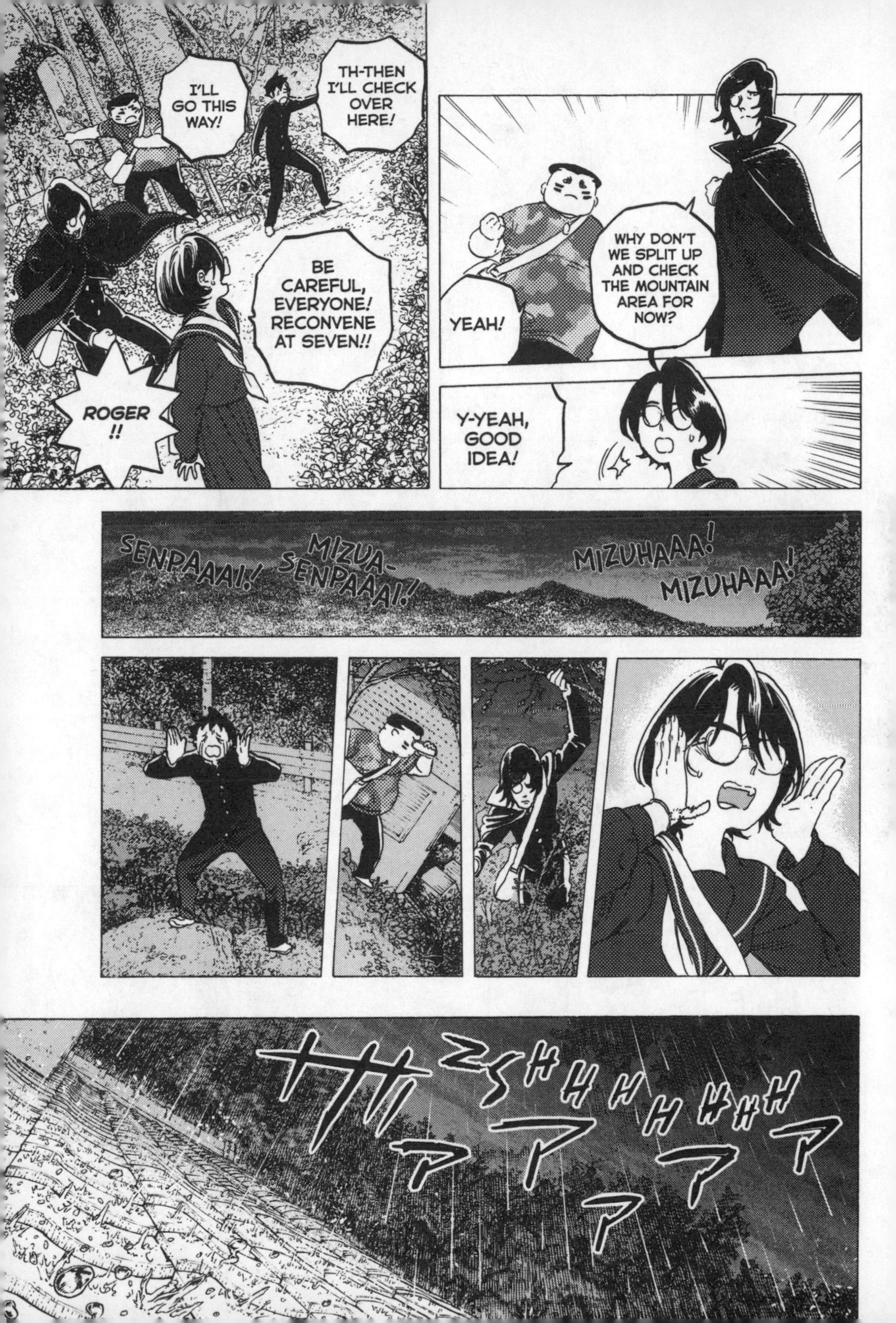
WHY DON'T WE SPLIT UP AND CHECK THE MOUNTAIN AREA FOR NOW?
YEAH!
Y-YEAH, GOOD IDEA!
TH-THEN I'LL CHECK OVER HERE!
I'LL GO THIS WAY!
BE CAREFUL, EVERYONE! RECONVENE AT SEVEN!!
ROGER !!
MIZUHAAA! MIZUHAAA!
MIZUA-SENPAAAI!
SENPAAAI!
ZSHHHHHHH

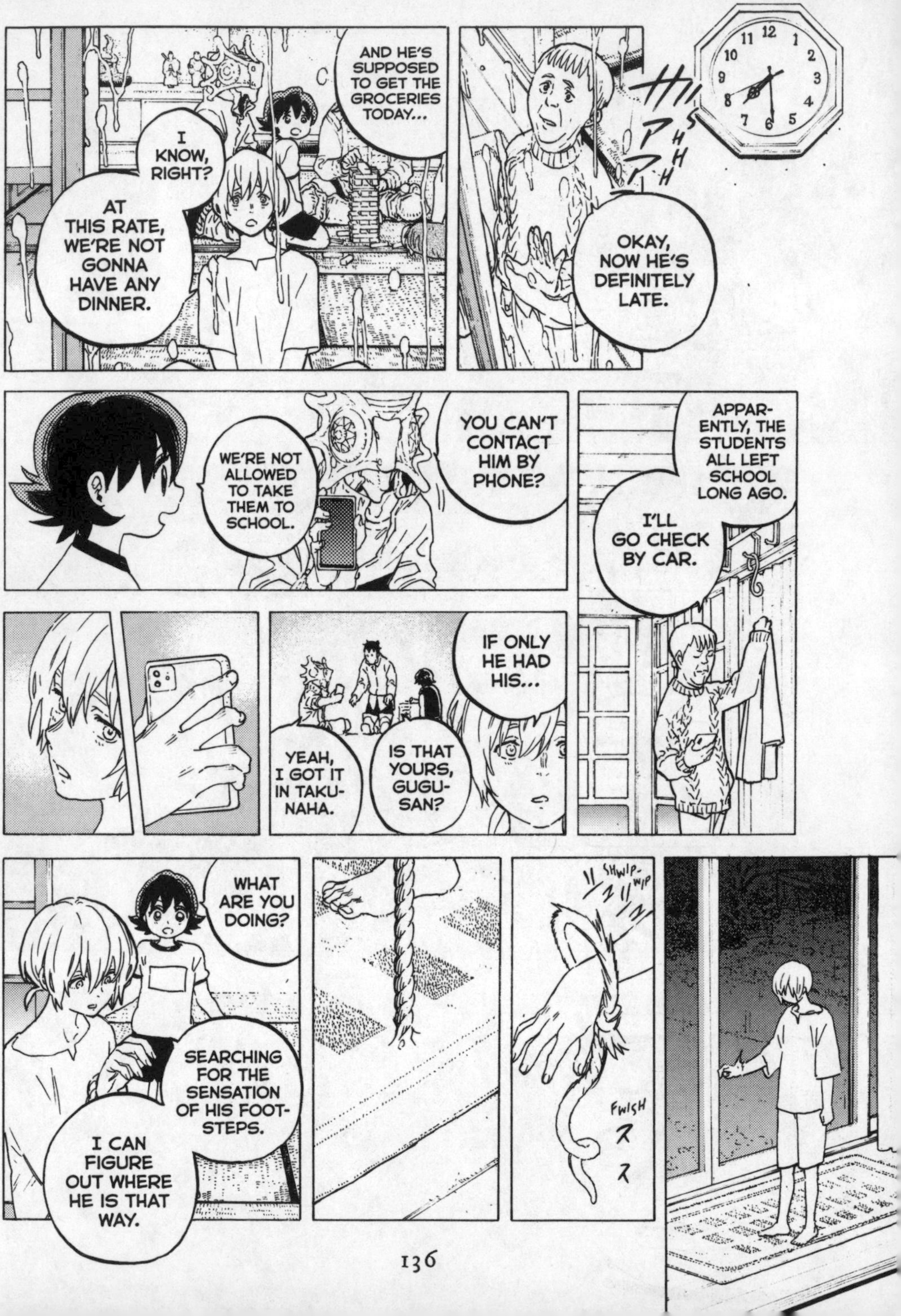
SHHH
OKAY, NOW HE'S DEFINITELY LATE.
AND HE'S SUPPOSED TO GET THE GROCERIES TODAY...
I KNOW, RIGHT?
AT THIS RATE, WE'RE NOT GONNA HAVE ANY DINNER.
APPARENTLY, THE STUDENTS ALL LEFT SCHOOL LONG AGO.
I'LL GO CHECK BY CAR.
YOU CAN'T CONTACT HIM BY PHONE?
WE'RE NOT ALLOWED TO TAKE THEM TO SCHOOL.
IF ONLY HE HAD HIS...
IS THAT YOURS, GUGU-SAN?
YEAH, I GOT IT IN TAKUNAHA.
SHWIP-WIP
FWISH
WHAT ARE YOU DOING?
SEARCHING FOR THE SENSATION OF HIS FOOTSTEPS.
I CAN FIGURE OUT WHERE HE IS THAT WAY.

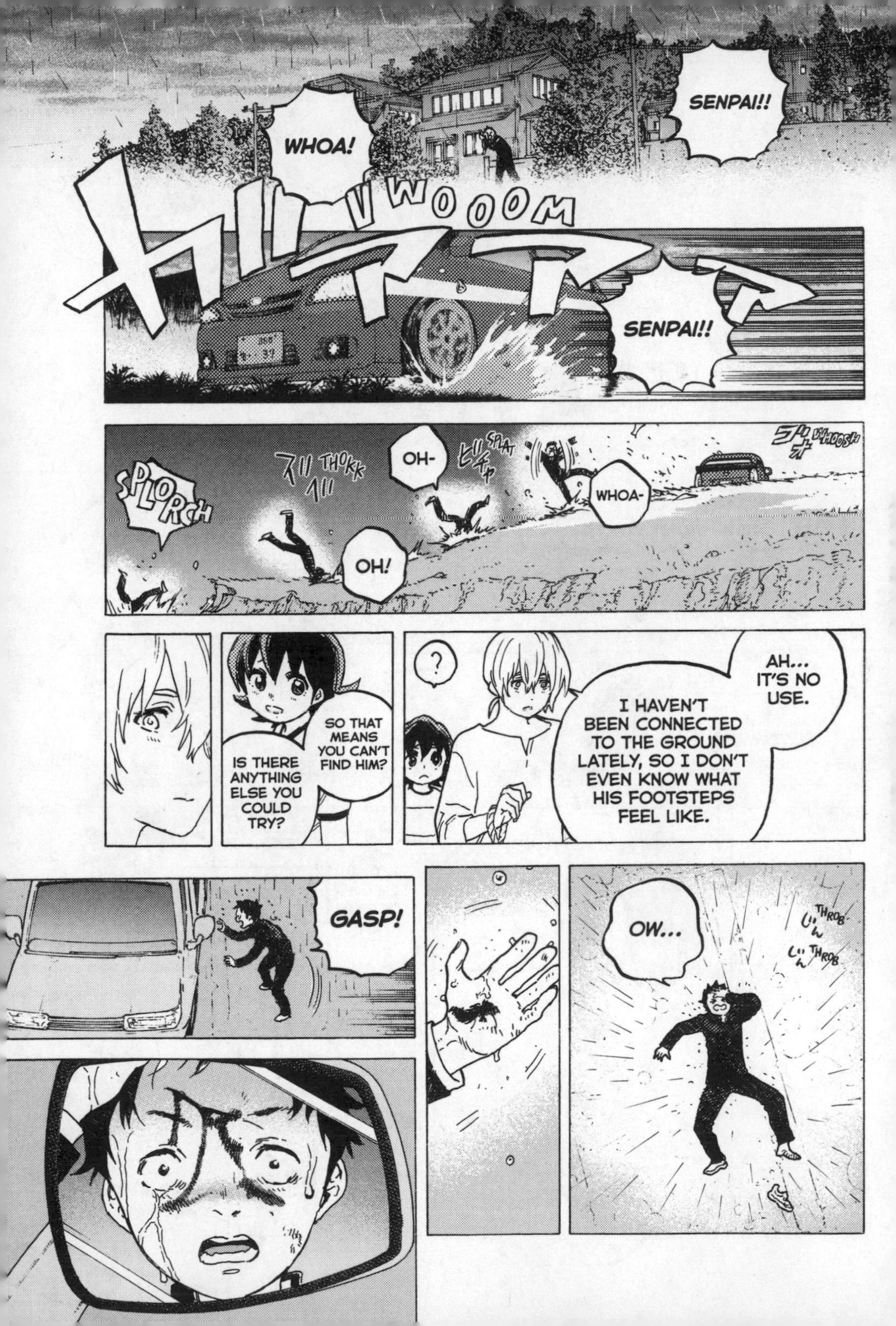
SENPAI!!
WHOA!
VWOOOM
SENPAI!!
WHOOSH
WHOA-
SPLAT
OH-
THOKK
OH!
SPLORCH
AH... IT'S NO USE.
I HAVEN'T BEEN CONNECTED TO THE GROUND LATELY, SO I DON'T EVEN KNOW WHAT HIS FOOTSTEPS FEEL LIKE.
?
SO THAT MEANS YOU CAN'T FIND HIM?
IS THERE ANYTHING ELSE YOU COULD TRY?
OW...
THROB
THROB
GASP!

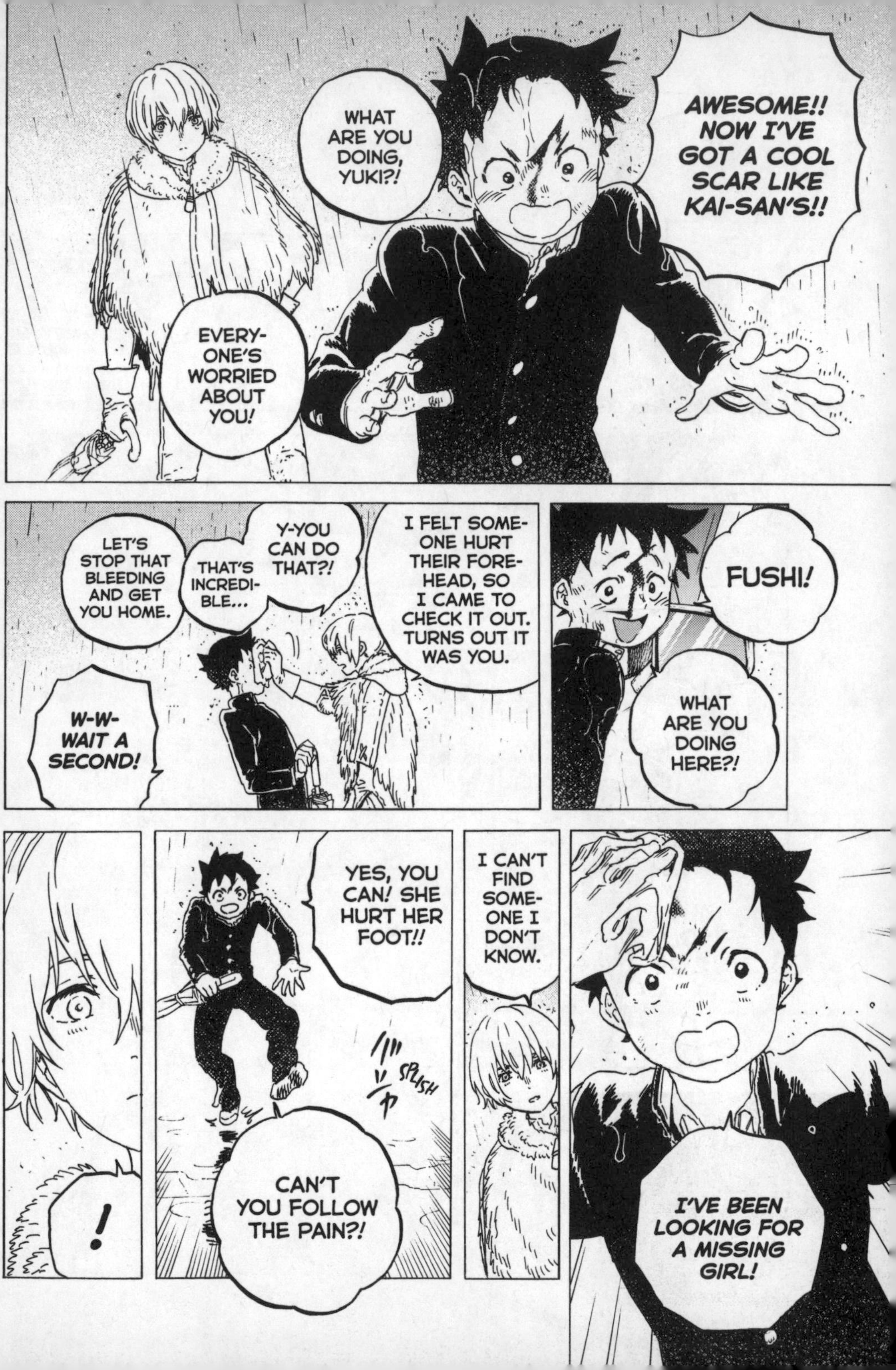
AWESOME!! NOW I'VE GOT A COOL SCAR LIKE KAI-SAN'S!!
WHAT ARE YOU DOING, YUKI?!
EVERY-ONE'S WORRIED ABOUT YOU!
FUSHI!
WHAT ARE YOU DOING HERE?!
I FELT SOME-ONE HURT THEIR FORE-HEAD, SO I CAME TO CHECK IT OUT. TURNS OUT IT WAS YOU.
Y-YOU CAN DO THAT?!
THAT'S INCREDI-BLE...
LET'S STOP THAT BLEEDING AND GET YOU HOME.
W-W-WAIT A SECOND!
I'VE BEEN LOOKING FOR A MISSING GIRL!
I CAN'T FIND SOME-ONE I DON'T KNOW.
YES, YOU CAN! SHE HURT HER FOOT!!
SPLISH
CAN'T YOU FOLLOW THE PAIN?!
!

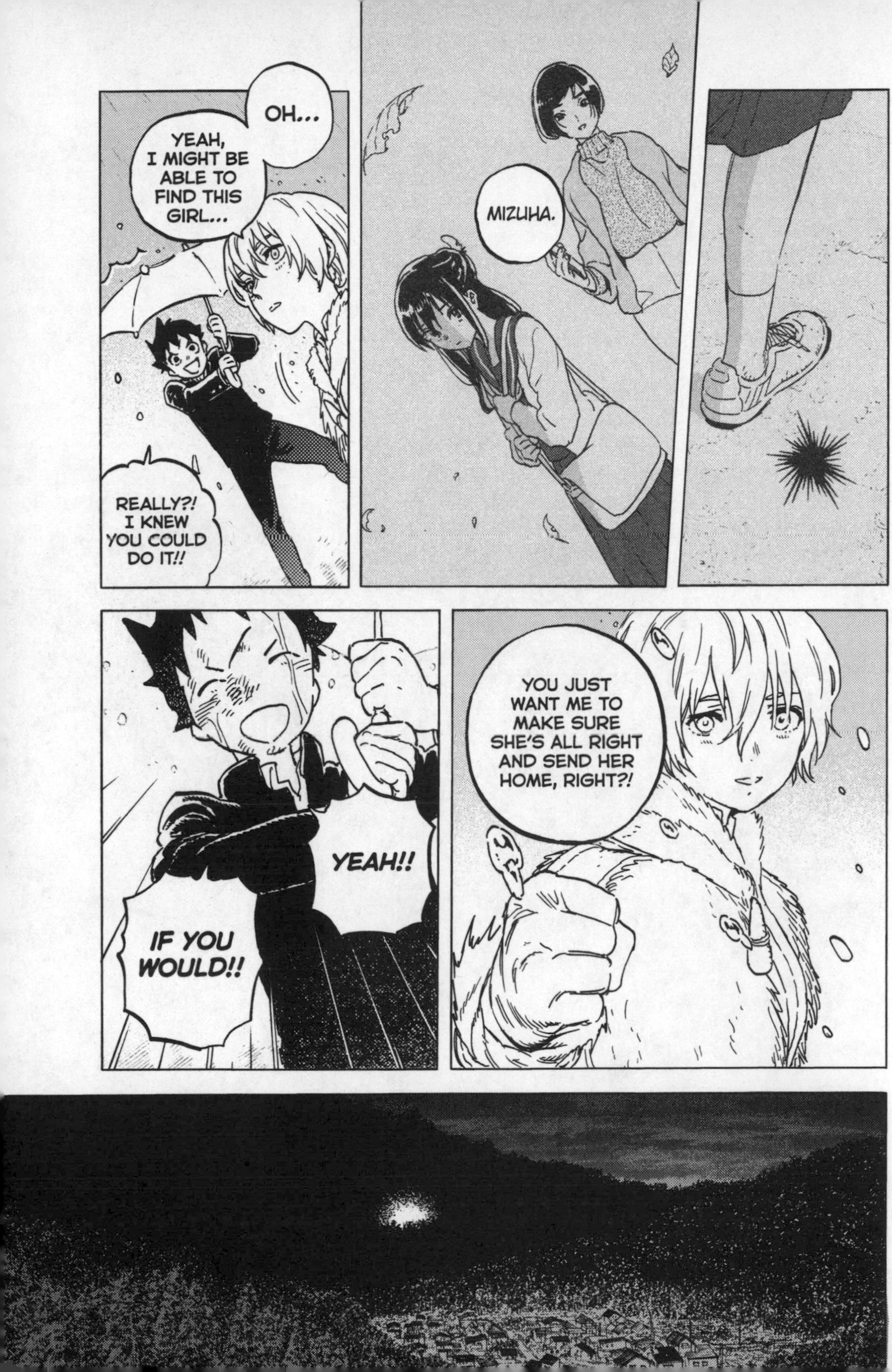
MIZUHA.
OH...
YEAH, I MIGHT BE ABLE TO FIND THIS GIRL...
REALLY?! I KNEW YOU COULD DO IT!!
YOU JUST WANT ME TO MAKE SURE SHE'S ALL RIGHT AND SEND HER HOME, RIGHT?!
YEAH!!
IF YOU WOULD!!

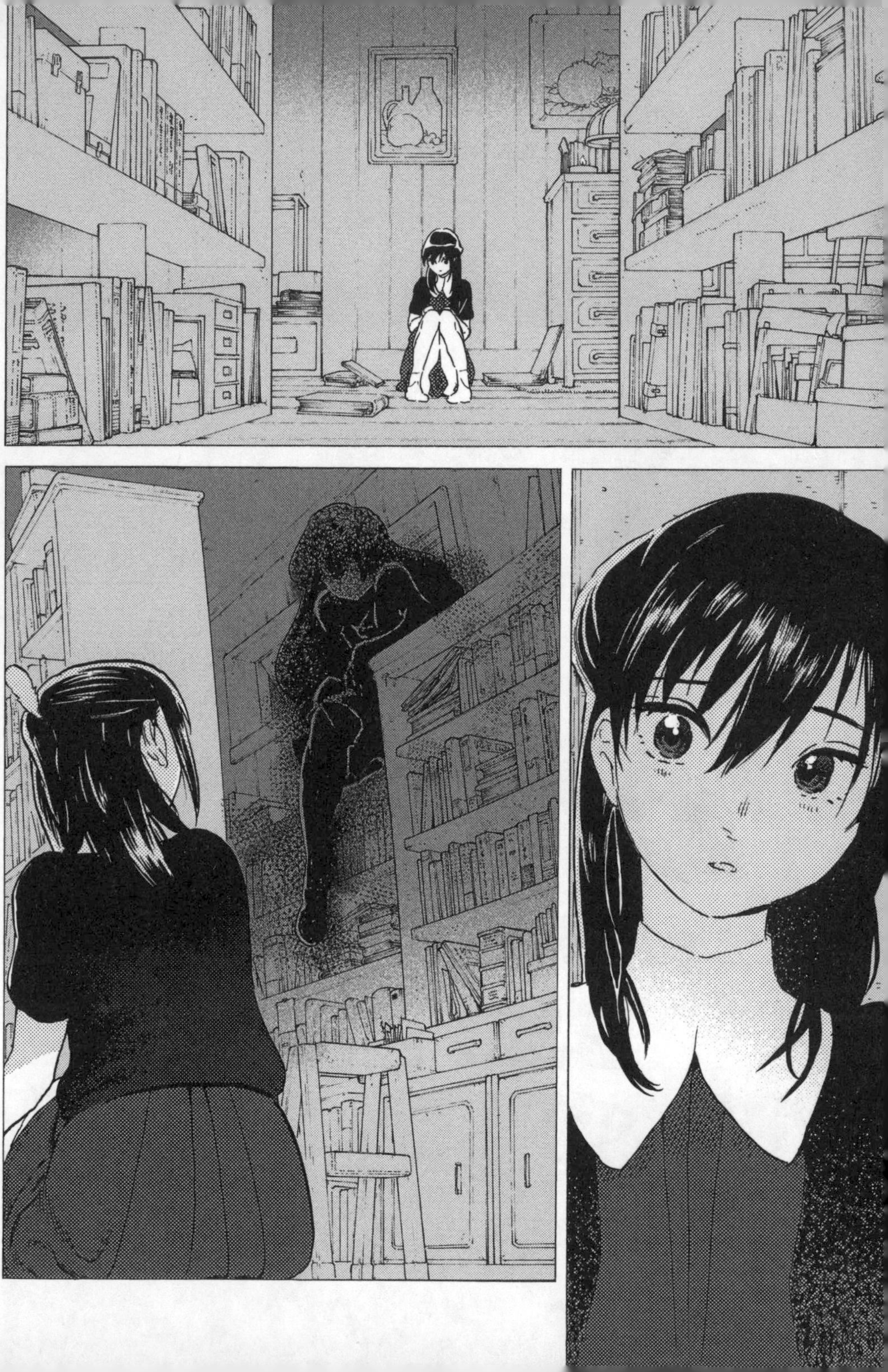

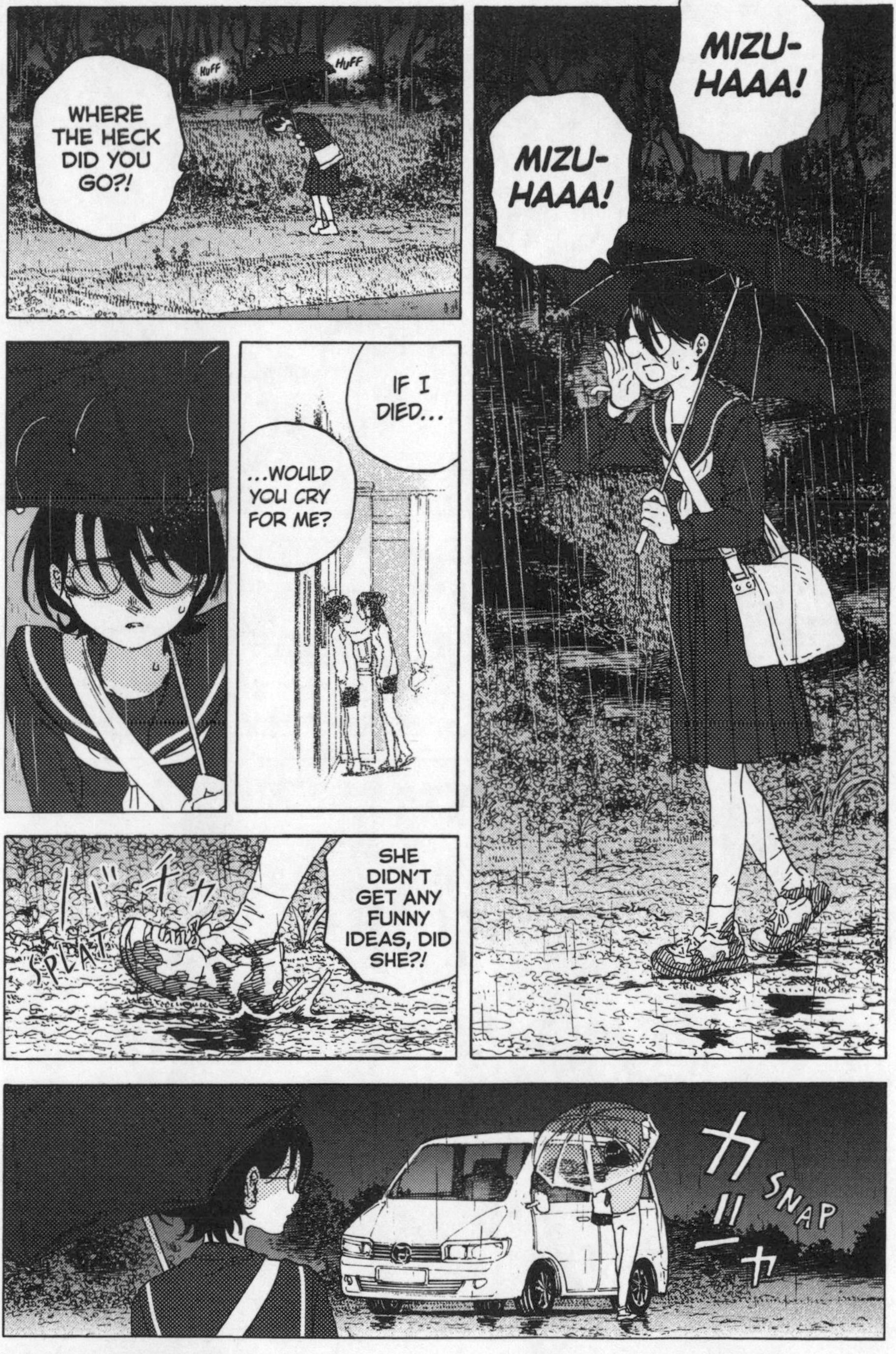
MIZU-HAAA!
MIZU-HAAA!
HUFF
HUFF
WHERE THE HECK DID YOU GO?!
IF I DIED...
...WOULD YOU CRY FOR ME?
SHE DIDN'T GET ANY FUNNY IDEAS, DID SHE?!
SPLAT
SNAP

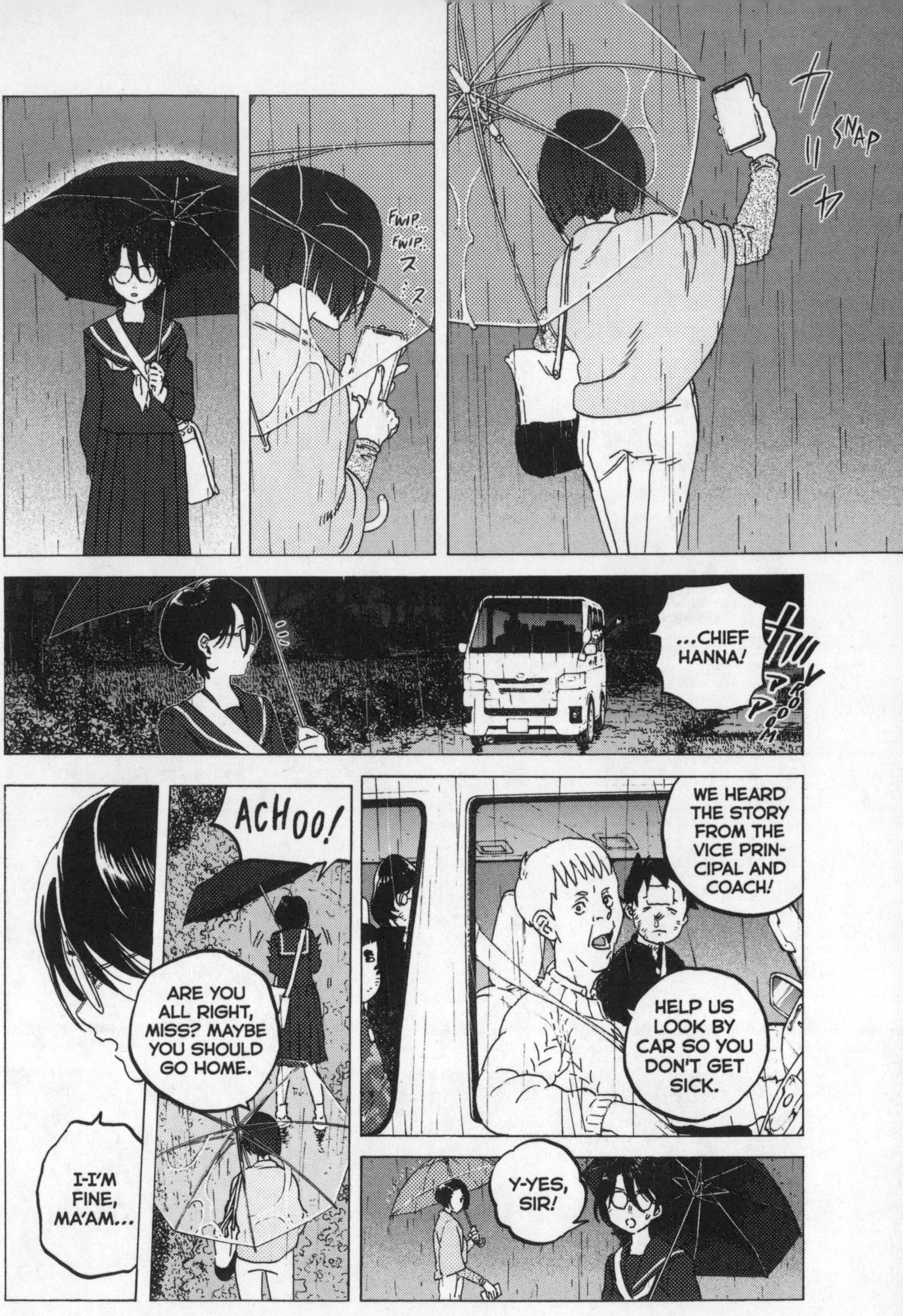
カリッャ
SNAP
FWIP FWIP
スス
...CHIEF HANNA!
VROOOOM
WE HEARD THE STORY FROM THE VICE PRINCIPAL AND COACH!
HELP US LOOK BY CAR SO YOU DON'T GET SICK.
Y-YES, SIR!
ACHOO!
ARE YOU ALL RIGHT, MISS? MAYBE YOU SHOULD GO HOME.
I-I'M FINE, MA'AM...

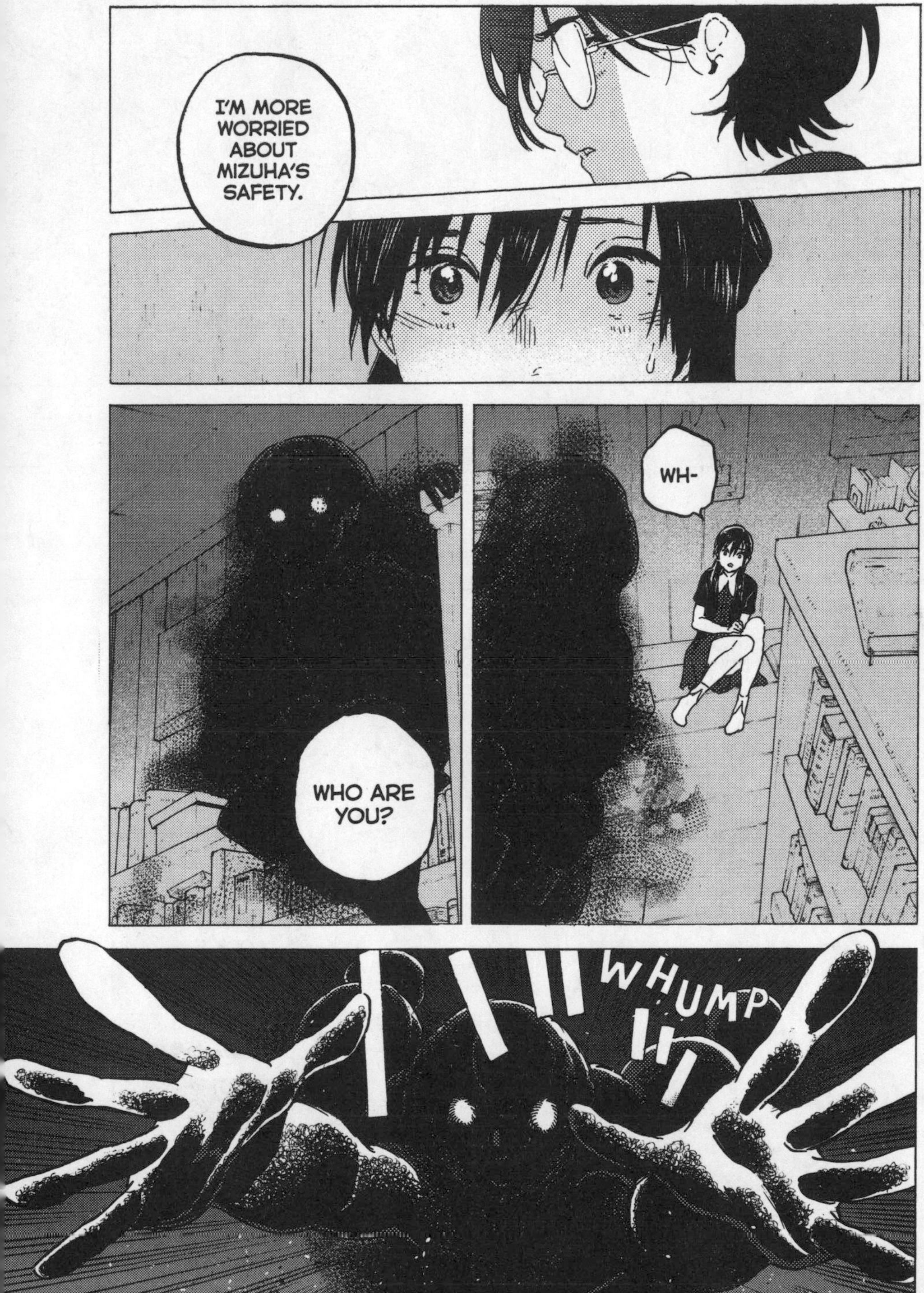
I'M MORE WORRIED ABOUT MIZUHA'S SAFETY.
WH-
WHO ARE YOU?
WHUMP

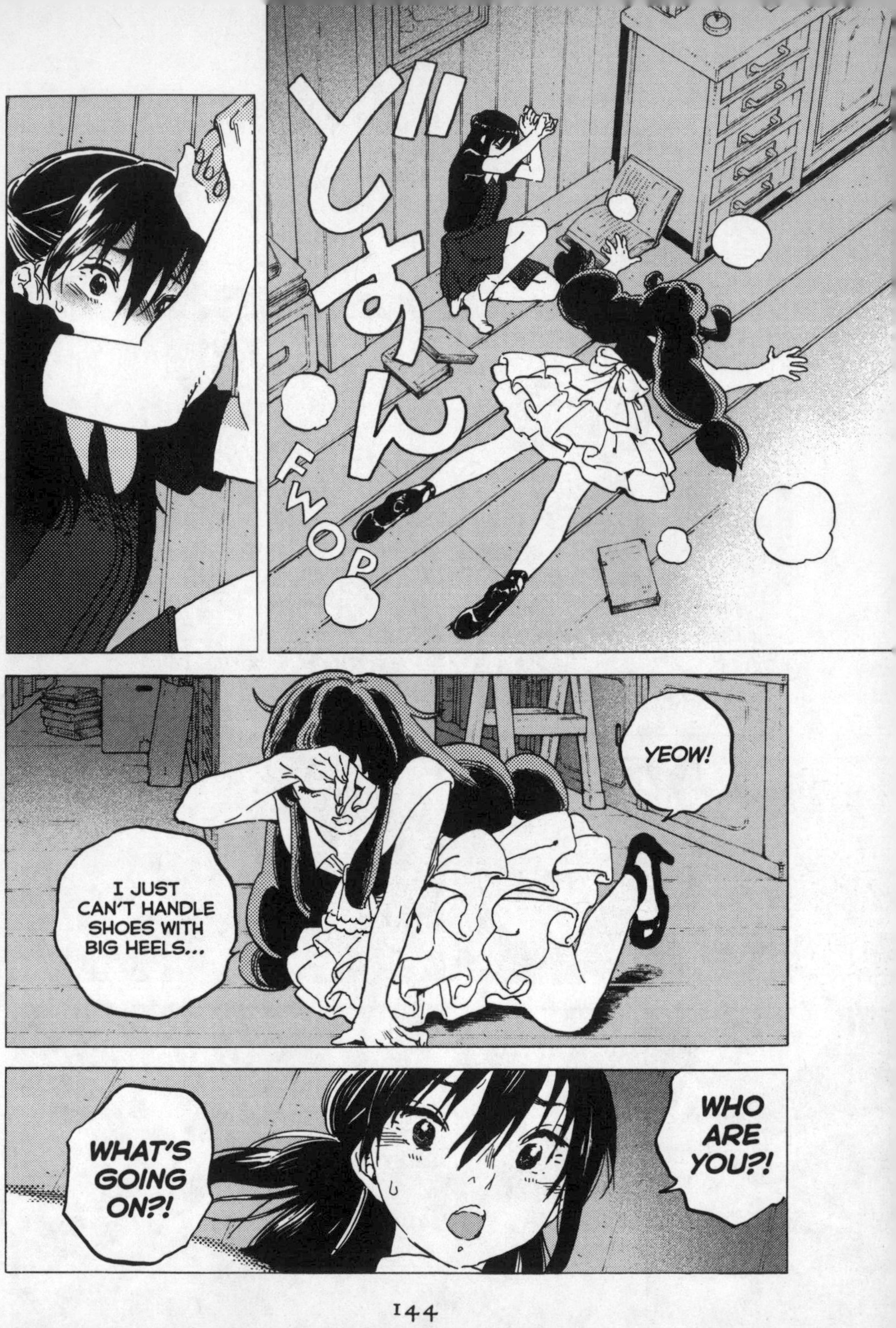
どすん
FWOP
YEOW!
I JUST CAN'T HANDLE SHOES WITH BIG HEELS...
WHO ARE YOU?!
WHAT'S GOING ON?!

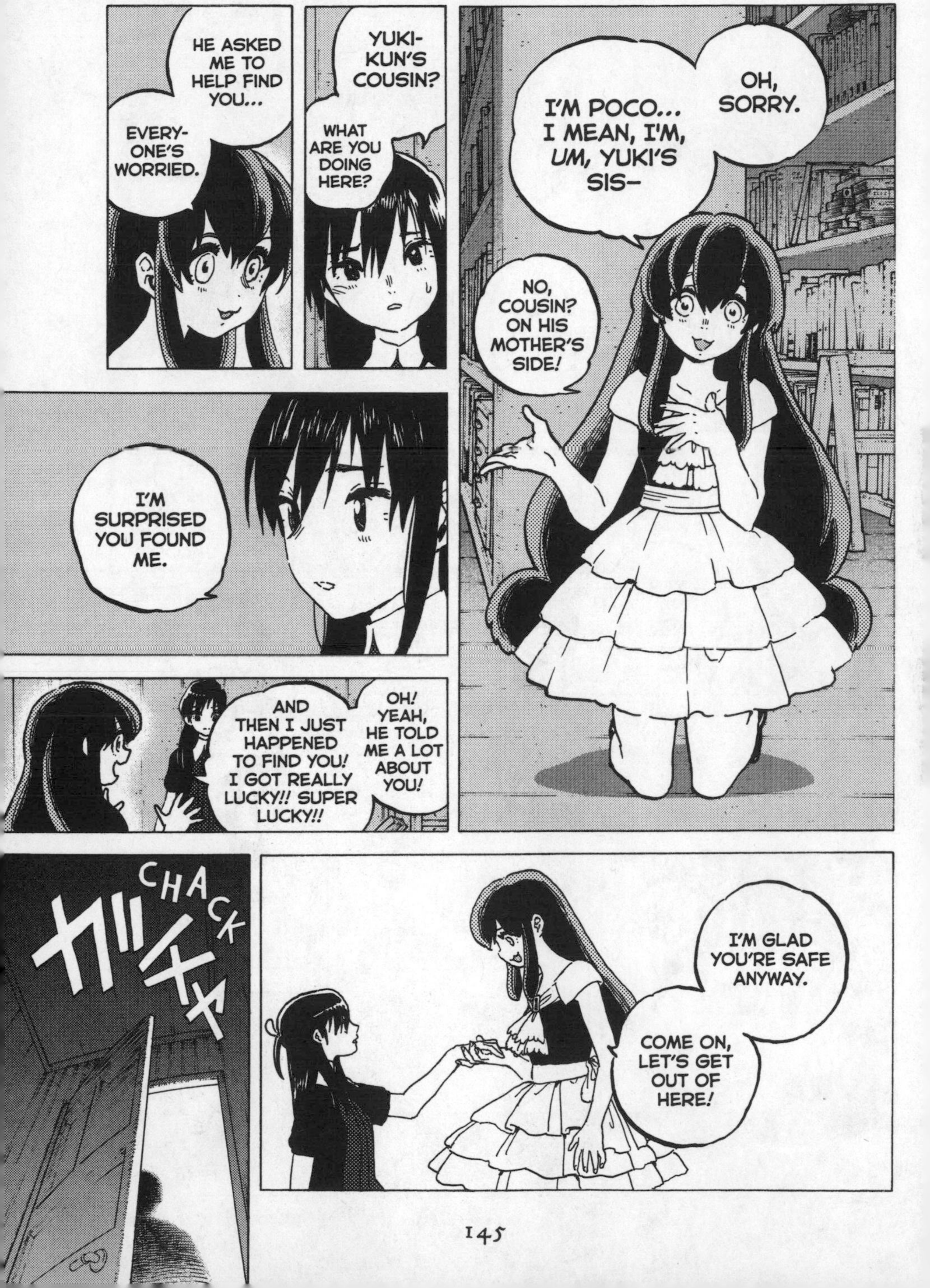
OH, SORRY.
I'M POCO... I MEAN, I'M, UM, YUKI'S SIS–
NO, COUSIN? ON HIS MOTHER'S SIDE!
YUKI-KUN'S COUSIN?
WHAT ARE YOU DOING HERE?
HE ASKED ME TO HELP FIND YOU...
EVERYONE'S WORRIED.
I'M SURPRISED YOU FOUND ME.
OH! YEAH, HE TOLD ME A LOT ABOUT YOU!
AND THEN I JUST HAPPENED TO FIND YOU! I GOT REALLY LUCKY!! SUPER LUCKY!!
I'M GLAD YOU'RE SAFE ANYWAY.
COME ON, LET'S GET OUT OF HERE!
CHACK

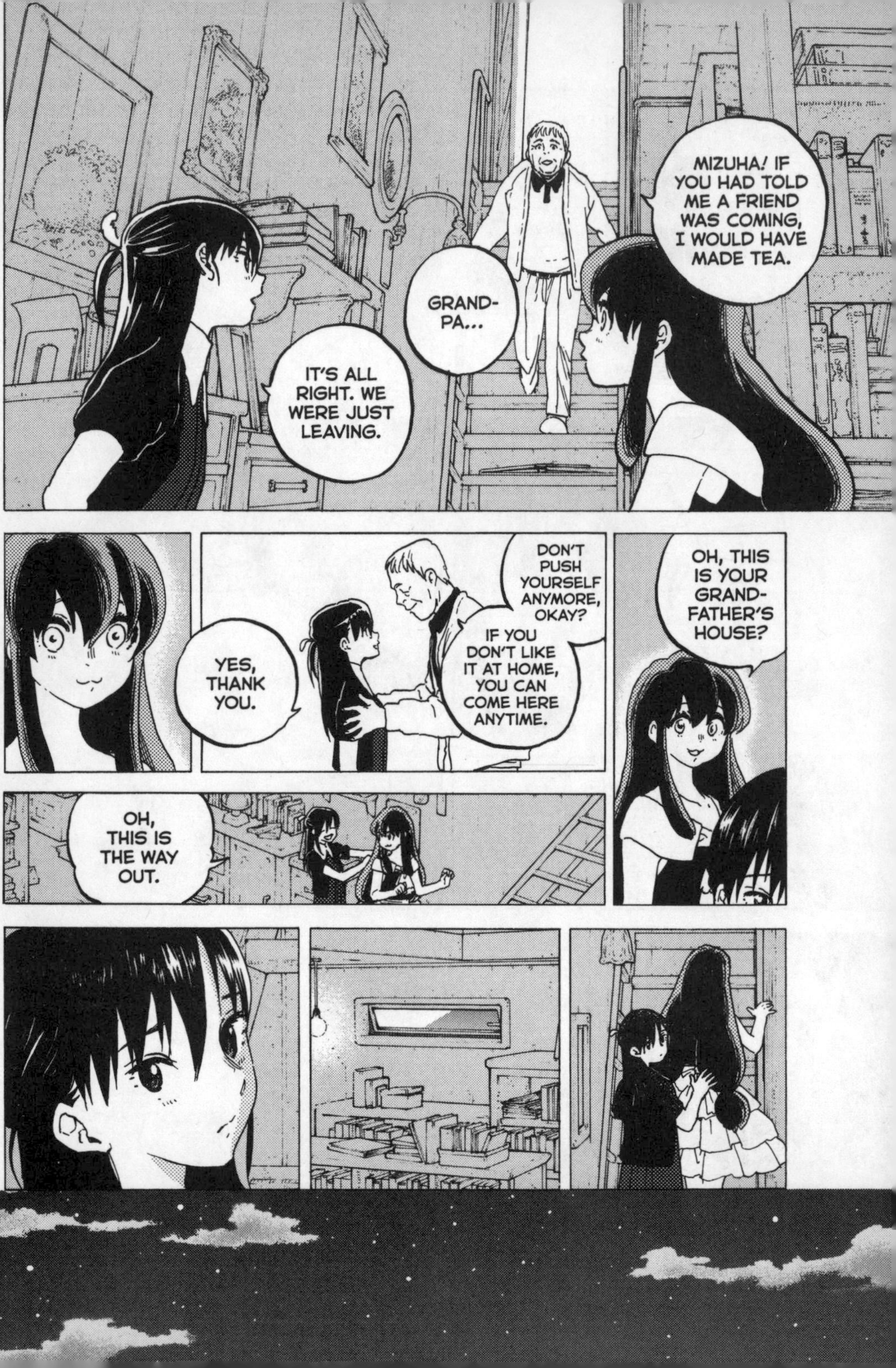
MIZUHA! IF YOU HAD TOLD ME A FRIEND WAS COMING, I WOULD HAVE MADE TEA.
GRAND-PA...
IT'S ALL RIGHT. WE WERE JUST LEAVING.
OH, THIS IS YOUR GRAND-FATHER'S HOUSE?
DON'T PUSH YOURSELF ANYMORE, OKAY?
IF YOU DON'T LIKE IT AT HOME, YOU CAN COME HERE ANYTIME.
YES, THANK YOU.
OH, THIS IS THE WAY OUT.

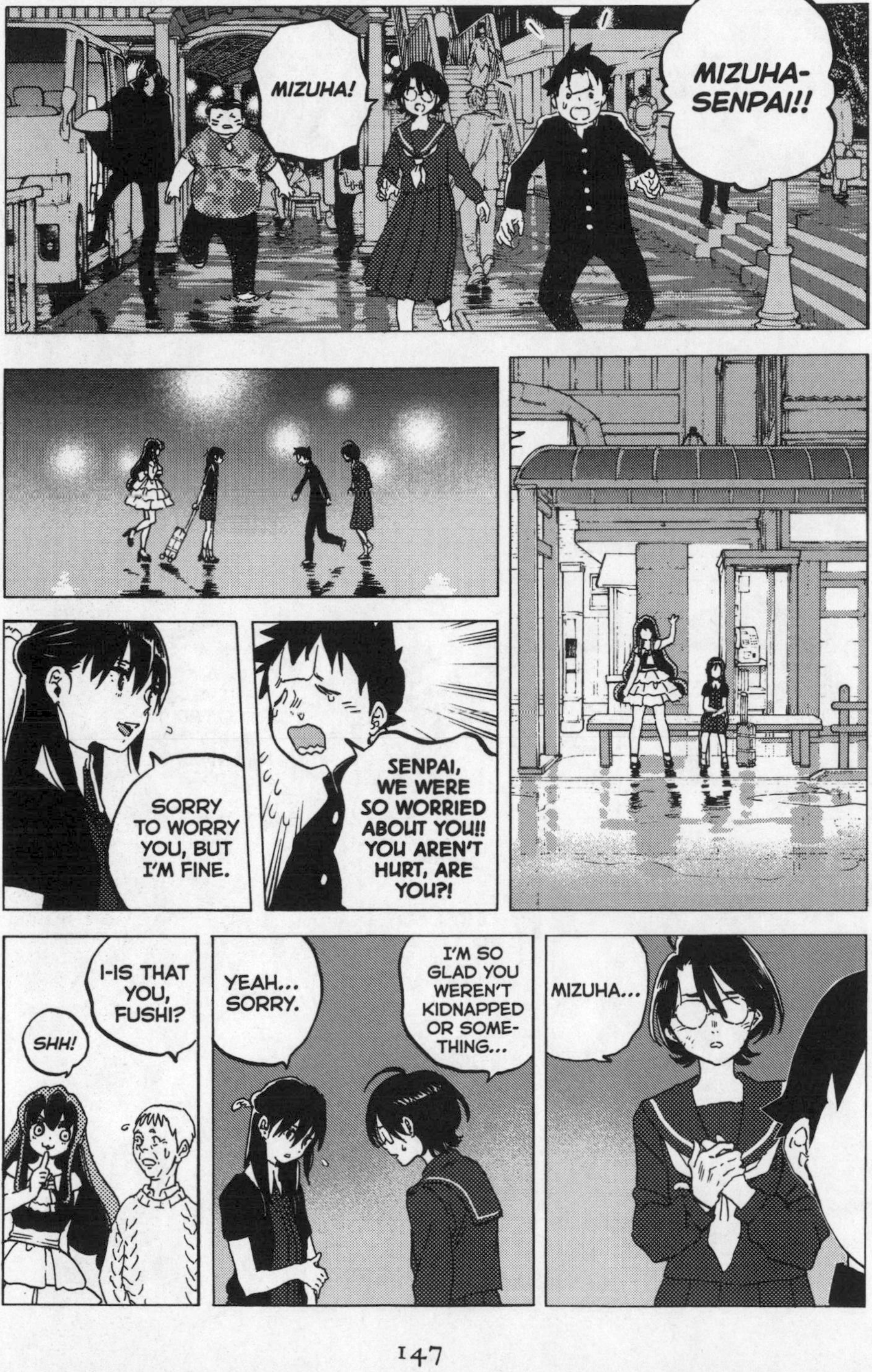

MIZUHA-SENPAI!!
MIZUHA!
SENPAI, WE WERE SO WORRIED ABOUT YOU!! YOU AREN'T HURT, ARE YOU?!
SORRY TO WORRY YOU, BUT I'M FINE.
MIZUHA...
I'M SO GLAD YOU WEREN'T KIDNAPPED OR SOME-THING...
YEAH... SORRY.
I-IS THAT YOU, FUSHI?
SHH!

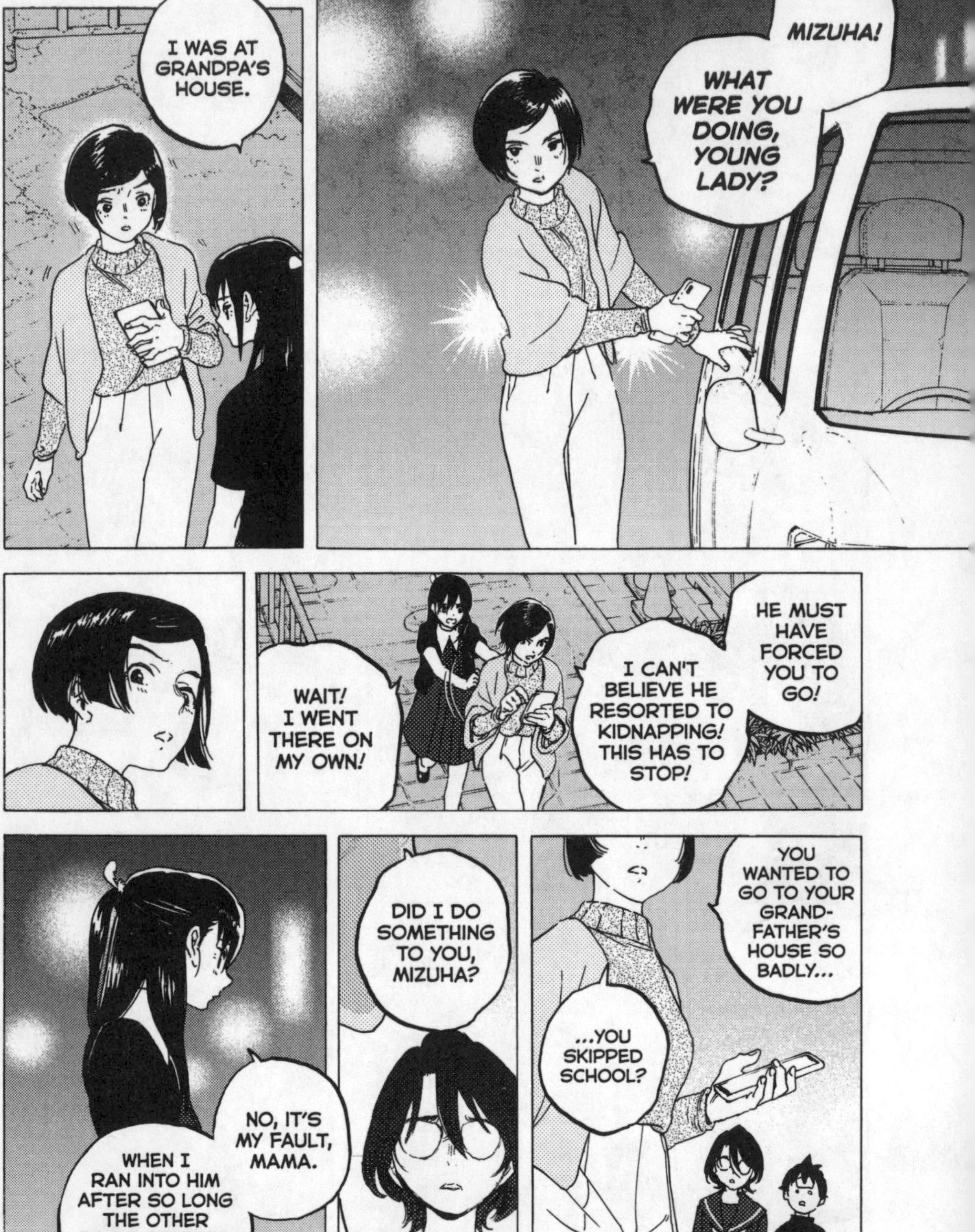
MIZUHA!
WHAT WERE YOU DOING, YOUNG LADY?
I WAS AT GRANDPA'S HOUSE.
HE MUST HAVE FORCED YOU TO GO!
I CAN'T BELIEVE HE RESORTED TO KIDNAPPING! THIS HAS TO STOP!
WAIT! I WENT THERE ON MY OWN!
YOU WANTED TO GO TO YOUR GRAND-FATHER'S HOUSE SO BADLY...
...YOU SKIPPED SCHOOL?
DID I DO SOMETHING TO YOU, MIZUHA?
NO, IT'S MY FAULT, MAMA.
WHEN I RAN INTO HIM AFTER SO LONG THE OTHER DAY, I STARTED GETTING LONELY...

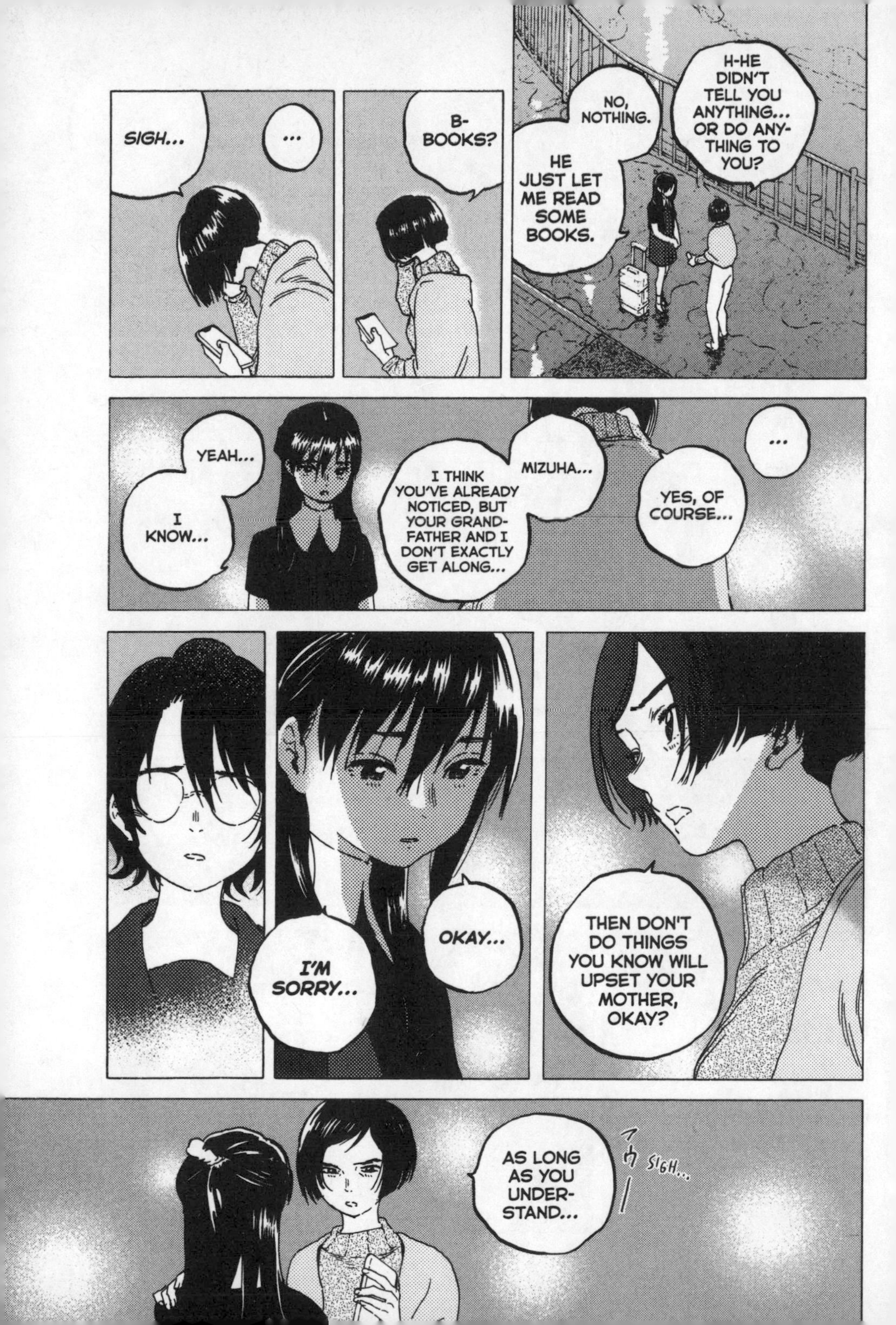
H-HE DIDN'T TELL YOU ANYTHING... OR DO ANYTHING TO YOU?
NO, NOTHING.
HE JUST LET ME READ SOME BOOKS.
B-BOOKS?
...
SIGH...
...
YES, OF COURSE...
MIZUHA...
I THINK YOU'VE ALREADY NOTICED, BUT YOUR GRANDFATHER AND I DON'T EXACTLY GET ALONG...
YEAH...
I KNOW...
THEN DON'T DO THINGS YOU KNOW WILL UPSET YOUR MOTHER, OKAY?
OKAY...
I'M SORRY...
フゥー
SIGH...
AS LONG AS YOU UNDERSTAND...

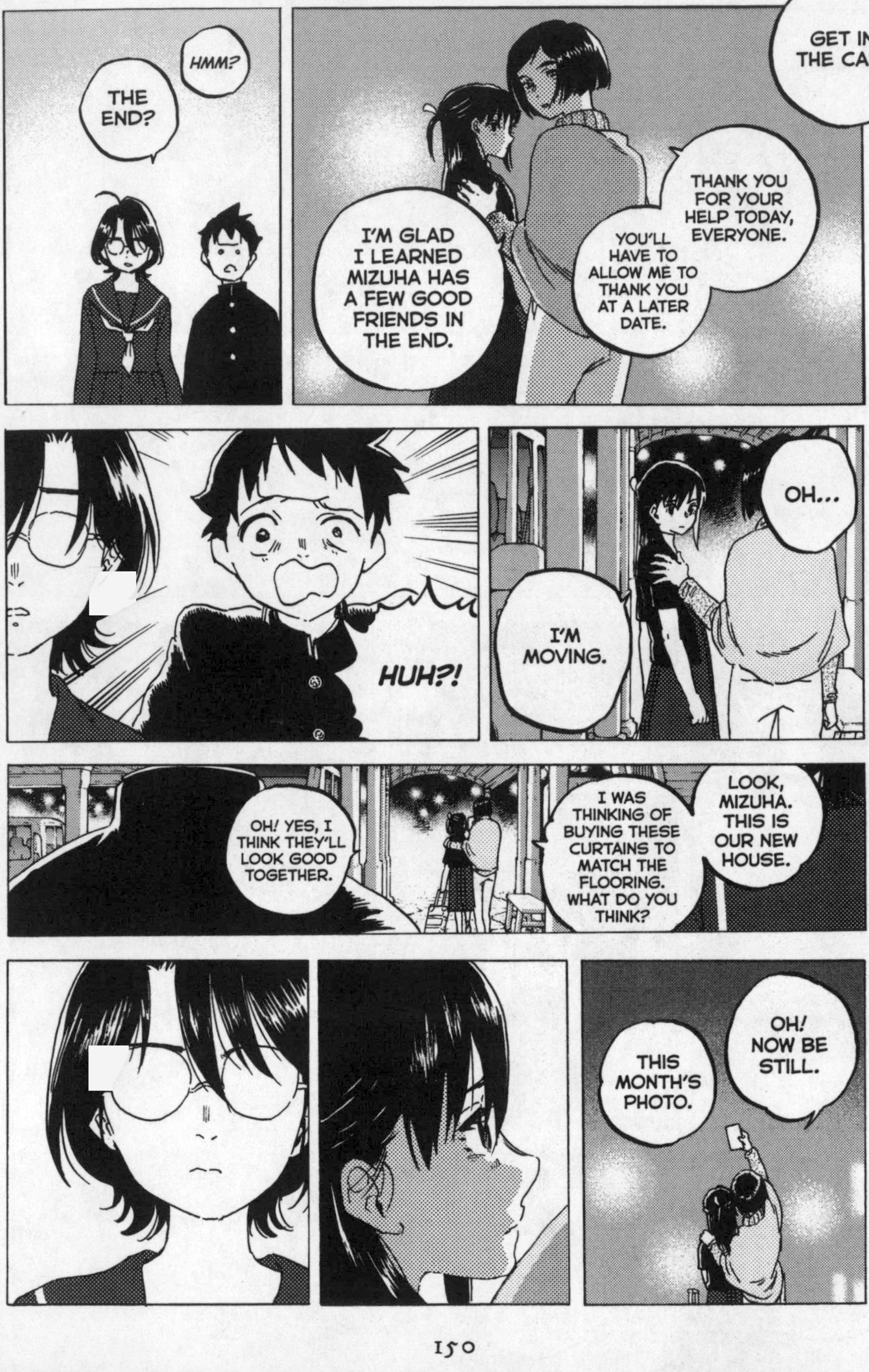
GET IN THE CAR.
THANK YOU FOR YOUR HELP TODAY, EVERYONE.
YOU'LL HAVE TO ALLOW ME TO THANK YOU AT A LATER DATE.
I'M GLAD I LEARNED MIZUHA HAS A FEW GOOD FRIENDS IN THE END.
HMM?
THE END?
OH...
I'M MOVING.
HUH?!
LOOK, MIZUHA. THIS IS OUR NEW HOUSE.
I WAS THINKING OF BUYING THESE CURTAINS TO MATCH THE FLOORING. WHAT DO YOU THINK?
OH! YES, I THINK THEY'LL LOOK GOOD TOGETHER.
OH! NOW BE STILL.
THIS MONTH'S PHOTO.

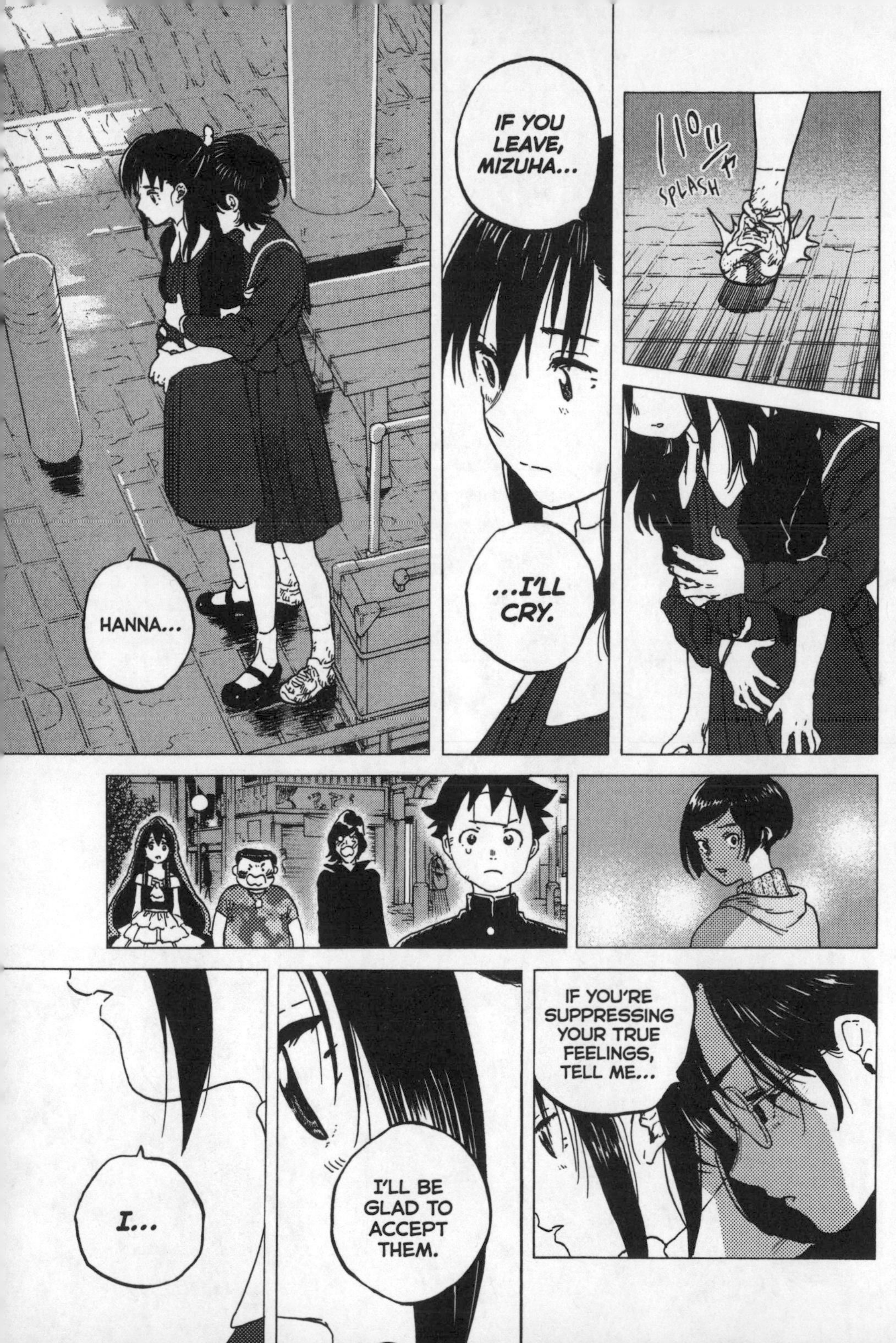
SPLASH
IF YOU LEAVE, MIZUHA...
...I'LL CRY.
HANNA...
IF YOU'RE SUPPRESSING YOUR TRUE FEELINGS, TELL ME...
I'LL BE GLAD TO ACCEPT THEM.
I...

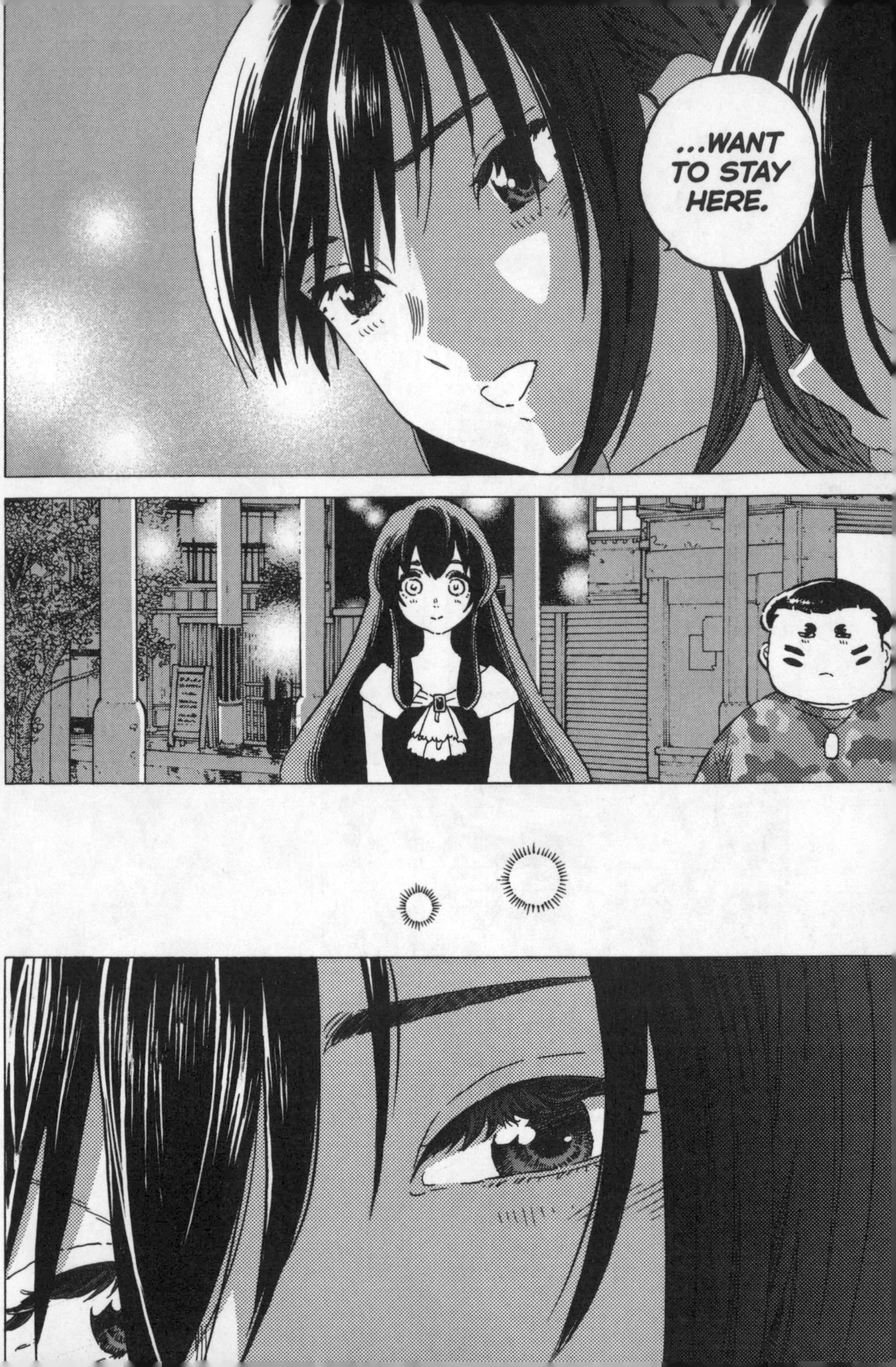
...WANT TO STAY HERE.

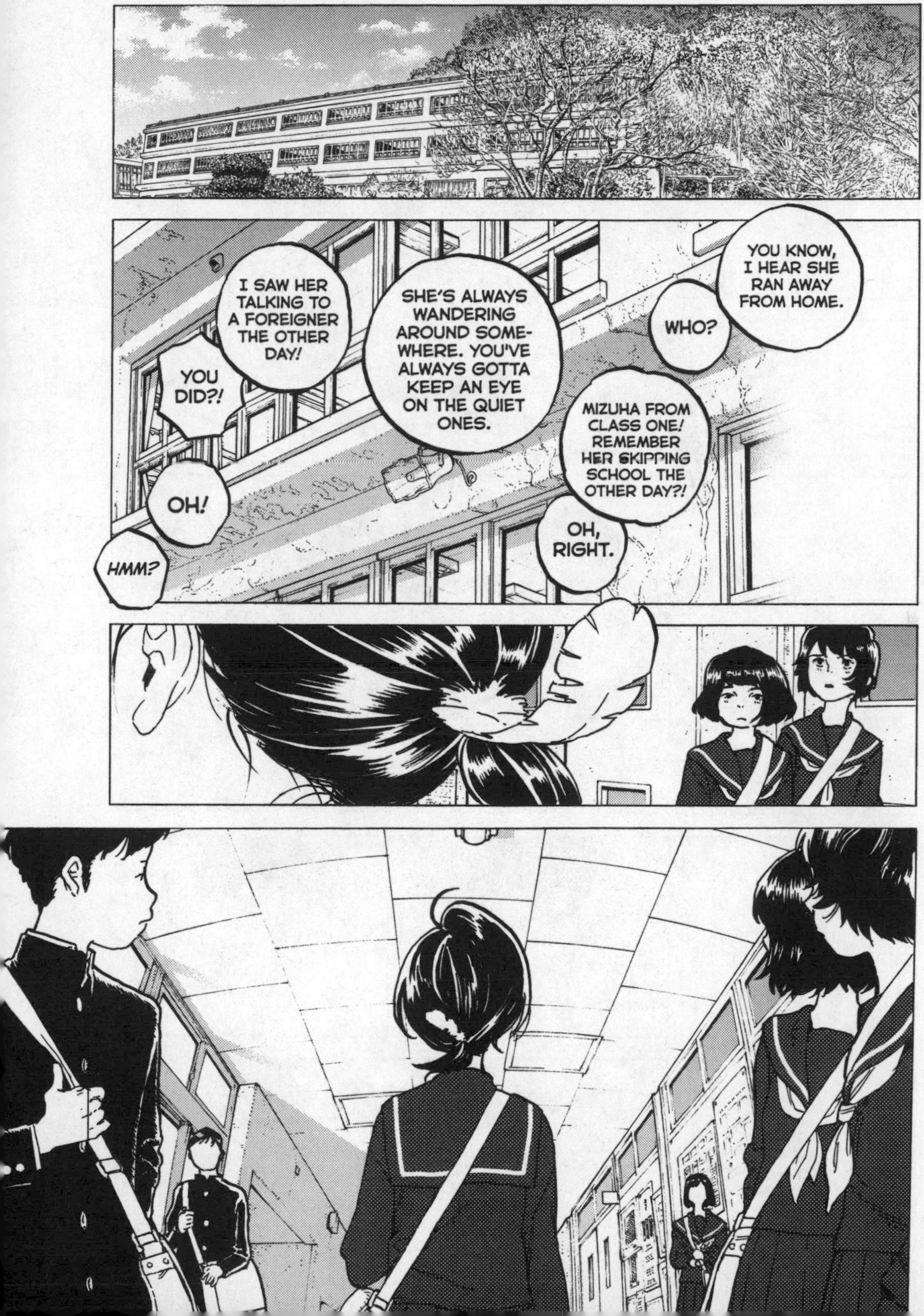
YOU KNOW, I HEAR SHE RAN AWAY FROM HOME.
WHO?
MIZUHA FROM CLASS ONE! REMEMBER HER SKIPPING SCHOOL THE OTHER DAY?!
OH, RIGHT.
SHE'S ALWAYS WANDERING AROUND SOME-WHERE. YOU'VE ALWAYS GOTTA KEEP AN EYE ON THE QUIET ONES.
I SAW HER TALKING TO A FOREIGNER THE OTHER DAY!
YOU DID?!
OH!
HMM?

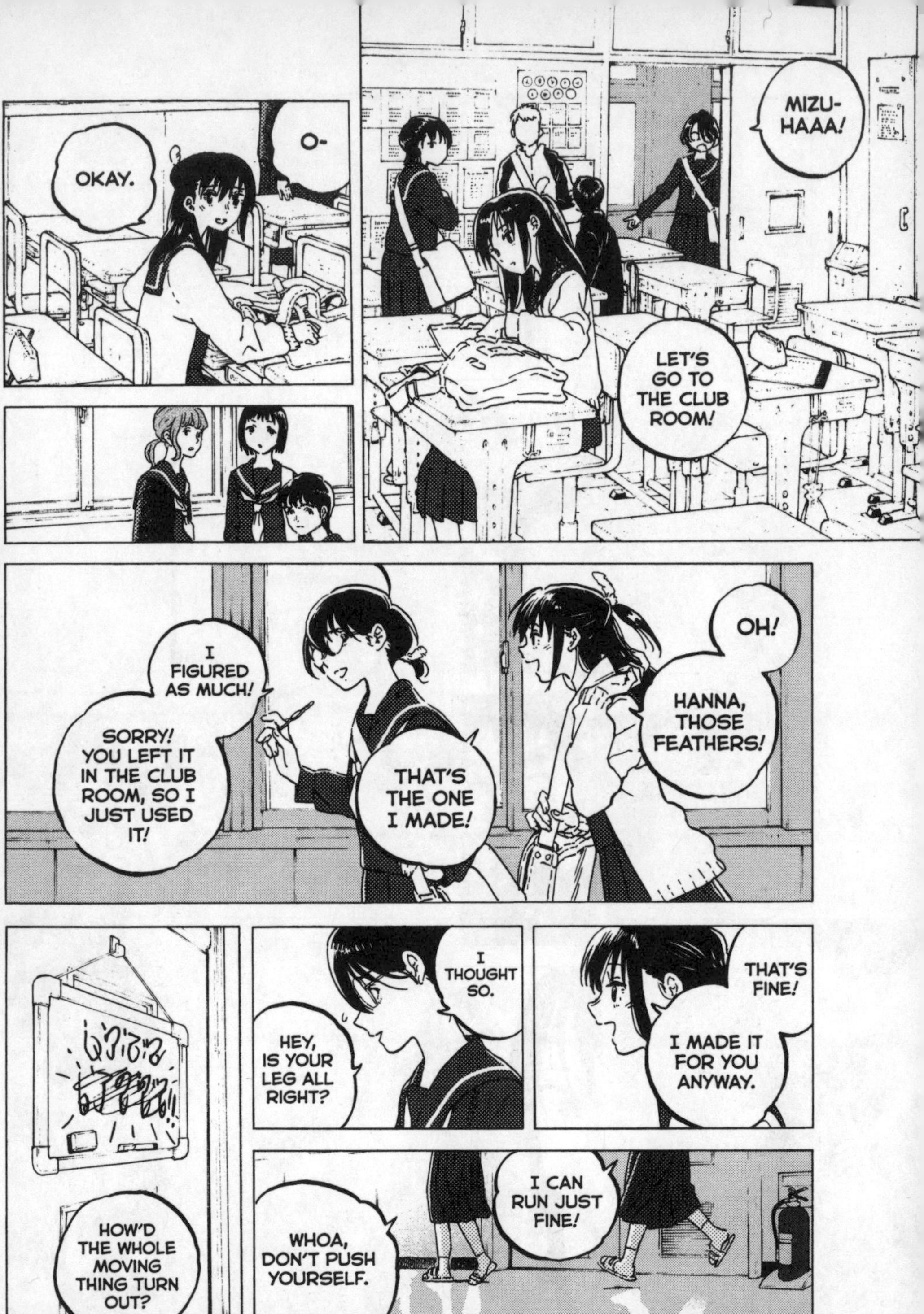
MIZU-HAAA!
LET'S GO TO THE CLUB ROOM!
O-
OKAY.
OH!
HANNA, THOSE FEATHERS!
THAT'S THE ONE I MADE!
I FIGURED AS MUCH!
SORRY! YOU LEFT IT IN THE CLUB ROOM, SO I JUST USED IT!
THAT'S FINE!
I MADE IT FOR YOU ANYWAY.
I THOUGHT SO.
HEY, IS YOUR LEG ALL RIGHT?
I CAN RUN JUST FINE!
WHOA, DON'T PUSH YOURSELF.
HOW'D THE WHOLE MOVING THING TURN OUT?

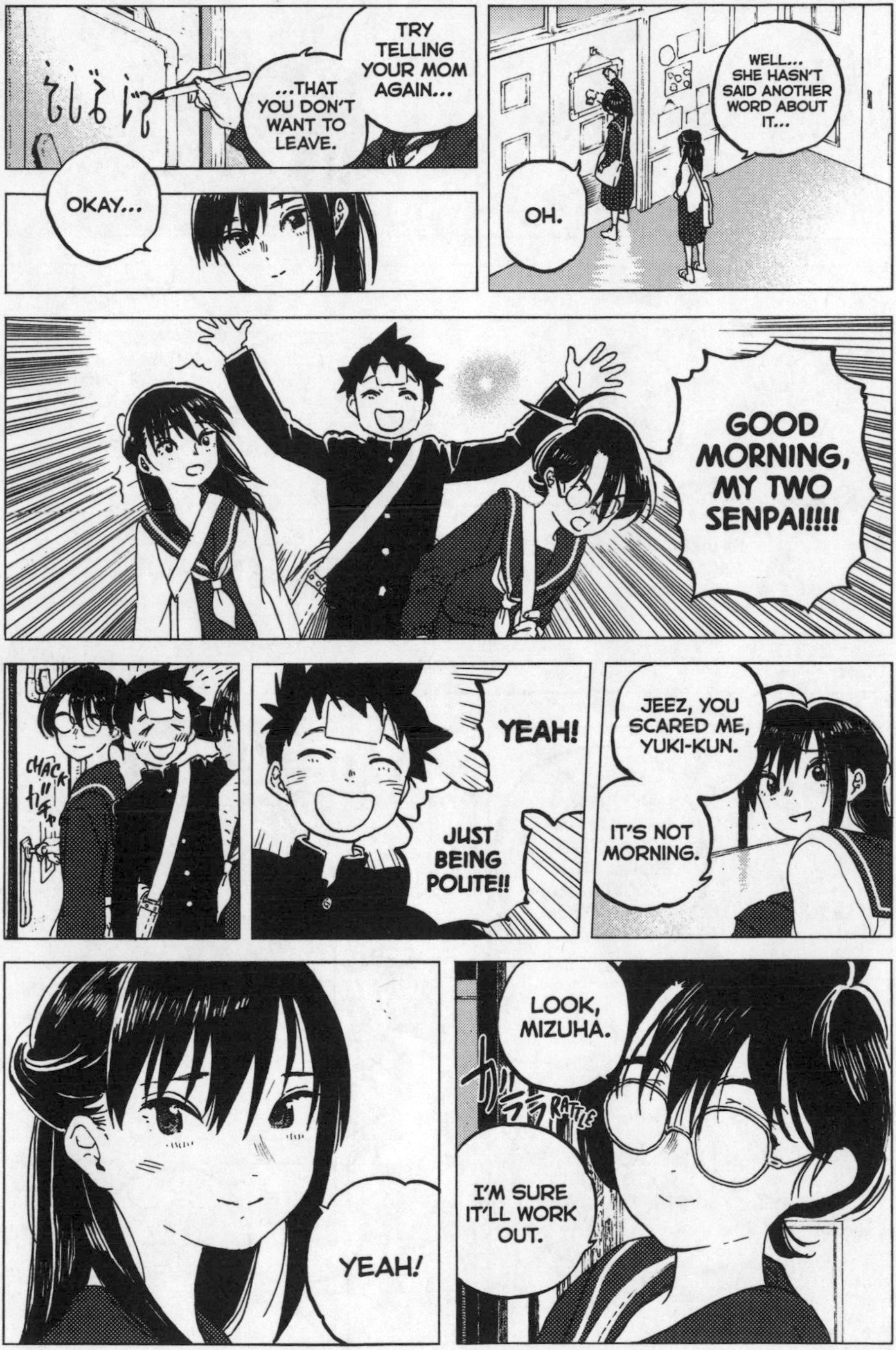
WELL... SHE HASN'T SAID ANOTHER WORD ABOUT IT...
OH.
TRY TELLING YOUR MOM AGAIN...
...THAT YOU DON'T WANT TO LEAVE.
OKAY...
GOOD MORNING, MY TWO SENPAI!!!!!
JEEZ, YOU SCARED ME, YUKI-KUN.
IT'S NOT MORNING.
YEAH!
JUST BEING POLITE!!
ガチャ CHACK
LOOK, MIZUHA.
カラ RATTLE
I'M SURE IT'LL WORK OUT.
YEAH!

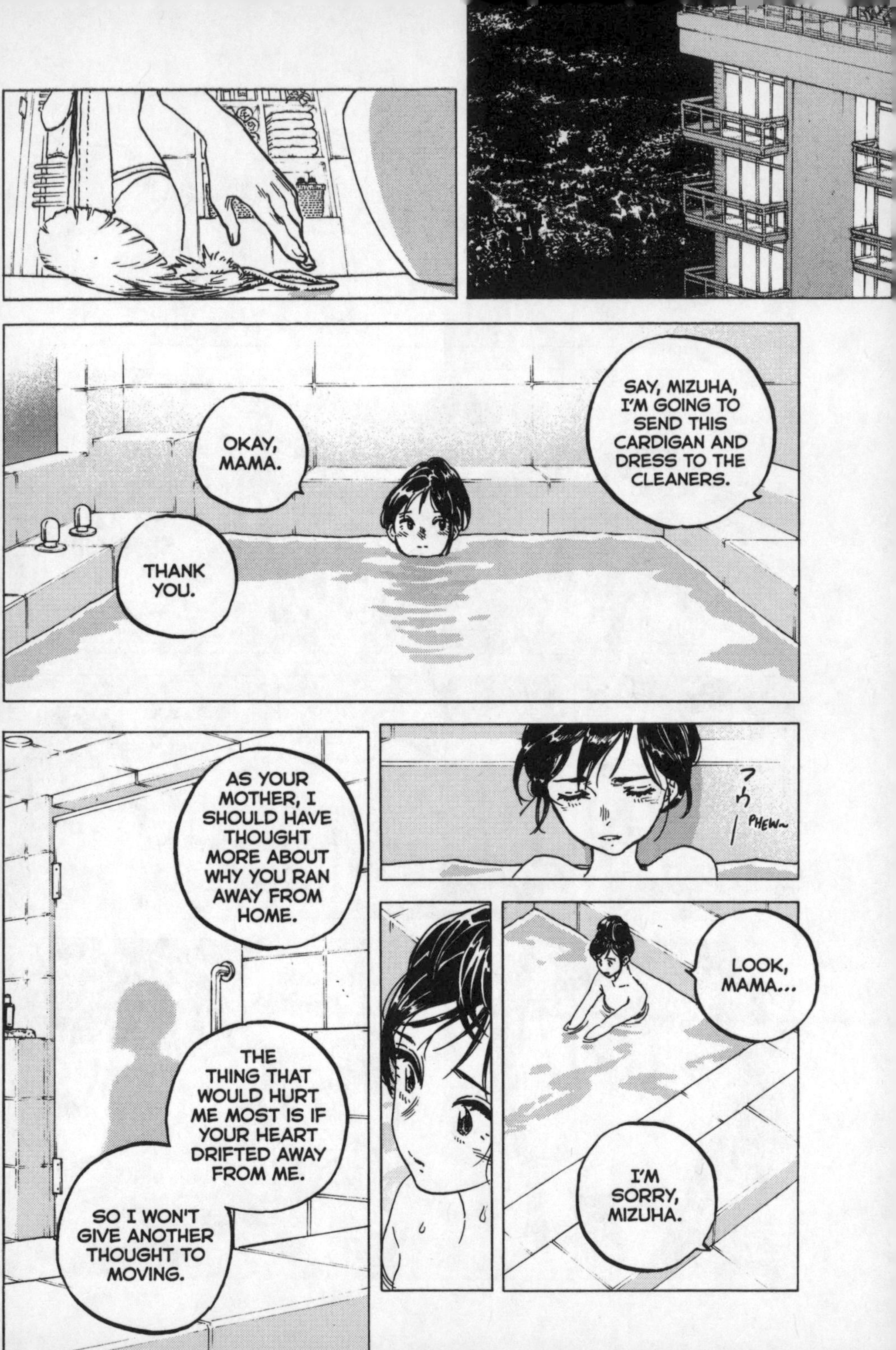

SAY, MIZUHA, I'M GOING TO SEND THIS CARDIGAN AND DRESS TO THE CLEANERS.
OKAY, MAMA.
THANK YOU.
フゥ
PHEW~
LOOK, MAMA...
I'M SORRY, MIZUHA.
AS YOUR MOTHER, I SHOULD HAVE THOUGHT MORE ABOUT WHY YOU RAN AWAY FROM HOME.
THE THING THAT WOULD HURT ME MOST IS IF YOUR HEART DRIFTED AWAY FROM ME.
SO I WON'T GIVE ANOTHER THOUGHT TO MOVING.

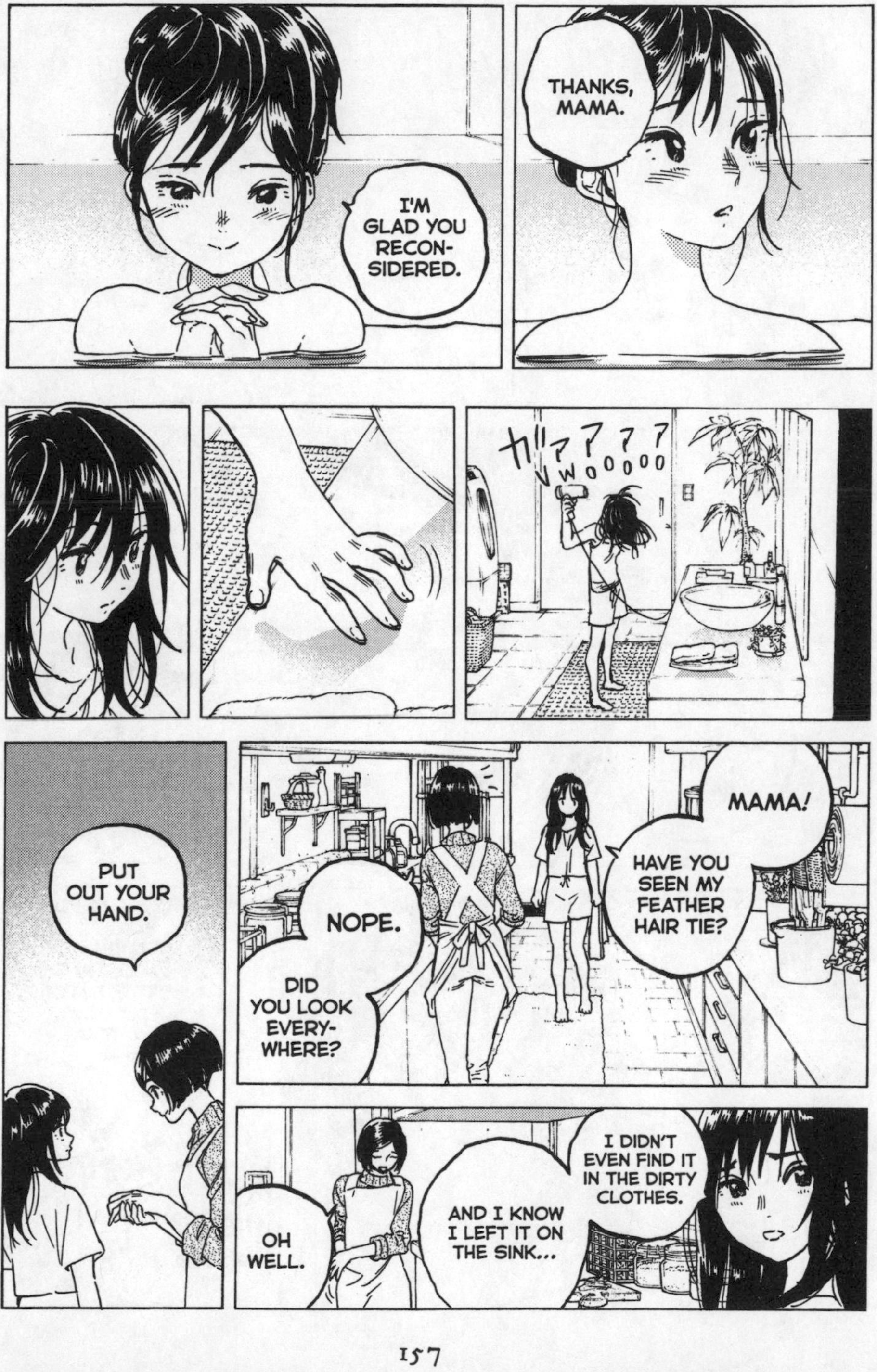
THANKS, MAMA.
I'M GLAD YOU RECON-SIDERED.
VWOOOOOO
MAMA!
HAVE YOU SEEN MY FEATHER HAIR TIE?
NOPE.
DID YOU LOOK EVERY-WHERE?
I DIDN'T EVEN FIND IT IN THE DIRTY CLOTHES.
AND I KNOW I LEFT IT ON THE SINK...
OH WELL.
PUT OUT YOUR HAND.

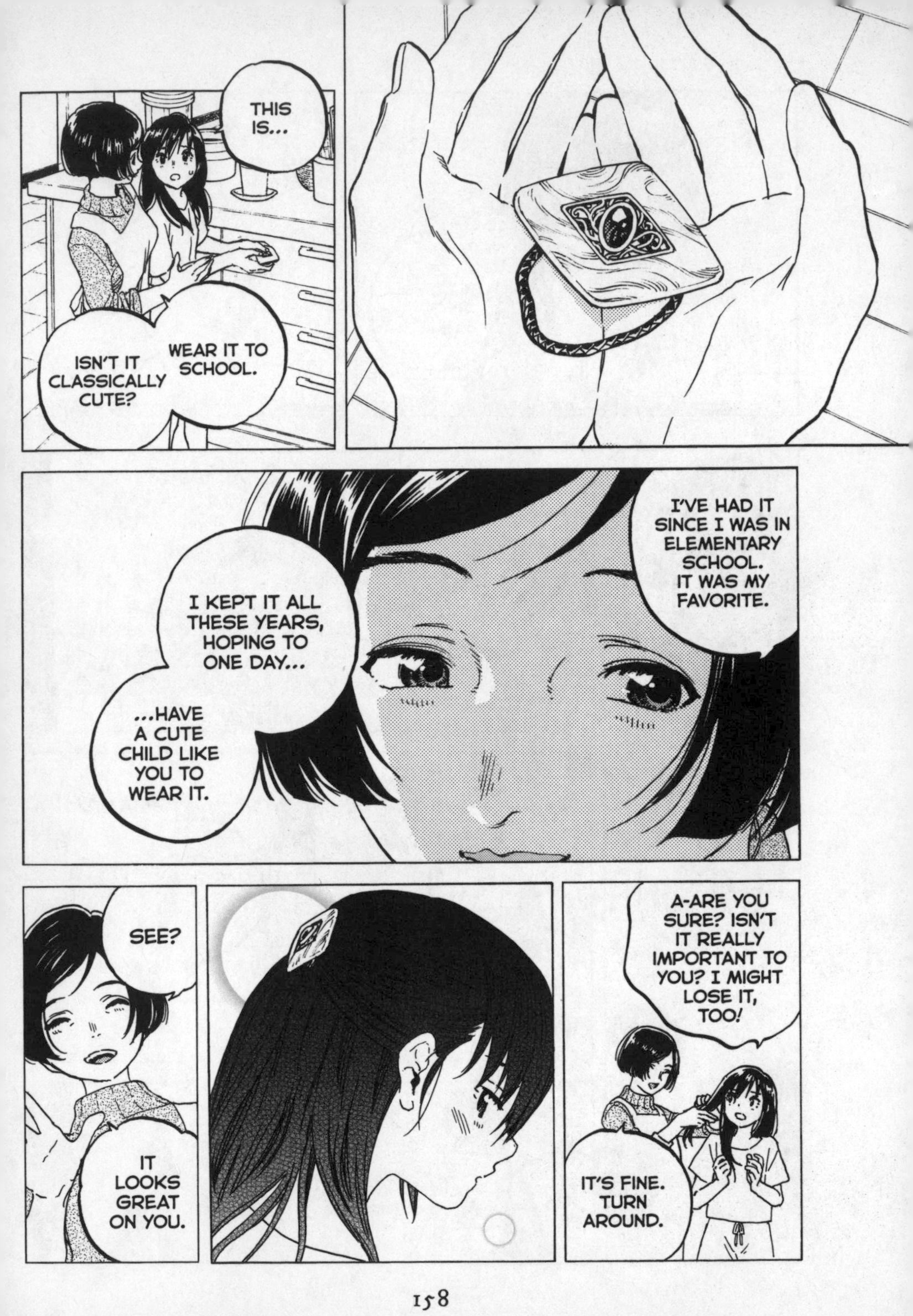
THIS IS...
WEAR IT TO SCHOOL.
ISN'T IT CLASSICALLY CUTE?
I'VE HAD IT SINCE I WAS IN ELEMENTARY SCHOOL. IT WAS MY FAVORITE.
I KEPT IT ALL THESE YEARS, HOPING TO ONE DAY...
...HAVE A CUTE CHILD LIKE YOU TO WEAR IT.
A-ARE YOU SURE? ISN'T IT REALLY IMPORTANT TO YOU? I MIGHT LOSE IT, TOO!
IT'S FINE. TURN AROUND.
SEE?
IT LOOKS GREAT ON YOU.

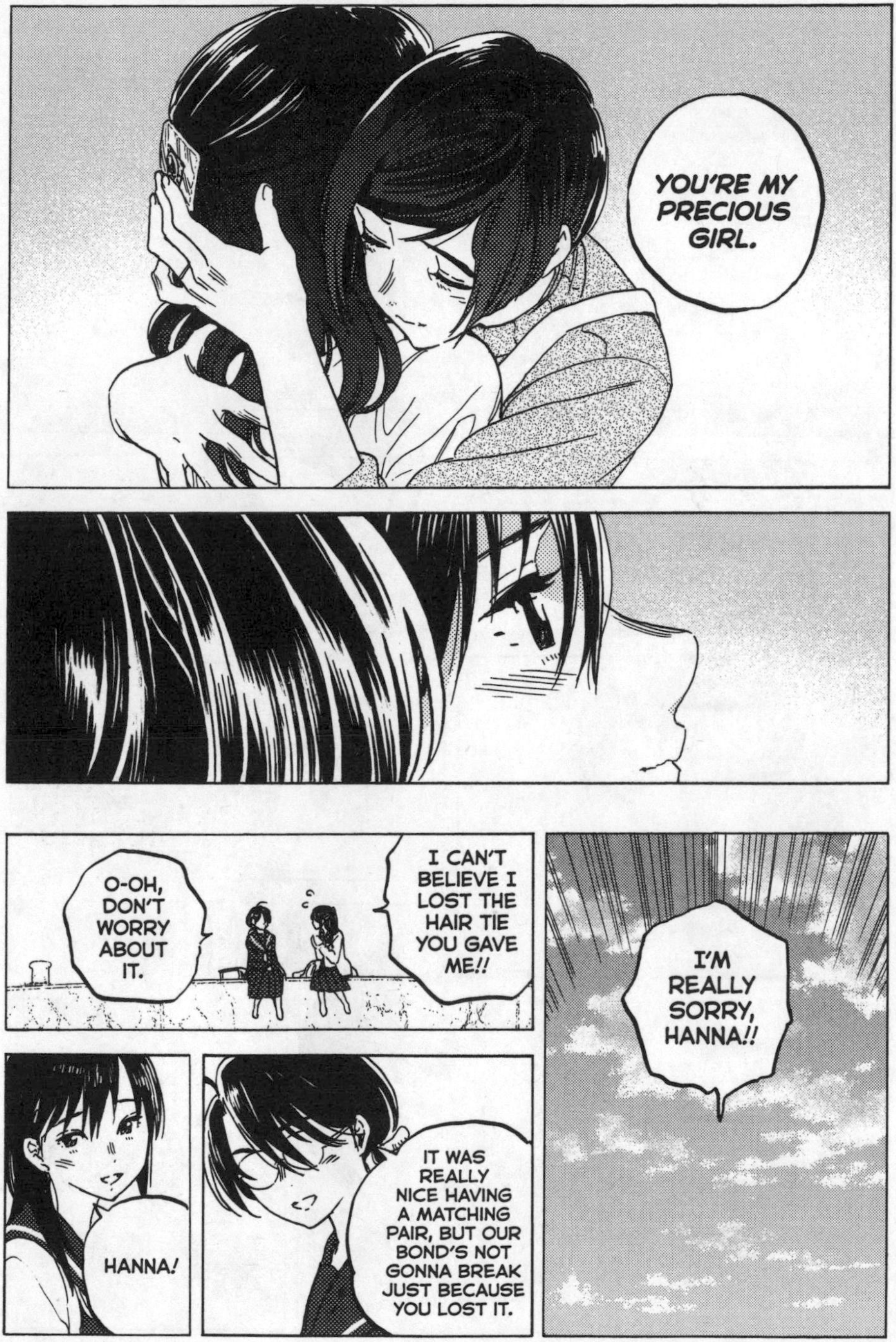
YOU'RE MY PRECIOUS GIRL.
I'M REALLY SORRY, HANNA!!
I CAN'T BELIEVE I LOST THE HAIR TIE YOU GAVE ME!!
O-OH, DON'T WORRY ABOUT IT.
IT WAS REALLY NICE HAVING A MATCHING PAIR, BUT OUR BOND'S NOT GONNA BREAK JUST BECAUSE YOU LOST IT.
HANNA!

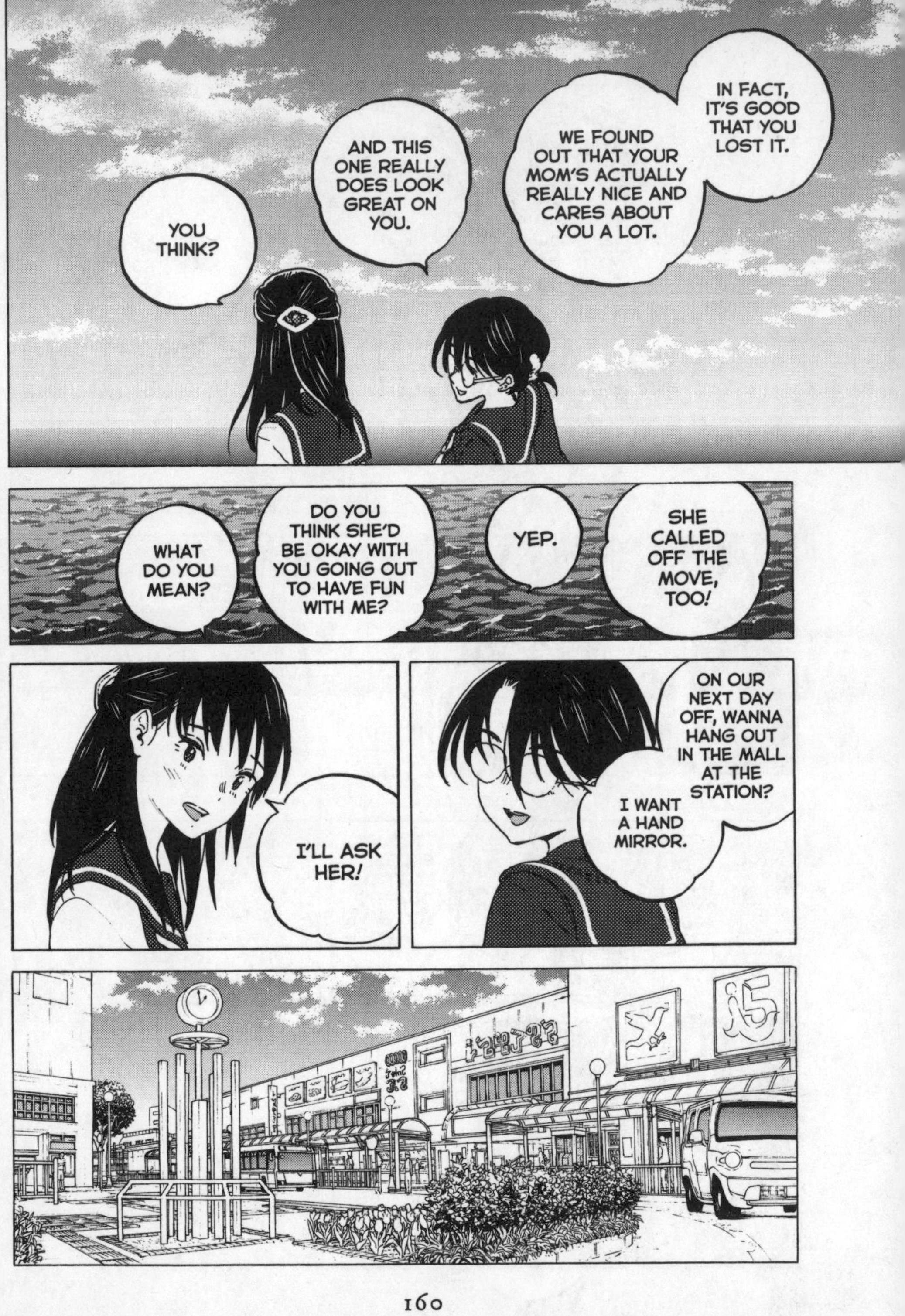
IN FACT, IT'S GOOD THAT YOU LOST IT.
WE FOUND OUT THAT YOUR MOM'S ACTUALLY REALLY NICE AND CARES ABOUT YOU A LOT.
AND THIS ONE REALLY DOES LOOK GREAT ON YOU.
YOU THINK?
SHE CALLED OFF THE MOVE, TOO!
YEP.
DO YOU THINK SHE'D BE OKAY WITH YOU GOING OUT TO HAVE FUN WITH ME?
WHAT DO YOU MEAN?
ON OUR NEXT DAY OFF, WANNA HANG OUT IN THE MALL AT THE STATION?
I WANT A HAND MIRROR.
I'LL ASK HER!

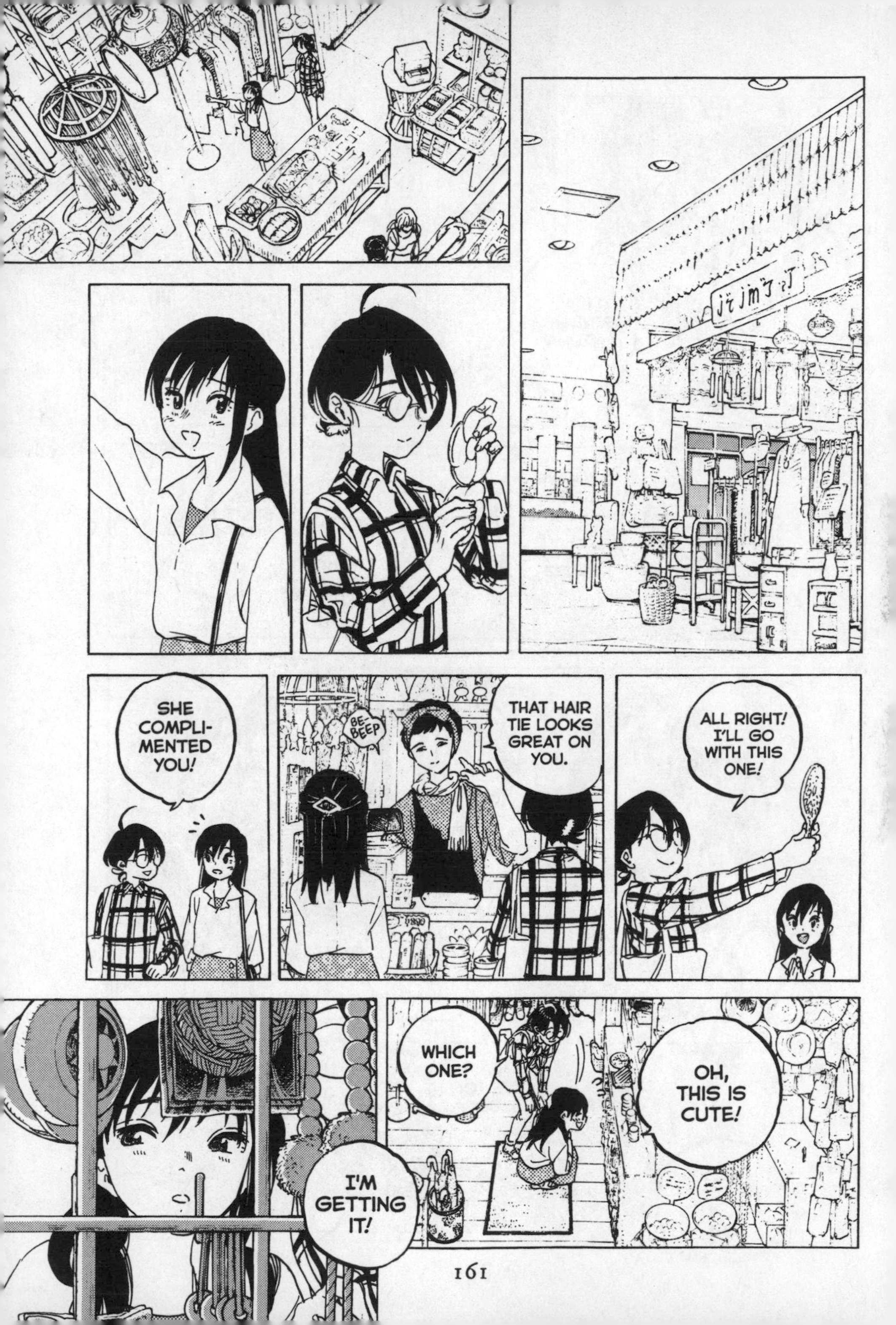
ALL RIGHT! I'LL GO WITH THIS ONE!
THAT HAIR TIE LOOKS GREAT ON YOU.
BE-BEEP
SHE COMPLIMENTED YOU!
OH, THIS IS CUTE!
WHICH ONE?
I'M GETTING IT!

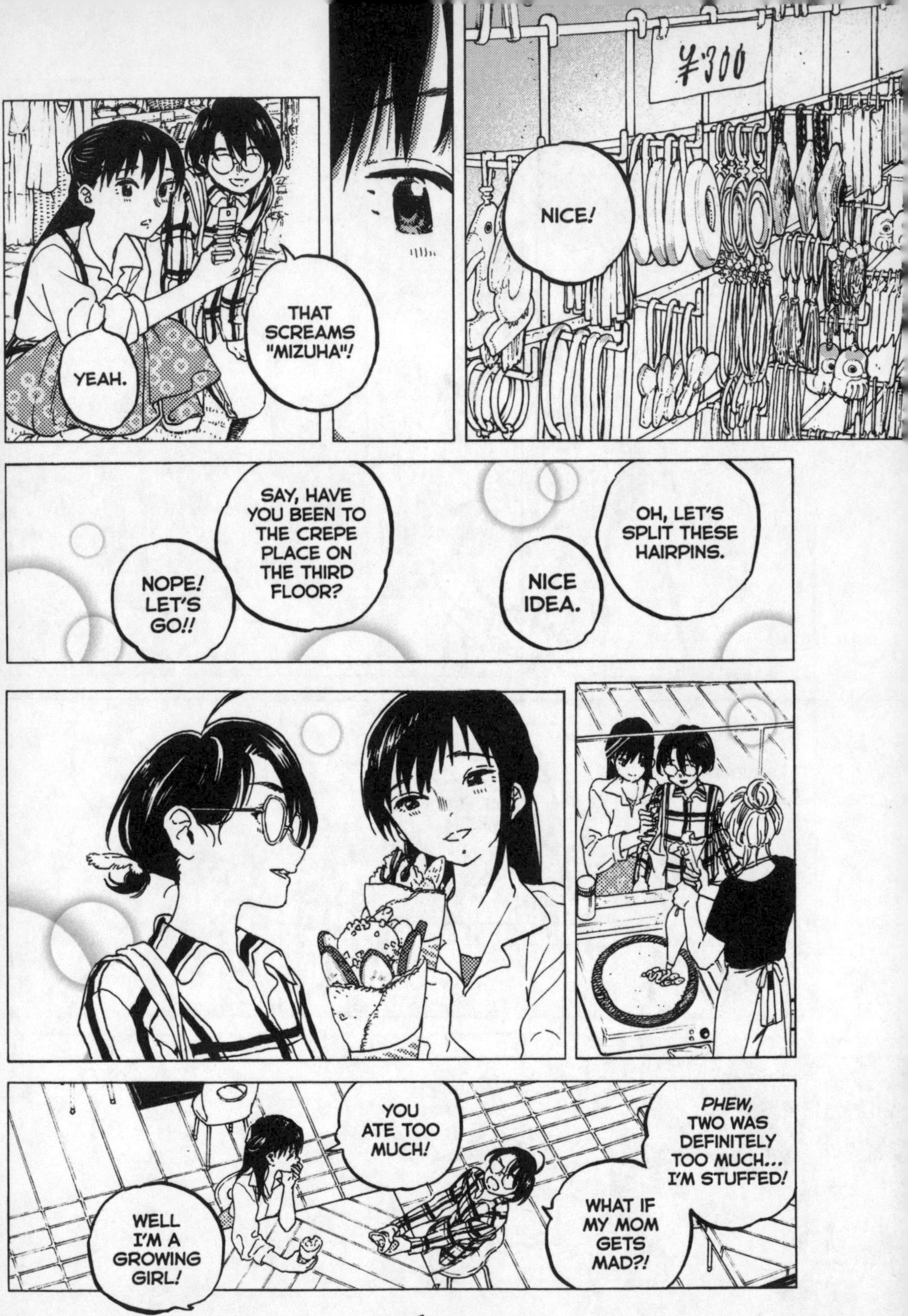

¥300
NICE!
THAT SCREAMS "MIZUHA"!
YEAH.
OH, LET'S SPLIT THESE HAIRPINS.
NICE IDEA.
SAY, HAVE YOU BEEN TO THE CREPE PLACE ON THE THIRD FLOOR?
NOPE! LET'S GO!!
PHEW, TWO WAS DEFINITELY TOO MUCH... I'M STUFFED!
WHAT IF MY MOM GETS MAD?!
YOU ATE TOO MUCH!
WELL I'M A GROWING GIRL!

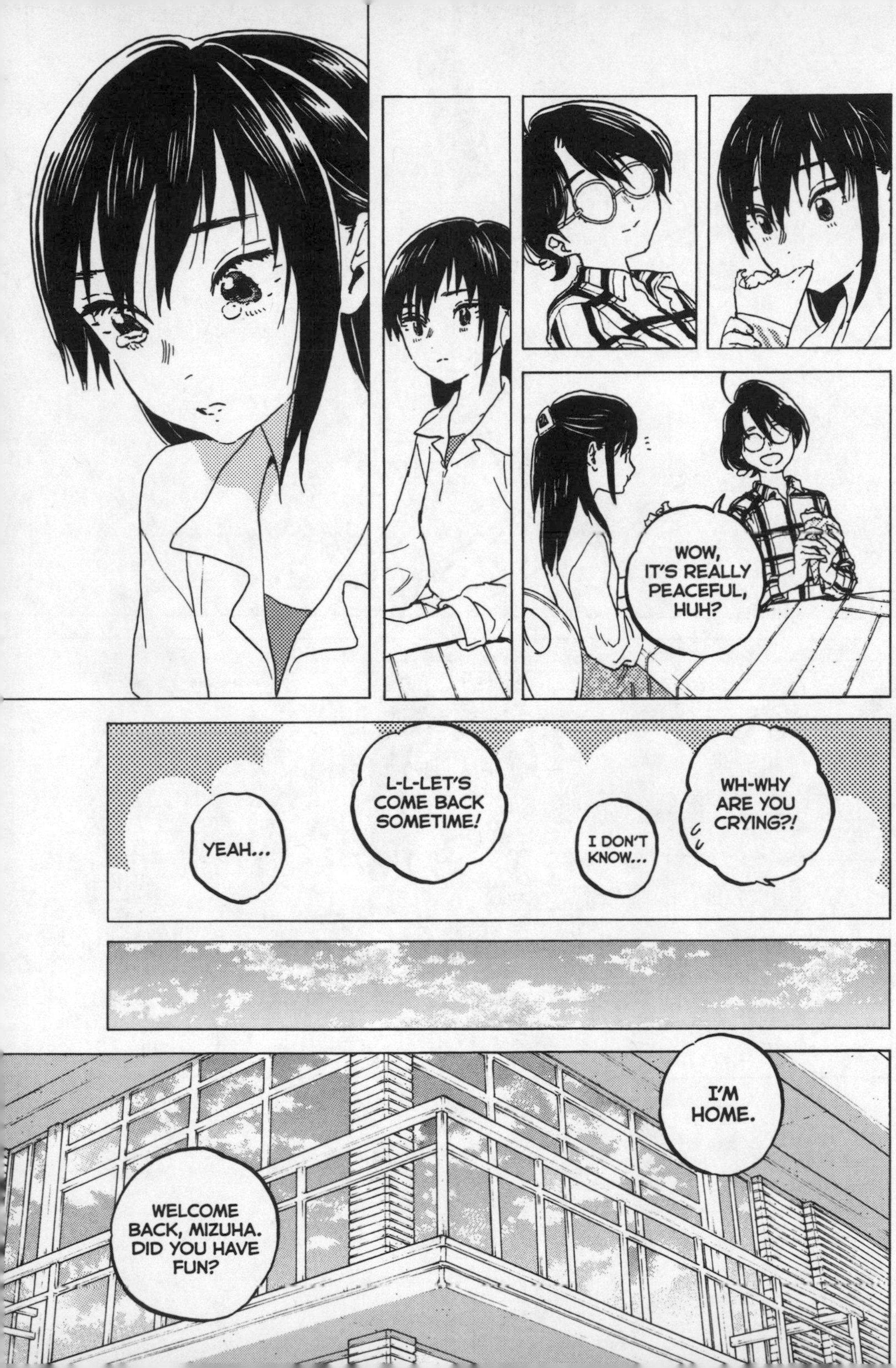
WOW, IT'S REALLY PEACEFUL, HUH?
WH-WHY ARE YOU CRYING?!
I DON'T KNOW...
L-L-LET'S COME BACK SOMETIME!
YEAH...
I'M HOME.
WELCOME BACK, MIZUHA. DID YOU HAVE FUN?

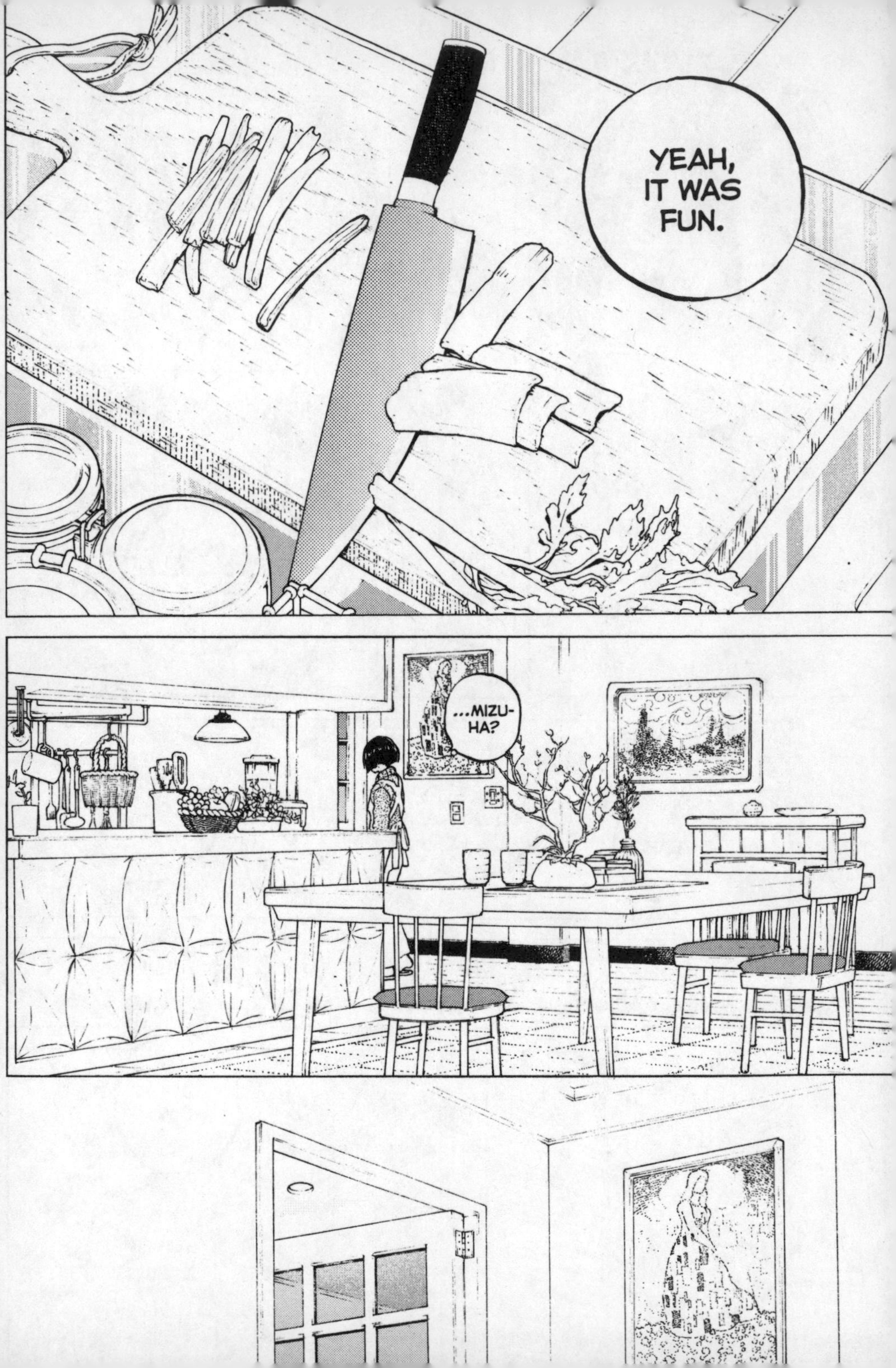
YEAH, IT WAS FUN.
...MIZU-HA?

#124 Mizuha

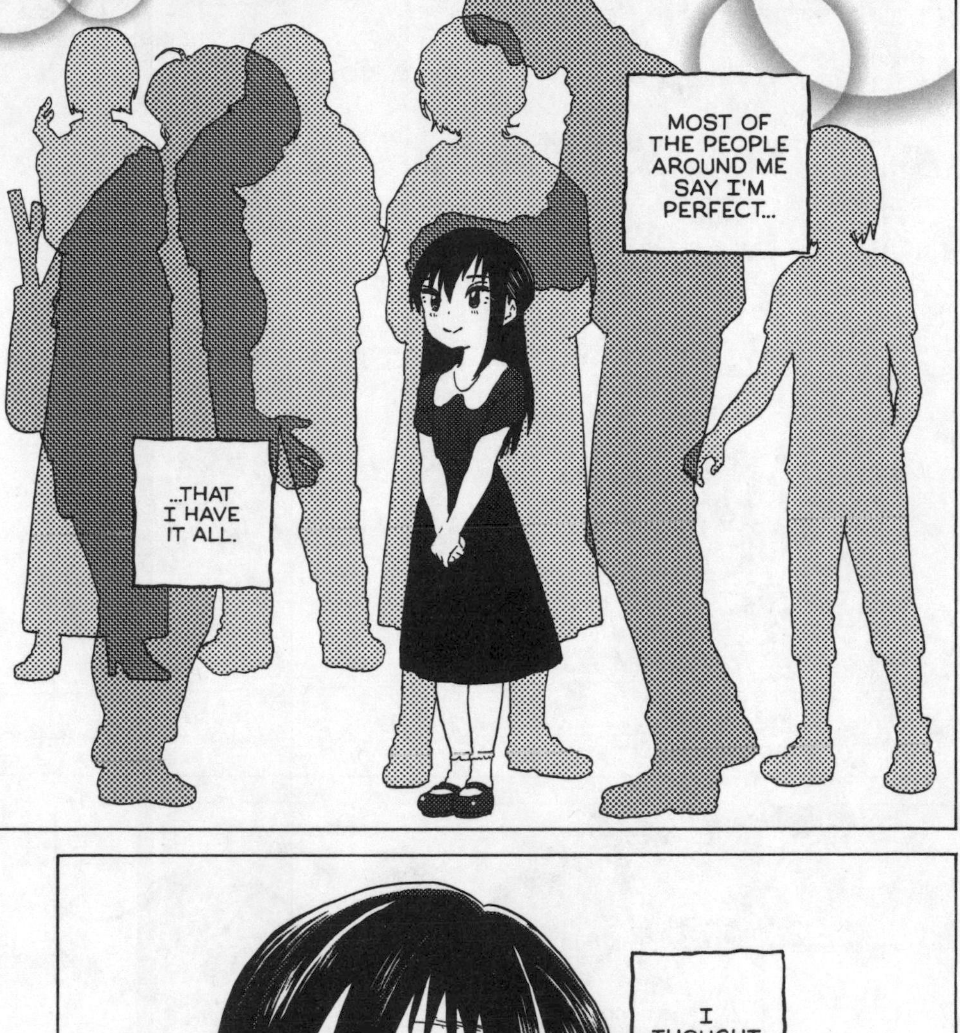
MOST OF THE PEOPLE AROUND ME SAY I'M PERFECT...
...THAT I HAVE IT ALL.

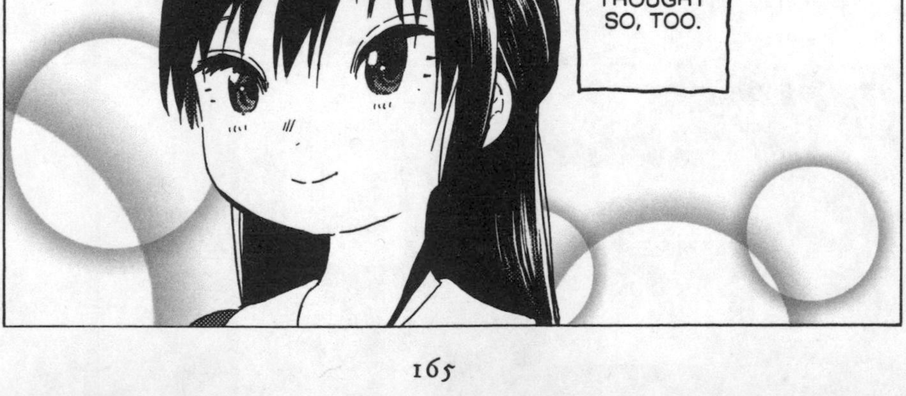
I THOUGHT SO, TOO.

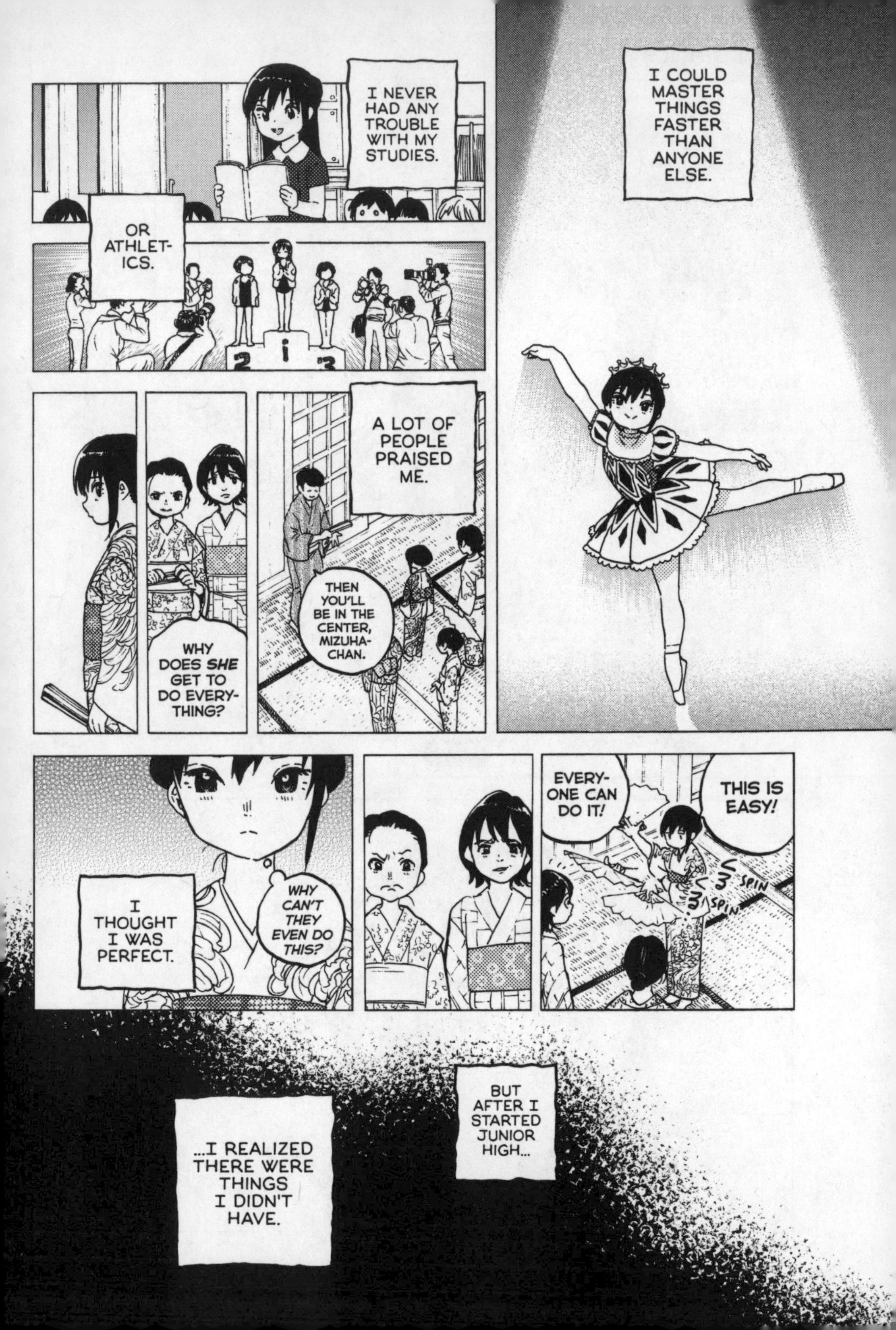
I COULD MASTER THINGS FASTER THAN ANYONE ELSE.
I NEVER HAD ANY TROUBLE WITH MY STUDIES.
OR ATHLETICS.
A LOT OF PEOPLE PRAISED ME.
THEN YOU'LL BE IN THE CENTER, MIZUHA-CHAN.
WHY DOES *SHE* GET TO DO EVERYTHING?
THIS IS EASY!
EVERYONE CAN DO IT!
SPIN
SPIN
WHY CAN'T THEY EVEN DO THIS?
I THOUGHT I WAS PERFECT.
BUT AFTER I STARTED JUNIOR HIGH...
...I REALIZED THERE WERE THINGS I DIDN'T HAVE.

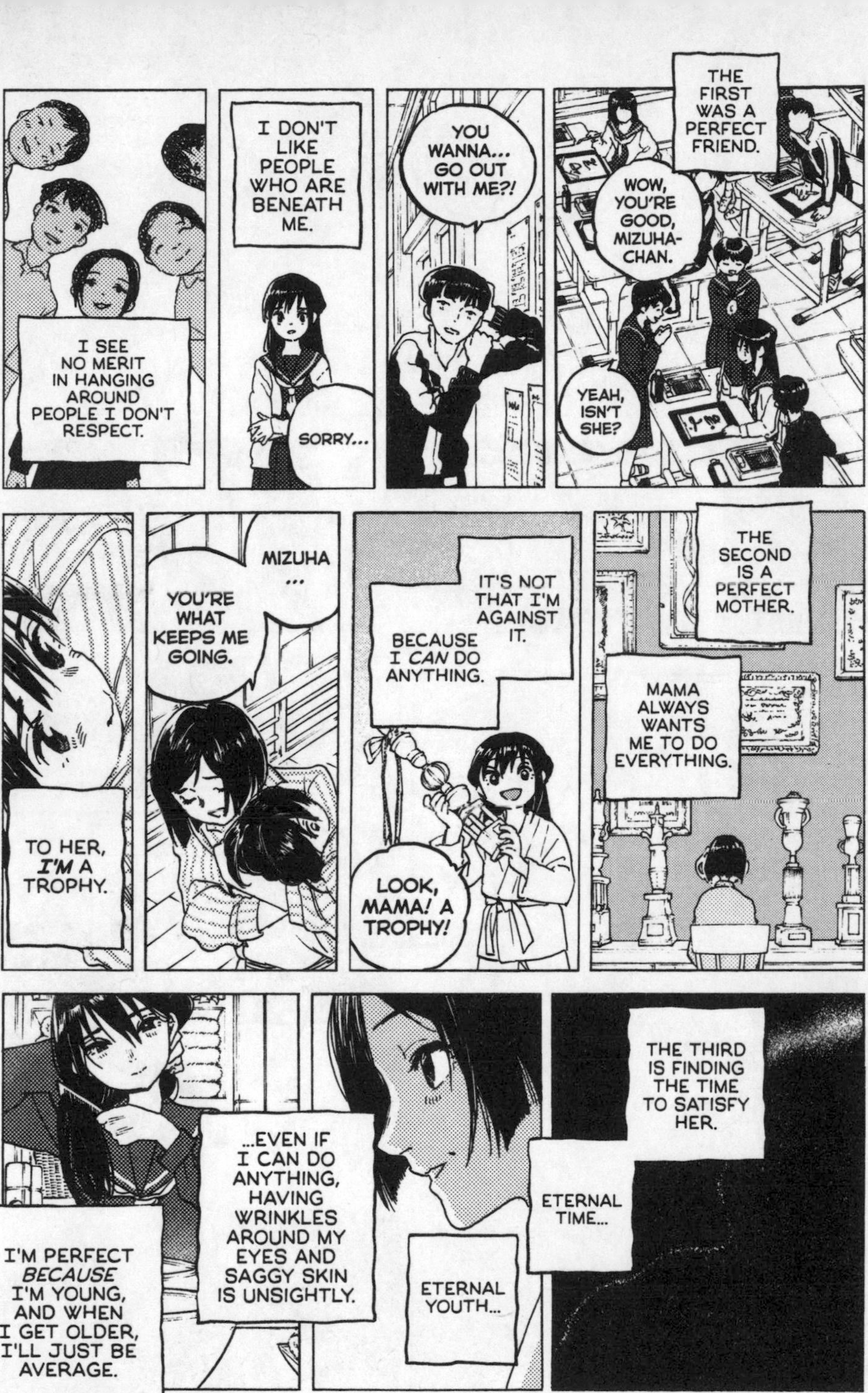
THE FIRST WAS A PERFECT FRIEND.
WOW, YOU'RE GOOD, MIZUHA-CHAN.
YEAH, ISN'T SHE?
YOU WANNA... GO OUT WITH ME?!
I DON'T LIKE PEOPLE WHO ARE BENEATH ME.
SORRY...
I SEE NO MERIT IN HANGING AROUND PEOPLE I DON'T RESPECT.
THE SECOND IS A PERFECT MOTHER.
MAMA ALWAYS WANTS ME TO DO EVERYTHING.
IT'S NOT THAT I'M AGAINST IT.
BECAUSE I *CAN* DO ANYTHING.
LOOK, MAMA! A TROPHY!
MIZUHA...
YOU'RE WHAT KEEPS ME GOING.
TO HER, *I'M* A TROPHY.
THE THIRD IS FINDING THE TIME TO SATISFY HER.
ETERNAL TIME...
ETERNAL YOUTH...
I'M PERFECT *BECAUSE* I'M YOUNG, AND WHEN I GET OLDER, I'LL JUST BE AVERAGE.
...EVEN IF I CAN DO ANYTHING, HAVING WRINKLES AROUND MY EYES AND SAGGY SKIN IS UNSIGHTLY.

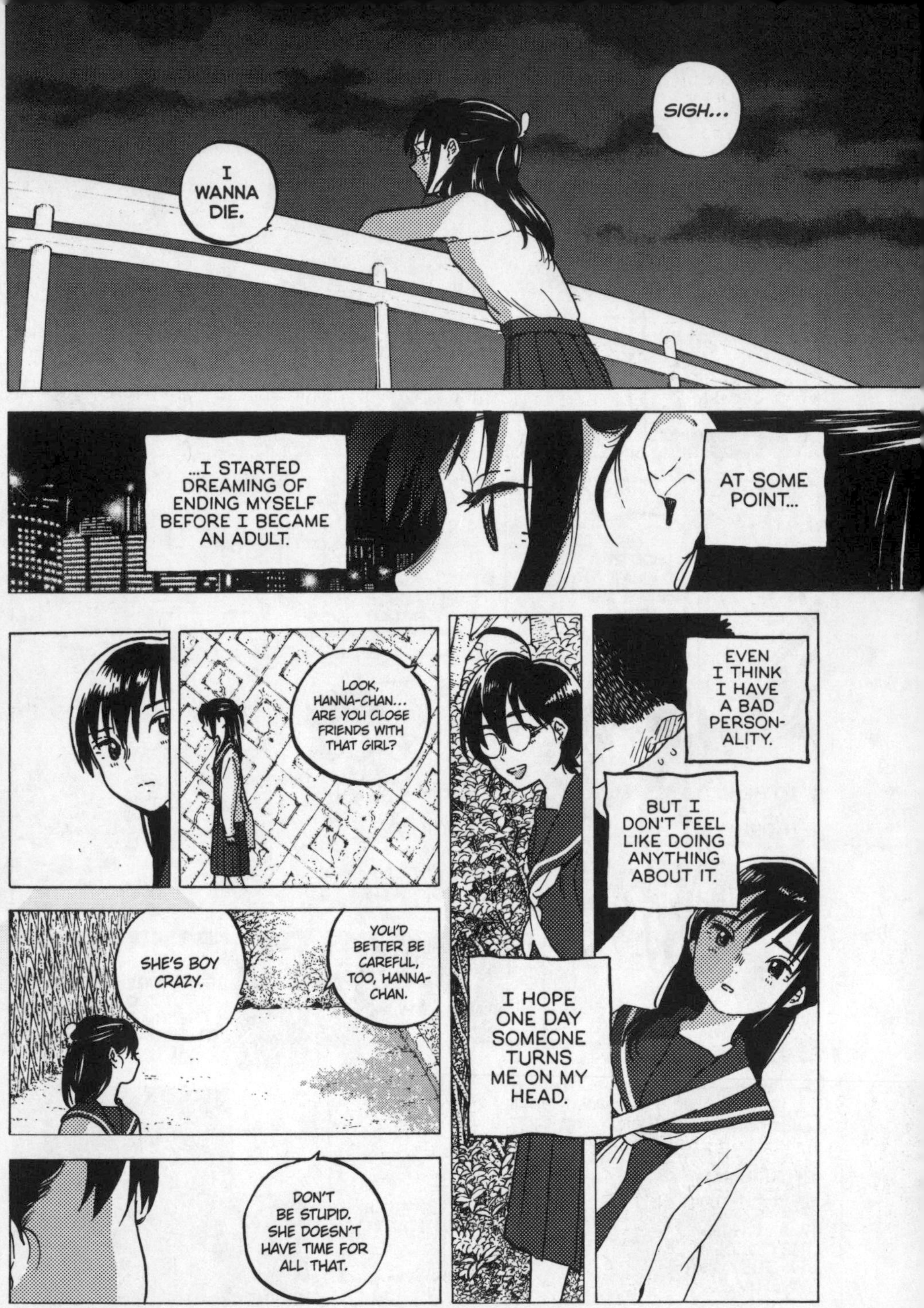
SIGH...
I WANNA DIE.
AT SOME POINT...
...I STARTED DREAMING OF ENDING MYSELF BEFORE I BECAME AN ADULT.
EVEN I THINK I HAVE A BAD PERSON-ALITY.
BUT I DON'T FEEL LIKE DOING ANYTHING ABOUT IT.
I HOPE ONE DAY SOMEONE TURNS ME ON MY HEAD.
LOOK, HANNA-CHAN... ARE YOU CLOSE FRIENDS WITH THAT GIRL?
YOU'D BETTER BE CAREFUL, TOO, HANNA-CHAN.
SHE'S BOY CRAZY.
DON'T BE STUPID. SHE DOESN'T HAVE TIME FOR ALL THAT.

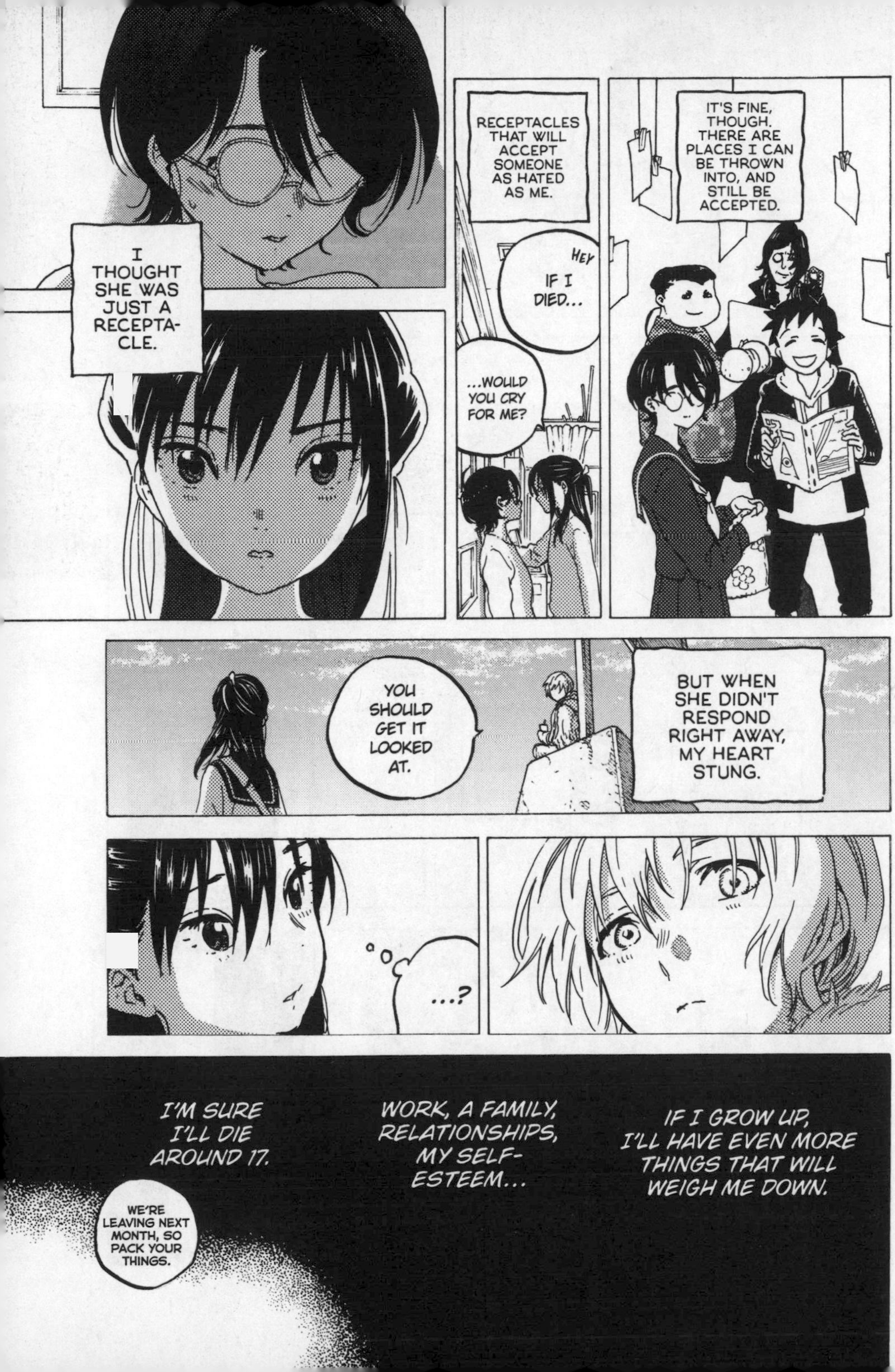
IT'S FINE, THOUGH. THERE ARE PLACES I CAN BE THROWN INTO, AND STILL BE ACCEPTED.
RECEPTACLES THAT WILL ACCEPT SOMEONE AS HATED AS ME.
HEY
IF I DIED...
...WOULD YOU CRY FOR ME?
I THOUGHT SHE WAS JUST A RECEPTACLE.
BUT WHEN SHE DIDN'T RESPOND RIGHT AWAY, MY HEART STUNG.
YOU SHOULD GET IT LOOKED AT.
...?
IF I GROW UP, I'LL HAVE EVEN MORE THINGS THAT WILL WEIGH ME DOWN.
WORK, A FAMILY, RELATIONSHIPS, MY SELF-ESTEEM...
I'M SURE I'LL DIE AROUND 17.
WE'RE LEAVING NEXT MONTH, SO PACK YOUR THINGS.

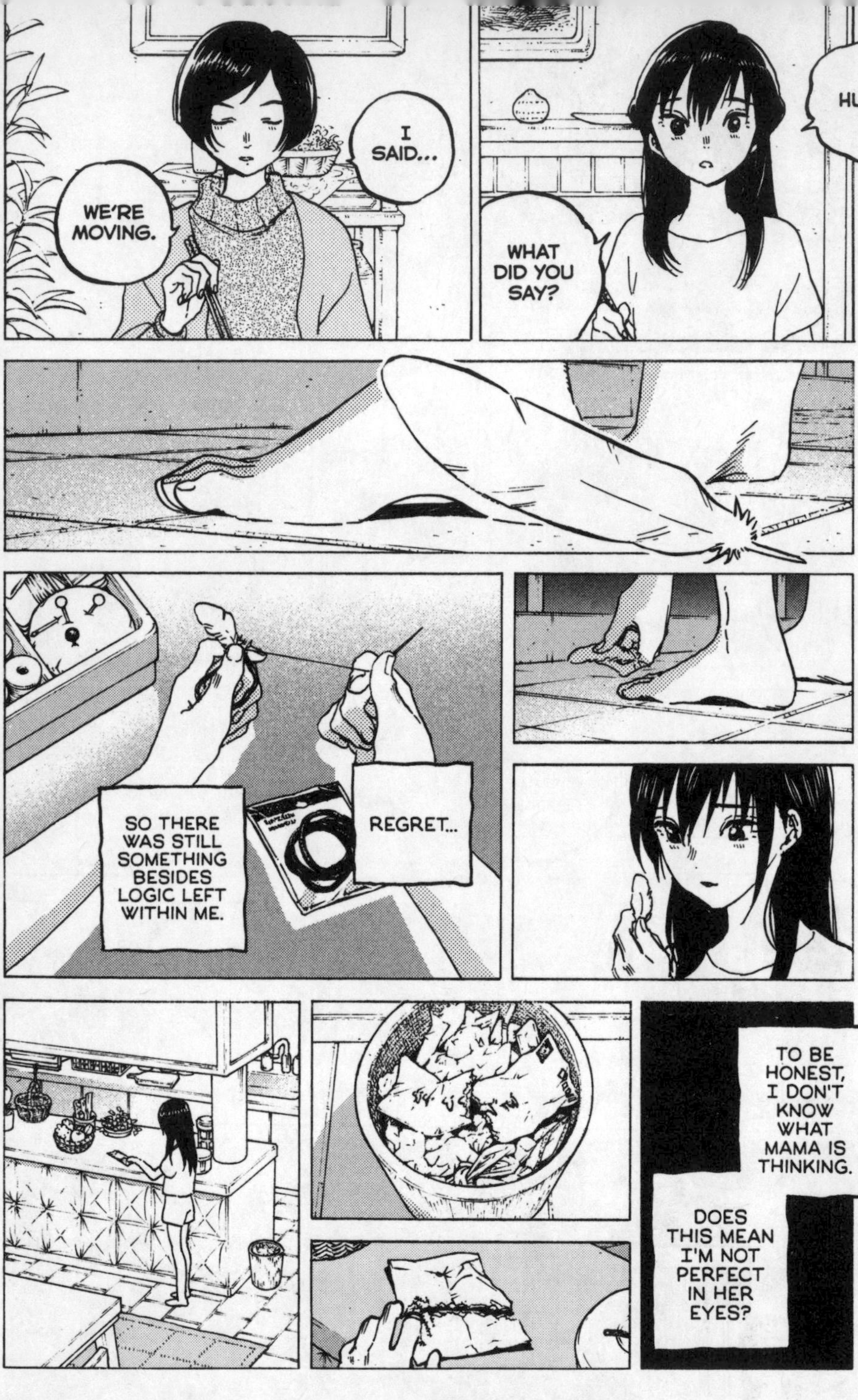
HUH?
WHAT DID YOU SAY?
I SAID...
WE'RE MOVING.
REGRET...
SO THERE WAS STILL SOMETHING BESIDES LOGIC LEFT WITHIN ME.
TO BE HONEST, I DON'T KNOW WHAT MAMA IS THINKING.
DOES THIS MEAN I'M NOT PERFECT IN HER EYES?

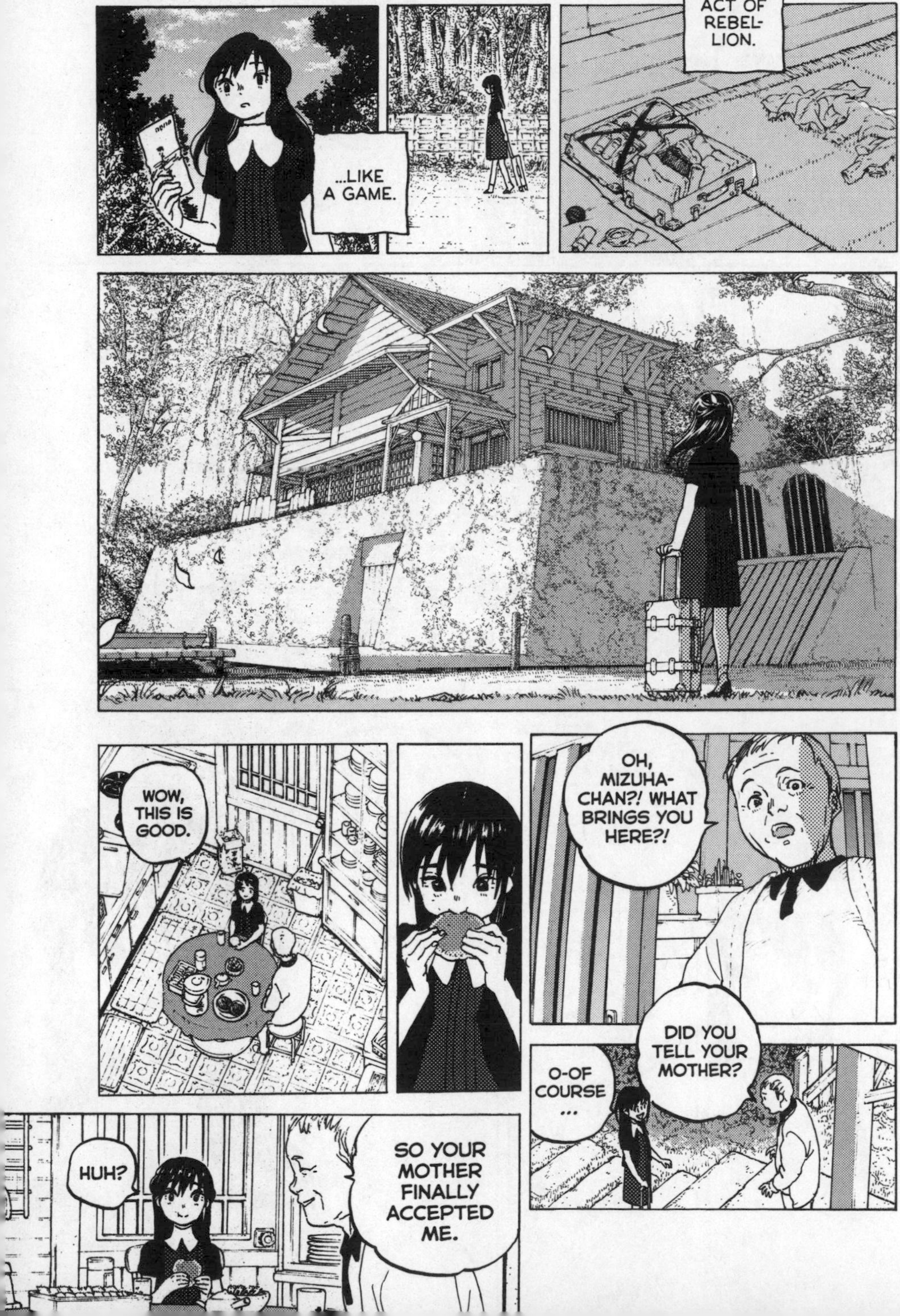
A TINY ACT OF REBEL-LION.
...LIKE A GAME.
OH, MIZUHA-CHAN?! WHAT BRINGS YOU HERE?!
DID YOU TELL YOUR MOTHER?
O-OF COURSE ...
WOW, THIS IS GOOD.
SO YOUR MOTHER FINALLY ACCEPTED ME.
HUH?

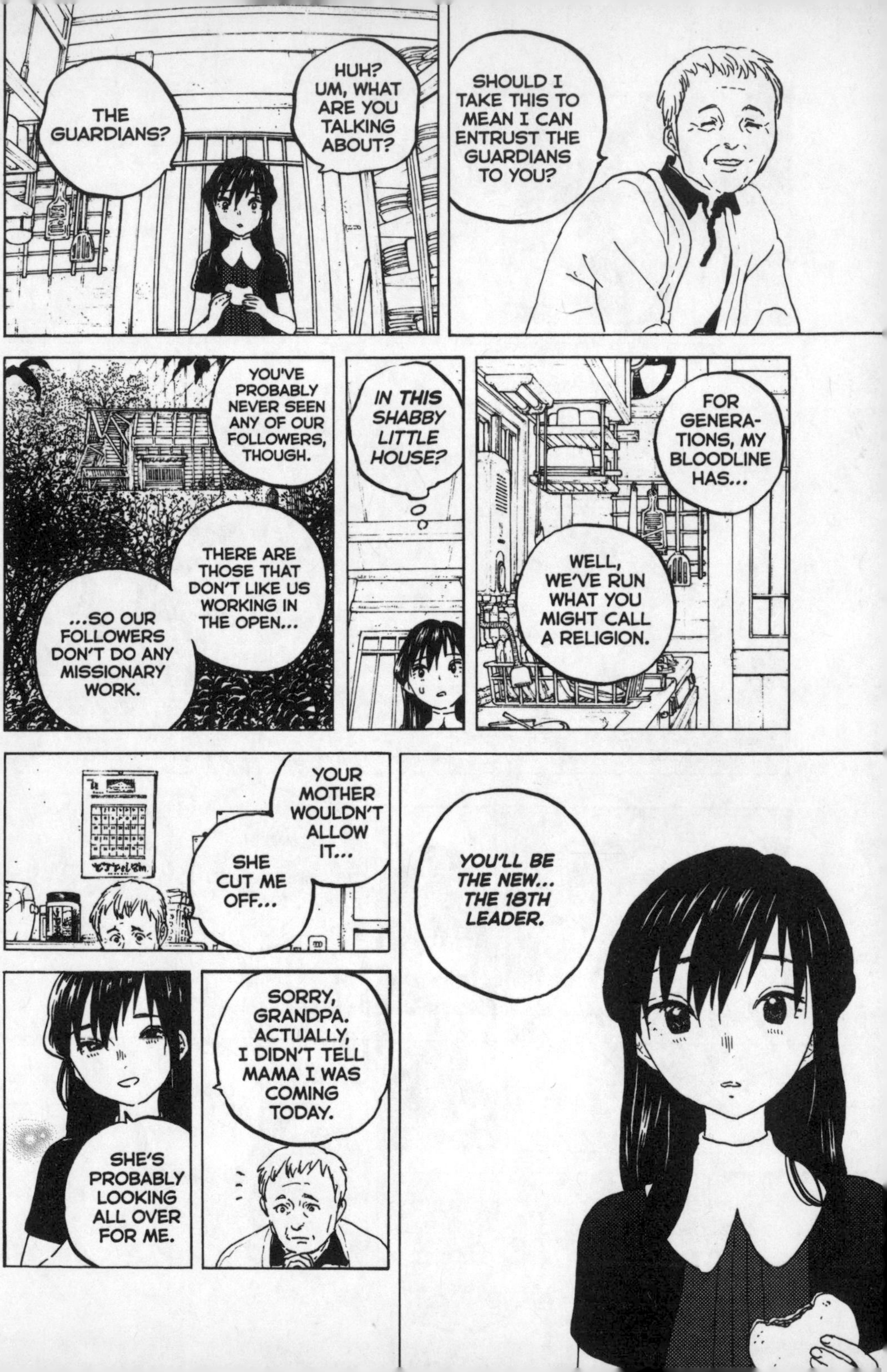
SHOULD I TAKE THIS TO MEAN I CAN ENTRUST THE GUARDIANS TO YOU?
HUH? UM, WHAT ARE YOU TALKING ABOUT?
THE GUARDIANS?
FOR GENERATIONS, MY BLOODLINE HAS...
WELL, WE'VE RUN WHAT YOU MIGHT CALL A RELIGION.
IN THIS SHABBY LITTLE HOUSE?
YOU'VE PROBABLY NEVER SEEN ANY OF OUR FOLLOWERS, THOUGH.
THERE ARE THOSE THAT DON'T LIKE US WORKING IN THE OPEN...
...SO OUR FOLLOWERS DON'T DO ANY MISSIONARY WORK.
YOU'LL BE THE NEW... THE 18TH LEADER.
YOUR MOTHER WOULDN'T ALLOW IT...
SHE CUT ME OFF...
SORRY, GRANDPA. ACTUALLY, I DIDN'T TELL MAMA I WAS COMING TODAY.
SHE'S PROBABLY LOOKING ALL OVER FOR ME.

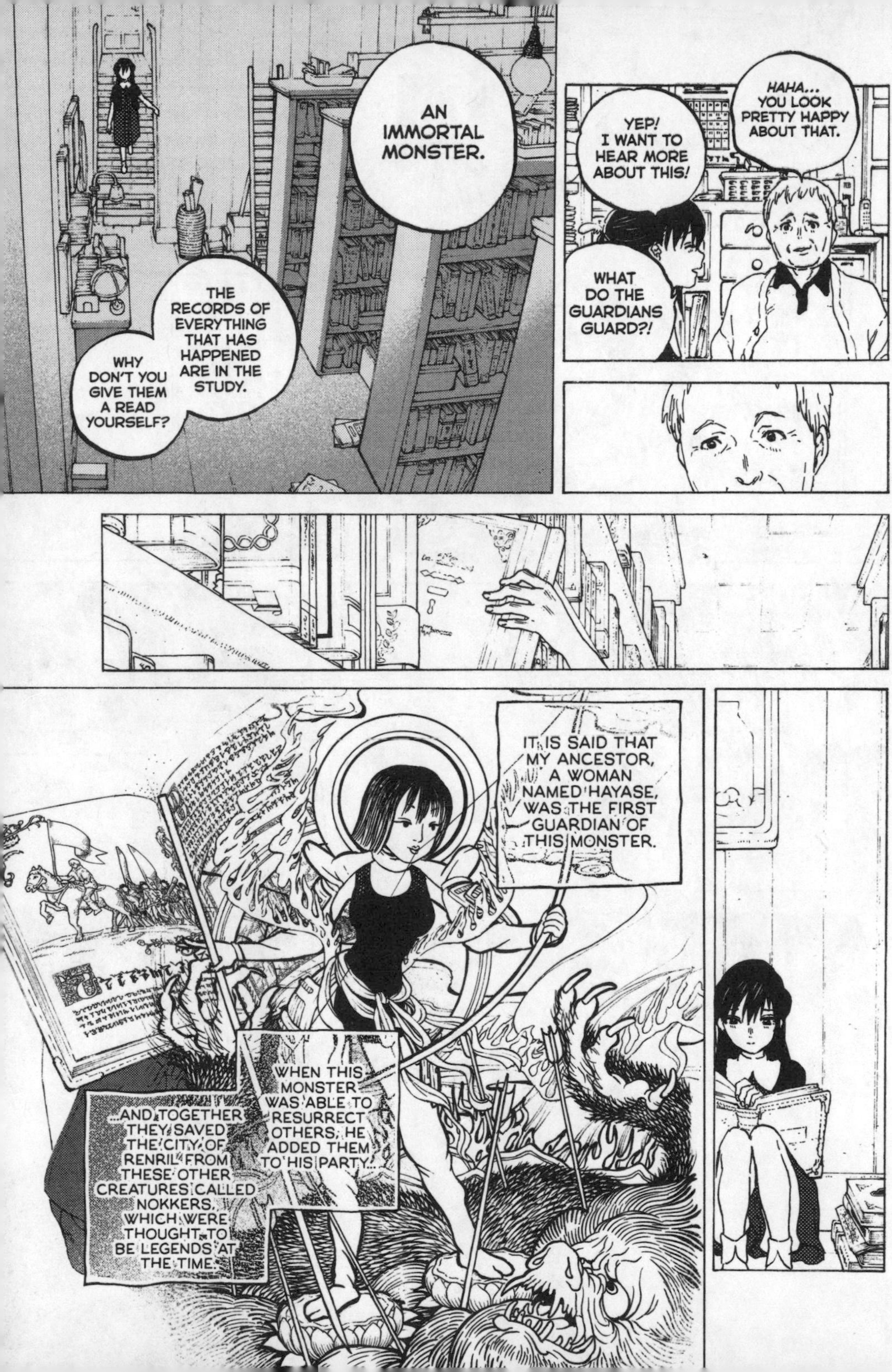
HAHA... YOU LOOK PRETTY HAPPY ABOUT THAT.
YEP! I WANT TO HEAR MORE ABOUT THIS!
WHAT DO THE GUARDIANS GUARD?!
AN IMMORTAL MONSTER.
THE RECORDS OF EVERYTHING THAT HAS HAPPENED ARE IN THE STUDY.
WHY DON'T YOU GIVE THEM A READ YOURSELF?
IT IS SAID THAT MY ANCESTOR, A WOMAN NAMED HAYASE, WAS THE FIRST GUARDIAN OF THIS MONSTER.
WHEN THIS MONSTER WAS ABLE TO RESURRECT OTHERS, HE ADDED THEM TO HIS PARTY...
...AND TOGETHER THEY SAVED THE CITY OF RENRIL FROM THESE OTHER CREATURES CALLED NOKKERS, WHICH WERE THOUGHT TO BE LEGENDS AT THE TIME.

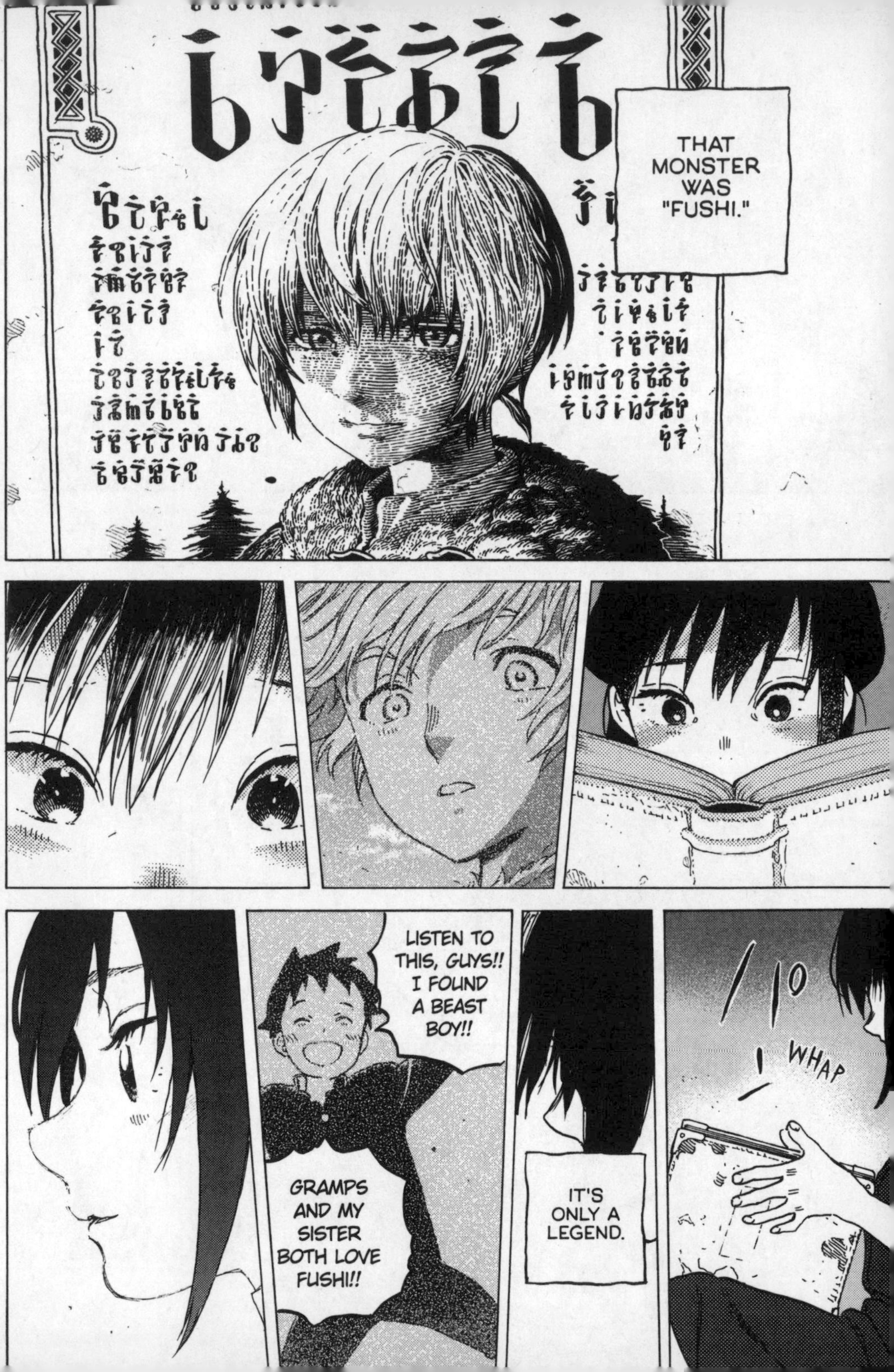
THAT MONSTER WAS "FUSHI."
WHAP
IT'S ONLY A LEGEND.
LISTEN TO THIS, GUYS!! I FOUND A BEAST BOY!!
GRAMPS AND MY SISTER BOTH LOVE FUSHI!!

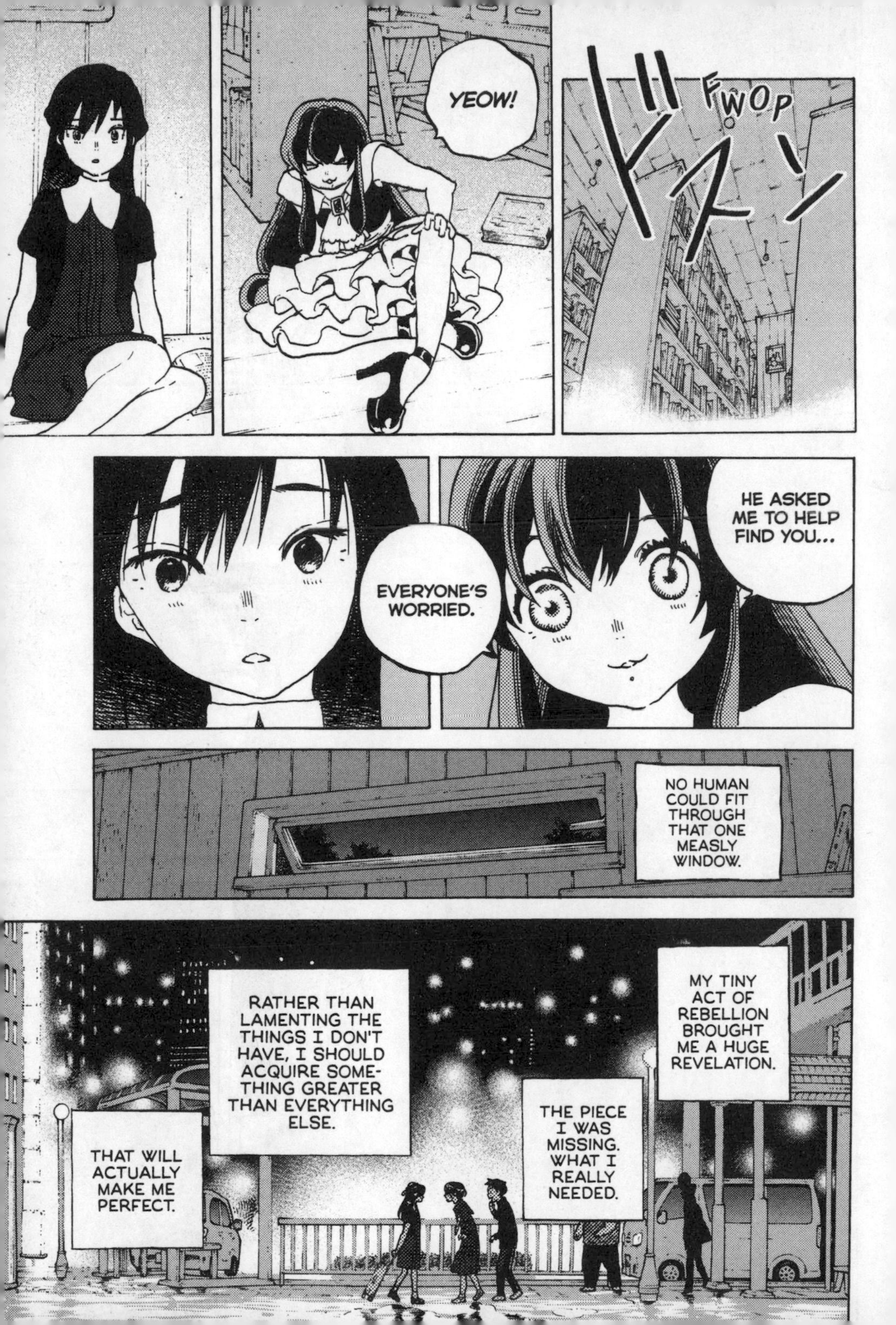
ドスン
FWOP
YEOW!
HE ASKED ME TO HELP FIND YOU...
EVERYONE'S WORRIED.
NO HUMAN COULD FIT THROUGH THAT ONE MEASLY WINDOW.
MY TINY ACT OF REBELLION BROUGHT ME A HUGE REVELATION.
THE PIECE I WAS MISSING. WHAT I REALLY NEEDED.
RATHER THAN LAMENTING THE THINGS I DON'T HAVE, I SHOULD ACQUIRE SOME-THING GREATER THAN EVERYTHING ELSE.
THAT WILL ACTUALLY MAKE ME PERFECT.

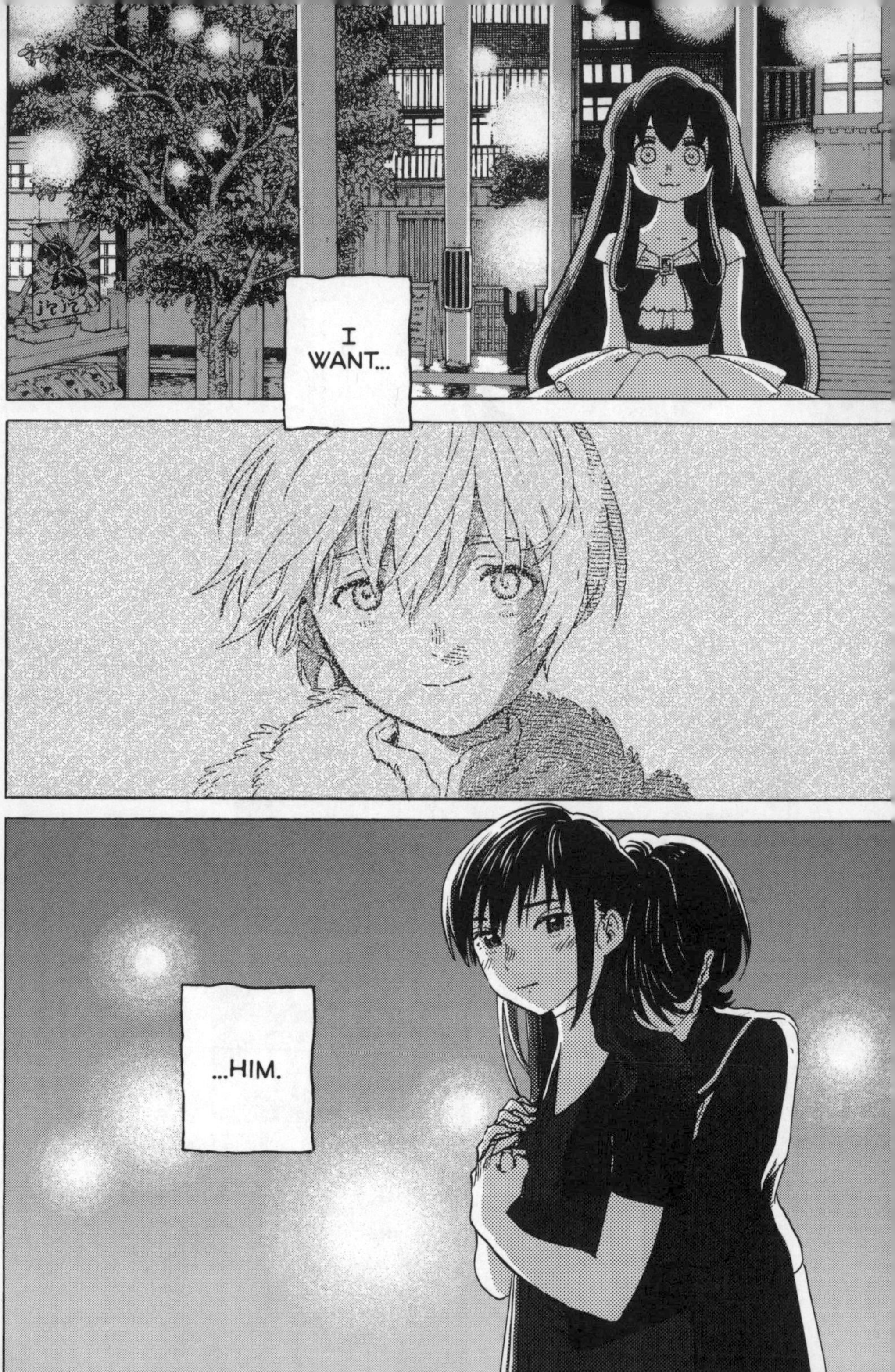
I WANT...
...HIM.

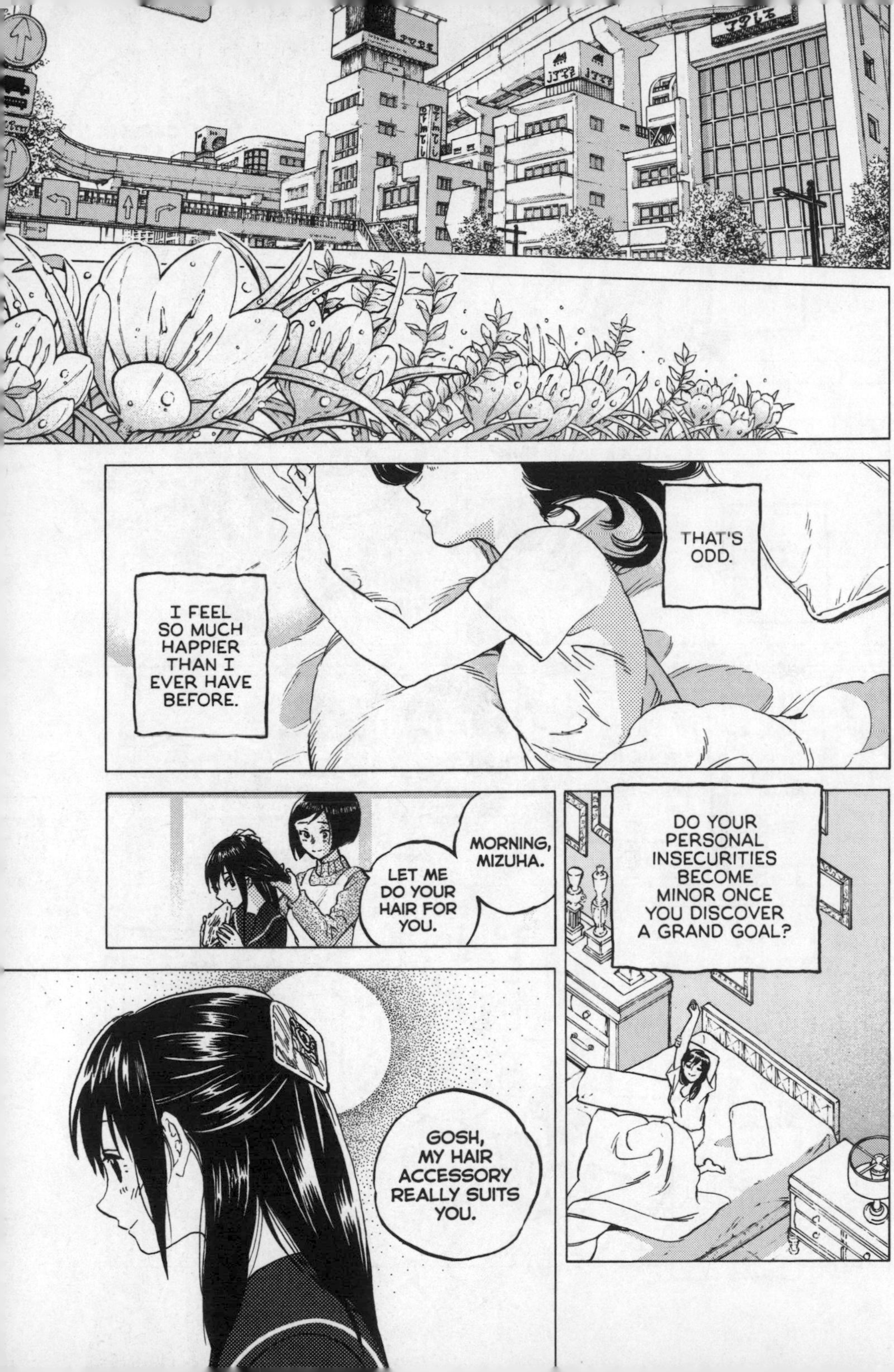
THAT'S ODD.
I FEEL SO MUCH HAPPIER THAN I EVER HAVE BEFORE.
DO YOUR PERSONAL INSECURITIES BECOME MINOR ONCE YOU DISCOVER A GRAND GOAL?
MORNING, MIZUHA.
LET ME DO YOUR HAIR FOR YOU.
GOSH, MY HAIR ACCESSORY REALLY SUITS YOU.

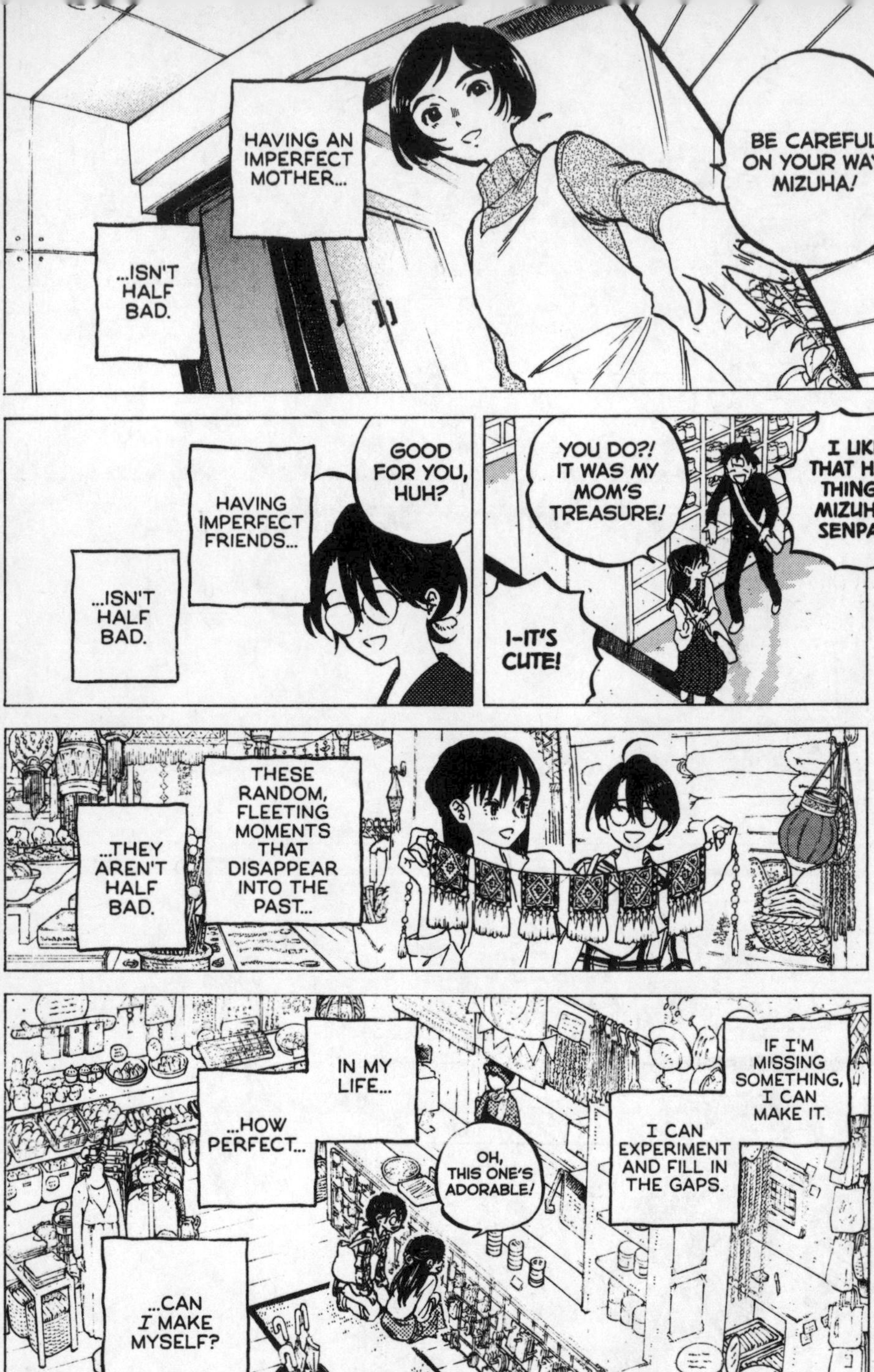
BE CAREFUL ON YOUR WAY, MIZUHA!
HAVING AN IMPERFECT MOTHER...
...ISN'T HALF BAD.
I LIKE THAT HAIR THINGY, MIZUHA-SENPAI!!!
YOU DO?! IT WAS MY MOM'S TREASURE!
I-IT'S CUTE!
GOOD FOR YOU, HUH?
HAVING IMPERFECT FRIENDS...
...ISN'T HALF BAD.
THESE RANDOM, FLEETING MOMENTS THAT DISAPPEAR INTO THE PAST...
...THEY AREN'T HALF BAD.
IF I'M MISSING SOMETHING, I CAN MAKE IT.
I CAN EXPERIMENT AND FILL IN THE GAPS.
OH, THIS ONE'S ADORABLE!
IN MY LIFE...
...HOW PERFECT...
...CAN *I* MAKE MYSELF?

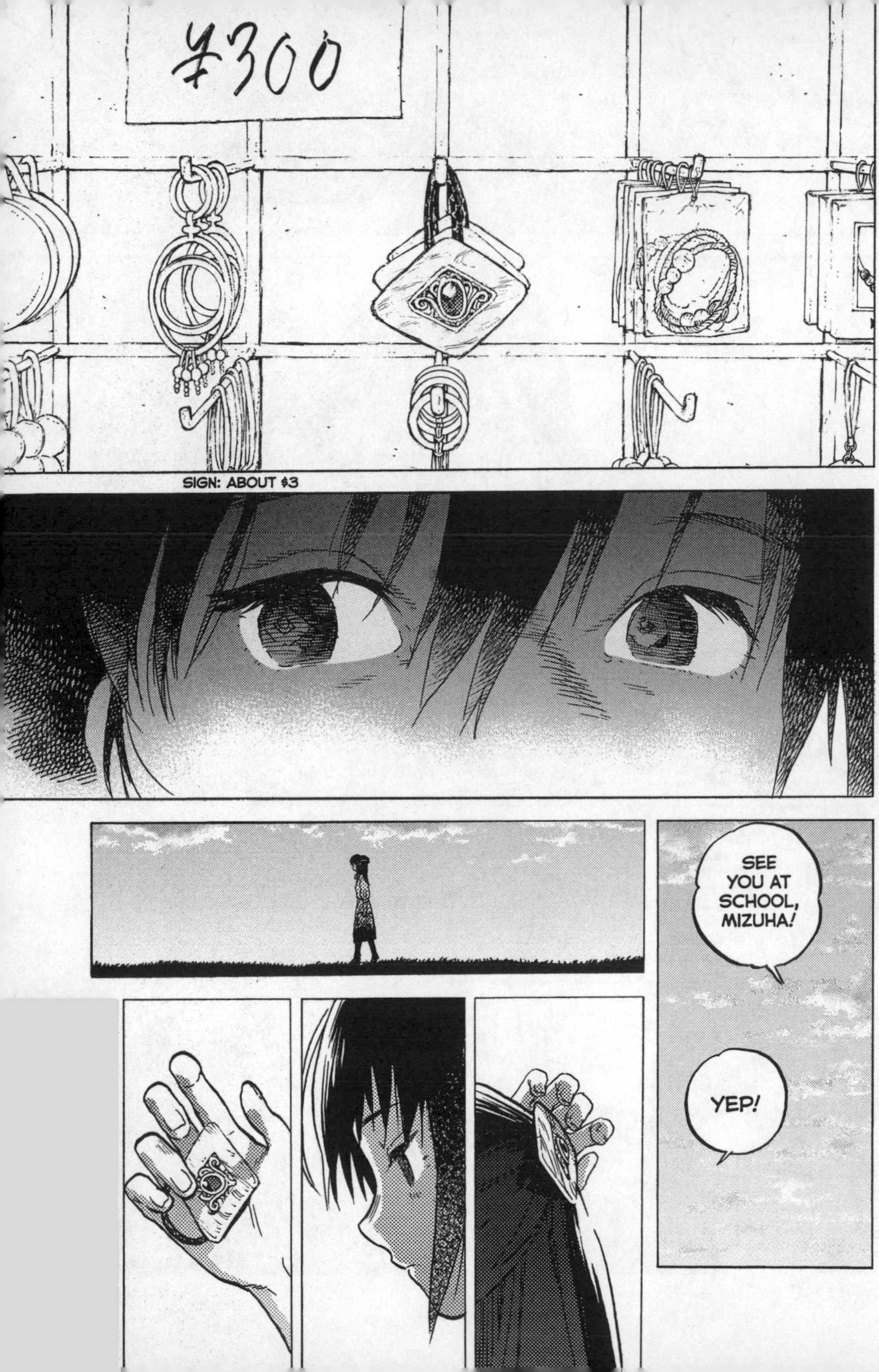
¥300
SIGN: ABOUT $3
SEE YOU AT SCHOOL, MIZUHA!
YEP!

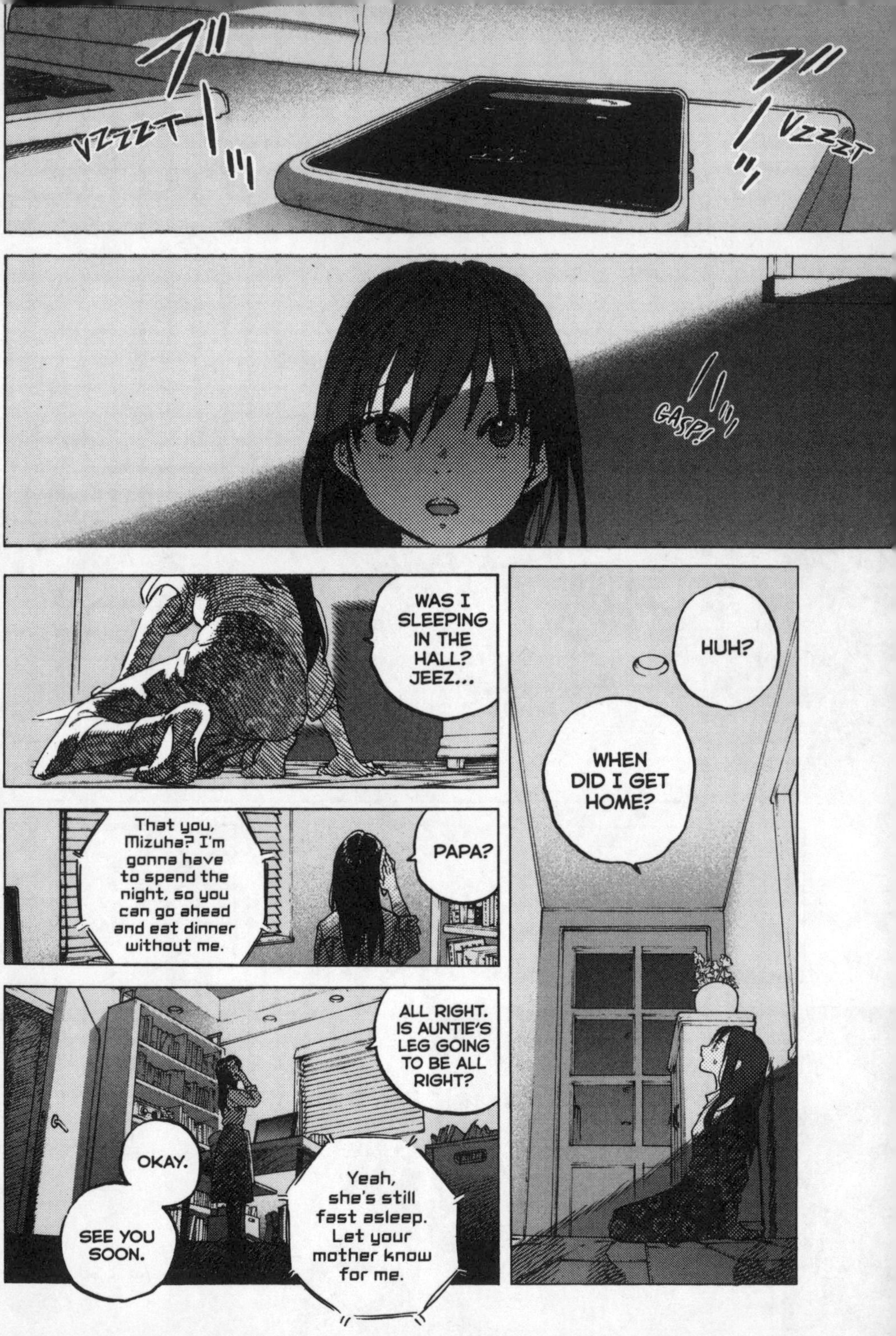
VZZZT
VZZZT
GASP!
HUH?
WHEN DID I GET HOME?
WAS I SLEEPING IN THE HALL? JEEZ...
PAPA?
That you, Mizuha? I'm gonna have to spend the night, so you can go ahead and eat dinner without me.
ALL RIGHT. IS AUNTIE'S LEG GOING TO BE ALL RIGHT?
Yeah, she's still fast asleep. Let your mother know for me.
OKAY.
SEE YOU SOON.

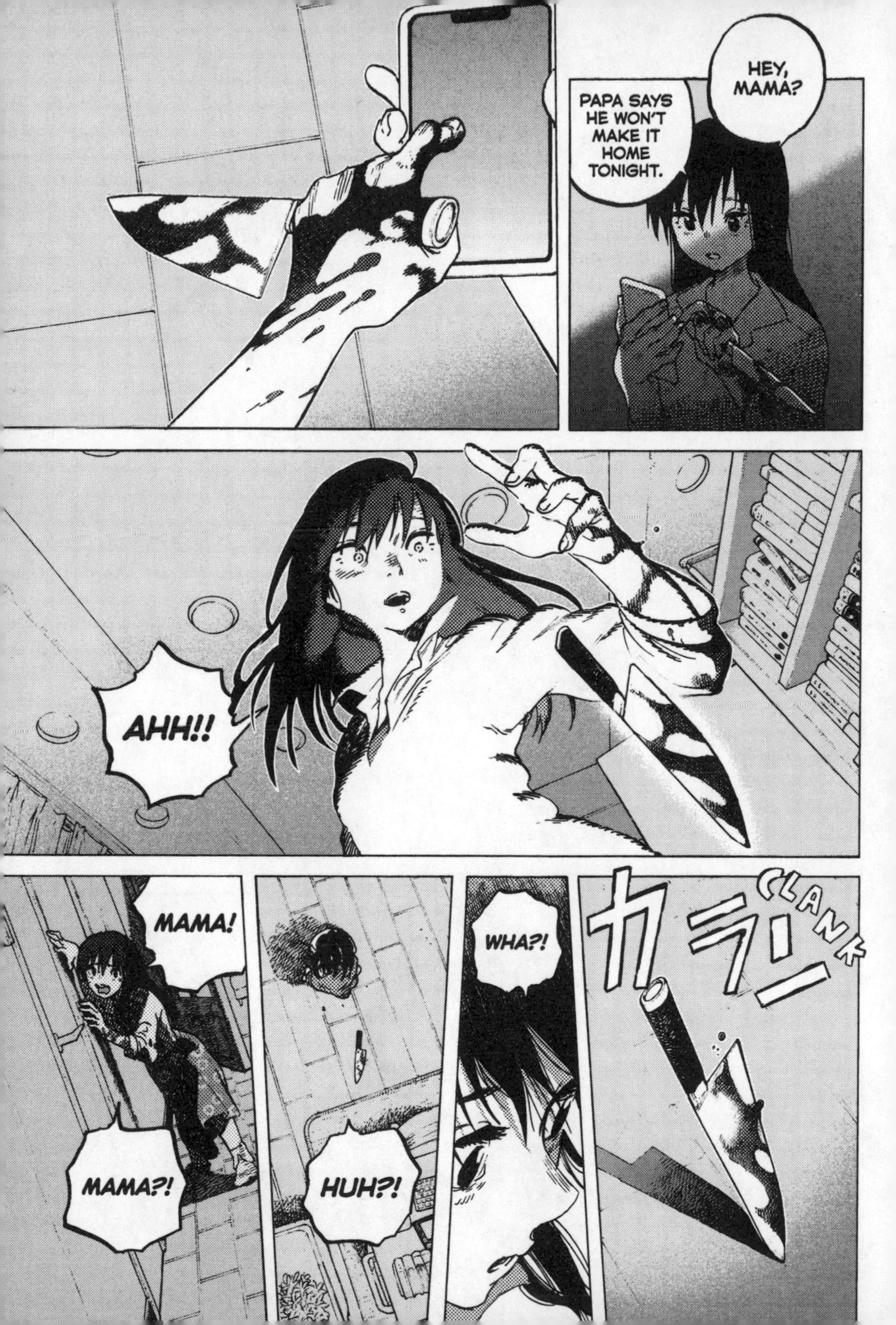
HEY, MAMA?
PAPA SAYS HE WON'T MAKE IT HOME TONIGHT.
AHH!!
カランー
CLANK
WHA?!
HUH?!
MAMA!
MAMA?!

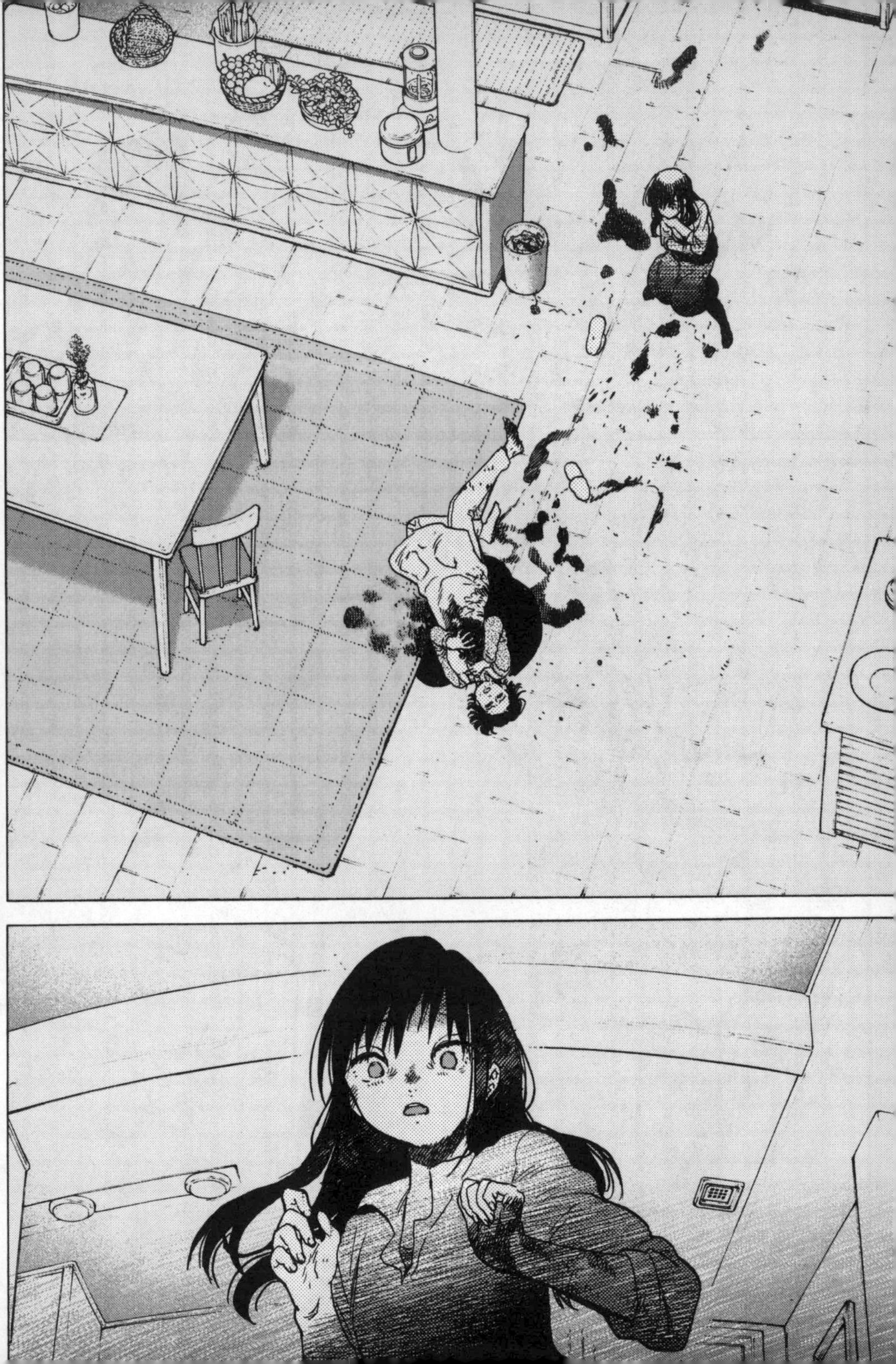

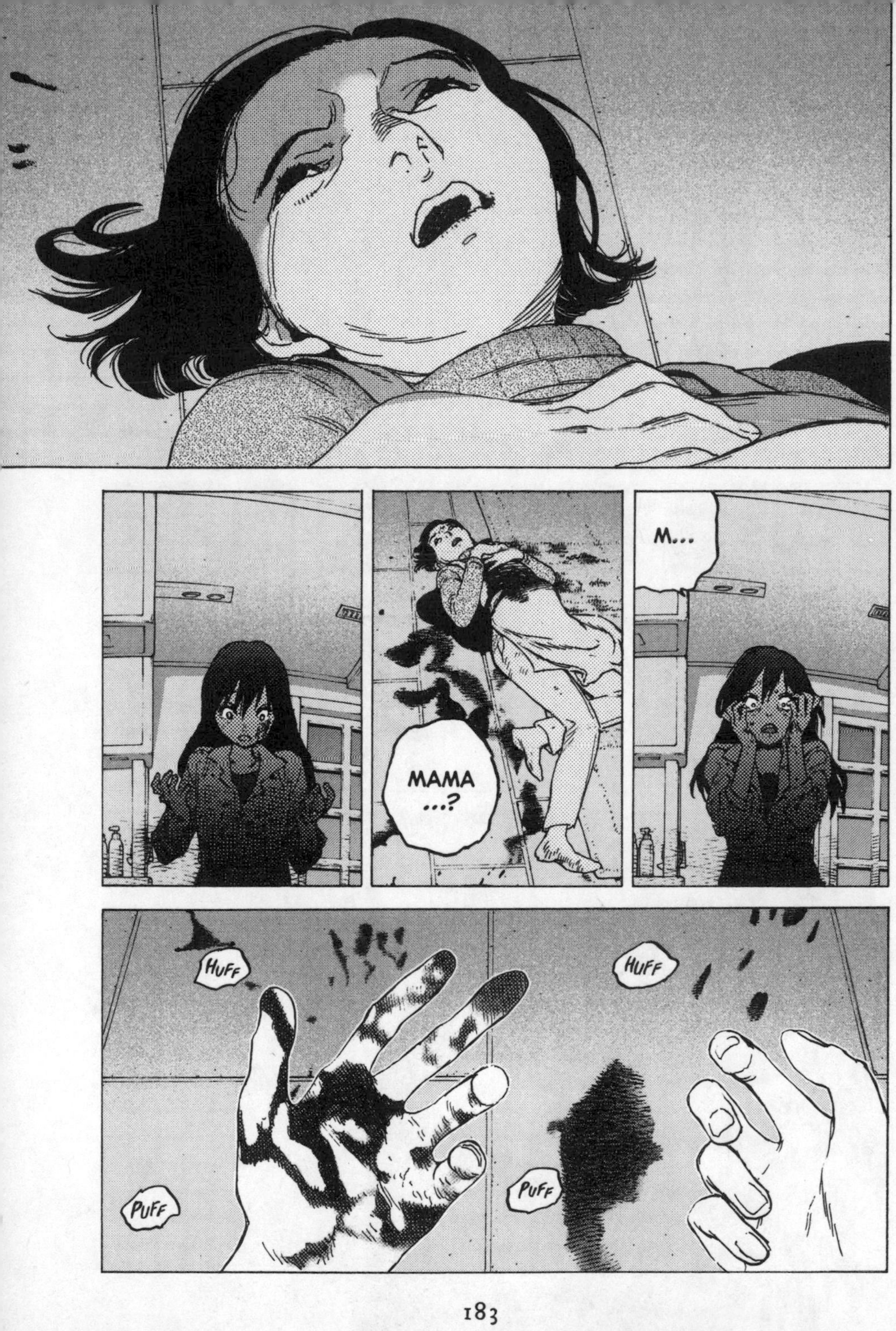
M...
MAMA ...?
HUFF
HUFF
PUFF
PUFF

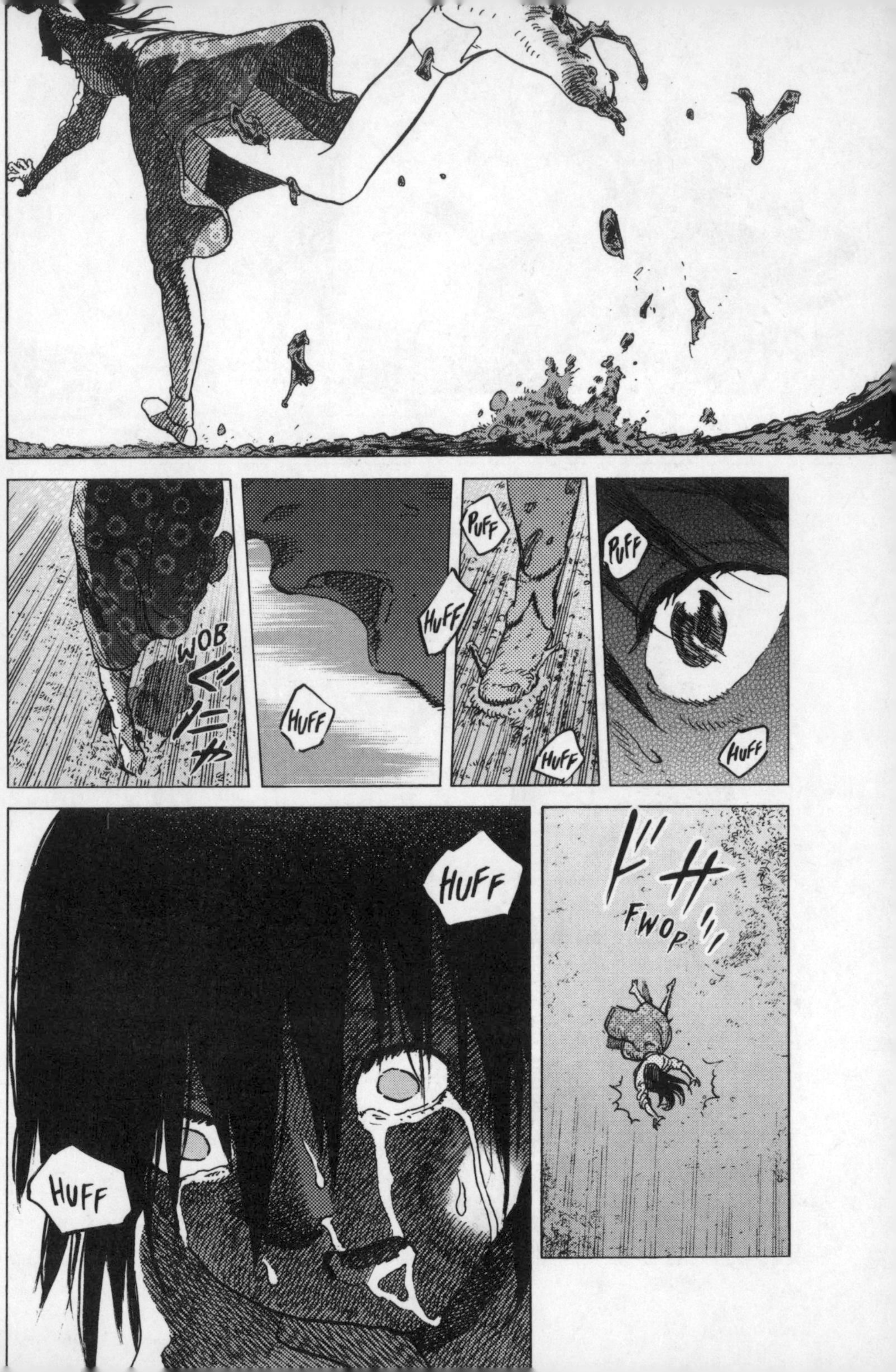
PUFF
HUFF
PUFF
HUFF
HUFF
HUFF
WOB
FWOP
HUFF
HUFF

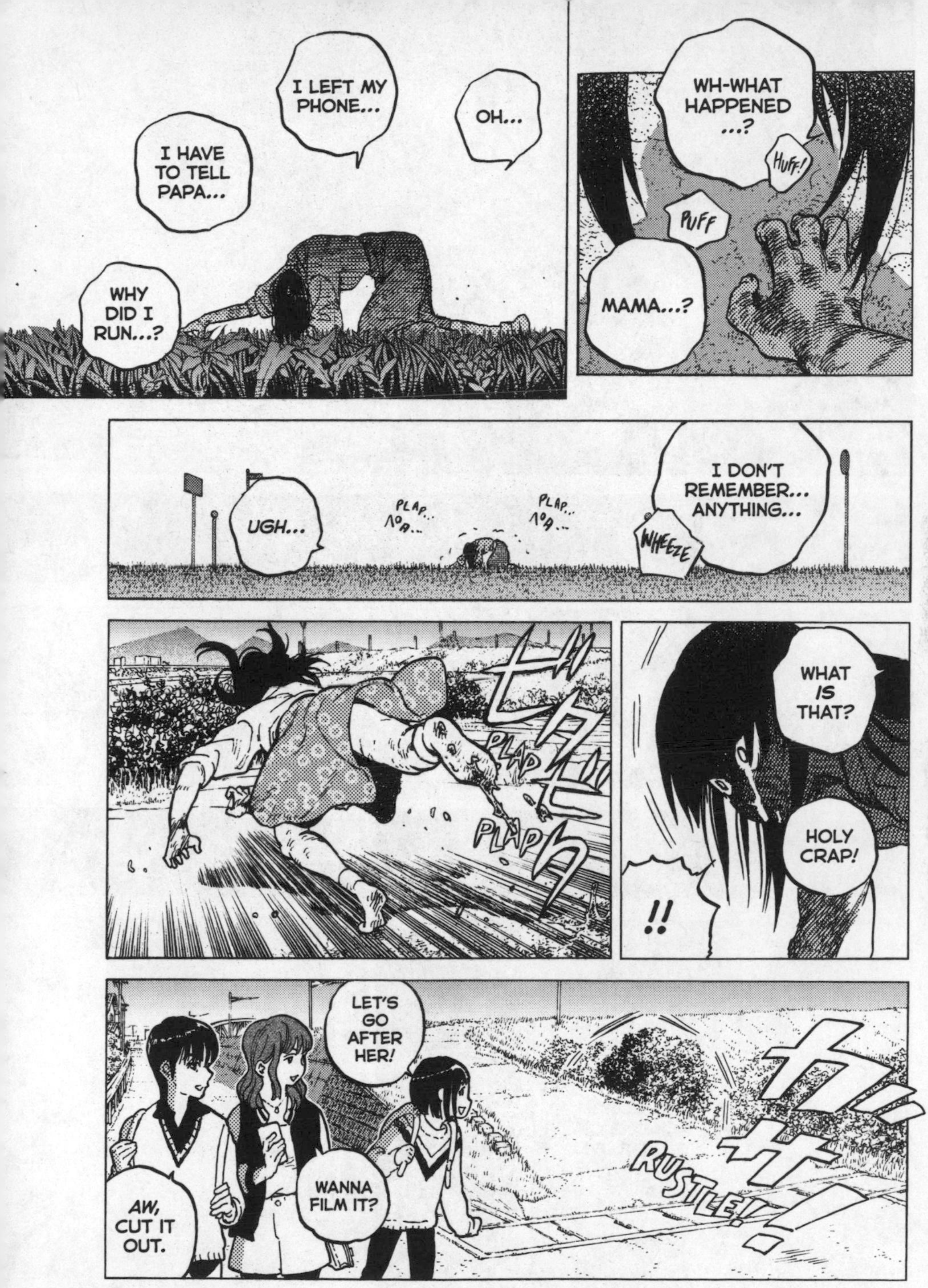
WH-WHAT HAPPENED ...?
HUFF!
PUFF
MAMA...?
OH...
I LEFT MY PHONE...
I HAVE TO TELL PAPA...
WHY DID I RUN...?
I DON'T REMEMBER... ANYTHING...
WHEEZE
PLAP...
PLAP...
UGH...
WHAT IS THAT?
HOLY CRAP!
!!
PLAP
PLAP
RUSTLE!
LET'S GO AFTER HER!
WANNA FILM IT?
AW, CUT IT OUT.

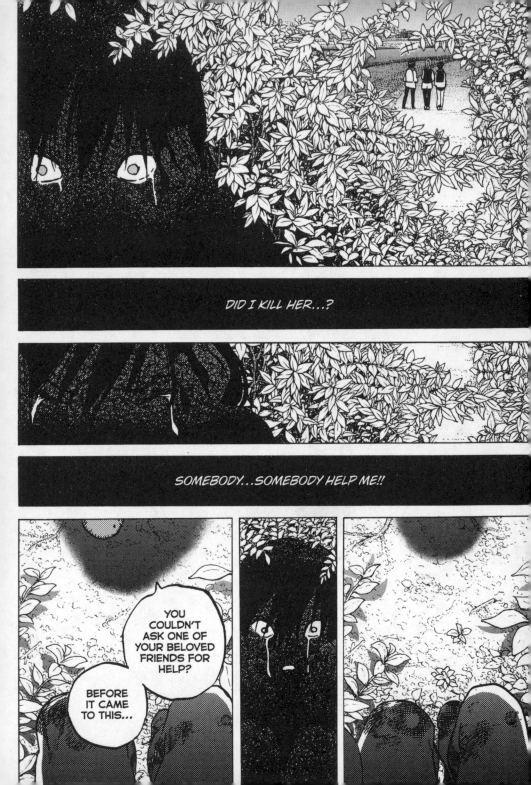

DID I KILL HER...?

SOMEBODY...SOMEBODY HELP ME!!

YOU COULDN'T ASK ONE OF YOUR BELOVED FRIENDS FOR HELP?

BEFORE IT CAME TO THIS...

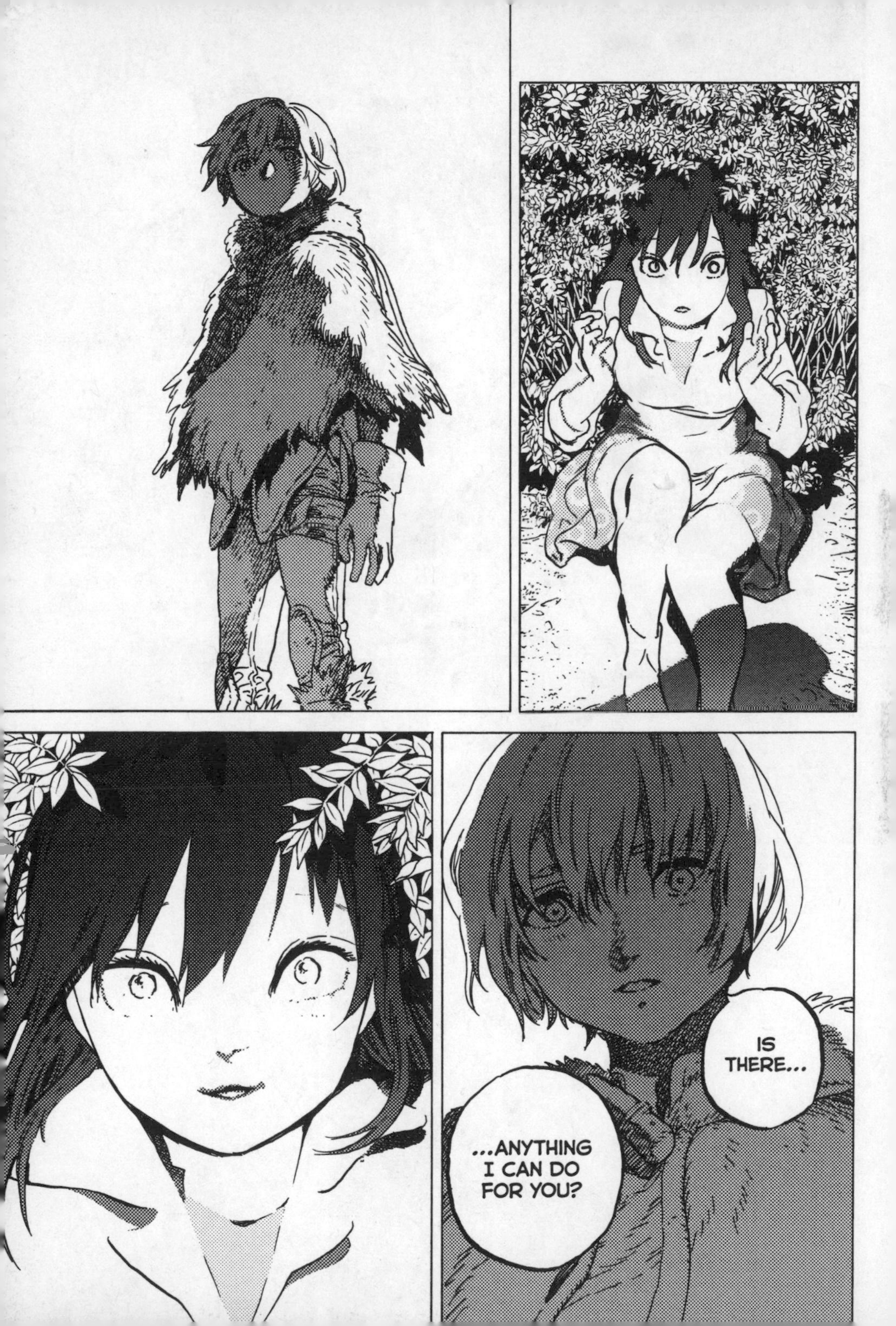
IS THERE...
...ANYTHING I CAN DO FOR YOU?

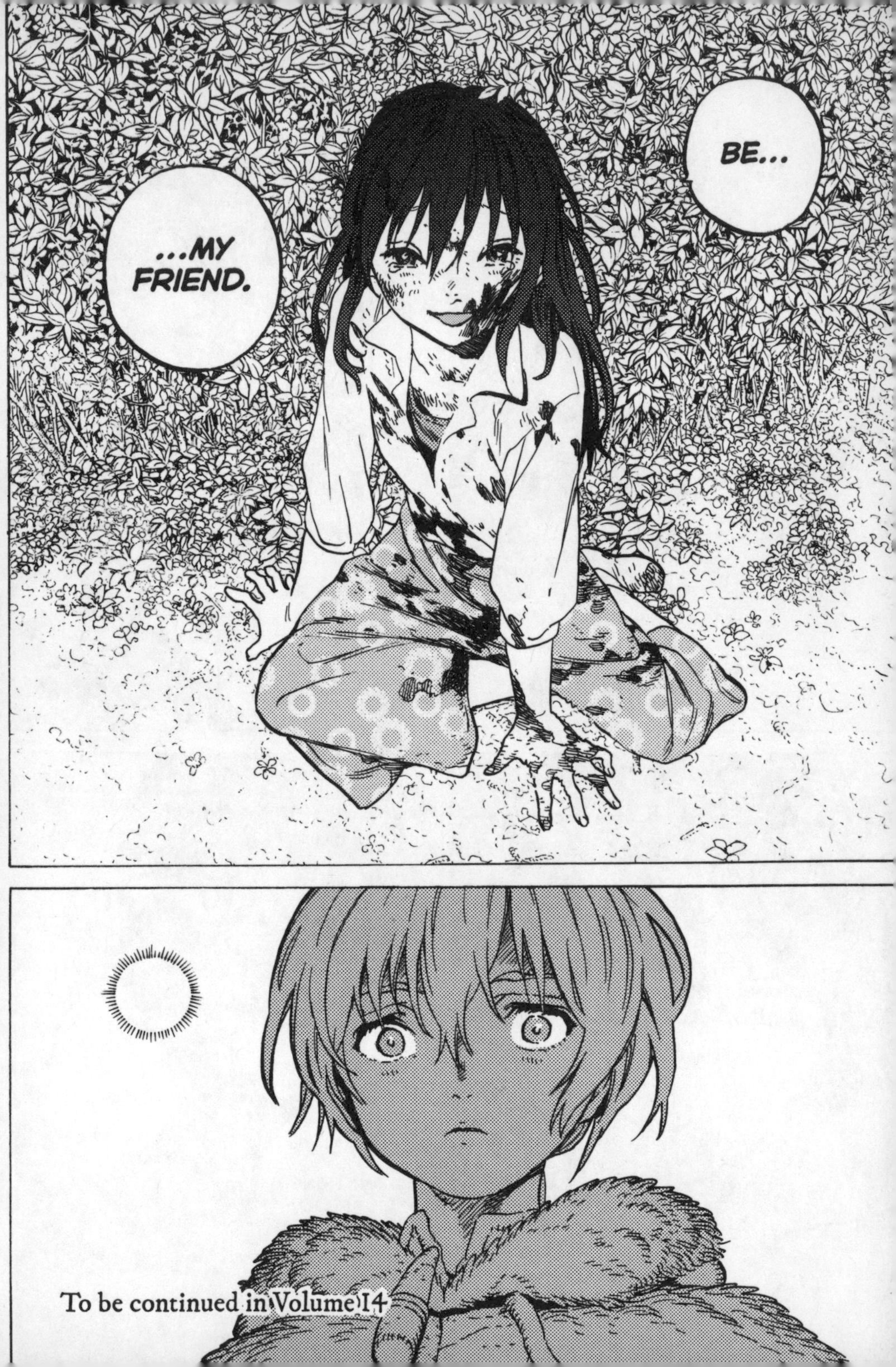
BE...
...MY FRIEND.
To be continued in Volume 14

TO YOUR ETERNITY

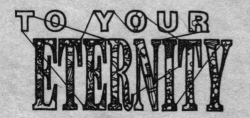

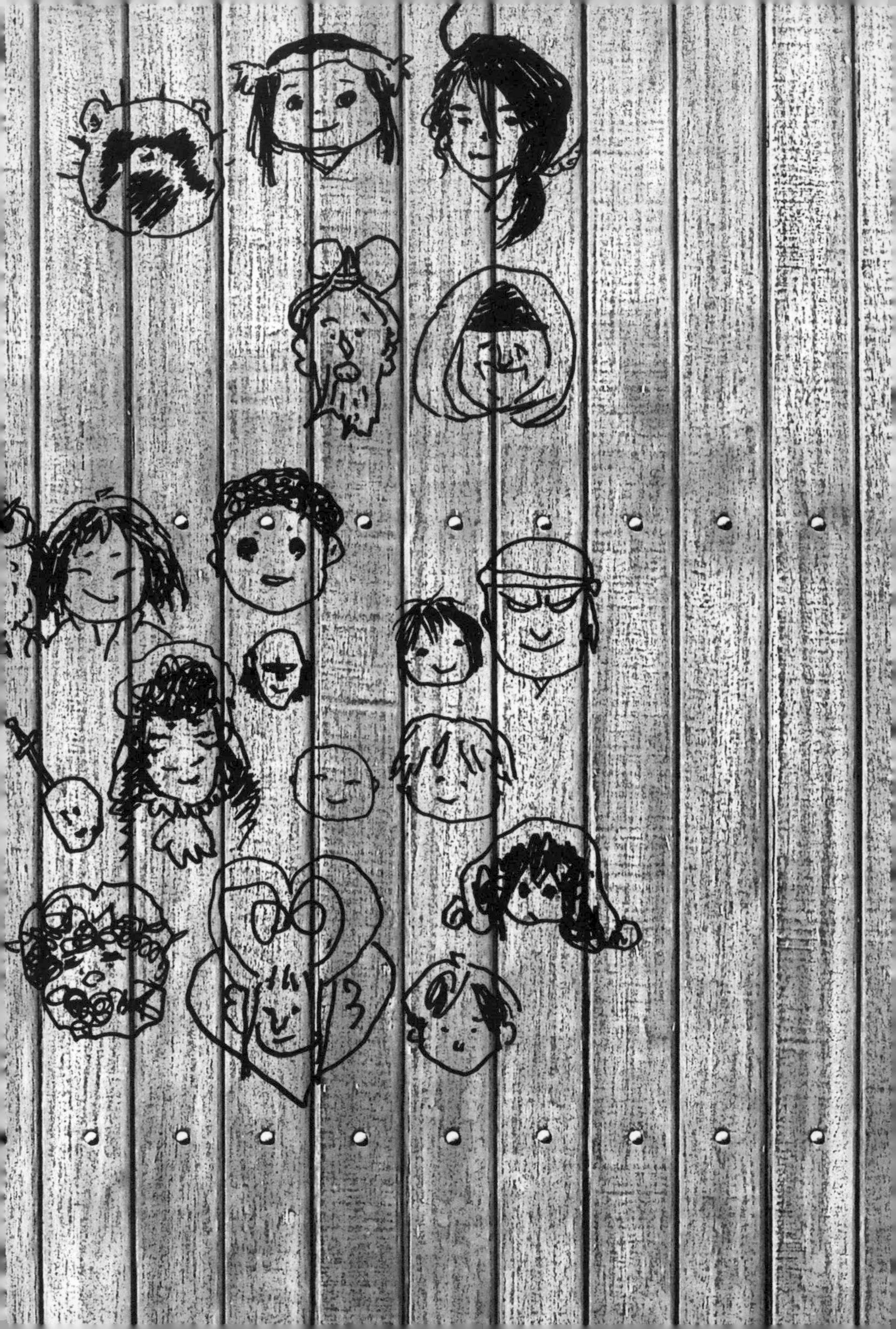

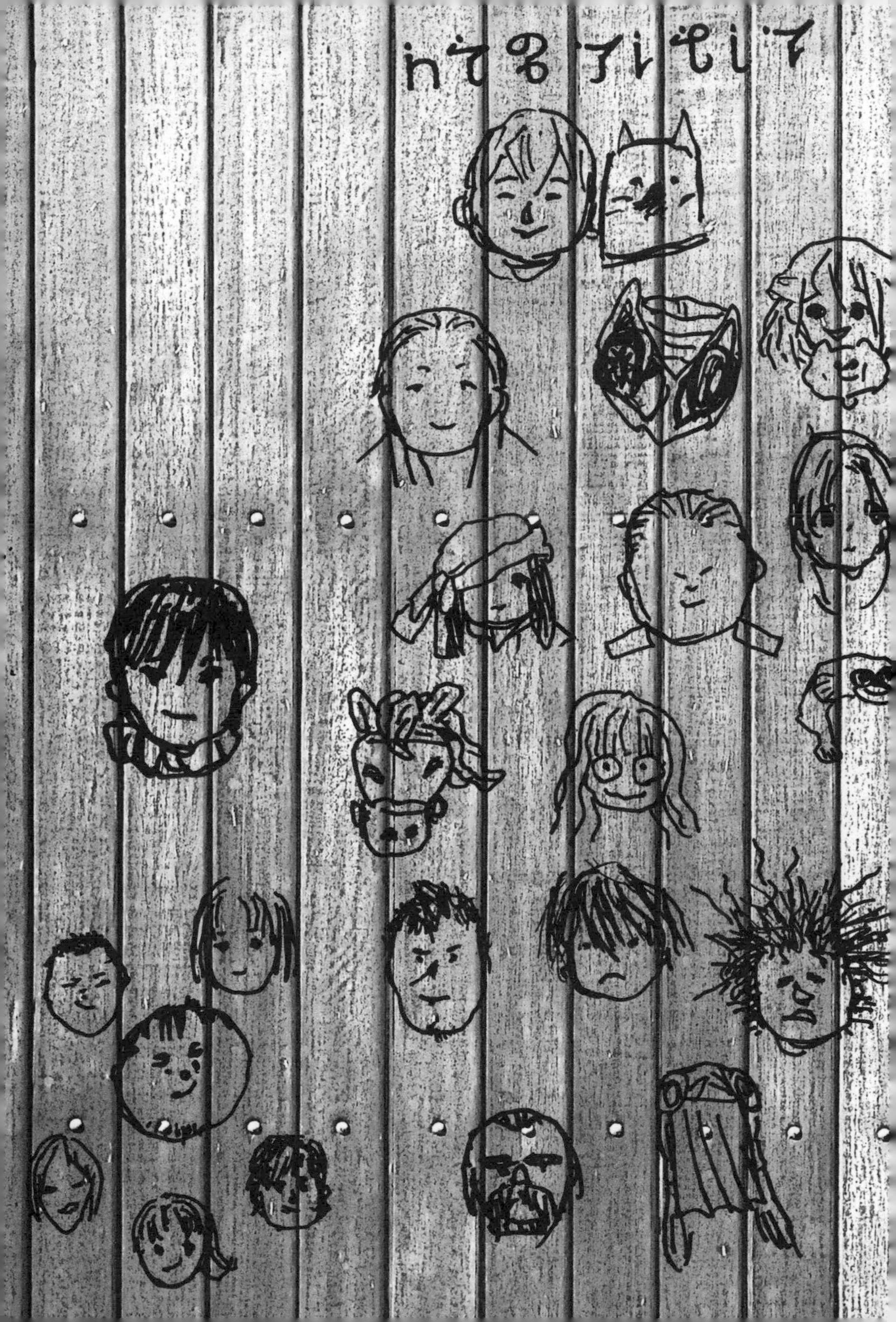

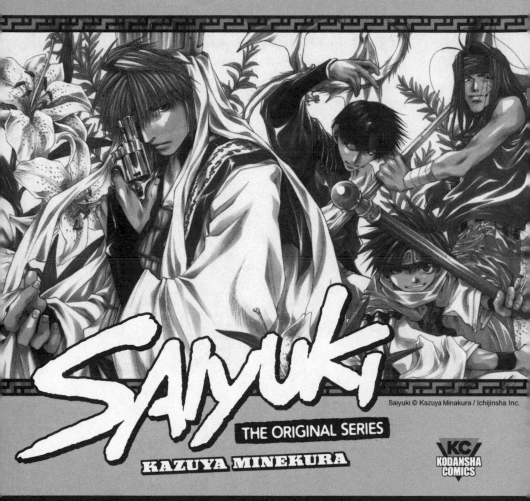

Young characters and steampunk setting, like *Howl's Moving Castle* and *Battle Angel Alita*

Beyond the Clouds © 2018 Nicke / Ki-oon

A boy with a talent for machines and a mysterious girl whose wings he's fixed will take you beyond the clouds! In the tradition of the high-flying, resonant adventure stories of Studio Ghibli comes a gorgeous tale about the longing of young hearts for adventure and friendship!

The art-deco cyberpunk classic from the creators of *xxxHOLiC* and *Cardcaptor Sakura!*

"Starred Review.
This experimental
sci-fi work from
CLAMP reads like a
romantic version of
AKIRA."
—Publishers Weekly

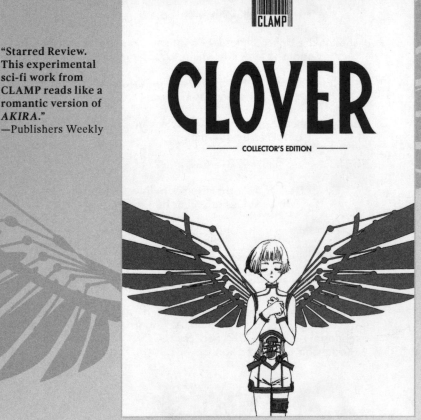

CLOVER © CLAMP ShigatsuTsuitachi CO.,LTD./Kodansha Ltd.

Su was born into a bleak future, where the government keeps
tight control over children with magical powers—codenamed
"Clovers." With Su being the only "four-leaf" Clover in the
world, she has been kept isolated nearly her whole life. Can
ex-military agent Kazuhiko deliver her to the happiness she
seeks? Experience the complete series in this hardcover
edition, which also includes over twenty pages of ravishing
color art!

KC
KODANSHA
COMICS

A Kodansha Comics Trade Paperback Original
To Your Eternity 13 copyright © 2020 Yoshitoki Oima
English translation copyright © 2020 Yoshitoki Oima

All rights reserved.

Published in the United States by Kodansha Comics, an imprint of Kodansha USA Publishing, LLC, New York.

Publication rights for this English edition arranged through Kodansha Ltd., Tokyo.

First published in Japan in 2020 by Kodansha Ltd., Tokyo as *Fumetsu no Anata e*, volume 13.

ISBN 978-1-63236-927-7

Cover Design: Tadashi Hisamochi (hive&co., Ltd.)
Title Logo Design: Shinobu Ohashi

Printed in the United States of America.

www.kodanshacomics.com

9 8 7 6 5 4 3 2 1
Translation: Steven LeCroy
Lettering: Darren Smith
Editing: Haruko Hashimoto, Alexandra Swanson
Editorial Assistance: YKS Services LLC/SKY Japan, INC.
Kodansha Comics Edition Cover Design: Phil Balsman

Publisher: Kiichiro Sugawara
Vice president of marketing & publicity: Naho Yamada

Director of publishing services: Ben Applegate
Associate director of operations: Stephen Pakula
Publishing services managing editor: Noelle Webster
Assistant production manager: Emi Lotto, Angela Zurlo